The History Men

The History Men

◆ ◆

The Historical Profession in England
since the Renaissance

John Kenyon

University of Pittsburgh Press

George Weidenfeld and Nicolson Limited, London
Published 1984 in the U.S.A. by the University of Pittsburgh Press, Pittsburgh, Pa., 15260
Copyright © 1983 John Kenyon
Manufactured in the United States of America

Library of Congress Cataloging in Publication Data

Kenyon, J. P. (John Philips), 1927-
  The history men.

  Includes bibliographical references and index.
  1. Great Britain—Historiography. 2. Historians—
England. I. Title.
DA1.K43 1983b   907'.2042   83-16649
ISBN 0-8229-5900-3 (pbk.)

In Memoriam
George Richard Potter

Contents

Preface

This book has a dual origin. Parts of it are based on a series of articles I wrote for the *Observer Magazine* in 1976 on 'Great Historians'. This caused me to take a new look at figures like Macaulay and Acton, whom I thought I knew fairly well, and sharpened my interest in men like Tawney and Namier, whose careers had overlapped mine. I am grateful to John Silverlight for giving me this commission, and to the *Observer* for allowing me to recycle some of the material I gave them.

Secondly, teaching a new first-year course at Hull University a few years ago, I was reminded of how little students know about historians they commonly read. To most of them a book by Tawney, Namier, Elton or Trevor-Roper is just a book, its author ageless and unreal (or no more real than Clarendon), and unaffected by pressures of class, religion, politics, education or professional animosity. It seemed worthwhile to try and place historians in their professional background, and show how our thinking about the past reshapes itself in their hands from generation to generation.

I have chosen to begin with the Renaissance because, as I explain later, it is soon after that, or even during it, that men first begin to appreciate that the past is, or can be, radically different from the present; a viewpoint which first made possible the writing of history as we understand it, and which is still its principal justification. The invention of printing is perhaps an even more important landmark.

Originally, I intended to cover all history published in Britain, but at an early stage I decided that the few remnants I had of a classical education did not equip me to assess the relative contribution to ancient history of, for instance, Grote, Bury and Sir Moses Finley – though I have not been consistent in this, and Edmund Gibbon could not be left out. Nor did the contribution of British historians to European history constitute an important or influential corpus of work, if we except Robertson's *Charles V* and exclude John Lothrop Motley as an American. I have therefore focused my attention on the history of England, and in a sense I have tried to expand and bring up

to date Sir Herbert Butterfield's little book on *The Englishman and his History*,
published in 1944. I have tried also to go beyond Butterfield and discuss
history as an occupation or a profession – again, I have found that many
people do not realize what a comparatively recent development the writing of
history by 'professional historians' is.

In the penultimate chapter I have surveyed a number of fields of historical
research over the past hundred years. These should be seen as case studies,
and I have not aimed at a comprehensive coverage; such a coverage, embrac-
ing the ardent technicalities of medieval history and the increasingly intensive
mapping-out of the nineteenth century, would have increased the size of the
book by fifty per cent, and taken me too far beyond my field of competence
for comfort.

I have incurred many debts in the preparation of this book. Lord Dacre of
Glanton and Professor G.R. Elton answered various queries of mine with
great patience, and told me a lot unprompted. (Perhaps it is unnecessary to
add that I did not discuss their own work with them, or what I proposed to
say about them.) Several people gave me private reminiscences of Sir Lewis
Namier; John Brooke was particularly helpful in this respect, also Professor
Douglas Johnson and Professor R.F. Leslie. Professor John Cannon provided me with a transcript of an excellent programme on Namier which he
edited for the BBC.

Professor Owen Chadwick answered my queries about Acton, Dr R.G.
Cant dealt with questions about the Scottish university system, and Randolph
Bufano, who is preparing a definitive bibliography of Macaulay, set me right
on a number of points. I also profited from discussions and correspondence
with Dr Edmund King, chiefly about medieval historians. The Secretary of
the Board of Graduate Studies, Cambridge, Mr C.W. Farrow, very kindly
sent me a copy of an unpublished paper on 'The Status of Research Student',
drafted by the late W.J. Sartain in 1955, and Christopher Parker was generous
in allowing me full use of his dissertation on 'The Development of History
Courses in British Universities 1850-1975' (Exeter 1976).

I am particularly grateful to Dr W.R. Robson for allowing me to use his
typed transcript of Macaulay's Journal at Trinity College, without which it
would have been impossible for me to make much use of this journal in the
time then available; also to Mrs Mary Moorman for granting me permission
to consult the papers of her father, G.M. Trevelyan. I am grateful, too, to Dr
J.R.L. Highfield, Dr J.S.G. Simmons, Professor Harold Brooks, Professor
P.H. Hardacre, Mrs Christina Colvin, Dr E.S. de Beer and Mr James Firth
for sending me material on Sir Charles Firth or reminiscences of him.
(Unfortunately much of this information could not be incorporated in the

present book, but it will appear in a separate study of Firth I am now preparing.)

Finally, a fruitful correspondence with Professor G.R. Potter, also about Firth, was tragically cut short by his sudden death in 1981. The dedication of this book expresses something of my great debt to this old friend and mentor, and I only wish he had lived to see it.

J.P.K.

Note. The major part of this book was complete by the autumn of 1981, and I was therefore unable to make full use of John Burrow's seminal study, *A Liberal Descent: Victorian Historians and the English Past*. The same applies to *The Transformation of Intellectual Life in Victorian England*, by T.W. Heyck.

One

◆ ◆

Introduction

There has always been a public eager to read or hear the narration of past events, usually presented in a nationalist or patriotic frame. Even in the Middle Ages a historical tradition was kept alive, and there was a steady demand for the work of chroniclers like Bede, Matthew Paris and Froissart. But with the coming of the Renaissance the prestige of history soared, and the invention of printing widened its dimensions overnight. Books were not only cheaper, but lighter and more portable. Libraries and affluent individuals could build up considerable collections, while at the same time it was very much easier to compare one account of any given historical episode with another.

From the first history was a discipline pregnant with moral purpose, abrim with latent edification. To Richard Stanyhurst, editor of Holinshed's *Chronicles*, who shared the optimistic enthusiasm of publishers down the ages, history was:

'The marrow of reason, the cream of experience, the sap of wisdom, the pith of judgment, the library of knowledge, the kernel of policy, the unfoldress of treachery, the calendar of time, the lantern of truth, the life of memory, the doctress of behaviour, the register of antiquity, the trumpet of chivalry'.

On the other hand, some savants had so elevated a view of the historian's function that they deprecated any attempt to win casual readers by stylistic embroidery or embellishment – 'I would to God', growled Simon Grinaeus, 'that the writers of histories, for the most part, sought not so much to please and entice the reader.'[1]

It also had a much more direct application. Machiavelli was not the only one who believed that through the study of history man could perfect present government. In the words of Sir Walter Raleigh: 'We may gather out of history a policy no less wise than eternal; by the comparison and application of other men's forepassed miseries with our own like errors and ill-deservings.'² Moreover, with the growth of European diplomacy the sheer utility of history as a source of precedent and a means of establishing norms was evident enough. Sir Robert Cotton advised Queen Elizabeth to establish an academy for the study of history in order to train young noblemen for government service, and he reminded her of the importance of historical evidence in establishing Edward I's claim to the throne of Scotland or Henry VIII's to the headship of the English Church. In 1677, when the rakehell Earl of Rochester decided to take his duties in the House of Lords more seriously, 'he began to inform himself of the wisdom of our laws and the excellent constitution of the English government'. 'He was inquisitive after all kinds of histories that concerned England, both ancient and modern, and set himself to read the journals of parliament proceedings.'³

Unfortunately, even in Rochester's time the histories of their own nation available to Englishmen were defective enough. In the early sixteenth century their understanding of the past was based, directly or indirectly, on Geoffrey of Monmouth's *Historia Regum Britanniae*, published in 1136, a work of abiding popularity but great eccentricity, which continued to dominate the thinking even of educated men well into the seventeenth century.⁴ Geoffrey, whose sources (if any) have resisted discovery, told how the Trojan hero Aeneas, who fled the doomed city to conquer Italy and found Rome, also had a grandson, Brutus, who, after many colourful adventures in and around the Mediterranean, sailed north and landed in the deserted isle of Albion – at Totnes, in fact; Geoffrey could be very specific – colonized it with his faithful band of Trojans, and renamed it Britain after himself. His descendants included the legendary Lear and King Bellinus, who among other exploits sacked the city of Rome, and Cymbeline (Cunobellinus), King Cole and King Lud, who founded Londinium of course; these nursery-rhyme characters jostling grotesquely with evident historical figures like Julius Caesar, Claudius and Vespasian. But after the Roman interlude, which was confusingly presented as an overlordship rather than an occupation, with English kings continuing to rule, there arose a leader greater even than Brutus, in the person of Arthur, son of Uther Pendragon. Not only did Arthur hold the Saxon hordes at bay for a generation, before his magical kingdom perished in treachery and blood, but at one time or another in a crowded reign he invaded France and conquered most of northwest Europe, transferred Stonehenge *en bloc* from Ireland to Salisbury Plain, and founded the University of Oxford.

Apart from sheer ignorance, two factors assisted the survival of this fabulous epic. The first was men's reluctance to admit to gaps in the historical record. The 'Brut', as the Trojan legend was known, filled two such gaps, one just before and the other just after the Roman occupation. Secondly, it had considerable patriotic appeal. Geoffrey of Monmouth showed that England had never been an isolated and backward island; on the contrary, her links with Rome through the Trojan royal house put her in the van of European civilization from the beginning, and Bellinus's and Arthur's invasions of the Continent foreshadowed those of Edward III and Henry V. In the person of Constantine the Great, born at York, she had even given the world its first Christian emperor. King Arthur, a great general as well as the epitome of knightly chivalry, was a proto-hero of whom any nation could be justly proud. Henry VII, groping for popular support, and conscious of his Welsh ancestry (Welsh = Old English = Trojan), christened his elder son Arthur in 1486, and the Brut's continuing prestige is demonstrated by the hostile reception given in some quarters to the first post-renaissance historian of England, Polydore Vergil, who would have nothing to do with such tales.

In fact, Vergil enjoyed the patronage of Henry VII, too, and Henry VIII was not prepared to abandon him, though his break with Rome enhanced the value of the Brut in some important respects. Geoffrey's account of the entry of Christianity into England with St Augustine in 797, independently confirmed by Bede, was crucial to the status in Christendom of the *ecclesia anglicana*, and this continued to be an important element in Anglican teaching at least to 1642. Yet, in order to secure 'the sanction of international humanism' the early Tudor kings were willing to play down the more blatantly nationalistic element in these myths. Vergil's *Anglicae Historicae*, written in the international language of Latin and constructed according to the most fashionable Italian conventions, was intended to present Europe with an account of English medieval history in the form of a prelude to the inevitable and entirely beneficial emergence of the Tudors.[5] In this it succeeded, and it at once established itself on the Continent as the standard history of England. In the same way, and for the same reasons, Louis XII commissioned another Italian humanist, Paolo Emili of Verona, to write a similar history of France, *De rebus gestis Francorum* (1517).

Vergil came to England in 1502 as the sub-collector of Peter's Pence, a member of the papal civil service. He found favour with Henry VII, and probably began to write the *Historia* in 1506 or 1507, whether at the king's direct suggestion or not we do not know. But he was speedily given lucrative preferments in the English Church, culminating in the archdeaconry of Wells in 1508, and apart from a brief spell of imprisonment in 1515 at the capricious hands of Henry VIII and Wolsey he survived all the perils and upheavals of the Reformation without apparently sacrificing his loyalty to Rome. He did not finally retire to Italy until the very end of Edward VI's reign, in 1553. He seems to have completed the *Historia* in manuscript by 1515, when he probably presented a copy to the king. The main section, up to the death of Henry

VII, was printed in 1534, but he held up the concluding portion, from 1509 to 1537, until he was safely back in Italy, in 1555.

Vergil's total rejection of Geoffrey of Monmouth was not well taken, and he was predictably denounced as an undercover agent, 'polluting our English chronicles most shamefully with his Romish lies and other Italish beggaries'. Nevertheless, such was the stature of the *Historia*, as a product of European humanism, that it was shamelessly pillaged by chroniclers of the next generation, who were safe in the knowledge that few of their readers would have tackled it in the Latin.[6] His influence was therefore wide, and on the whole beneficial. He used no new sources, but those he used he used as exactly and accurately as he could, with some attempt to assess their comparative value. His static view of the Middle Ages, inevitable at this stage of intellectual development, was taken over entire; and though he discussed such institutions as parliament, the central law courts and the jury with a new fullness and accuracy, he tended to affix arbitrary dates to their introduction, which were also slavishly copied, and he envisaged little or no subsequent development. His underlying assumption was that the uncertainty and unpredictability of human life were mitigated by the ruler alone, whose policy and actions were the crucial factor in political development; society reacted to the king, never vice-versa. Thus his account was divided into reigns, one book (or chapter) per reign – an obvious enough device, perhaps, but someone had to use it for the first time. The line of steady regnal progress was broken by the Wars of the Roses, which had their origins in Henry IV's usurpation, a sin for which atonement could only be made by the mutual destruction of the warring houses of York and Lancaster. This finally opened the way for the establishment of peace and stability under the Tudors.[7]

This framework, then, and these moral assumptions, were taken over almost entirely by the chroniclers in the vernacular, whose dull, mechanical narratives enjoyed a ready sale, and were in turn taken over by Shakespeare. In their pages power equalled right and right always triumphed. They had no concept of causality, still less any sense of anachronism; to them history was a seamless robe, a rolling belt on which everything which had ever happened or was to happen had existed from the beginning, each episode coming into view at the predestined moment.[8] This implied that any lessons to be learnt from the past could be immediately and uncritically applied to the present. Decisions taken by Richard II, for instance, were directly relevant to those taken by Elizabeth I, irrespective of – indeed, in blissful ignorance of – the differing circumstances. This was reinforced by the attitude of the common lawyers, who insisted on regarding precedents in case law from any period as binding upon them; the limit of 'legal memory', beyond which no claim could be pressed, no legal title disputed, was still 1189, the year of Richard the

Lionheart's accession. This had important consequences, for in the pressing debates between seventeenth-century kings and their parliaments, particularly on taxation, so much hinged on medieval precedents which neither side was capable of putting in perspective. As Gardiner said:

'It is impossible to read the arguments which were used in the long debate [on import duties in 1610] without perceiving that all the speakers agreed in attributing to the constitution of [the thirteenth and fourteenth] centuries far more of a settled character than it in reality possessed. They all seem to have imagined that on important points there was some fixed rule to which all had assented, the contravention of which was known to be a breach of constitutional law'.[9]

Moreover, 'literary' evidence for medieval history was limited in scope, and the proper study of charters only began in the late sixteenth century and was not regularized for another hundred years; meanwhile chroniclers had to rely on their medieval predecessors, who were concerned only with facts, not motives or causes. No one, of course, was much concerned with what we would call economic or social history, and the emphasis was on war rather than policy. Hobbes remarked in his saturnine way in 1629:

'For the greatest part, men come to the reading of history with an affection much like that of the people in Rome, who came to the spectacle of the gladiators with more delight to behold their blood, than their skill in fencing. For they be far more in number that love to read of great armies, bloody battles, and many thousands slain at once, than that mind the art by which the affairs both of armies and cities be conducted to their ends'.[10]

More to the point, the Tudor chroniclers were understandably biased in favour of royal authority. In their accounts kings (except for an occasional aberrant like Richard II) were always right, their opponents wrong; the barons' revolts against John and Henry III were condemned outright, and it was cheerfully accepted that the Norman Conquest brought to an end a period of near-barbarism and conferred on William I and his successors pre-eminent right. The status of King John is a case in point. In Shakespeare's play, which reflected current assumptions, he was not a villainous tyrant from whom liberal concessions were wrung by a statesmanlike baronage, but the hero of a national struggle against papal domination, stabbed in the back by his own nobility and clergy, and subsequently traduced by 'monkish chroniclers'. The comparison between Henry VIII and Wolsey on the one hand, and John and Stephen Langton on the other, was too obvious to be missed.

Ignorance of the Anglo-Saxons was almost total. They were squeezed between the resplendent Arthur, whose golden age they had brutally terminated, and the much-admired Normans, the harbingers of a new and im-

proved civilization. Richard Harvey said in 1593: 'What have I to do with
[the Saxons], unless it were to make them tributary to the Britains? Let them
lie in dead forgetfulness.'[11] A greater understanding of the Anglo-Saxons
waited on the elucidation of their language, which did not come until the
seventeenth century; not until then, for instance, was the way clear for the
emergence of King Alfred as a national hero. It was also unfortunate that the
Venerable Bede, author of *The History of the English Church and Nation*
(731), was now tarred with the papist brush; much of the chronology of the
Dark Ages, defective as it is, we owe to him. His works were first printed at
Strasbourg in the 1470s, but the first popular edition of the *History* was edited
by John de Grave and published at Antwerp in 1550, the editor hoping 'that
this proof of the antiquity of Christianity in England will discomfort those
who hope they can reform it'. The first English translation was published by
the recusant Thomas Stapleton, also at Antwerp, in 1565; it was dedicated to
Queen Elizabeth, with the expressed hope that it would lead her back to the
true faith. It was reprinted by the Jesuits at St Omer in 1622 and 1626, and as
late as 1658 an anonymous paraphrase was published at Antwerp entitled,
'England's Old Religion faithfully gathered out of the History of the Church
of England as it was written almost a thousand years ago'. The first edition to
be published in England was by a scholar for other scholars, the magnificent
Latin and Old English version on facing pages edited by Abraham Wheloc
and published by the Cambridge University Press in 1643.

One obvious reason for the confusion in historical scholarship at this time,
and the failure to build up any plausible picture of the English past, was that
history, despite its great prestige, had no foothold in higher education – nor
was it to gain such a foothold until the nineteenth century. For all the nagging
of reformers and humanists, Oxford and Cambridge continued to base their
syllabus on the medieval *trivium* of grammar, rhetoric and logic, followed by
the *quadrivium* of arithmetic, geometry, astronomy and music (none of these
last four bearing much relationship to their twentieth-century namesakes).
Such reform as was undertaken was in the teaching of Greek and mathematics. The pre-eminent English historians of the sixteenth century, Vergil,
Stow and Camden, were all outside the universities: Stow was the son of a
London merchant tailor, Camden of a Lichfield craftsman. Camden did in
fact go to Oxford, but he went down without taking a degree, and had no
further contact with the place until his old age. In this he followed the example
of most middle- and upper-class undergraduates of his day, and it is a matter
of no small importance that if the sons of the seventeenth-century ruling class
learned any history at all, it was at school or from the lawyers at the Inns of
Court.

The grammar schools certainly taught plenty of history, but it was almost exclusively the history of Rome, with a smattering of Ancient Greece. Boys studied Livy, direct or through his various paraphrasers, like Florus or Eutropius, Tacitus in the better schools, and the surviving fragments of Ammianus's *History of the Roman Empire*, which covered the period 353–378 AD. Most educated men were also familiar with Plutarch's *Lives of the Noble Graecians and Romans*, at least in North's famous translation. Hobbes was not the first to point out that this regimen, with its emphasis, through Livy and Plutarch, on republican virtues and, through Tacitus and Ammianus, on imperial sadism and degradation, was not calculated to enhance men's devotion to monarchy.[12] In 1582 the Privy Council asked the High Commission to prescribe for schools a new history of England in Latin verse by one Christopher Ocland, which was 'heroical and of good instruction', unlike the 'divers heathen poets' now in use, 'from which the youth of the realm do rather receive infection in manners than advancement in virtue'.[13] But when the emphasis in teaching was on the memorization of grammatical rules and the perfection of a correct style such exhortations had little effect.

But in historiography, as in many other fields, the seventeenth century saw decisive changes. There is a fundamental difference between the modern and the 'pre-modern' approach to historical studies, which is conclusively and concisely explained by the great Italian historian, Arnaldo Momigliano:

'The whole modern method of historical research is founded upon the distinction between original and derivative authorities. By original authorities we mean statements by eye witnesses, or documents and other material remains that are contemporary with the events they attest. By derivative authorities we mean historians and chroniclers who relate and discuss events which they have not witnessed, but which they have heard of or inferred directly or indirectly from original authorities. We praise original authorities, or sources, for being reliable, but we praise non-contemporary historians, or derivative authorities, for displaying sound judgment in the interpretation and evaluation of the original sources. This distinction between original authorities and non-contemporary historians became the common patrimony of historical research in the late seventeenth century. The distinction, of course, is to be found before that time, but it was not formulated with any degree of accuracy or generally considered to be a necessary presupposition of historical study.'[14]

It is often difficult to make this distinction, particularly in a transitional period. Even later, a general historian like David Hume could compile his account of the Middle Ages largely from secondary authorities without being thought any the worse for it. Also England lagged behind the Continent in this respect. By 1600 Etienne Pasquier was reconstructing the history of France in the Middle Ages with a remarkable degree of sophistication, and he was not alone.[15] In England as in France, a desire to recover the history of the law was the main impetus to progress, a desire expressed and to some extent satisfied by the great Sir Edward Coke. By mid-century a number of English scholars were labouring to establish a new factual skeleton for medieval history; editing charters, elucidating the mysteries of landholding and military obligation, establishing accurate texts of the medieval chronicles. But this work was not at once collated and utilized in any work of general import. As we shall see, the first work of historical synthesis in Momigliano's sense was published as late as 1679, by Gilbert Burnet.

Meanwhile the prevailing tone of sixteenth-century English history was set by Ralph Holinshed, who published his *Chronicles of England, Scotland and Ireland* in 1577. These were simply an agglomeration of all the known facts (and fancies) about the Middle Ages, with no attempt to criticize or assess the evidence at all, still less draw conclusions from it. The only message which came through was that civil strife, even political contestation, was inimical to the development of the nation.[16] This was put more explicitly by Edward Hall, whose chronicles were completed after his death by his friend Richard Grafton. The Hall–Grafton Chronicles painted a disastrous picture of the late Middle Ages, reaching a climax in the Wars of the Roses. The answer was strong monarchical rule, handsomely provided by the Tudors. Burnet, writing a century later, dismissed the lot of them with contempt:

'Hall was but a superficial writer, and was more careful to get full information of the clothes that were worn at the interviews of princes, jousts, tournaments and great solemnities, than about the counsels or secret transactions of the time he lived in. Holinshed, Speed and Stow give bare relations of things that were public, and commit many faults'.[17]

He was perhaps not entirely fair, and certainly not to Stow, whose career illustrates the operation of Gresham's Law. He published *A Summary of English Chronicles* in 1565, followed by a much enlarged version, *The Annals or General Chronicle of England*, in 1580. He was experienced in handling record material, he had some idea of judging contemporary evidence, and he was really concerned to establish the truth of events – unlike most of his rivals, who merely made pious noises to this effect. Moreover, he had a dawning sense of anachronism – he realized, for instance, that in assessing Geoffrey of Monmouth's reliability we should consider the times in which he wrote – and he had a vague understanding, at least, of the fact that institutions and political habits changed over the centuries. Yet in competition with

Holinshed he could not find a publisher for his final 'History of England', and the manuscript is now lost. He turned instead to topography, and he is best known for his great *Survey of London*, published in 1598.[18]

However, his pupil and friend, William Camden (1551–1623), was more fortunate; he even ventured with success into the field of recent history, where the precedents were not encouraging. Even Holinshed had fallen foul of authority, albeit posthumously. When he died in 1580 his publishers recruited a consortium of writers to revise his *Chronicles* and bring them down to the present day. It was published in 1586, and at once incurred the full wrath of the Privy Council, which ordered whole sections on the then ministers, particularly the Earl of Leicester, to be removed. (They were not restored until 1723.)[19] In 1599 Sir John Hayward even found medieval history a minefield. When he published a detailed account of the first year of Henry IV's reign, including the deposition and murder of Richard II, Queen Elizabeth's suspicions were at once aroused, especially since the book was dedicated to Hayward's patron, the Earl of Essex. Francis Bacon defended Hayward before the Privy Council, though a mite ambiguously – he said that he had stolen so much from other authors that he might be indicted for felony, but there was no treason in it. Nevertheless, Hayward went to the Tower, where he stayed until after Essex's trial and execution in 1601.[20] James I, learned as he liked to be thought, refused to permit the revival of the Society of Antiquaries, even though the members assured him that they 'had resolved to decline all matters of state'.[21] As late as 1627 Sir Robert Cotton was closely questioned by the Council about his *Short View of the Long Life and Reign of King Henry the Third*, which was thought to imply criticism of Charles I's government.[22]

However, under Elizabeth Camden was fortunate in the patronage of her chief minister, Lord Burleigh, and the assistance of the aforesaid Sir Robert Cotton. Cotton wrote little himself, but he was an assiduous collector of rare books and documents, which he was glad to place at the disposal of other scholars, and his library still forms the core of the British Museum's medieval collections. Camden also established a solid and uncontroversial reputation at the outset of his career with his famous *Britannia* (1586), a comprehensive account of British antiquities arranged on a topographical basis. He enlarged it in successive editions, but that of 1600, dedicated to the Queen, is usually accepted as definitive. As late as 1695 Edmund Gibson thought it worthwhile to bring it up to date for a new edition, and it is still the work on which Camden's reputation principally rests.

Burleigh then encouraged Camden to write on Queen Elizabeth herself; the more objectively recent events were scrutinized the more acceptable the politic historian's central message, of undeviating support for the government, would be. It was in this spirit that Camden undertook his *Annales Rerum*

Anglicarum et Hibernicorum Regnante Elizabethae, begun in 1607 and published in 1615, though it was not translated into English until 1625.

He has been criticized for submitting the first draft to King James I, but it would have been folly to do otherwise in the circumstances. As it was, the king's attempts to bully Camden into moderating the tone of the book, and particularly his references to Mary Queen of Scots, were largely unavailing, and faced by the much more serious 'libels' on his mother put about by George Buchanan and the Frenchman de Thou, whose works he banned in England and Scotland, he had to let Camden go ahead.[23] The result is a work whose subtlety many modern historians would envy, and whose total picture of 'The Elizabethan Age', in war, trade, exploration and the arts, has fixed our concept of the reign right down to the present day; in fact, it was Camden who first viewed the later sixteenth century as a great explosion of the national genius, controlled and orchestrated by the great queen. As Hugh Trevor-Roper remarks: 'It is thanks to Camden that we ascribe to Queen Elizabeth a consistent policy of *via media* rather than an inconsequent series of unresolved conflicts and paralysed indecisions.'[24]

As an under-master and later headmaster of Westminster School, and a correspondent of most of the leading European scholars of his time, Camden is the first historian who to some extent fits our picture of an 'academic', and he used some of the wealth his books brought him to endow the first chair of history at Oxford in 1622, insisting that the holder should practise 'civil history'. Unfortunately, the Camden professors did not have his courage nor his influence in high places, and they rapidly gravitated to ancient history; in any case, before the nineteenth century none of them had any serious pretensions to scholarship.[25] But Camden's technique and approach were not without their influence on medieval history, as in the case of his friend, John Speed.

Speed is now best remembered for his famous county maps, published between 1608 and 1610, and collected together in 1611 as *The Theatre of the Empire of Great Britain*. But he was as much a historian as a cartographer, and these twin interests merged in a highly ambitious map of 'The Invasions of England and Ireland with all their Civil Wars since the Conquest', in 1610. This was followed in 1611 by his *History of Great Britain*. Speed was a great sceptic, in a field in which scepticism had hitherto been a rarity. He simply dismissed early British history as of no account, and began with the Roman invasion; he denounced the medieval chronicles as 'vulgar annals', and sneered at their preoccupation with 'apparel, jewels, pageants, banquets, guests and other princely compliments, the only weighty business of many weaker brains'. His account of each reign was roughly proportionate to the amount of evidence available – a greater innovation than one might suppose

– and he judged kings strictly by their capacity to rule, not by their standards of morality or their sense of justice, a criterion he ruthlessly applied to monarchs like Henry vi.[26]

But even more sophisticated was a contemporary of Speed's, Samuel Daniel, remembered now, if at all, as a minor poet in the Sidney circle.[27] But between 1595 and 1609 Daniel published a long narrative poem, in eight books, on 'The Civil Wars between the two Houses of Lancaster and York', and in 1612, under the patronage of Queen Anne of Denmark, he published the first part of a prose history of England, down to the end of Stephen's reign. The second part, down to the death of Edward iii, appeared in 1617. They enjoyed considerable success, and were reprinted together, as *A Collection of the History of England*, in 1618, 1621, 1626 and 1650. The 1650 edition had a continuation down to 1485 by 'John Thrussell, gent.', which had already appeared separately in 1636; this joint edition was reprinted in 1685, and it is reasonable to suppose that it is from this book that many, if not most, seventeenth-century Englishmen took their view of medieval history. In fact, in 1706 the Whig editors of a new compendium called 'A Complete History of England' thought it worth reprinting Daniel's original *Collection*, minus Thrussel, with a new continuation up to the death of Henry v, 'all new writ in Mr Daniel's method', even though many of his conclusions ran counter to the prevailing Whig myth.

Daniel owed something of his initial prestige to his sturdy support of monarchical right in the Middle Ages, a sentiment to be expected of a writer who enjoyed the patronage of James i and his queen, but his essentially Tory, establishment view of medieval history maintained its popularity right down the seventeenth century, in the face of the new Whig interpretation on which the attention of most modern historians and political theorists has been focused. But Daniel was far from being a mere Tory hack, and after centuries of neglect he is now coming to be recognized for the original that he was, not for his general outlook, which was traditional enough, but for his ruthless approach to the sources. More sceptical even than Speed, he did not think it was possible to write credible history at all prior to 1066, so his account began with the Conquest. Moreover, his main concern was not with right but with power; how authority was secured, maintained, lost, restored. In this respect he is arguably the first true writer of political history in England, and a recognizable contemporary of Thomas Hobbes. His rumination on the Tudors, in the preface to the *Collection*, is almost breath-taking in its modernity:

'A time not of that virility as the former, but more subtle, and let out into wider notions, and bolder discoveries of what lay hidden before. A time wherein began a great improvement of the sovereignty, and more came to be effected by wit [*sc.* intelligence] than the sword; equal and just encounters, of State and State in forces, and of Prince and Prince in sufficiency. The opening of a new world, which strangely altered the manner of this, enhancing both the rate of all things, by the induction of infinite treasure, and opened a wider way to corruption, whereby princes got much without their swords. Protections, and confederations to counterpoise, and prevent over-growing powers, came to be maintained with larger pensions. Ledger [*sc.* resident] ambassadors first employed abroad for intelligences. Common banks erected, to return and furnish moneys for these businesses. Besides strange alterations in the state ecclesiastical; religion brought forth to be an actor in the greatest designs of ambition and faction. To conclude, a time stored with all variety of accidents fit for example and instruction'.[28]

Of course, the most remarkable product of the new 'politic' history was Francis Bacon's *The History of the Reign of King Henry the Seventh*, in 1622. Because of its literary quality, for which it is still bought and read in the twentieth century, and because it has fostered some remarkably enduring historical myths (such as that of Henry's financial rapacity), it has been unfairly judged by standards which were not its own. Of course, it is derivative in form, taking its approach and structure from Tacitus and Seneca, and its ethos from Machiavelli; and its sources were restricted, much more so than Bacon pretended – almost all his quotations are invented. It is really little more than an impressionistic sketch. Yet it is the first historical biography in the English language which comes near to meeting our own standards in form and content. In fact, it was accepted as a more or less accurate account of Henry's reign until the publication of a revisionist analysis by the German, Wilhelm Busch, in 1892.

In prose of a lucidity, economy and grace we would expect of the author of the famous *Essays*, Bacon delivered himself of a commentary on kingship which was obviously relevant to the 1620s but still had some of the timeless quality of Machiavelli's apothegms. It is characteristic that he should have the nerve to dedicate it to the Prince of Wales, the future Charles I, only a year after pleading guilty to corruption and resigning the Lord Chancellorship. Here is Bacon on the fall of Sir William Stanley, who had deserted Richard III to turn the tide of battle in favour of Henry Tudor at Bosworth:

'It was conceived that he trusted much to his former merits, and the interest that his brother had in the king. But those helps were overweighed by divers things that made against him, and were predominant in the king's nature and mind. First, an over-merit; for convenient merit, unto which reward may easily reach, doth best with kings. Next, the sense of his power; for the king thought that he that could set him up was the more dangerous to pull him down. Thirdly, the glimmering of a confiscation; for he was the richest subject for value in the kingdom . . . Lastly, the nature of the time; for if the king had been out of fear for his own estate, it was not unlike he would have spared his life, but the cloud of so great a rebellion hanging over his head made him work sure. Therefore, after some six weeks' distance of time – which the king did honourably interpose . . . to show to the world that he had a conflict with himself what he should do – he was arraigned of high treason, and condemned, and presently after beheaded'.[29]

His final summation on Henry VII is justly famous; it created a familiar image which modern scholarship has altered in some respects but not destroyed. It begins:

'He was of an high mind, and loved his own will and his own way, as one that revered himself and would reign indeed. Had he been a private man, he would have been termed proud. But in a wise prince it was but keeping of distance – which indeed he did towards all, not admitting any near or full approach either to his power or to his secrets, for he was governed by none . . . [As] for any person agreeable to him for society, such as was Hastings to King Edward IV, or Charles Brandon afterwards to King Henry VIII – he had none'.

And it ends:

'As for the disposition of his subjects in general towards him, it stood thus with him; that of the three affections which naturally tie the hearts of the subjects to their sovereigns, love, fear and reverence, he had the last in height, the second in good measure, and so little of the first as he was beholden to the other two . . . [As] for his pleasures, there is no news of them'.[30]

As a work of historical literature Bacon's *Henry VII* was not to be excelled for the best part of a century, if then. But his ignorance of the Middle Ages exceeded his knowledge. The same could be said of all his contemporaries, of course, and Samuel Daniel, for one, was well aware of it. Even Stow and Camden could only peer through the narrow portholes offered by a charter here, a cartulary there. The advance of general historical knowledge was dependent on the detailed work of individual scholars who, unlike the historians themselves, were often established in the universities.

Such were the archival discoveries and the linguistic advances made in the reigns of Elizabeth and James I that some historians have tried to drape the period in the modish flag of revolution, proclaiming this as 'The Historical Revolution'.[31] Scholarship's most impressive achievement was the 'recovery' of the Anglo-Saxons. Some progress was made under Elizabeth I; Robert Nowell and William Lambarde published a selection of Anglo-Saxon laws in 1568, and in 1572 Archbishop Parker published a corrupt text of Asser's *Life of Alfred*, in Latin. In 1605, however, there appeared *A Restitution of Decayed Intelligence in Antiquities concerning the most Noble and Renowned English Nation*, by an exiled Catholic scholar, Richard Rowlands, who wrote under the alias 'Richard Verstegan', and pretended to be an anglophile Dutchman. 'Verstegan' berated the English for seeking their origins in a gang of Levantine pirates when they were blessed with ancestors of real worth like Offa, Edwin and Alfred. His emphasis on the Teutonic origins of the Anglo-Saxons lent weight to the concept of 'Gothic Constitution', and influenced not only linguists but men of affairs like the great jurist Sir Edward Coke.[32] Coke's *Second Institutes*, written in the 1620s though not published until 1642, made great play with the virtue of 'primitive' Anglo-Saxon institutions, set in a free society. Naturally he was entranced by Verstegan's account of the Witenagemot, which he at once visualized as the precursor of parliament.

Anglo-Saxon Christianity was also of vital importance to those who wished to affirm the antiquity of the Church of England, and it engaged the attention of James Ussher, archbishop of Armagh, one of the leading ecclesiastical scholars of the age. (He established a famous chronology of the Bible, in use until the nineteenth century, which dated the Creation in 4004 BC.) Ussher realized that what was lacking was a knowledge of Old English, and in 1640 he persuaded Sir Henry Spelman to endow a lectureship at Cambridge for the study of 'domestic antiquities touching our Church, and reviving the Saxon tongue'.[33] The first holder of the Spelman lectureship was Abraham Wheloc, who in the 1640s, in the midst of the Civil War, brought out a corpus of printed material on which Anglo-Saxon scholarship was to rest for the next fifty years – an edition of the Old English Laws, an edition of Bede in Anglo-Saxon and Latin, and the first printed edition of the Anglo-Saxon Chronicle. The second Spelman lecturer, William Somner, did even better: his Anglo-Saxon Dictionary, published in 1659, was the first comprehensive key to Old English, and the basis for all subsequent studies in the language. Work continued after the Restoration, of course, and in 1691 Thomas Gale, dean of York, published the first definitive editions of Gildas's *Chronicle*, Nennius's *Historia Britonum*, and Eddi's *Life of Wilfred*, and interest in the Anglo-Saxon Church was sustained by the violent controversy in Queen Anne's reign over the powers and status of Convocation. But these specialized studies owed most to the universities; in fact, only the university presses could afford to invest in the special type required. In 1722 Cambridge University Press celebrated the culmination of the 'Saxonist' movement by issuing the first definitive edition of the Anglo-Saxon Chronicle, edited by William Smith.

Much of this material was only slowly assimilated, and general histories of the Anglo-Saxons were slow to appear. In 1694, when a group of Whig divines was planning a general history of England, Edmund Gibson angrily refused to tackle the pre-1066 section:

'We, forsooth, are to thrash amongst the Saxons and Danes, where the materials for a history are so narrow and have in them so little of connexion, that after a man had done all he could, it should look more like dry annals than a just history ... But those that cut out these shares for others had the wit to reserve a better for themselves; and while we are drudging and endeavouring in vain to piece up little scraps, others must have the satisfaction of flourishing in a variety of matter'.[34]

Nevertheless, no one could now imagine that the period before the Conquest was one of unrelieved barbarism. Though there were still great gaps in the story, the Anglo-Saxons were established as a cultivated, almost sophisticated race, with well-defined laws based on self-discipline and mutual trust, a heroic record of national defence against the Danes, and even a literature of their own. The pendulum had begun to swing back; the status of the Normans as harbingers of civilization was now open to question.

The 'recovery' of feudalism, which proceeded at much the same time, was mainly the work of Sir Henry Spelman. Contemporary jurists like Coke knew almost everything we know about feudalism, but they could not put them together in their mind to make a unified legal, tenurial and military system; this intellectual breakthrough was achieved by Spelman, and it seems that his conclusions were widely known amongst the cognoscenti before they were published.[35] In his treatise on 'The Growth, Propagation and Condition of Tenures by Knight Service' in 1641, consolidated in the second edition of the *Archaeologus* in 1664, and a further 'Treatise of Tenures and Feuds by Knight Service', published long after his death, in 1698, Spelman first demonstrated the relationship between military service, or labour services, and land tenure, which has ever afterwards been acknowledged to be the framework of feudalism, bolted together by the feudal oath. It has been described as 'the most important single discovery that has ever been made in the historiography of the medieval constitution',[36] and its implications were vast; for in a feudal system established by the king, and focusing on him as ultimate lord of land, there could be no place for parliament as a free institution – or for that matter, for independent courts of law.

The result was to impose on medieval history a concept of 'progression'. Camden was the first to use the term 'Middle Ages', in his *Britannia*. Now Spelman's demonstration that feudalism was a Norman import – a proposition open to considerable qualification today, of course, but accepted in all its stark simplicity by Spelman's contemporaries – implied a three-stage scenario: a pre-feudal age, a feudal age, ending about 1485, and a post-feudal age. This in itself assumed a process of linear development, especially as it soon came to be understood that feudalism had decayed gradually, and had not been wiped out in one day by Henry VII at Bosworth. The steady decline in the credibility of Geoffrey of Monmouth, and the corresponding rise of the Anglo-Saxons, added a fourth stage, though the nature of the pre-Anglo-Saxon age continued to be a matter for debate, and the deposition of King Arthur cannot be regarded as complete even today.[37] So great was the reluctance of the English to admit that they were descended from 'savages' that alternatives were still sought to the Trojans, and as late as 1676 Aylett Sammes, fellow of Christ's College, Cambridge, wrote a 500-page treatise, *Britannia Antiqua Illustrata*, arguing that Britain was first settled by the Phoenicians.[38]

However, the Romans, too, were now coming to the fore. Caesar and Tacitus had long been available in definitive Latin texts, and as early as 1591 Sir Henry Savile, Warden of Merton College, published translations of Tacitus's *Histories* and *Agricola*. He also wrote 'A View of Certain Military Matters, for the better understanding of Ancient Roman Stories', which first suggested the sophistication and complexity of the Roman road and fort system in England.[39] A translation of Caesar's *Commentaries* followed in 1601. Such texts made it quite clear that what the Romans found in Britain when they came was certainly not the Trojans, nor indeed the Phoenicians, nor any other civilized race; and a proper understanding of the nature of the Roman occupation wiped out most of Geoffrey of Monmouth's fabled kings. At the same time contacts now being made with aboriginal natives in America and Africa forced everyone to reassess the probable level of civilization attained by the Ancient Britons. It is noticeable that in the illustrations to Speed's *History* in 1611, the Ancient Britons have shed their togas and body armour, previously *de rigueur*, and now appear in little more than loin cloths and paint. In 1612 Samuel Daniel acknowledged that the British before the advent of Caesar must have existed in a state of almost continuous tribal warfare, like the American Indians 'in the West World lately discovered'. In 1659 John Aubrey admitted that the Ancient Britons were 'as savage as the beasts whose skins were their only raiment', though he speculated that they might have been 'two or three degrees less savage than the Americans'.[40]

Also, throughout the seventeenth century interest in prehistoric graves and monuments was growing. Improvements in mathematics, particularly in geometry and mensuration, induced some antiquaries like William Stukeley to move out of their studies and onto the road. Random perambulation of the countryside became more feasible as the breed of horses improved, highway robbery declined and inns and hostels improved. Of course, this did not imply an increase in accurate knowledge. When James I asked his Surveyor General, Inigo Jones, to investigate Stonehenge he came back with the answer that it had been built by the Romans; others argued that it was the tomb of Boudicca, or Boadicea. In the 1690s Aubrey assigned it to the Druids, and Stukeley agreed. However, science kept peeping out from among the prevailing credulity. Stukeley could fairly be described as fixated on the Druids – he saw them everywhere – but his 'Society of Roman Knights', founded in 1722, despite all its masonic-adolescent flummery – uniforms, oaths, secret meetings – was seriously devoted to the study of Roman remains.[41]

The discovery of the Druids certainly inspired a new interest in pre-Roman Britain, but with their sorceries, their spells, their sympathetic oaths, their human sacrifices, they did nothing to suggest that the Britons had attained a high level of civilization. So a new picture began to emerge, in which the Romans had hauled the nation up out of barbarism, only to abandon it 400 years later to a fate from which it had been rescued by the Anglo-Saxons. The weak point was the Norman Conquest: had it really been a conquest, or an occupation, or merely a take-over? Had it advanced or retarded English civilization? This was a debate which still had life in the nineteenth-century world of Edward Augustus Freeman and William Stubbs, and it was directly relevant to the squabbles between king and parliament which dominated seventeenth-century thinking. Medieval historians and antiquarians found themselves obliged, with varying degrees of reluctance, to arbitrate on live constitutional issues.

Two

◆ ◆

The Seventeenth Century

It is arguable that Sir Walter Raleigh was the first Whig historian. His *History of the World*, written between 1608 and 1614 while he lay under suspended sentence of death in the Tower, and published in 1614, only went down to 130 BC. But he had plenty of incidental comments to make on English history, and his general belief that history was directed by Providence, which monitored even the actions of kings and brought them to judgment in this world (not just the next), ran clean counter to the prevailing doctrine of the Divine Right of Kings. He preached the evanescence of regal power, for:

> 'Who hath not observed what labour, practice, peril, bloodshed and cruelty the kings and princes of this world have undergone, exercised, taken upon them and committed, to make themselves and their issues masters of the world? And yet Babylon, Persia, Egypt, Syria, Macedon, Carthage, Rome and the rest, no fruit, no flower, no grass, no leaf, springing upon the earth, of those deeds: No, their very roots and ruins do hardly remain'.

And after a scathing review of the English monarchy from the beginning he lighted upon Henry VIII, for whom no words in his vocabulary were bad enough:

> 'If all the pictures and patterns of a merciless prince were lost to the world, they might all again be painted to the life, out of the story of this king. For how many servants did he advance in haste, (but for what virtue no man could suspect), and with the change of his fancy ruined again, no man knowing for what offence? To how many others of more desert gave he abundant flowers whence to gather honey, and in the end the harvest burned them in the hive? How many wives did he cut off, and cast off, as his fancy and affection changed? How many princes of the blood, (whereof some of them for age could scarcely crawl towards the block), with a world of others of all degrees, (of whom our common chroniclers have kept the account), did he execute? Yea, in his very death bed, and when he was at

the point to have given his account to God for the abundance of blood already spilt, he imprisoned the Duke of Norfolk the father, and executed the Earl of Surrey the son'.[1]

He was careful to praise Henry VII, James's direct ancestor, which Henry VIII was not – 'a politick prince he was if ever there were any, who by the engines of his wisdom beat down and overturned as many strong oppositions both before and after he wore the crown as ever king of England did' – but it is not surprising that the king thought him 'too saucy in censuring princes'. (It is also said that James thought he and his mother were satirized in the persons of the effeminate Ninus, king of Persia, and his nymphomaniac mother, Queen Semiramis.) James fumed, but it is typical of his essentially uncombative nature that his attempt to suppress the first edition merely led to the removal of the author's name from the title-page. Amassing retrospective glamour from Raleigh's execution in 1618, it emerged as one of the most popular books of the century, especially amongst opponents of the monarchy. Its moral tone particularly recommended it to the Puritans, and it was heartily endorsed by Cromwell. It was reprinted eleven times between 1617 and 1687.

By illuminating the moral and political uses to which history could be put, Raleigh gave additional impetus to a developing theory of English history which was more or less self-consciously designed to serve political purposes. The need for such a history was pressing. The need to reunite the nation after the disastrous Wars of the Roses, then the need to fend off the damage latent in the rule of a child followed by two women, then the need to defend the Protestant Reformation against external invasion and internal conspiracy – all this had caused the government and the governing classes persistently to exalt the authority of the crown. It was not easy now to reverse the process, though the succession was assured in the Stuart line, the country was firmly united, and the Counter-Reformation had been repulsed.

The discontinuity involved in James's accession in 1603 was traumatic. Not only was he a foreigner, he was a king, succeeding two queens who together had reigned fifty years. He was in fact the first male to exercise full regal authority since the death of Henry VIII in 1547. A queen, however effective and however popular, was always a woman in a man's world; her tactics must be defensive, her policy one of survival. It is significant that even Elizabeth I never dared marry. A king, a foreign king, and one who like James had already reigned successfully for twenty years elsewhere, might be expected to adopt a more aggressive stance, not least in his attitude towards his subjects' rights. As his first House of Commons, in 1604, mournfully observed: 'The prerogatives of princes may easily and do daily grow; the privileges of the subject are for the most part at an everlasting stand.'[2]

Their fears were accentuated by James's known views on the powers of the monarchy. In fact, his notorious *True Law of Free Monarchies* said nothing about the Divine Right of Kings which had not been implicit in the policy and practice of the Tudors, nor explicit in the teaching of the Church of England on the civil obligations of a Christian man, but it was unusual for a ruler to nail his colours to the mast so blatantly. Throughout Europe the 'estates' or elected assemblies of the Middle Ages had already disappeared or were on their way out, and there seemed no reason why the Westminster parliament should not follow them, especially if it failed to reach agreement with the king, an agreement which seemed less and less likely. Apart from a brief interlude in 1614, James I dispensed with parliament from 1611 to 1621; his son revived old quarrels and found new ones, and in 1629 put his threats into operation by announcing that he intended to rule indefinitely without a parliament at all.

Therefore parliament was on the defensive, and the parliamentarians summoned history to their aid. The result was a decisive reshaping of medieval history, using the latest scholarly aids as they were then understood. The process was a gradual one, nor was it marked by the emergence of any significant or memorable works. The message was conveyed indirectly, through speeches, pamphlets and legal textbooks; the great historians of the century, like Clarendon, wrote in another tradition. But, as we have seen, a better understanding of medieval feudalism began to permeate the intellectual world long before it emerged in published form, and so did a better appreciation of the nature of Anglo-Saxon institutions and society. From this emerged the theory of the 'Ancient Constitution'.

In its most fully developed form, 'The Ancient Constitution' was visualized as almost ageless. According to Sir Edward Coke, the representative element which was the basis of a balanced constitution was to be found in the Anglo-Saxon Witenagemot, and it had crossed the divide between 1066 and Simon de Montfort's parliament of 1265 over the bridge provided by the Anglo-Norman *curia regis*, which had achieved its perfect form, though fleetingly, in Henry I's assembly of barons and knights in 1116. The surviving records were patchy, but the general picture was clear enough, for those who wanted it to be clear. And as the antiquity of the Commons was exaggerated, so was its representative nature. In 1604 the Commons claimed to represent the whole nation, but the king replied: 'This house doth not so represent the whole commons of the realm as the shadow doth the body, but representatively. Impossible it was for them to know all that would be propounded here, much more all those answers that you would make to all propositions.'[3] The Commons were undeterred. Coke said of them in 1624: 'They appear for multitudes, and bind multitudes ... They are the representative body of the

realm, for all the people are present in parliament by person representative.'[4]
By the outbreak of Civil War in 1642 William Prynne was asserting that in
some far-off past the people had not only elected parliaments but kings.[5]

The danger of this kind of constitutional theory was that, when challenged,
it could only push the origins of the constitution farther back in time. What
lay at the beginning? No one knew, but Thomas Hobbes argued that man
was inherently evil – something the Church could not very well deny, since it
preached Original Sin – and therefore the origin of society must be coercive
and authoritarian. The Whig answer was to execute a smart left turn, and
pursue the origins of the Ancient Constitution across the North Sea and into
Germany. There, it was said, the wandering armies of the Teutonic tribes
which had beset the Roman Empire in its decline had been led by elected
generals who were obliged to seek the opinion of their followers in war
councils. As the tribes settled down in new lands, and turned farmers, the
habit of consultation passed over into civil society, together with the practice
of electing chiefs, then kings. The Saxons had then brought this 'Gothic
Constitution' to England. The more radical exponents of this theory continued to stress the elective nature of kingship and the reciprocal rights and
duties of the ruler and the ruled, strong traces of which survived in the
coronation service; in the oath of fealty then taken by the lords, and the
coronation oath taken by the monarch. Thus, they argued, William I was an
elected war leader, whose right arose not from conquest but from free election
by the people. There was therefore no real break in 1066: if inheritance were
the key, William had a better title than Harold; if election, then he was elected
at his coronation, six months after the battle of Hastings. Moreover, at that
coronation William confirmed to his subjects the rights they had enjoyed in
the Anglo-Saxon free society, and this confirmation was repeated by successive rulers; by William II, Henry I, Henry II and, most spectacularly, by John.
Parliament meanwhile continued, dropping the name 'Witan' and adopting
the name '*communitas regni*' or some such. This theory of the Gothic origins
of English society had additional advantages: it conclusively explained England's loyalty to the Common Law and her refusal to accept Roman Law,
and it justified her rejection of Roman Catholicism, a mere Mediterranean
superstition.

Undoubtedly the most dramatic impact of the new history was on Magna
Carta. It is ironic that at the same time as it was being pinned down by
scholars and identified as an essentially feudal document it should have been
picked up by smart politicians and lawyers and paraded as a charter of rights
and liberties of almost unlimited scope.[6] In the parliaments of the 1620s
almost any unpopular innovation, even a patent for the sole engrossing of
wills, was held to be against the sacred Charter, and it formed the backbone

of the Petition of Right in 1628. Sir Dudley Digges likened its rediscovery to 'the finding of the Book of the Law in the days of good King Josiah'.[7] The importance now attached to antiquarian research is shown by Charles I's decision to close Sir Robert Cotton's library in 1629 on the grounds that the possession of such records by a private citizen was a danger to the state.[8] Charles also seized Coke's papers on his death in 1634, including his unpublished commentary on Magna Carta. Nor was he imprudent. Such was the cult of the Charter that in 1643, in *The Sovereign Powers of Parliaments and Kingdoms*, Prynne argued that the king's veto on legislation, and his right to dissolve parliament at will, were infractions of it.[9]

On the other hand, the theory of the Ancient Constitution was never flatly rejected by the crown. James I readily acknowledged the pre-eminent importance of parliament, as did Charles I, despite his fears that the Commons were trying to encroach on his sovereign power. In 1628 he agreed that Magna Carta was in full force, and offered to issue a declaration to that effect. James acknowledged in 1610 that the high claims he had made for the royal prerogative applied only to 'the state of kings in their first original', and 'every just king in a settled kingdom' – which he acknowledged England to be – 'is bound to observe that paction made to his people by his laws'.[10] The idea of an Original Contract between king and people, renewed by the coronation oath, was already in vogue, though it was very far from being defined in strict terms. Brought to bay in 1642, Charles I found it politic to liberalize his views still further, and in his 'Answer to the Nineteen Propositions' he over-trumped his opponents by positing the existence of a balanced constitution of King, Lords and Commons, which horrified many royalists because it made the king merely one of three co-equal 'estates'.[11] It accorded with the theory of 'mixed monarchy' put forward by the parliamentarian Philip Hunton, and neither theory was seriously out of line with constitutional practice.

However, the Civil Wars, the defeat of the king and his trial and execution had drastic implications for the theory of the Ancient Constitution. In the revulsion which followed the king's death, blame attached to any theory which had questioned his authority and status. Worse still, it was discredited by its association with the Levellers, an extreme radical, republican group which enjoyed considerable influence in London and in the Army in 1647 and 1648. The Levellers wholeheartedly embraced the Ancient Constitution, and went on to argue that in the beginning all men had enjoyed equal political and social rights, which had been unjustly abrogated by the Normans. Monarchy in its present form was, in fact, a Norman invention; it should be abolished and replaced by a republic in which all men would have the vote and enjoy complete equality before the law. Some Levellers, like William Walwyn, even dismissed Magna Carta as a feudal document, reeking of despotism, and irrelevant, even prejudicial, to their cause. It is not surprising that the Republic which was in fact established in 1649 was sternly conservative and elitist, as was the Protectorate set up by Cromwell in 1653, nor that the Restoration of Charles II was accompanied by a hysterical reaffirmation of supreme monarchical authority in Church and state, and a studied dismissal of any doctrine which sought to qualifty it.

But the eclipse of the Ancient Constitution was only temporary. The ultra-royalism of the Restoration was a superficial phenomenon, which ran counter to political realities, denying as it did the pre-eminent place which parliament had won for itself in the 1640s. Lip-service was generally paid to the Divine Right of Kings, now propagated by the Church in a more extreme form than ever before, but the conduct of most Englishmen in 1688 and 1689, including the clergy themselves, demonstrated its irrationality. Similarly, the extreme 'patriarchal' theories of Sir Robert Filmer, which became fashionable in the Exclusion Crisis of 1679-81, though they enjoyed a longer vogue than was once thought, also proved too strong for English tastes in the end. Moreover, the Exclusion Crisis, involving as it did an attempt by parliament to alter the succession to the throne, raised fundamental questions the answer to which, it was agreed, could only be found in history, and a new generation of politicians was now able to draw on the results of the scholarly work which had been going forward over the last generation. The result was that academic scholarship was increasingly pressed into the service of politics.

But the royalists still had the best of it, for the simple reason that they were right. William Petyt's *The Ancient Right of the Commons of England Asserted*, in 1680, was the most comprehensive and scholarly attempt yet to prove what was in fact not true: that the Commons were of immemorial antiquity, that their history had been continuous, that they had always been freely elected, that they had always been independent of the Lords, and that they had always had the deciding voice in the operation of the constitution. He was easy meat, however, for the erudite and combative Dr Robert Brady, Master of Caius College, Cambridge, and a staunch royalist. He at once published *A Full and Clear Answer*, and followed this up in 1684 with *An Introduction to the Old English History*. The first volume of his *Complete History of England*, up to 1272, appeared in 1685, though the second volume had to wait until 1700.[12]

In his desire to crush his opponents Brady sometimes overreached himself on technical points. But in general his account of English constitutional history in the twelfth and thirteenth centuries is the one now accepted. He argued that William I had in fact conquered England, and he had confiscated and re-allocated all the land therein, making a complete break in continuity. Any subsequent grant or 'confirmation' of the subjects' rights, by him or his successors, was merely an act of grace; documents like Magna Carta were of limited import, and could only be understood in a feudal context. As for the history of parliament, the Anglo-Saxon Witan was almost certainly not elected, and in any case it did not survive the Conquest. The post-Conquest *communitas regni* was merely an assembly of feudal tenants-in-chief summoned largely for military purposes. Parliament as such could not be pushed back beyond 1265, and even then its function and its mode of election were obscure, and until the late fifteenth century it sat together with the Lords.

This fell message was not seriously contested for the time being – indeed, it was difficult to contest. The Revolution of 1688 seemed to serve as a practical confirmation and demonstration of the Ancient Constitution and the Whig interpretation of history, but the new settlement was by no means firm, Tory feeling remained strong, and the need for retrospective justification was as urgent as ever. In particular, the Norman Conquest was even more of a problem than before; if Brady's view of the matter was correct, then all kings after 1066 enjoyed untrammelled power, therefore James II was in the right, and the Revolution of 1688 was a true revolution, not a return to proper and hallowed forms of government, as the Whigs claimed. The problem was exacerbated by the fact that the history books which enjoyed the largest circulation, though they are now forgotten, were mostly written in a Tory way, or at least they were simpleminded enough to accept the Norman Conquest, for instance, as being what it said it was.[13] Sir Richard Baker's *A Chronicle of the Kings of England* is a case in point. First published in 1643, it conveyed a picture of English kingship which was positively hair-raising to any good Whig; yet it was reprinted in 1653, 1660, 1665, 1670, 1674 and 1684, and was apparently much favoured by country gentlemen of a conservative cast. Addison, for instance, twice mentions Sir Roger de Coverley as consulting it, and tells us that 'it always lay in his hall window'. Fielding, in *Joseph Andrews*, placed it amongst Sir Thomas Booby's best-used books. Whig theory, in fact, ran counter to popular culture.

This explains why even Locke, who eschewed any consideration of history, devoted a gnomic chapter in his *Second Treatise* on government to the problem of conquest – to the mystification of his latest editor.[14] Locke's friend, James Tyrrell, took up the matter more directly, and at great length, in his *Bibliotheca Politica* in 1694. In this atmosphere it is scarcely surprising that journalists like John Tutchin under Queen Anne should devote issue after issue of his *Observator* to the consideration of such knotty problems as whether the barons who opposed King John or Henry III were in a state of rebellion or not. Tutchin was reluctant even to refer to William I as 'William the Conqueror'; to him he was 'William the Norman', or 'William, commonly called the Conqueror'. Nobody supposed that such matters were not directly relevant to current politics; how could this be otherwise when as late as 1708 a leading non-juror, who had declined the oath of allegiance since 1689, was suddenly converted by reading a book on medieval history?[15]

The Convocation Controversy of 1697–1717 provoked a further wave of historical research. The claim of the High Church party that Convocation was independent of parliament and the crown forced academically-minded clergymen on both sides to undertake a thorough re-examination of the early history of the Church in England. The enormous tomes which resulted, from Edmund Gibson, William Wake, White Kennett, Francis Atterbury and many more, peacefully gather dust today on the shelves of college and minster libraries, but in their time they were the very stuff of debate, and they did much to encourage the exact scrutiny of records and the perfection of research techniques.

At the same time, there was no need to go back to the Middle Ages in search of historical controversy. The Great Rebellion was a live issue within the memory of men still living. Since the very outbreak of war in 1642 debate had raged on the rights and wrongs of the matter, and it showed no signs of subsiding; and by 1688, and certainly by 1700, a considerable amount of direct evidence was available in print.

Initially at least, and perhaps rather strangely, there was no attempt to relate the Great Rebellion to the civil wars of the thirteenth or fifteenth centuries, though these were well enough known. It was a unique catastrophe, which must be considered in isolation.

The early 'histories' written in the 1640s and 1650s – many of them little more than essays – had the merit of frankness; a frankness not always possible after the Restoration. For instance, in the 1640s there was what seems a concerted attempt by many quite disparate authors to blame Charles I's misfortunes on his father. A few royalists leaped to the defence, but it was in fact the ultra-royalist Peter Heylyn, disciple of William Laud, who handed down the most devastating indictment of King James I:

'It is true indeed, that he much pleased himself with boasting of his "king-craft", as he used to call it, but ... I have heard many wise men say, that they could never find out what that kingcraft was, it being no hard matter to prove, that in all public treaties and negotiations, and many private conferences and debates of council, he was outwitted, and made use of unto other men's ends, by almost all that undertook him, and one might say (I fear too truly) that by putting off the majesty belonging to a king of England, that so he might more liberally enjoy himself, neglecting the affairs of state, and cares of government, to hunt after pleasure; deserting the imperial city, to sport himself at Royston, Newmarket and such obscure places, (which were to him as the Isle of Capri to Tiberius Caesar), and finally by letting loose the golden reins of discipline held by his predecessors with so strict a hand, he opened the first gap unto those confusions, of which we have since found the miserable and woeful consequences'.[16]

Most of the other explanations offered were similarly straightforward, even simplistic. Sir William Dugdale's *A Short View of the Late Troubles* plumped for the 'conspiracy' theory of rebellion, which was naturally a favourite with many royalist writers.[17] (Like many such apologists, Dugdale did not publish his book until after the Restoration, but it was composed, in draft at least, long before.) Several – like Sir Edward Waller, Peter Heylyn, and for that matter Thomas Hobbes, in *Behemoth* – put much of the blame on the teaching of the Puritan clergy, though Hobbes also criticized the use in schools and universities of classical authors who were strongly republican in sentiment. Heylyn also accused the Catholics of being at the bottom of the whole thing; an expression of prejudice, of course, rather than a historical assessment, but one which found much favour at the time.[18] Under Charles II the idea that the Puritan opposition to Charles I had been infiltrated by Catholic 'cells' was put forward as an alibi by radical Nonconformists, and it was even entertained by some right-wing Anglicans like Nalson, who, much as they loathed the Puritans, still acknowledged them to be fellow-Protestants, and preferred to believe that they had been deceived by the Papists.[19]

But others achieved a much higher degree of sophistication. Sir Edward Walker looked for the origin of the Troubles in a displacement of the natural social order of rank and degree; like James Harrington, he also guessed that the dissolution of the monasteries was the beginning of the process. Like Hobbes, he also saw the undue size of London, and its instability as an economic unit, as an important factor; likewise James I's mass creation of peers and his extravagant generosity in general.[20] Matthew Wren's brief essay, 'Of the Origins and Progress of the Revolutions in England', is a highly intellectual schema going back to the Reformation, which, with very slight adjustments, could be taken for something published in the present century; it is certainly more sophisticated than anything written in the nineteenth.

Supporters of parliament were not behindhand, of course. In 1647 the Secretary to the Long Parliament, Thomas May, published what must be regarded as an official apologia for its doings, as well as several treatises on parliamentary history relevant to his purpose. He showed considerable ingenuity in arguing from medieval history that periods of prerogative rule, whatever their merits or demerits, always led, as in 1640, to the election of a radical or reforming parliament. But he had enough sense of 'anachronism' to criticize measures like the Triennial Act of 1641; whether the king ought to have complete control of the meetings of parliament or not, he said, he had exercised this control for so long that any attempt to restrict it constituted an encroachment on his legitimate authority.[21] Then there is the remarkable case of James Howell, a man whose royalism was considerably modified by his commitment to the Fleet prison from 1643 to 1651. He worked his way out by a relentless programme of writing, thus paying off his debts, and he emerged as an enthusiastic and uncritical supporter of Oliver Cromwell. Nevertheless, his more important historical and political tracts were put together in one volume in 1661 under the title *Twelve Treatises of the Later Revolutions*, and he was appointed historiographer-royal to Charles II.

Howell was almost unique in portraying the Rebellion and Civil Wars as a direct contest for physical ascendancy through military power. This may seem an obvious point, but it was not often made at the time; contemporaries preferred to ascribe almost any other motive to the combatants, whether moral, intellectual or religious. One of the most teasing aspects of the problem is that the English, who even before the Civil Wars were regarded in Europe as a bellicose and combative race, should have been so unwilling to admit that the mid-century revolution was a contest for political authority. But Howell was unusual in other ways. For instance, he was the only writer in this period who thought to compare the Great Rebellion with contemporaneous revolts in Spain, France, Sicily and the Netherlands, and thus in a tentative way he anticipated modern theories on the 'General Crisis of the Seventeenth Century'. He also argued that the House of Commons was now basically unstable because the landed gentry had taken over most of the seats originally allotted to townsmen – a conclusion reached with some éclat by Sir John Neale three hundred years later.[22]

The return of Charles II, and the passage of the 'Licensing' or press censorship Act in 1662, put a moratorium on further discussion for nearly twenty years. The 'murder' of Charles I was now the central event in recent history, and since the official attitude, expressed in the Act of 1661 attainting the regicides, and in the special church services now commissioned for 30 January, was that this foul act was the result of a conspiracy by a minority of 'cruel and bloody men', it was natural to extend this conspiracy theory back ten years and use it as a blanket explanation for the Rebellion as a whole. This received some support from the *Eikon Basiliké*, Charles I's best-selling apologia, but it was not expounded in any official or officially inspired history. For it was Charles II's aim, expressed in the Act of Indemnity and Oblivion in 1660, 'to bury all seeds of future discords and remembrance of the former, as well in his own heart as in the breasts of his subjects one towards another'. It was this as much as anything which led him, for instance, to forbid the publication of Hobbes's *Behemoth* in his lifetime. In fact, apart from a few pious memoirs of the martyr-king, and a few violently hostile pieces on Cromwell and the other regicides, the burden of royalist propaganda was left to the clergy, and no one would wish to take the sermons even of the great Caroline bishops as a serious contribution to history.

However, the expiry of the Licensing Act in 1679 brought a flood of new material, much of it reflecting the new critical attitude towards the monarchy evinced in the Exclusion Crisis. Most notable was the second volume of John Rushworth's *Historical Collections*, covering the years 1629 to 1640. Rushworth's sympathies were never in doubt. He had been clerk-assistant to the Long Parliament and secretary to Fairfax, the Commander of the New Model Army, and he had acted for the Protectorate government in various capacities. He had taken shorthand notes of Commons debates over many years, and copied as many state papers as he could, and the first volume of his *Collections*, in 1659, was dedicated to Richard Cromwell. There was a brisk market for this kind of authentic material. In 1663 Samuel Pepys ordered a copy for the Navy Office Library, and sat up all night reading it. 'It is', he wrote, 'a book the best worth reading for a man of my condition, or any man that hopes to come to any public condition in the world.' He purchased all the subsequent volumes as they appeared.[23]

In 1680 Rushworth also published a verbatim account of Strafford's trial in 1641, but the interruption in the censorship was short-lived, and the publication of his remaining volumes had to wait until after his death, and, more important, after the Revolution of 1688. Volume three, covering the years 1640–44, appeared in 1692, and the last volume, up to 1648, in 1701. The counter to Rushworth was John Nalson's *Impartial Collection of the Great Affairs of State*, covering the years 1639 to 1649, which was published in two volumes in 1682 and 1683. Nalson displayed a violent royalist bias, but he printed many further documents omitted by Rushworth or unknown to him.[24] Also in 1682 came Bulstrode Whitelocke's *Memorials of the English Affairs* (from 1625 to 1660), a curiously ambiguous document, though not untypical of the time in that it reflected Whitelocke's progression, over a long career, from being a doubtful parliamentarian to being a questioning Cromwellian, and finally a hesitant royalist.[25]

There was a hiatus after 1682, when the Anglican-Tory reaction began to bite, but after the Revolution the flood resumed, the high points being Edmund Ludlow's *Memoirs* (1698), and on the royalist side *The Memoirs of the Reign of King Charles I* by Sir Philip Warwick (1701–2). Most of these works were naturally published posthumously, and when any editorial direction is discernible at all it is corrupt and partial, but the end result was to make the period 1640–1660 one of the best documented in English history. Nor should we forget the early newspapers, or 'newsbooks', published throughout the Civil Wars – *Mercurius Britannicus* in London and *Mercurius Aulicus* in Oxford. The latter petered out, of course, in 1646, but the former persisted through the Interregnum, though in 1650 it changed its name to *Mercurius Politicus*. The use to which subsequent writers put these newsbooks is uncertain, but straight runs were available in many libraries; they were tendentious and biased, but they did provide a solid background of fact.

But the major debate on the Great Rebellion began in earnest in 1689, and it took on new life in 1694, when the Licensing Act, renewed in 1685, was finally allowed to expire. For the next fifteen or twenty years recent history was the very stuff of political debate. At the heart of the problem was the fact that Charles I's case so closely resembled James II's. It was difficult for the Whigs to criticize Charles without forfeiting considerable upper-class support, particularly in the Church; but if his trial and execution were utterly and irredeemably wrong – and this continued to be the official viewpoint, even after the Revolution – then it was difficult to justify James's deposition in 1689. (The pretence that James had 'abdicated' was never much more than a fig-leaf.) Many High Churchmen deliberately used the cult of Charles I, particularly in their 30 January sermons, to expose the inconsistencies of the Whig position, to express their own unease at the Revolution of 1688, which most of them nevertheless felt obliged to accept in legal terms, and to intensify their campaign against the Dissenters, who had been granted freedom of worship in 1689, but who could plausibly be associated with the regicide Puritans. Nor were the Whig leaders helped by their own left wing, who insisted on applauding republicanism and justifying regicide. Thus the memoirs of Edmund Ludlow, notorious regicide, republican and general, were drastically remodelled and abridged for publication in 1698 by the Whig publicist John Toland. They provoked a flurry of outraged comment, as did Toland's own biography of Milton the following year, which was regarded as unduly laudatory of a man who had done so much to justify regicide. But in 1700 Toland went on to publish a new edition of Harrington's *Oceana*, that notorious blueprint for a republican utopia, which had first appeared in 1657.[26]

It is upon this rather confused and rancorous scene that Lord Clarendon burst in 1702, with the first volume of his posthumous *History of the Rebellion and Civil Wars in England*; volumes two and three followed at twelve-monthly intervals. To put Clarendon in perspective as a historian is not difficult. We may agree that his was 'the profoundest and most magnanimous history of his times', but to say that 'with Clarendon we move unmistakably from quasi-history to the real thing' is going much too far.[27] His so-called *History* is in fact very much the kind of 'history' we have grown accustomed to in the twentieth century from Lloyd George, Winston Churchill, even Harold

Wilson: a melange of personal reminiscence (often useful as direct historical evidence), accepted chronological fact, and autobiography.

After the king's defeat in 1646 Clarendon (then Sir Edward Hyde) fled with the Prince of Wales to Jersey, where he began to write an account of the 1630s and 1640s. It was intended as a royalist apologia, for fairly prompt publication; the king knew of it, and sent material for it; in other circumstances he would no doubt have read and approved it. As it was, he was executed, Clarendon was recalled to Charles II's service, and the manuscript, which had been taken up to the year 1644, was laid aside and forgotten. However, after his fall in 1667 Clarendon was exiled again, this time to Montpellier, where between 1668 and 1671 he wrote a detailed autobiography which was intended as a personal exculpation. His sons were then given permission to visit him, and he asked them to bring over the text of his 'history', up to 1644. The two manuscripts were dovetailed together, with the cut-off at 1660, and when he died in 1674 he left it to his sons to decide when it was to be published, though he stipulated that this should not be during the lifetime of any person mentioned in it.[28] His younger son, Lawrence Hyde, Earl of Rochester, finally decided to release it on Queen Anne's accession, prefacing each of the three volumes with a tendentious introduction which was avowedly a party manifesto. However, despite the advice of various clerical adjutants, he declined to alter the text one iota.

It was a runaway success, and it made a great impact on the reading public as the authentic voice of a man who had walked and talked with all the heroes and villains of a bygone generation, with kings and princes, statesmen and soldiers, bishops and politicians. The fact that his knowledge was gappy, particularly for the years of exile from 1646 to 1660, did not affect the validity of his judgments in the public eye. Though as a political narrative it was sadly lacking in structure, something only partly explained by the circumstances of its composition, and though much of its prose was dense and confused, its general scope was of epic dimensions, and it was distinguished by a series of brilliant, biting character sketches of his contemporaries.

But whether it was really a Tory propaganda work became more doubtful as successive volumes appeared, in 1703 and 1704. Its purpose was set out in the first paragraph, one long, swaying, Clarendonian sentence rising up from the page like a boa-constrictor roused from sleep:

'That posterity may not be deceived, by the prosperous wickedness of these times, into an opinion that less than a general combination, and universal apostasy in the whole nation from their religion and allegiance, could, in so short a time, have produced such a total and prodigious alteration and confusion over the whole kingdom; and so the memory of those few who, out of duty and conscience, have opposed and resisted that torrent which hath overwhelmed them may lose the recompense due to their virtue, and, having undergone the injuries and reproaches of this, may not find a vindication in a better age; it will not be unuseful (at least to the curiosity if not the conscience of men) to present to the world a full and clear narration of the grounds, circumstances and artifices of this rebellion, not only from the time since the flame hath been visible in a civil war, but, looking farther back, from those former passages, accidents and actions, by which the seed-plots were made and framed from whence these mischiefs have successively grown to the height they are now at'.

But for all Clarendon's talk of 'seed-plots' and 'artifices', his explanation of the causes of the Rebellion is strangly evasive. By declining to go back beyond 1625 he automatically exculpated James I, though this meant that he put the blame on his son, at least by implication. And though he painted an unflattering picture of Pym, Hampden and the other opposition leaders, he saw them as devil-driven, victims as much as victors, and since he himself, as plain Edward Hyde, MP, had taken a leading role in the opposition up to the summer of 1641, he could not very well portray it as arising from a malevolent conspiracy of long standing. Unable to say much that was derogatory of Charles I, either, he operated within very narrow limits. He wriggled out of these confines by attributing the Rebellion to (a) an accidental concatenation of circumstances, (b) God's retribution on a nation swollen with pride and softened by easy living, and (c) the follies of Charles I's ministers, particularly Buckingham and Laud.

He painted a classic picture of his master, Charles I. In fact, with Van Dyk's portraits, it has imposed on posterity a model which is almost certainly inaccurate, and yet difficult to counter. Charles emerges from Clarendon's account as a frail, rather pusillanimous ruler, too diffident of his own judgment, too easily swayed by others. There is some truth in this, but other evidence shows that Charles was often aggressive, dogmatic, impatient of advice. But Clarendon's version, uninspiring and even unflattering as it was, accorded with the rather sickly Charles-the-Martyr image created by the Anglican Church, and it enabled him to excuse the king in most circumstances; he was, after all, a mere leaf blown by the winds of Providence. Thus:

'He was very fearless in his person, but not enterprising; and had an excellent understanding but was not confident enough of it; which made him often times change his own opinion for a worse, and follow the advice of a man that did not judge so well as himself. And this made him more irresolute than the conjuncture of his affairs would admit. If he had been of a rougher and more imperious nature, he would have found more respect and duty; and his not applying some severe cures to approaching evils proceeded from the lenity of his nature and the tenderness of his conscience, which in all cases of blood made him choose the softer way'.[29]

Clearly Clarendon did not like him very much, and this becomes more apparent as the *History* proceeds:

'His kingly virtues had some mixture and allay that hindered them from shining in full lustre, and from producing those fruits they should have been attended with. He was not in his nature bountiful, though he gave very much, ... and he paused too long in giving, which made those to whom he gave less sensible of the benefit. He kept state to the full, which made his Court very orderly, no man presuming to be seen in a place where he had no pretence to be. He saw and observed men long before he received any about his person, and did not love strangers, nor very confident men'.

And he summed him up in these celebrated words:

'He was the worthiest gentleman, the best master, the best friend, the best husband, the best father, and the best Christian, that the age in which he lived had produced. And if he was not the best king, if he was without some parts and qualities which have made some kings great and happy, no other prince was ever unhappy who was possessed of half his virtues and endowments, and so much without any kind of vice'.[30]

At the same time his scathing portrait of Queen Henrietta Maria, whom he loathed, chimed in with the anti-Catholic, anti-French propensities of the Whigs, and his account of Archbishop Laud reflected little credit on the Church which had surrendered itself to his leadership. He had curiously little to say about Puritanism. His contempt for all but a few of the royalist nobility was obvious, nor was his famous summing-up on Oliver Cromwell as derogatory as might have been expected:

'Without doubt, no man with more wickedness ever attempted anything, or brought to pass what he desired more wickedly, more in the face and contempt of religion and moral honesty; yet wickedness as great as his could never have accomplished these trophies without the assistance of a great spirit, an admirable circumspection and sagacity, and a most magnanimous resolution ... To reduce three nations, which perfectly hated him, to an entire obedience to all his dictates, to awe and govern these nations by an army that was indevoted to him and wished his ruin; was an instance of a very prodigious address ... In a word, as he had all the wickedness against which damnation is denounced and for which hell fire is prepared, so he had some virtues which have caused the memory of some men in all ages to be celebrated; and he will be looked upon by posterity as a brave, bad man'.[31]

But though it was not a mere work of propaganda, nor was this history as we understand it. The contrast is evident in the life and works of a publicist of the next generation, Gilbert Burnet, bishop of Salisbury, whose pioneering work as a historian is still largely unrecognized. Throughout a long and intensely active career in politics and the Church Burnet kept a detailed diary, which in 1683 he began to convert into an autobiography, similar to Clarendon's. Since he was from time to time on intimate terms with Charles II, James II as Duke of York, William III and most of their ministers of state, these memoirs still have considerable evidential value. In 1703, directly inspired by Clarendon, he began to turn this autobiography into a narrative history, taking it back to the Restoration and taking it forward, eventually, to the Peace of Utrecht in 1713. He was no theorist, and his Whig views on the constitution were published separately as pamphlets in 1687, 1688 and 1689, but his avowed aim in his history was to justify the Revolution of 1688, just as Clarendon's had been to justify the Restoration. He also hoped to educate the English upper classes, who to him, raised as he was in Scotland, seemed 'the worst instructed and the least knowing of any of their rank I ever went amongst, ... ill taught and ill bred'. 'Plutarch's Lives', he said, 'with the Greek and Roman history, ought to be early put in their hands; they ought to be well acquainted with all history, more particularly that of their own nation, which they should not read in abridgements, but in the fullest and most copious collections of it; that they may see to the bottom what is our constitution and what are our laws, what are the methods bad princes have taken to enslave us, and by what conduct we have been preserved.' He hoped that his own *History* would make a contribution, and enable his readers to 'form just reflections and sound principles of religion and virtue, of duty to our princes, and of love to our country, with a sincere and incorruptible zeal to preserve our religion, and maintain our liberty and property'.[32]

Unfortunately he missed his mark. He died in 1715, and the first volume of the *History of My Own Time* was not published until 1724, the second following ten years later. It sold well, but largely for its scandal value. His version of many events, and his judgments on particular men, were hotly contested by the survivors or by their descendants, and the second volume, in fact, would probably never have been published at all if his son Thomas Burnet had not been in need of the money. In any case his ardent and rather naive 'revolution whiggery' was out of fashion in the Age of Walpole, and 'honest Burnet', 'noble, valuable and great', found a more appreciative audience amongst the American colonists, who still cherished an uncomplicated view of liberty, and revered the testimony of a man who had been a friend of Russell and Sidney and a confidant of the Great Deliverer.[33]

Yet in his lifetime Burnet's main claim to literary fame was his *History of the Reformation in England*, which he wrote as a comparatively young man, and which is now almost entirely forgotten. This book was a milestone, for Burnet was the first historian in the English language who attempted to reconstruct the history of an episode in modern times, yet far beyond any man's memory, from original documents, going back beyond chronicles and narratives to letters, charters and proclamations. He drew heavily on the Cottonian Library, sought government records when he could gain access to the State Paper Office, and he even consulted diocesan records. He kept up a wide correspondence with foreign scholars, and while he was abroad, from 1684 to 1688, he made copious transcripts from other records, in France, Italy and Holland, some of which he published in a supplementary volume in 1715.

The first volume, covering the reign of Henry VIII, took him two years, and he was happy in his publishing date, in May 1679, when the Popish Plot scare was still at its height and the first Exclusion Parliament was sitting. He received the thanks of the House of Commons, and an honorary D.D. from Oxford University, as well as a royal warrant giving him unrestricted access to government records. Private owners, notably Corpus Christi College, Cambridge, also threw open archives previously shut, and Lord Chancellor Finch, Lord Halifax and Lord Russell all undertook to subsidize his further research.[34] The second volume, up to the accession of Elizabeth I, appeared at a less auspicious time, just before the Oxford Parliament of March 1681, when Charles II broke finally with the Whigs. Burnet was also in disgrace with the government, but his book continued to sell well. In 1683 he fell into even deeper disfavour by espousing the cause of his patron, Lord Russell, who was convicted of treason and executed for his supposed share in the Rye House Plot. But when he paid a visit to Paris later that year he found himself lionized; he was even received in audience by Louis XIV, much to Charles II's irritation.[35] He had already made a one-volume abridgement for the English market the year before, and a French translation was now in hand; this appeared in 1684, followed by translations of the original volumes in 1687 and 1694. When he went to Rome in 1685 he had immediate access to important members of the Curia, who were prepared to discuss the problems of the Catholic Church with him fairly freely; later, when he settled in the Netherlands, he was warmly welcomed in academic circles. His work was subject to strong criticism on points of detail even then, but to the end of his long life he was accepted as the leading, if not the only authority on the English Reformation.

Posterity has not been kind. He was always a controversial and unpopular man, with an element of buffoonery about him which has rubbed off on his subsequent reputation:

> '... A big-boned northern priest,
> With pliant body and with brawny fist;
> Whose weighty blows the dusty cushions thrash,
> And make the trembling pulpit's wainscot crash'.[36]

The fact that he was Scots was enough in itself to arouse dislike and suspicion in the England of his day, and even the fact that he married two wealthy and handsome women in succession, one much older and the other much younger than himself, was the subject of unkind satire. It was Dryden who described him as 'Broad-backed and brawny, built for love's delight,/A prophet formed to make a female proselyte.' And his methods of composition gave hostages to fortune. He wrote with enviable speed – or indiscriminate haste, according to one's point of view – and he unwisely boasted that he had written the second volume of the *History of the Reformation* in six weeks. Moreover, as his biographer admits: 'The minute vigilance required [of a historian] fretted his active spirit; a rapid imagination often jumped at a conclusion; and he seems to have specially chafed against the demands of chronological precision.' He admitted himself that this last was 'one of the most necessary but ... one of the most unacceptable (to me, at least) of the labours of a historian'.[37]

Yet Burnet was disarmingly ready to admit his mistakes. Volume II contained long *corrigenda* to volume I, and volume III had a whole section devoted to them. In the preface to volume II he also paid ungrudging tribute to one of his most severe critics, one Mr Felman, rector of Hampton Mersey in Gloucestershire – 'that learned divine, and most exact inquirer into historical knowledge' – who had sent him a portmanteau-size list of errors he had detected in volume I. 'He has for many years applied his thoughts with a very searching care to the same subject', said Burnet complacently:

> 'and so was able to judge more critically of it than other readers. Some of those [errors] had escaped me, others had not come within my view; in some particulars my vouchers were not good, and in others I had mistaken my authors. These I publish at the end of this volume, being neither ashamed to confess my faults, nor unwilling to acknowledge from what hand I received better information. My design in writing is to discover truth, and to deliver it down impartially to the next age; so I should think it both a mean and criminal piece of vanity to suppress this discovery of my errors. And though the number and consequence of them had been greater

than it is, I should rather have submitted to a much severer penance, than have left the world in the mistakes I had led them into'.

True, he was disposed to regard these mistakes as being of slight importance, 'chiefly about dates', he said airily, 'or small variations in the order of time'. Nevertheless, he told his readers that he had submitted the manuscript of this second volume to the redoubtable Mr Felman beforehand, and even then, if 'there is anything left', he said, 'that may require a further recantation, I shall not decline to make it so soon as I see there is need of it; being, I hope, raised above the poor vanity of seeking my own reputation, by sacrificing truth to it'.[38]

In other words, he was certainly conscious of the need for accuracy even if he found it difficult to achieve, and he had a ninteenth-century reverence for archive or record material. Even the great Ranke commented on Burnet's 'passion for primitive sources of information', and noted with approval that 'he had a natural instinct, confirmed by study, always to go back to first sources'.[39] His *History* was, of course, a work of propaganda, but this fact was trumpeted aloud, and bias of this kind never led anyone unwittingly astray. The first two volumes were intended to counter the creeping Romanism of Charles II's reign, and in his dedication to the king he gave as the proper objectives of the Church of England 'the composing our differences at home, the establishing a closer correspondence with the reformed churches abroad, [and] the securing us from the restless and wicked practices of [the Church of Rome]'. 'For attaining these ends', he went on, 'it will be of great use to trace the steps of our first reformers; for if the landmarks they set be observed, we can hardly go out of the way.'[40] In other words, it offered a measure of academic reinforcement for that emotional and subjective account of Protestant fortitude and suffering, John Foxe's *Acts and Monuments of these Latter and Perilous Days* (usually known as the 'Book of Martyrs'), first published in 1563, and reprinted for the ninth time in 1684.

Burnet was remarkably shrewd, and by his own lights fair. He dealt gently with the question of Henry VIII's divorce, arguing that it arose from a genuine religious scruple – a position not entirely abandoned today – though his attempts to exculpate Anne Boleyn were obviously dictated by a reverence for her 'incomparable daughter', Queen Elizabeth. But he was unsparing in his criticizm of Henry's treatment of his wives, of More and Fisher, and even of Thomas Cromwell. 'These are', he admitted, 'such remarkable blemishes, that, as no man of ingenuity [*sc.* ingenuousness] can go about the whitening them, so the poor reformers drunk so deep of that bitter cup, that it very ill becomes any of their followers to endeavour to give fair colours to those red and bloody characters, with which so much of his reign is stained.' His general attitude was very much that of James Anthony Froude two hundred years later. 'If we consider the great things that were done by [King Henry]', he said, 'we must acknowledge that there was a signal providence of God in raising up a king of his temper, for clearing the way to that blessed work that followed; and that could hardly have been done, but by a man of his humour.' 'As the postilion of reformation, [he] made way for it through a great deal of mire and filth', and Almighty God 'has often showed his power and wisdom in raising up unlikely and unpromising instruments to do great services in the world, not always employing the best men in them, lest good instruments should share too deep in the praises of that which is only due to the supreme creator and governor of the world.'[41]

But his greatest merit is that he was one of the first English historians to understand the importance of causation, and the need to explain great religious movements not solely by reference to religion itself or to the actions of individuals. He said himself: 'There is no part of history better received than the account of great changes, and revolutions of states and governments, in which the variety of unlooked-for accidents and events both entertains the reader and improves him.'[42] His was a new approach, which was not taken up again until the nineteenth century; or at least until the advent of Hume. Until then this brief period 1529–58 was the only segment of English history which had been treated in a truly historical manner. As H.W.C. Davis recognized:

'He is less concerned with persons than with the genesis of new ideas in the turmoil of events. His vindication of reformed religion rests on a contrast between the system into which the earliest reformers were born and that which was established as a consequence of their revolt. His interest in the visible causes by which the transition was effected is almost purely scientific'.[43]

Sir George Clark regarded it as 'the first English book which told the story of a great historical change as a coherent whole, and in the light of the great issues which it decided'.[44]

Moreover, with all its glaring faults, the *History of the Reformation* held its own as a historical authority until well into the nineteenth century; in fact it was reprinted in six volumes by Oxford University Press in 1816, and by a London publisher in 1820 and 1825. Oxford University Press then commissioned a new edition from Edward Nares, which was published in four volumes in 1829. Of course, this must be associated with the burning contemporary issue of Catholic Emancipation, and the Catholic Question persisted, no doubt encouraging a London publisher to reissue Nares's edition in 1838, followed by an abridgement in 1841, which was reprinted in 1850 and 1857.

(Foxe's 'Book of Martyrs', in one form or another, came back into vogue at much the same time.)

It might have been expected that the first four volumes of Froude's *History*, published between 1854 and 1858, would blot Burnet out.* In the eyes of the public this was probably so, but Froude's churchmanship was distinctly questionable, and Oxford University Press went ahead and commissioned a definitive seven-volume edition from Nicholas Pocock, which it published in 1865. It survived in the reading lists for the Oxford School of Law and History, and then Modern History, for another twenty years, and the old two-volume edition of 1841 was reprinted in 1873 and 1880. So his fall from grace has been comparatively recent – if it has ever occurred. In 1902 the Oxford historian H.W.C. Davis wrote a perceptive piece on Burnet, and interest in him was heightened by the publication of a solid, though unfortunately very dull biography in 1907, to which Charles Firth contributed an introduction in which he compared Clarendon unfavourably with Burnet.[45] Strangely enough, even his prose style, for which he was castigated by the Victorians, has now swung back into favour. To James Sutherland his style is entirely acceptable – 'Natural, unpretentious, colloquial, and like the author himself, busy, bold and abundantly alive'. His conclusion is that: 'He is a bigger man, and perhaps a better historian, than he has usually been allowed to be.'[46]

* See p. 116 below.

Three

◆ ◆

The Enlightenment and Neo-Whiggism

Party animosity continued to govern the writing of history well into the eighteenth century, though it was difficult sometimes to be sure which party authors were supporting. Lawrence Echard, who published the first volumes of his *History of England* in 1707, and two further volumes, up to 1689, in 1718, is described as 'steeped in the Tory moderation of Clarendon', though he enjoyed the patronage of George I and Archbishop William Wake, the leading Whig prelate of his generation.[1] The bent of Paul de Rapin-Thoyras's *Histoire de l'Angleterre*, published 1723-5, was much clearer; not surprisingly, since Rapin-Thoyras was an exiled Huguenot officer who had sailed with William III in 1688 and subsequently fought in the Irish campaign. It was painstaking, enormously long (fifteen volumes) and impeccably Whig as Whiggism was understood at the end of the seventeenth century. It was soon translated into English by Nicholas Tindal (1726-31), with a continuation up to the death of George I in 1727, and established itself as the nearest thing to a standard history of England, though in 1744 the Whig journalist James Ralph published a detailed history of the reigns of William III, Anne and George I, 'with an introductory review of the reigns of the royal brothers Charles and James, in which are to be found the seeds of the Revolution'.

However, by this time there had been a dizzying switch in party ideology, initiated mainly by the Tory leader Bolingbroke. Bolingbroke fled abroad in 1715 in fear of impeachment, and was attainted of high treason in his absence. Pardoned in 1725, he returned to England to find his arch-rival Robert Walpole firmly established in power, and the political ethos of establishment Whiggism invulnerable to attack on the usual front. Accordingly, he set out to turn received opinion on its head. In a long series of articles for his journal *The Craftsman*, from 1726 through 1735, he and his associates shamelessly appropriated the Whig theory of the Ancient Constitution. They now agreed that England had always been a free nation, and that she had had to defend

her liberties tenaciously against a succession of authoritarian kings and their
unscrupulous favourites. (A parallel series of articles demolished the reputation of these favourites, from the Despensers via Cardinal Wolsey to Robert
Walpole.) The last great assault on English liberties, by the Stuarts, had been
repulsed at the Revolution, but this Revolution, said Bolingbroke, had never
been fully consummated, and instead of restoring English freedom under the
law it had allowed it to be undermined by a subtle process of corruption,
culminating in the long, unconstitutional 'reign' of Walpole as chief minister.
He now called for a return to an idyllic 'Old England', in which the social and
political balance would be maintained by annual general elections, a strong
citizen militia, and the exclusion of office-holders from parliament.[2]

This 'Country' programme was dangerously seductive; it had enjoyed
strong support in the parliaments of William III, and was still espoused by an
important minority of Whigs ('The Old Whigs'). Its adoption by Bolingbroke
therefore forced the ministry's defenders to embrace a Tory view of English
history which their fathers and grandfathers had passionately rejected. With
a cynicism which matched Bolingbroke's they now adopted Brady's theories
on the medieval past entire, and even extended them. Neither Brady nor
Spelman had explained the decline of feudalism; the Whigs now attributed it
to the growth of a strong middle class with its roots in trade, which had then
been given a more extensive landed base by the redistribution of monastic
estates under Henry VIII. Moreover, they drove Brady's ideas to a logical
conclusion, which even he had not dared to do, except by implication. The
Norman Conquest, they said, had enslaved England, and any subsequent
concessions, such as the issue of Magna Carta or the introduction of parliaments, were a byproduct of rivalry between the king and the aristocracy.
Parliament had not appeared at all until 1265, and then it had remained a
docile tool of monarchical or baronial power well into the sixteenth century.
Even Elizabeth I, hitherto sacrosanct in Whig mythology, was now characterized as just another tyrant, as bad as the rest, if not worse; in fact, 'never
were the reins of prerogative held with a stricter hand, or the yoke of slavery
faster bound upon the people's neck than at this period of time'. That the
Stuarts were despots, one and all, went without saying. So, the Revolution of
1688 was a heroic and dramatic reversal of all previous trends, bringing to
fruition the botched attempt in the previous generation against Charles I; it
was 'The Year I of English Liberty'.[3]

The paradoxes involved could be painful. It was no use the Whigs denying
that they were using Brady, and they made the best of a bad job by freely
admitting it. They also admitted that they were discarding several distinguished Whig theorists who had dealt with the Ancient Constitution, notably
the martyr Algernon Sidney. In fact, if we are to find echoes of Sidney's

Discourses concerning Government in the eighteenth century it is in Boling-broke's *Remarks on the History of England*. In 1735 the government-controlled *Daily Gazetteer* referred condescendingly to Sidney as an immortal hero, 'who, had he lived in these days, would never have wrote his book'.[4] Like Burnet, he found a posthumous refuge in the American colonies. Similarly, it was Bolingbroke who most often cited Rapin-Thoyras, and declared him to be the best of historians; it was the Whig Lord Hervey who dismissed him as 'The Craftsman's own political evangelist'. The *Daily Gazetteer* sneered at his devotion to the Ancient Constitution, and dismissed him as being 'without genius, or perfect knowledge of the subject'.[5]

In fact, there was a crying need for a new synthesis of English history which would overcome the prejudices of party and restore the discipline's aesthetic and moral status. But it was mortifying that this should come at the hands of a foreigner, and the first volume of David Hume's *History of England*, in 1754, met with a stormy reception on this ground alone.

Hume was born at Ninewells, in Berwickshire, in 1711. He studied law at Edinburgh University, but declined to practise it. Instead he went to France in 1734, and spent most of the next fifteen years abroad in a variety of tutorial and secretarial posts far beneath his ability, while he wrote the great philosophical works which have gained him his present reputation. But in his lifetime they were disregarded – his *Treatise of Human Nature*, published 1739-40, was not reprinted until 1817 – and in any case his notorious scepticism frustrated his ambitions for a university career in Scotland. It was not until 1752 that he was appointed Keeper of the Library of Advocates in Edinburgh, and began to write the *History*.

But he was deeply influenced by the Enlightenment, and to him history was an alternative means of propagating his philosophical ideas, or perhaps even an essential adjunct to philosophy. He read Montesquieu's *De l'Esprit des Lois* at Turin in 1749, and was at once converted to the view of history as a continuing process, governed by geography, climate, economic forces, laws, institutions, religion, which could be affected to a limited extent, but not controlled, by the intervention of individuals. It was at this stage that he drafted a first rough outline of his *History of England*. He corresponded with Montesquieu, and they exchanged copies of their works. Hume brought *De l'Esprit des Lois* back to Edinburgh and translated and published the first two chapters. It was this that determined his direction as a historian, at a time when in England history was still regarded at best as a moral or political exemplar, or as a means of civilized recreation. Hume's aim was to reduce history to a science by the close study of man in his environment, or, as he defined it in the second edition of his *Essay Concerning Human Understanding*, in 1751:

'To discover the constant and universal principles of human nature, by showing men in all varieties of circumstances and situations, and furnishing us with materials, from which we may form our observations, and become acquainted with the regular springs of human action and behaviour. These records of wars, intrigues, factions and revolutions are so many collections of experiments, by which the politician or moral philosopher fixes the principles of his science; in the same manner as the physician or natural philosopher becomes acquainted with the nature of plants, minerals, and other external objects by the experiments which he forms concerning them'.

Hugh Trevor-Roper contrasts this with the attitude of Dr Johnson, the cultural arbiter of Augustan London; to him history was 'mere mechanical compilation, in which "there is but a shallow stream of thought" and "all the greatest powers of the human mind are quiescent"'.[6]

Already, in his *Essays Moral and Political*, in 1741, Hume had attacked the concept of an Original Contract of government, regarded by many as the prime philosophical justification for the Revolution of 1688. He doubted the relevance of a concept which in the nature of things predated recorded history and could never be proved, and which ignored the fact that most states had their foundation in conquest or usurpation. Such ventures into the past were irrelevant; the structure of politics and law must be seen as an organic entity with entirely conjectural beginnings, steadily developing and mutating; and since the prime objective of man in society must be to preserve political stability and social security, he agreed with Hobbes that civil war, rebellion or revolution could never be justified.[7] And although the British constitution as it then existed might be taken to represent his ideal, his attitude towards it was more than a little ambivalent. In the first edition of his *History* he referred to it as 'that singular and happy government which we enjoy at present'. In 1772, in a fit of pique, he struck out the words 'and happy', then wrote to his publisher asking him to restore them, remarking that: 'The English government is certainly happy, though probably not calculated for duration by reason of its excessive liberty.' (Even then, Duncan Forbes reminds us that 'singular' had, and has, more than one meaning.) At the very end of the *History* he ambiguously observed: 'We, in this land, have ever since [1688] enjoyed, if not the best system of government, at least the most entire system of liberty, that was ever known amongst mankind.'[8]

His complacency was remarkable. He told a correspondent in 1753: 'You know there is no post of honour in the English Parnassus more vacant than that of history. Style, judgment, impartiality, care – everything is wanting in our historians.' And again: 'The more I advance in my undertaking, the more I am convinced that the History of England has never yet been written, not only for style, which is notorious to all the world, but also for matter; such is the ignorance and partiality of all our historians.' In the *History* he took notice of the virtues of Camden's *Elizabeth*, but seemed rather surprised at it – 'Tis well known', he said, 'that the English have not much excelled in that kind of literature.'[9] It was a justifiable attitude, certainly, but not one to endear him to the English, who still regarded the Scots as a somewhat inferior race.

It was particularly unfortunate that he chose as the subject of his first volume, published in 1754, 'that permanent historical minefield', the reigns of James I and Charles I.[10] The reaction to it in London rankled on and off for the rest of his life, seeming to fluctuate with his Scots nationalism. (It is typical that in his autobiography he parades the fact – if fact it was – that it only sold forty-five copies in London in the first year, and neglects to remind us that in Edinburgh it sold 450 copies in five weeks.) He affected to imagine that by the 1750s there was a market for impartial history, and, lacking direct experience of England, he may even have believed it. He had even chosen to begin in 1603 deliberately, because that was when 'the misrepresentation of faction began chiefly to take place'. 'I was', he said later, 'the only historian that had at once neglected present power, interest and authority, and the cry of popular prejudice; and as the subject was suited to every capacity, I expected proportional applause.' 'Instead', he went on, 'I was assailed by one cry of reproach, disapprobation and even detestation; English, Scotch and Irish, Whig and Tory, churchman and sectary, freethinker and religionist, patriot and courtier, united in their rage against the man who had presumed to shed a generous tear for the fate of Charles I and the Earl of Strafford.'[11]

He was disillusioned, of course, but he exaggerated the animosity with which the book was received, and his biographers have followed his example.[12] It received a slashing attack, certainly, in the *Monthly Review*, but otherwise its main opponent was the Revd William Warburton, and his criticisms, for what they were worth, were not published until 1756; William Pitt's hostility, which upset Hume more than anything, was never voiced in print, and seems to belong to the 1760s. Certainly it met with some hostility from the start – Horace Walpole remarked that it was 'more decried than ever book was' – but this gave it a certain cachet, as did Hume's reputation for atheism, in an age when it was becoming chic to be non-Christian. It is an exaggeration to speak of an 'uproar' or a 'hue and cry', though Hume himself used such terms.

However, party loyalties were far from dead in England, and certainly not in the press, and the time was not yet ripe for a judicious assessment of the failings of the Stuart kings, whom Old Whigs and New, and even the Tories under Bolingbroke, united to denounce as tyrants. For Hume saw the parliaments of the early Stuarts as the aggressors, not the crown; and though he admitted that much of Charles I's policy was indefensible, he argued that he was entitled to claim the protection of the Ancient Constitution and his opponents were not. His regime might not be sanctioned by express law, but it offered the only natural and generally accepted authority, and:

> 'The true rule of government ... during any period, is that to which the people, from time immemorial, have been accustomed, and to which they naturally pay a prompt obedience. A practice which has ever struck their senses, and of which they have seen and heard innumerable precedents, has another mind of authority with them, than maxims derived from antiquated statutes and mouldy records'.[13]

In other words, Hume refused to acknowledge an Ancient Constitution at all, in the sense of a permanent construct handed down intact from generation to generation; instead he offered the novel and rather giddying idea of a developing, changing constitution, adapting itself to the needs of successive generations.

His attitude was the more offensive in that many of the conventions he was attacking or dismissing, though they were retained through ingrained sentiment or political prejudice, were in fact contrary to the political life-style of most eighteenth-century Englishmen. As Macaulay said: 'The Whig who, during three parliaments, had never given one vote against the Court, and who was ready to sell his soul for the Comptroller's staff or for the Great Wardrobe, still professed to draw his political opinions from Locke and Milton, still worshipped the memory of Pym and Hampden, and would still on the thirtieth of January take his glass, first to the man in the mask, and then to the man who would do it without a mask.' Even Horace Walpole, 'the most eccentric, the most artificial, the most fastidious, the most capricious of men', kept a framed reproduction of Charles I's death warrant on his wall, inscribed 'Major Charta'.[14]

To men like this, who were conditioned to regard the reign of Charles I as one long, total conspiracy against the constitution, a period in which all Englishmen except the despot's immediate followers languished in Egyptian bondage, it was irritating, to say the least, to be assured that during the 'tyranny' of the 1630s 'the grievances under which the English laboured, when considered in themselves, scarce deserve the name; nor were they either burdensome on the people's revenues, or any way shocking to the natural humanity of mankind'.[15] To men brought up to regard Pym, Vane and Hampden as national heroes, equal to the great tribunes of Rome, it was infuriating to see Hume dismiss the comparison with scorn: 'The leisure of the noble ancients', he said, 'was totally employed in the study of Grecian eloquence and philosophy; in the cultivation of polite letters and civilized society. The whole discourse and language of the moderns were polluted with mysterious jargon, and full of the lowest and most vulgar hypocrisy.'[16]

His hostility to Puritanism was fundamental, and was the focus of the *Monthly Review*'s attack on his first volume. But his readers' reaction was ambivalent. It was generally agreed that Puritanism was the motive force behind the Great Rebellion, and that this Rebellion, whatever its outcome, was a political event of acknowledged virtue. But in an age of Reason civilized men could only regard Puritanism as an 'enthusiastic' delusion, and it was galling to be reminded that: 'Of all European nations the British were at that time, and till long after, sunk into the lowest and most odious bigotry',* or that: 'many men of the greatest parts and most extensive knowledge whom the nation at that time produced could not enjoy any peace of mind, because [they were] obliged to hear prayers offered up to the Divinity by a priest covered with a white linen vestment', or to be told that it was 'the disgrace of that age and of this island ... that the disorders in Scotland entirely, and those in England mostly, proceeded from so mean and contemptible an origin'.[17]

Also, it is easy to see why contemporaries boggled at his picture of Charles I – his 'generous tear', as he called it. The issue was not so much his temperate exposition of Charles's virtues – most historians were, and still are, ready to acknowledge his personal rectitude – but his assumption that his policy was basically correct, and that it was his opponents who were the aggressors. In fact, his interpretation was modelled on Clarendon's, and he acknowledged the debt, but this was not the time to resurrect this late-Tory thesis, which was deeply respected but largely unread. What Hume said was:

'He deserves the epithet of a good rather than a great man, and was more fitted to rule in a regular, established government, than either to give way to the encroachments of a popular assembly or finally subdue their pretensions. He wanted [*sc.* lacked] suppleness and dexterity sufficient for the first measure; he was not endowed with the vigour requisite for the second. Had he been born an absolute prince, his humanity and good sense had rendered his reign happy and his memory precious; has the limitations on prerogative been, in his time, quite fixed and ascertained, his integrity had made him regard as sacred the boundaries of the constitution. Unhappily, his fate threw him into a period, when the precedents of many former reigns savoured strongly of arbitrary power, and the genius of the people ran violently towards liberty. And if his political prudence was insufficient to

* Altered in later editions to, 'under the influence of that religious spirit which tends rather to inflame bigotry than increase peace and mutual charity'.

extricate him from so perilous a situation he may be excused, since even
after the event, when it is commonly easy to correct all errors, one is at a
loss to determine what conduct, in his circumstances, could have maintained the authority of the crown and preserved the peace of the nation.
Exposed to the assaults of furious, implacable and bigoted factions, it was
never permitted him, without the most fatal consequences, to commit the
smallest mistake; a condition too rigorous to be imposed on the greatest
human capacity'.[18]

His second volume, taking the story up to 1688, appeared in 1756, and he
thought he had made a serious error in not issuing the two together, because
the second rectified the balance of the narrative. He poured scorn on the
superstitious bigotry and intolerance of the Interregnum governments, and
applauded the Restoration. Unfortunately, he said, the chance of a new start
after 1660, a rebirth, was thrown away, and if the discords in the first half of
the century had been provoked largely by parliament, in the second they were
almost entirely provoked by the monarchy; he had few excuses to offer for
Charles II and none for James II. Nevertheless, placing himself on the side
of the Walpolean Whigs, he argued that the Revolution of 1688 marked 'a
new epoch in the constitution', and those who portrayed it entirely as a
reaction against monarchical aggression were in danger of diminishing its
novelty:

> 'To decry with such violence, as is affected by some, the whole line of
> Stuart, to maintain that their administration was one continued encroach-
> ment on the incontestable rights of the people, is not giving due honour to
> that great event, which not only put a period to their hereditary succession,
> but made a new settlement of the whole constitution'.[19]

This gave him the opportunity to restate, with even greater sharpness, his
defence of James I and Charles I:

> 'While the parliaments in these reigns were taking advantage of the necess-
> ities of the prince, and attempting every session to abolish or circumscribe
> or define some prerogative of the crown, and innovate in the usual tenor of
> government, what could be expected, but that the prince would exert
> himself in defending against such inveterate enemies an authority which,
> during the most regular course of English government, had been exercised
> without dispute or controversy?[20]

Finally, his animosity sharpened by hostile criticism, he launched a comprehensive attack on the Whig historians, and on the Whig politicians of his
own day. The history of the previous century, he said, had for too long been

'clouded and obscured' by 'the representations of faction'. He was now the first to reveal the truth, 'without covering or disguise'. The Whig party, which had always boasted of its regard for liberty, had had no regard for liberty of thought. Indeed, 'obliged to court the favour of the populace, they found it necessary to comply with their rage and folly, and have even, on many occasions, by propagating calumnies and by promoting violence, served to infatuate as well as corrupt that people, to whom they made a tender of liberty and justice'. The prime example, of course, was the Popish Plot – 'a fiction which exceeds the ordinary bounds of vulgar credulity'.[21] Yet in the middle of the next century it was still propagating the same falsehoods:

'The Whig Party, for a course of near seventy years, has almost without interruption enjoyed the whole authority of government, and no honours or office could be obtained but by their countenance and protection. But this event, which in some particulars has been advantageous to the state, has proved destructive to the truth of history, and has established many gross falsehoods, which it is unaccountable how any civilized nation could have embraced with regard to its domestic occurrences. Compositions the most despicable, both for style and matter, have been extolled and propagated and read, as if they equalled the most celebrated remains of antiquity.* And forgetting that a regard to liberty, though a laudable passion, ought commonly to be subordinate to a reverence for established government, the prevailing faction has celebrated only the partisans of the former, who pursued as their object the perfection of civil society, and has extolled them at the expense of their antagonists, who maintained those maxims that are essential to its very existence'.[22]

The Whigs took this on the chin. The second volume was issued by a London publisher and sold well; so did a reprint of the first. It now appeared that the poor sales of the first volume in London reflected as much as anything the fact that it had been handled by an inexperienced Edinburgh firm. Certainly Hume was emboldened to go on, and his research into the Tudors soon convinced him that he ought to have begun with Henry VII, as Adam Smith had originally advised, for in the authoritarian regime established by Henry VIII and reinforced by Elizabeth he found ample justification for the claims of the first two Stuarts to absolute power. *England under the House of Tudor* was published in 1759, and Richard Hurd sarcastically remarked that Hume obviously 'judged it necessary to the charm to reverse the order of things, and to evoke this frightful spectre [of absolute monarchy] by writing (as witches used to say their prayers) backwards'.[23]

* In a footnote Hume cited Rapin-Thoyras, Locke, Sidney and Benjamin Hoadly.

The catalogue of Henry VIII's vices did not call for improvement either way, and since Hume did not regard the Reformation with any enthusiasm, the king's share in it did not have the palliative charm for him it had had for Burnet. Nor was his 'absolute uncontrolled authority' in doubt, or 'that entire dominion, by which his reign is so much distinguished in English history'. What surprised him was that 'notwithstanding his cruelty, his extortion, his violence, his arbitrary administration, this prince not only acquired the regard of his subjects, but never was the object of their hatred'. He comfortably concluded that: 'The English in that age were so thoroughly subdued, that, like eastern slaves, they were inclined to admire those acts of violence and tyranny which were exercised over themselves, and at their own expense.'[24]

The logical extension of this thesis to cover the reign of Elizabeth was less acceptable, but Hume unhesitatingly made it. Elizabeth's singular reputation had not withered with age, and as the seventeenth century progressed it was increasingly felt that she was the last ruler who had understood the Ancient Constitution, her reign the last in which there had been a perfect understanding between the monarch and the people; it was an assumption scarcely questioned by Whig historians like Rapin-Thoyras. True, like many ripe Whig myths this had been taken over by Bolingbroke, who extolled Elizabeth as the archetype of a moderate Tory ruler, and this had driven the Whig establishment onto the opposite tack. In his *Ancient and Modern Liberty Stated and Compared*, in 1734, Lord Hervey had refused to use the word 'liberty' in relation to any regime before 1688.[25] But how far this had penetrated the popular consciousness is doubtful, and Hume's studied demolition of the Elizabethan legend must have been a shock to the sensibilities of many readers, though his interpretation, once established, held its own well into the twentieth century.

He acknowledged Elizabeth's great abilities. As he rather quaintly put it: 'We may find it difficult to reconcile our fancy to her as a wife or mistress, but her qualities as a sovereign are the object of undisputed applause.' But approbation was no excuse for adulation. The Whig historians had 'long indulged their prejudices against the succeeding race of princes by bestowing unbounded panegyrics on the virtue and wisdom of Elizabeth'; unfortunately, in their ignorance and partiality they had extolled her for 'a quality which, of all others, she was the least possessed of – a tender regard for the constitution, and a concern for the liberties and privileges of her people'.[26] In fact, she had exercised her authority in a manner 'contrary to all the ideas which we at present entertain of a legal constitution'. Not surprisingly, since there was no 'legal constitution' in her day; the legislative authority of parliament was 'a mere fallacy', and its power over taxation meaningless, since it never refused any taxes demanded of it.* He went so far as to liken England to contemporary Turkey – the favourite whipping-boy of the Whig historians – and Elizabeth to Peter the Great of Russia. Far from being a more temperate and enlightened ruler than the Stuart kings, she was much less so, for:

> 'The prerogatives of this princess were scarcely ever disputed, and she therefore employed them without scruple; her imperious temper, a circumstance in which she went far beyond her successors, rendered her exertions of power violent and frequent, and discovered the whole extent of her authority'.[27]

It was then almost inevitable, given the success of the *History* so far, that Hume should turn back to the Middle Ages. In fact, for the first time he took an advance from his publisher, of £1,400. He approached the task with his usual drive and competence, and the final section of the *History*, from the landing of Julius Caesar to the battle of Bosworth, appeared in 1761.

His treatment of the Middle Ages was detached, but comparatively uncontentious. He concluded that prior to the Norman Conquest the English polity was so barbarous and uncivilized that there could be no question of the survival of immemorial rights; if the king was strong, then government was despotic, if he was weak, popular. In any case, he agreed with Brady that the Norman Conquest was absolute and final, and destroyed any precedent popular rights which might have survived. Nor was Magna Carta a charter of general liberty, and the best he could say of it was that it inaugurated a new kind of government which outlasted the Middle Ages – baronial despotism instead of royal despotism. However, he admitted that it provided 'all the chief outlines of a legal government', particularly 'the equal distribution of justice and free enjoyment of property; the great objects for which political society was at first founded by men'; so that, 'without seeming anywise to innovate in the distribution of political power, [it] became a kind of epoch in the constitution'.

As for the great controversy over the date of parliament's foundation, he blandly assumed – with some justice – that the verdict had already gone against the Whigs:

> 'The question was once disputed in England with great acrimony, but such is the force of time and evidence that they can sometimes prevail even over faction; and the question seems, by general consent and by their own, to be at last determined against the ruling party'.

* A point firmly made by G.R. Elton in recent years; for instance, in *TRHS*, 5th series, xxiv (1974), 190–1. In fact, Hume's jaundiced view of Elizabeth is now coming back into fashion. See p. 208 below.

But in any case it was a fallacy, he smugly informed them, to appeal to the example of past generations:

> 'The only rule of government which is intelligible, or carries any authority with it, is the established practice of the age, and the maxims of administration which were at the time prevalent and universally assented to. Those who, from a pretended respect to antiquity, appeal at every turn to an original plan of the constitution, only cover their turbulent spirit and their private ambition under the appearance of venerable forms'.[28]

In any case, as a man of the Enlightenment he had no interest in, or sympathy with, the Middle Ages, and his relief was manifest as he approached 1485. 'We have pursued the history of England', he said, 'through a series of many barbarous ages, till we have at last reached the dawn of civility and science, and have the prospect both of greater certainty in our historical narrations, and of being able to present to the reader a spectacle more worthy of his attention.'[29]

But by now his *History* had attained the recognition it deserved, and he had assuaged what he confessed to be his 'ruling passion', a 'love of literary fame'. The *Annual Register* gave him its highest accolade in 1761, when it wrote:

> 'Our writers had commonly so ill succeeded in history, the Italians, and even the French, had so long continued our acknowledged superiors, that it was almost feared that the British genius, which had so happily displayed itself in every other kind of writing, and gained the prize in most, yet could not enter in this. The historical work Mr Hume has published discharged our country from this opprobrium'.

And the young Edward Gibbon gladly acknowledged him as the master, not only in interpretation but in style – 'The calm philosophy, the careless, inimitable beauties', he said, 'often forced me to close the volume with a mixed sensation of delight and despair.'[30] He sold the copyright for a new, complete edition in 1763 for the then unprecedented sum of £3,000.

He was so far mollified as to come down to London in 1758, with some intention of settling there. But he found the Hanoverian capital much more philistine than the new Edinburgh of the Scottish Enlightenment, and he soon retreated to the company of his friends there, who now included another brilliant historian in William Robertson. 'I believe this is the historical age', he said later, 'and this is the historical nation.'[31] He was neurotically sensitive to criticism, and for the rest of his life he worked away at the *History*, revising it for successive editions, and consciously and defiantly reinforcing its so-called Tory bias. His sensitivity had a strong nationalist tinge, at times mounting to paranoia; in 1761 he told a friend: 'I do not believe that there is one Englishman in fifty, who, if he heard that I had broke my neck tonight, would not be rejoiced with it. Some hate me because I am not a Tory, some because I am not a Whig, some because I am not a Christian, and all because I am a Scotsman.' No doubt this had its basis in a very thick Scots accent, which he tried in vain to eradicate. He was haunted by the fear that it might taint his writing; as he told John Wilkes in 1754: 'Notwithstanding all the pains I have taken in the study of the English language, I am still jealous [*sc.* suspicious] of my pen. As to my tongue, you have seen that I regard it as totally desperate and irreclaimable.'[32]

But in 1763 he was granted a civil list pension of £200 a year on the intercession of George III's Scots favourite, Lord Bute. The king wanted him to continue his *History* beyond 1688, and approached Robertson on the same quest. Even more splendid and consoling was the unsolicited offer in 1764 of the post of secretary to the new British ambassador to Paris, the Earl of Hertford. Hume was astonished by his reception in Paris, where his *History*, in the original and in translation, had made an overwhelming impression, and was acclaimed in the most extravagant terms. Voltaire, for instance, admitted that nothing he could say could add to the prestige of the *History*, which was 'perhaps the best written in any language'.[33] 'Le bon David' found himself lionized in the salons, and cosseted by the royal family. The Dauphin was one of his greatest admirers; indeed, as Louis XVI he was to model his conduct at his trial and execution on Charles I's, as described by Hume.[34] To his delighted embarrassment he even found himself pursued by one of the great beauties of France, the comtesse de Boufflers. This adulation was sustained for the whole period of his stay, and sophisticated visitors from London like Horace Walpole, who were clearly accustomed to treating him with some condescension, had to adjust their conduct accordingly or risk disfavour with the great.[35]

Still fighting off the fair comtesse, he returned to England in 1765 a much more self-confident and well-adjusted man: 'You have saved me', he told her, 'from a total indifference towards everything in human life.'[36] He needed little urging from Lord Hertford, now his close friend, to accept an under-secretaryship of state under his brother, General Conway. Through the Conway family he had the entree to the houses of all the Whig aristocracy; he was elected to Almack's, the exclusive gambling club, and he was almost as much in demand for dinner parties, soirées and country house weekends as he had been in France. Nor was his intellectual eminence forgotten. Gibbon sent him the first part of his history of Switzerland, in French, and bowed to his decision that he should thenceforth write in English, the language of the future. 'Let the French triumph', said Hume, 'in the present diffusion of their tongue; our solid and increasing establishments in America, where we need less dread the inundations of barbarians, promise a superior stability and duration to the English language.'[37] His civil list pension, doubled in 1765, was increased again, to £600, in 1767, and no doubt he needed it, despite his high literary earnings; but he found London so congenial that he stayed on for another eighteen months after General Conway's resignation, and his own, in January 1768.

He finally returned to Edinburgh in August 1769, ostensibly to continue his *History* into the eighteenth century. But he had no such intention, though his publisher told him it was 'the only thing wanting to fill up the measure of your glory as the Great Historian and Philosopher of the Eighteenth Century'. He declined, as he said, for four reasons: 'Because I am too old, too fat, too lazy and too rich.'[38] Also he had returned home to die; a longstanding bowel disorder, perhaps cancer, was pulling him down. He continued to correspond with friends in London, but his animosity towards the English was only dormant. Resisting the further importunities of his publisher, he told him: 'Considering the treatment I have met with, it would have been very silly of me at my years to continue writing any more; and still more blameable to warp my principles and sentiments in conformity to the prejudices of a stupid, factious nation, with whom I am heartily disgusted.' As for finding an English-man to continue the task, 'That nation', he said, 'is so sunk in stupidity and barbarism and faction that you may as well think of Lapland for an author', and when Gibbon sent him the first volume of his *Decline and Fall of the Roman Empire* in 1776 he acknowledged the gift in these words: 'If I had not previously had the happiness of your personal acquaintance, such a perform-ance from an Englishman of our age would have given me some surprise.'[39]

He died a few months later, on 25 August 1776, amid considerable publicity and deeply philosophic to the end. (One of the penalties of blatant atheism was that you never died in peace.) In fact he was in a state of high compla-cency, and confident of his fame. In his will he asked that: 'A monument be built over my body at an expense not exceeding £100, with an inscription containing only my name, with the year of my birth and death, leaving it to posterity to add the rest.'[40]

Posterity has added a great deal, of course, though it is his philosophy, largely derided in his own lifetime, which has ensured his fame, his history being studied as an adjunct to it. He would not have quarrelled with this view; he saw his *History* as a philosophic construct, and never aimed at a complete or accurate recapitulation of events. So he had none of that devotion to sources which had inspired Burnet, and which William Robertson thought obligatory; in the first edition of volume I he did not provide any references at all. From the footnotes to subsequent editions, and his correspondence, it is clear that he used the expected printed sources: Clarendon, Whitelocke, Rushworth, Dudley Carleton's letters, Walker's *History of Independency*, Rymer's *Foedera*, and so on. He also made good use of the *Commons Journals*, which had only recently been printed. The notes to later volumes show a similar pattern. He took his responsibilities seriously, and when he was preparing for the last volume he ordered a large number of medieval collections for the Advocates' Library; the facilities the Library offered him were probably one reason why he preferred to write in Edinburgh.[41] But he was indifferent to manuscript collections unless they were thrust under his nose, and during his extended visits to London he made no effort to study in the British Museum, though he was not above appropriating an important letter found there by his rival Mrs Macaulay and inserting it in later editions.[42] There is only one exception. At the Scots College in Paris he was shown the manuscript 'memoirs' of James II, from which he learned of the secret Treaty of Dover. He recommended his friend Sir John Dalrymple to look further into the French archives, and incorporated some of his discoveries in his final version. This added to the gravamen of his charges against Charles II, but it is the only example of his making use of manuscripts, and even then it is unfortunately typical of the man that he got Dalrymple to do the hard work for him, then sneered at the result. When volume I of Dalrymple's *Memoirs of Great Britain and Ireland* appeared in 1771 he said: 'There is not a new circumstance of the least importance from the beginning to the end of the work.' He could not very well say this of volume II, in 1773, but he dismissed it as 'curious, but far from being agreeable reading'.[43]*

In fact, his attitude towards evidence in general is somewhat suspect. Many modern historians have secretly wished that their evidence were less abundant, but few would admit it as openly as Hume, in a letter to the editor of the Clarendon Papers:

> 'Do you intend to publish all Clarendon's papers, or only the more material ones? I should think the last method more satisfying to everybody except historians; and even they would not be displeased that you spare them a great deal of superfluous reading. Had Thurloe's papers† been reduced to one volume, they had been more useful as well as more entertaining'.[44]

After his death one of his friends gave a rather disconcerting picture of his working methods. When some of Hume's mistakes were pointed out to him he replied: 'Why, man, David read a vast deal before he set about a piece of his book, but his usual seat was the sofa, and he often wrote with his legs up;

---

* For Dalrymple see pp. 64–5 below.

† Published in seven volumes in 1742, and already consulted by Hume, of course.

and it would have been unco' fashious [intolerably inconvenient] to have moved across the room when any little doubt appeared'.[45] However, he was more prone to omission than inaccuracy, and his account of the seventeenth century, which he always regarded as the most important part of the *History*, is particularly difficult to fault on that score.

In any case it was manner rather than matter which preoccupied him, and he deliberately rejected the anxious method of his predecessors, particularly Echard and Rapin, who interlarded their narrative with copious extracts from, and often complete transcripts of original documents; in contrast he rarely quoted at all. In 1754 he told one of his friends:

'I have more proposed as my model the concise manner of the ancient historians than the prolix, tedious style of some modern compilers. I have inserted no original papers, and entered into no detail of minute, uninteresting facts. The philosophical spirit, which I have so much indulged in all my writings, finds here ample materials to work upon'.[46]

He must have worked hard on his style, though he gives us no detail of his method, and it was his urbanity and grace, and the ease with which he moved his narrative along, which brought him so large an audience. It is a style recently described as 'the fastest and smoothest vehicle in historical literature'.[47]

In his lifetime he had many critics, of course, but only one serious rival, Catherine Macaulay. Mrs Macaulay (who was no relation to Thomas Babington Macaulay) was a celebrated, even notorious figure in her generation. With her brother, Alderman John Sawbridge, MP, and Thomas Hollis, she dominated a miscellaneous group of radicals and republicans contemptuously dismissed by Hume as 'the Sanhedrin at Mrs Macaulay's'. She was a big woman of striking physical beauty and irrepressible energy, who was constantly in the public eye. Her second marriage, in 1778, to a man more than twenty-five years her junior occasioned predictable public comment, and there is no doubt that she was hampered by the prejudices of a misogynistic age. Mary Wollstonecraft called her 'the woman of the greatest abilities that this country has ever produced'.[48]

The study of Roman history had given her an almost hysterical passion for liberty, and she reacted quite violently against Hume's portrayal of the seventeenth century.[49] In 1763 she published the first of eight volumes on the history of England from the accession of James I to the death of Anne, which provoked an exchange of letters with Hume, at his most urbane. Apologizing for the delay in acknowledging the presentation copy she had sent him, which had been delayed in transit to Paris, he said:

'I should not otherwise have been so long wanting to express my thanks for the pleasure your performance has given me, even when you oppose my sentiments. I find, indeed, that you often do me the honour to keep me in your eye during the course of your narration; and I flatter myself that we differ less in facts than in our interpretation and construction of them'.

However, it was more than a matter of interpretation, and she drew from him an important statement of principle. He told her firmly:

'I look upon all kinds of subdivision of power, from the monarchy of France to the freest democracy of some Swiss cantons, to be equally legal, if established by custom and authority. I cannot but think that the mixed monarchy of England, such as it was left by Queen Elizabeth, was a lawful form of government, and carried obligations to obedience and allegiance; at least it must be acknowledged that the princes and ministers who supported that form, though somewhat arbitrarily, could not incur much blame on that account, and that there is more reason to make an apology for their antagonists than for them. I grant that the cause of liberty which you, madam, with the Pyms and Hampdens, have adopted, is noble and generous; but most of the partisans of that cause in the last century disgraced it with their violence, and also by their cant, hypocrisy and bigotry, which, more than the principles of civil liberty, seem to have been the motive of all their actions'.[50]

He ended in a blaze of gallantry – 'had those principles always appeared in the amiable light which they receive both from your person and writings, it would have been impossible to resist them' – but the gulf between them continued to widen, particularly with the publication of her third volume in 1767, in which she lauded the leaders of the Long Parliament, so condescendingly deflated by Hume, with the most extravagant praise.[51] Her progress was slow, and on his death in 1776 she had only reached 1660, in five volumes. An occasional reference in his correspondence betrays a simmering irritation,[52] and he resented the fact that she was supported by prominent politicians, notably Chatham. It is as well that he did not live to hear of her triumphal reception in Paris in 1777, which rivalled his own, or her even more splendid tour of the United States in 1784 and 1785, when she was received by Washington at Mount Vernon.

Fate dealt unfairly with her. Her coverage of the seventeenth century was obviously more extensive than Hume's, and it was deeper; she worked on documents and records at the British Museum and the State Paper Office, though in an episodic way. (She was very much of her era in that she went to the archives hoping to find support for her views on specific points.) She was not Hume's equal as a prose stylist, but she was far from being a dull writer, and she knew how to move her narrative along. However, her fame did not outlast her life; in the backwash of the French Revolution her flaunted republicanism became abruptly unfashionable, and even unpatriotic. She finished the book, but it was not reprinted, and in a generation it was forgotten.

To the leaders of Whig opinion the whole business of Hume was inexplicable. 'That he should have sided with the Tudors and the Stuarts against the people', said Francis Jeffrey, 'seems quite inconsistent with all the great traits of his character', and Charles James Fox found 'his partiality to kings and princes' intolerable.[53] As for Macaulay, he positively hated him. In an early essay for the *Edinburgh Review*, in 1828, he admitted that he was 'the ablest and most popular writer of his class', but he went on to denounce him as a dangerous and underhand manipulator of the record:

'Without positively asserting more than he can prove, he gives prominence to all the circumstances which support his case; he glides lightly over those which are unfavourable to it; his own witnesses are applauded and encouraged; the statements which seem to throw discredit on them are controverted; the contradictions into which they fall are explained away; a clear and connected abstract of their evidence is given. Everything that is offered on the other side is scrutinised with the utmost severity; every suspicious circumstance is a ground for comment and invective; what cannot be denied is extenuated, or passed by without notice; concessions even are sometimes made: but this insidious candour only increases the effect of the vast mass of sophistry'.[54]

Unfortunately, this sounds very much like Macaulay's own technique, and he may even have realized it; this particular essay was never reprinted in his lifetime.

Macaulay may genuinely have believed that Hume was poisoning the wells of truth, or he may simply have been jealous of his phenomenal success. Hume's *History of England* was reprinted three times in his lifetime, with successive amendments, and the final version, with a short autobiography, was published in 1778, two years after his death. This was reprinted in 1782, 1789 and 1791 – the French Revolution adding weight to his Tory interpretation of the past – followed by eleven more editions between 1808 and 1832, spawning on the way many curious byproducts, such as 'Hume's History of England revised for family use' by G.B. Mitchell, in 1816. A luxurious folio edition published between 1793 and 1806 contained more than a hundred illustrations commissioned from the leading artists of the day. The originals, exhibited at Robert Bowyer's 'Historic Gallery' in Pall Mall, had a seminal effect on the development of nineteenth-century history painting.[55] He even invaded the universities. William Smyth, the first active professor of history at Cambridge (1807–49), lectured almost exclusively from Hume. 'It is Hume', he said, 'who is read by everyone. Hume is the historian whose views and opinions insensibly become our own. He is respected and admired by the most enlightened reader; he is the guide and philosopher of the ordinary reader, to whose mind, on all the topics connected with our history, he entirely gives the tone and law.'[56]

Hume's *History*, as Smyth saw, operated on two levels, and he was a figure in popular culture in a way which his fellow Enlightenment historians, Robertson and Gibbon, were not. History made Robertson, just as it made Hume, and the emergence of both men in the same generation testifies to the vigour of the Scottish Enlightenment. Robertson published *A History of Scotland during the Reigns of Queen Mary and King James VI* in 1759, when he was only thirty-five, and it made an even greater impression in London than it did in Edinburgh – where he fell foul, in fact, of Mary's ardent defenders. It was wholeheartedly admired by Gibbon and Burke, and Lord Chesterfield declared it to be 'equal in beauty and elegance to [the histories] of Livy'. It straight away earned him the considerable sum of £600 – his publishers, Cadell & Millar, were reputed to have cleared ten times as much – and two years later it was no doubt an important factor in the translation of this promising but hitherto unknown young minister from a country parish to the Kirk of the Greyfriars in Edinburgh, one of the premier livings in the Church of Scotland. In 1762 he was appointed Principal of Edinburgh University, and the following year Moderator of the General Assembly of the Church of Scotland. George III and Lord Bute were anxious for him to write a new history of England – no doubt despairing of Hume – but he turned instead to European history, and in 1769 produced his masterpiece, *The Emperor Charles V*, for which he received the stupendous sum of £4,500, putting even Hume's royalties in the shade. In 1777 he published a *History of America*, and in 1779 *A Historical Disquisition concerning the Knowledge which the Ancients had of India*, showing himself sensitive, in an oblique way, to two of the most important public issues of his time.[57]

Of course, this was the bent of the Enlightenment mind; Robertson, like Hume, was deeply influenced by Montesquieu, and acknowledged a considerable debt to Voltaire. The art of history was to use a topic or a restricted period as a peg on which to hang philosophical reflections of universal relevance, or as the focus of a general sociological survey. Thus the most important part of his *History of Scotland* was his analysis of Scottish feudalism; of *Charles V* his extended introductory survey of the history of Germany since the fall of the Roman Empire.[58] Indeed, in Scotland at this time there was a marked reaction against narrative or biographical history. John Logan, in his *Elements of the Philosophy of History*, published in 1781, deprecated the current preoccupation with the achievements of great men – 'All that legislators, patriots, philosophers, statesmen and kings can do', he wrote, 'is to give a direction to that stream which is for ever flowing.'[59] The great Adam Ferguson, in his *Essay on the History of Civil Society* (1767), had already sketched out a 'total' history, covering commerce, social habits and the arts, as well as politics and war – indeed, he and his fellow Scots Dugald Stewart and Andrew Millar have been hailed as the fathers of modern sociology. The brief general chapters on trade and social trends tacked by Hume onto his account of each reign were a hesitant step in the same direction, and Robertson himself stressed the need for a much broader approach:

> 'It is a cruel mortification searching for what is instructive in the history of past times, to find that the exploits of conquerors who have desolated the earth, and the freaks of tyrants who have rendered nations unhappy, are recorded with minute and often disgusting accuracy, while the discovery of useful arts, and the progress of the most beneficial branches of commerce, are passed over in silence, and suffered to sink into oblivion'.[60]

Thus Robert Henry, an Edinburgh clergyman, published a six-volume *History of England* in 1771 arranged in 'themes': politics, religion, commerce, social life, and so on. Dull and conventional as it was, it brought its author £3,300 in royalties and a civil list pension of £100 a year.[61] In Scotland the feeling was growing that in order to understand *any* history it was necessary to study *all* history, a point which was put with great force by George Thompson, whose public lectures on history to Edinburgh audiences were published in 1791 under the title *The Spirit of General History*. He argued that it was the historian's mission 'to teach men to endeavour to remove the evils which are pernicious to society; to correct the faults of government, and establish public good upon a right foundation'. But to do this he must consider the whole of human history, not just a part of it, for, he said, 'The history of mankind, from the beginning of the world to the present time, is a chain consisting of many links; and to strike off one would be to discompose the whole.'[62]

This concern with history is reflected to some extent in the Scots universities. As early as 1692 a lectureship in Civil and Ecclesiastical History was established in Glasgow though this mutated into a chair of Ecclesiastical history alone in 1716. In 1719 a chair of Universal Civil History was founded at Edinburgh, and St Andrews followed suit in 1747. The Edinburgh chair was subsequently absorbed by the Faculty of Law, and the St Andrews chair degenerated into a sinecure, being refounded in 1850, rather remarkably, as a chair of Civil and Natural History.[63] But in England the regius chairs of modern history founded by George I at Oxford and Cambridge in 1724 were sinecures from the start. Since history, apart from ancient history, formed no part of the curriculum, there was no compulsion on the professor to teach, and his emoluments of £400 a year were princely by contemporary academic standards. After Lord Townshend's retirement in 1730 the government lost interest altogether in the original purpose of the scheme, which had been to train recruits for the diplomatic service.[64] By 1762 Gregory Sharpe, Fellow of Trinity, was applying to Lord Bute for the Cambridge chair in these terms: 'Unsuccessful in my profession, and infirm and lame, I am compelled to solicit for some addition to my present income.' Not surprisingly, perhaps, he failed, but as a professor he could not have been more of a scandal than his successful rival Lawrence Brockett, who had the advantage of being Bute's son-in-law. A man of 'free and luxurious' life, with no scholarly pretensions in any subject, he died prematurely in 1768 after falling dead drunk from his horse.[65] When the Oxford chair fell vacant in 1770 George III characteristically intervened with the novel demand that this prime piece of patronage should 'not be given by favour, but according to merit'. This secured the nomination for Thomas Nowell, Principal of St Mary's Hall, who was certainly a staunch Tory, and is said to have given regular lectures, though no account of them has survived. His main claim to fame is a sensationally royalist sermon preached before the House of Commons on 30 January 1772, the anniversary of Charles I's execution, for which he narrowly escaped censure because only about five MPs had been present.

In England, in fact, it was the dissenting academies which maintained the study of history. These academies had emerged and flourished since the Revolution of 1688 to serve the needs of the Protestant Nonconformists, who were still barred from the universities by the requirement that students as well as staff be practising members of the Church of England. Their syllabuses put the emphasis on practical career training, and though they did not ignore the classics altogether they found increasing room for modern language, modern history and rudimentary economics as well as modern history.[66] Moreover, they spurned the parochialism of so much British historical writing; the eternal verities which were still the bedrock of all education could best be learned through the study of world history, or universal history.

This produced a plethora of elementary 'cribs', skeletal outlines of events and compendia of 'useful facts', but at the other extreme it produced the series of brilliant lectures delivered by the scientist Joseph Priestley to his students at Warrington Academy. In 1788 he was persuaded to publish his introductory course on world history, under the title *Lectures on History and General Policy*. They opened with a wide-ranging review of the possible sources for history, including numismatics, heraldry and place-name studies, as well as books and manuscripts, followed by a survey of the ancillary sciences – philology, geography, economics, statistics and what we would call psychology. (Priestley called it 'knowledge of human nature'.) In the main body of the course he directed the hard-working student's attention not only to constitutional and political history, but to 'biography, politics, manufacturing and commerce, forms and problems of government and law, agriculture, the arts, colonies and colonisation, money, luxury and manners, religion, population, war and national finance'.[67] It is easy to mock this kind of omnicompetent compendium, but in fact Priestley's lectures were remarkably solid, and they were reprinted many times in the handy octavo edition of 1826. They had an immense influence, particularly in America, where they were still being used and recommended in the 1880s, and it is not too fanciful to suppose that it is this and similar books which have made courses in 'World History' or 'World Civilization' a compulsory element in the syllabuses of so many American colleges.*

But the only European historian whom England produced turned his back on the universities in the most ostentatious way. Edward Gibbon's *Decline and Fall of the Roman Empire* was one of the masterworks of the Enlightenment. Gibbon chose his theme, vast as it was, to illustrate a general process in history, and he neither hoped nor desired that it should be continued by others into a later era. He originally intended to write the history of Switzerland, a much more isolated and clinical specimen.[68] His contempt for superstition, his mistrust of Christianity, his condescension towards the Middle Ages, earned him a mixed reception in England, but in its assessment of political forms, its stress on the balance between monarchy, aristocracy and democracy, or king, Lords and Commons, the *Decline and Fall* was the culmination of establishment Whiggism.[69] Yet its central message, that even the greatest, the best-organized, the most powerful states can decay again into barbarism, sounded a chill note of pessimism, almost at once reinforced by the outbreak of the French Revolution.

Gibbon's learning was prodigious, and his scholarship almost immune to criticism. He was merciless with his critics, and G.M. Young says of his famous *Vindication*: 'It has at times a nightmarish effect, as of a dream in which we see the Great Pyramid eternally pursuing, and always about to tread on, a mouse.'[70] Richard Porson, the famous Cambridge classicist, checked every one of his references to the Byzantine historians and found not a single misquotation; Robertson said the same of the earlier classical authors. Yet in many ways it was a curiously static performance. Gibbon gained direct inspiration from his first visit to the decaying ruins of Rome, as he records in that famous passage in his autobiography: 'It was at Rome, on the fifteenth

* Alexander Frazer Tytler's lectures in Edinburgh, published in outline in 1782, and in full in 1801 as *Elements of General History*, had a similar influence in America.

of October 1764, as I sat musing amid the ruins of the Capitol, while the barefooted friars were singing vespers in the temple of Jupiter, that the idea of writing the decline and fall of the city first started to my mind.'[71] Yet he never went beyond this. Though so much of his work was concerned with the Byzantine Empire he never went to Greece or Asia Minor, nor, apparently, did it ever occur to him to do so. His enormous and all-embracing knowledge of geography, topography and climatic conditions in distant places was painfully reconstructed from books, maps and manuscripts.[72]

That is not to say that he was alone in this. His technique was typical of the age. Hume never thought it necessary, as Macaulay did, to visit the scenes of his narrative, even in Scotland. Robertson prided himself on his exact documentation, and published original material in supplementary volumes, but he rarely left Edinburgh, and then he never went further than London. In the preface to his history of the Americas he is proud to reveal that a Mr Waddilove, chaplain to the Madrid embassy, had laboured for five years on his behalf, procuring rare books, transcribing manuscripts in the Spanish archives, even distributing questionaires to government officials. Sir Murray Keith, ambassador to Vienna, had answered queries about the Habsburg archives there; Governor Hutchinson of Massachusetts had been most obliging; Dr Rogerson, physician to Catherine the Great, had been allowed access on his behalf to the jealously-guarded archives of the Tsars at St Petersburg; and so on.[73] The insistence of Ranke a generation later that true history could not be written without recourse to the archives gives the unfortunate impression that no one before him had used them; the difference is that in the nineteenth century the historian went to the archives,* in the eighteenth century they sometimes came to him.

As for Gibbon's *Decline and Fall*, it remained 'an enduring monument of research, an imperishable literary possession, and one of the highest encouragements to intellectual endeavour that can be found in the history of letters'.[74] But in the event its success was almost too conclusive. It was a monument whose very eminence made it unscalable. Gibbon had no followers, founded no school, and his chief bequest to posterity was in fact his style, one of the most distinctive in the English language, whose influence is now and again detectable in the prose of English historians down to the present day.[75]

Gibbon's stature is the more evident when we compare him with his friend

---

* There have always been exceptions. When Herbert Butterfield visited the archives at Hanover after the war, he was startled to find that Sir Adolphus William Ward, that great authority on Anglo-Hanoverian relations (and a Peterhouse man), had never been there at all; he had been content with selected transcripts sent over to him in England. (*TRHS*, 5th series, xix (1969), 165.)

and contemporary, William Mitford, like him a Hampshire gentleman of independent means who early turned his back on Oxford. His *History of Greece*, published between 1784 and 1810, was enormously popular in his generation and the next, not least because it filled an obvious gap. But its strident criticism of the inefficiency and irresponsibility of democracy was too obviously directed at the great problem of the age, the French Revolution. Nor was Mitford alone in this; many contemporaries, watching the dread virus of equality and unrestrained liberty spreading across Europe, found a melancholy consolation in classical parallels. Hearing of the Peterloo Massacre in 1819, Thomas Arnold wrote: 'I think daily of the Corcyrean sedition, and of the story of the French Revolution, and of the Cassandra-like fate of history, whose lessons are read in vain even to the very next generation.'[76]

It was fashionable to suppose that history was cyclic, and the Italian Vico and the German Niebuhr even regarded the state as a living organism, undergoing a process of birth, growth, decline, death and rebirth. Since the early eighteenth century the historians of the university of Gottingen, which was in Hanover and to that extent linked with England, had been concerned with the problem of writing general or universal history in the hope of establishing a pattern – a task later taken over by individuals right down to the present day: Buckle in his old age, Spengler and Toynbee. Strangely enough, the first, anonymous, attempt at a universal world history was made in England, with a huge compilation entitled *An Universal History from the Earliest Account of Time to the Present compiled from the Original Authors*, and published in thirty-eight volumes between 1736 and 1765. It was sufficiently well regarded to be translated into several European languages, but the German translation was left incomplete; the book was too rambling and discursive for the taste of the Gottingen school.[77] By the turn of the century the chief exponents of these Continental ideas in England were a group of men who have been dubbed the 'Liberal Anglicans', who are now largely forgotten. Mitford apart, their most celebrated member was Thomas Arnold, best remembered now as a great reforming headmaster, but in the year before his premature death in 1841 also regius professor of modern history at Oxford. He was a first-rate classical scholar, but his *History of Rome* leaned heavily on Niebuhr. However, if his confidence in his own authority as a historian seems to us exaggerated, it was one shared by many of his contemporaries, though their standards were not high. As he said himself of Mitford:

'His knowledge of the Greek language was limited, and so was his learning altogether; but because he was an English gentleman, who felt and understood the things around him and warmly entered into its parties, therefore he was able to write a history of Greece'.[78]

This bent towards ancient history, and the need to explain or rationalize the French Revolution, put English history in the shade for a generation, and perpetuated the ascendancy of Hume well into the nineteenth century. But in the meanwhile more and more source material was finding its way into print. There was obviously a considerable market for volumes of original documents, often with little or no commentary, and usually floated by private subscription. We have already seen how important material on the Great Rebellion began to appear under Charles II and William III, and the eighteenth century, perhaps mistrusting historians, continued to prefer its history in the raw. Thus in 1702 Thomas Brown published his *Miscellanea Aulica*, an undigested mass of correspondence relating to foreign policy between 1660 and 1675. Arthur Collins's *Letters and Memorials of State* (1746) was a random selection from the Sidney archives at Penshurst, and in 1767 Oxford University Press published the first three volumes of *Clarendon State Papers* from the Bodleian Library. The diary and correspondence of Clarendon's son, the 2nd Earl, for the reign of James II had already appeared in 1763, though an enlarged edition was later published in 1828. In 1778 the 2nd Earl of Hardwicke edited two volumes of *Miscellaneous State Papers 1501-1726*, including important fragments from Lord Somers's papers, most of which had been accidentally destroyed. The *Somers Tracts*, a basic collection of seventeenth- and early eighteenth-century pamphlets supposed to have been collected by the same lord, were published in sixteen volumes between 1748 and 1751; a revised and extended edition was later published by Walter Scott 1809-15.

In the meanwhile, under government patronage, Thomas Rymer and Robert Sanderson had edited twenty volumes of *Foedera*, from 1101 to 1654, covering diplomatic correspondence as well as actual treaties.* In 1737 David Wilkins followed with a four-volume record of *Concilia Magnae Britannicae et Hivernicae*, known to generations of scholars as 'Wilkins' Concilia', and in 1742 Thomas Birch published the papers of John Thurloe, Cromwell's Secretary of State – the compilation which Hume thought could with advantage have been shorter. In 1742 the Commons also began to release its records, ordering the printing of its Journals from their beginning in 1547, a task which took until 1762. In 1767 the Lords followed suit, though the project took until 1830. In the meanwhile the *Statutes of the Realm* up to 1714 were

---

* Its full title, in fact, is: *Foedera, conventiones, literae, et cuiuscunque generis acta publica, inter reges Angliae et alios quosvis imperatores, reges, pontifices, principes, vel communitates.*

published in eleven volumes between 1810 and 1828, though they were over-lapped in 1811 by a private venture, *The Statutes at Large*, which went up to 1800, though it was not so carefully edited. Parliamentary debates were much more sketchily recorded, but in 1742 Edward Timberland reprinted every scrap of information he could find on *The History and Proceedings of the House of Lords from the Restoration in 1660*. Chandler's *Debates* (1741–4) was a similar compilation for the House of Commons, by a rival bookseller. *The Parliamentary or Old Constitutional History of England*, usually known as 'The Old Parliamentary History', covered the period up to 1660 in twenty-four volumes, and was published between 1751 and 1761.[79] (Simonds d'Ewes's collection for Elizabeth's parliaments had been in print since 1682, Hayward Townshend's journals since 1680.) In 1763 came Anchitel Grey's vitally important parliamentary diary for the years 1667 to 1694, in ten volumes. Most of these sources were brought together by William Cobbett in *The Parliamentary History of England from 1066*, continued by T.G. Hansard. It appeared in thirty-six volumes between 1806 and 1820.

Hume used such material as was in print when he came to write each volume, but he seems to have ignored new material after that, not bothering to incorporate it into subsequent editions. For instance, he used the Commons Journals extensively, but he did not bother with Anchitel Grey's *Debates*, which appeared in 1763 and would have supplemented his account of the Exclusion Crisis significantly. The exception, as we have seen, was the material discovered by Sir John Dalrymple in the Paris archives; and even then, he incorporated most of this new and startling information in foot-notes.*

Certainly Dalrymple, who was a devoted Whig, found more than he bar-gained for at the Quai d'Orsay. He was delighted by the discovery that the Treaty of Dover in 1670 did indeed contain a clause obliging Charles II to turn Roman Catholic, and he also unearthed concrete evidence of the secret agreement between Charles and Louis XIV in March 1681. It was also he who discovered a cache of hitherto unknown documents bearing on the Revolu-tion of 1688 in an old wooden chest at Kensington Palace, to which George III had given him free access. (The Public Record Office call number for this class of documents is still 'KWC', for 'King William's Chest'.) They included the original of the Invitation of the Seven to William III in June 1688, the very sight of which filled Dalrymple with honest emotion – 'Immortal Seven!' he enthused, 'whose memories Britain can never sufficiently revere.'[80] The care-ful and accurate transcripts he published of these and other key documents have been a boon to other historians right down to the present day.

---

* Page 53 above.

Unfortunately he rushed his initial discoveries, which were highly preju-
dicial to the Stuarts, into print in the first volume of his *Memoirs of Great
Britain and Ireland*, in 1771. Returning to Paris a second time, he was aghast
to discover from the French ambassador's despatches that the leaders of the
Whig opposition had also been deep in intrigue with Louis XIV in 1678. 'When
I found Lord Russell', he said, 'intriguing with the Court of Versailles, and
Algernon Sidney taking money from it, I felt very near the same shock as if
I had seen a son turn his back in the day of battle.'[81] But with admirable
honesty he printed these documents, too, in a second volume in 1773, with
the rueful comment:

> 'Some of the following papers contradict facts contained in the first volume,
> the truth of which I believed on the credit of other publications. This would
> be a mortification, if truth, according to the best of my abilities to find it
> out, was not my first object. Whoever corrects the relations of history by
> the private letters of the times will learn at every step as he advances, to
> distrust the opinions of others and his own'.

He ended with the rather pathetic comment: 'I am certainly a very unfortunate
party man, and this is a very unfortunate party book.'[82]

Further revelations shortly followed from that shady littérateur, James
Macpherson of Ruthven. A penniless schoolmaster of poor farming stock,
Macpherson secured the patronage of Lord Bute in the early 1760s, and made
his name by publishing a series of epic poems supposedly translated from the
works of the legendary Celtic poet 'Ossian', orally transmitted from generation to generation, and only recently written down. Macpherson had his
believers and supporters to the end, but the 'Ossian' poems were at once
denounced as an imposture by Dr Johnson and other literary pundits. He was
then taken on as a hack writer of government pamphlets, with an absentee
post in Florida, which did nothing to enhance his reputation, and in 1771 he
published a tendentious and controversial *Introduction to the Ancient History
of Great Britain and Ireland*, asserting the racial and ethnic superiority of the
Celts to the English.

The booksellers, scenting a profitable scoop – for Macpherson was now so
sensational a figure that almost anything from his pen would sell – commissioned him to write a new *History of Great Britain* from 1660 to 1714, which
appeared in 1775. His sponsors must have found it disappointingly judicious
and temperate; his worst sin was to describe the Revolution of 1688 as an
unnecessary overreaction to the crackbrained and insubstantial schemes of
James II, if schemes they were. (Though this was at once denounced as a
heretical novelty, it was essentially the attitude of shrewd contemporary
observers like Halifax and Nottingham, as Dalrymple's *Memoirs* showed.) In

any case, he argued, the Revolution had been ineffective, for what the crown lost in the shape of obsolete legal prerogatives it more than regained in the form of revenue, military power and political patronage. 'Power had ceased to be splendid, but it became permanent and irresistible; and mankind may be imperceptibly surrounded with the toils of despotism, while they have the vanity to think themselves free' – a sentiment hardly likely to please his employers, the ministers of George III.[83]

But much more startling was Macpherson's companion volume, *Original Papers containing the Secret History of Great Britain*, largely drawn from the correspondence of David Nairne, the Old Pretender's secretary, which revealed the intrigues of various English politicians with the Court of St Germain after the Revolution. He also printed short extracts from James II's 'Memoirs', then at the Scots College in Paris and already viewed by David Hume. In view of Macpherson's reputation for forgery, this provoked a furious controversy which continued for many years.[84]

The French Revolution then intervened, consigning James II's original memoirs to oblivion, with much else, but Dalrymple and Macpherson had demonstrated the value of the French archives for party mud-slinging, and Charles James Fox took immediate advantage of the Peace of Amiens in 1802 to visit the Quai d'Orsay. The result is the careful (and carefully selected) transcripts of the French ambassador's despatches for 1685 printed as an appendix to his unfinished history of James II's reign, posthumously published in 1806. It was left to Lord John Russell to rehabilitate the reputation of his famous ancestor, after the charges made by Dalrymple, which he did in his *Life of William Lord Russell* in 1819. This was accompanied by Mary Berry's edition of the letters of Lord Russell's saintly widow, which went through nine editions in seven years. Mark Noble's *Memoirs of the Protectoral House of Cromwell* (1787) was to be invaluable to Carlyle fifty years later, though at the time it did little to retrieve Cromwell's rather battered reputation.

William Coxe took this process into the eighteenth century itself. His life of Sir Robert Walpole, in 1798, an unavailing attempt to retrieve that minister's reputation, had two volumes of manuscripts to one of narrative. Archdeacon Coxe, an indefatigable copyist and a much-beneficed hanger-on of the great, continued to ransack the archives of the nobility for the rest of a long life. His *Memoirs of Horatio Lord Walpole* (Sir Robert's brother) in 1802 and of *John Duke of Marlborough* in 1819 consisted largely of documents; his *Correspondence of Charles Talbot Duke of Shrewsbury*, in 1821, entirely so. Coxe was much too subservient to the demands of his noble patrons, but though he was ready to suppress evidence at their request he was not prepared to alter it, and his accuracy as a transcriber has given his work a lasting value.[85] The multitude of letters he printed from the Blenheim Archives were a particular boon to historians when they were closed in the 1930s at the whim of the then Duke of Marlborough.

Those who had brought this mass of material into print were for the most part incapable of using it, which is why Hume's brief and rather impressionistic account of English history retained its authority for so long. But in the aftermath of two generations of war some new synthesis was called for; above all it was necessary to key in the Revolution – the French Revolution was always '*The* Revolution' – with the history of England, and a new attempt was made by the Whig lawyer Henry Hallam in 1827, with his *Constitutional History of England from the Accession of Henry VII to the Death of George III*.

This was a remarkable book, no longer appreciated as it ought to be. The standard bibliography of the seventeenth century issued by the Royal Historical Society still denounces it as 'strongly Whig in bias', but it is a very strange Whig bias which leads a man to assert, for instance, that the Long Parliament was the aggressor in the Civil Wars, or enter a serious defence for Charles I. The young Macaulay read it with mixed feelings. He described it as the most impartial book he had ever read. 'Eulogy and invective', he went on, 'may be had for the asking; but for cold, rigid justice, the one weight and the one measure, we know not where else we can look.'[86] He then proceeded to criticize it for just those qualities. In fact, his review is a masterpiece in the art of damning by faint praise and undermining by innuendo.

However, we can see what upset Macaulay when we read Hallam's succinct and dispassionate analysis of Whiggism and Toryism. In his summing-up he said:

'It will be obvious that I have given to each of these political principles a moral character, and have considered them as they would subsist in upright and conscientious men, not as we may find them 'in the dregs of Romulus', suffocated by selfishness or distorted by faction. The Whigs appear to have taken a much more comprehensive view of the nature and ends of civil society; their principle is more virtuous, more flexible to the variations of time and circumstance, more congenial to large and masculine intellects. But it may probably be no small advantage that the two parties, or rather the sentiments which have been presumed to actuate them, should have been mingled, as we find them, in the complex mass of the English nation, whether the proportions may or may not have been always such as we might desire. They bear some analogy to the two forces which retain the planetary bodies in their orbits; the annihilation of one would disperse them into chaos, that of the other would drag them to a centre. And though I cannot reckon these old appellations by any means characteristic of our political factions in the nineteenth century, the names Whig and Tory are well applied to individuals. Nor can it be otherwise; since they are founded not on our laws and history, with which most have some acquaintance, but in the diversities of condition and moral temperament generally subsisting among mankind'.

Then came the chilling addition, which Macaulay, the great partisan, could never have penned: 'It is, however, one thing to prefer the Whig principle, another to justify, as an advocate, the party which bore that name.'[87]

Thomas Babington Macaulay is still, I suppose, the most celebrated of English historians, and certainly the best known, and known about. For most of his adult life he kept a detailed daily journal, and he was an indefatigable letter writer. His nephew, Sir George Trevelyan, used this great bulk of material to produce a classic biography in 1876; its replacement, by the Harvard historian John Clive, has already taken five hundred pages to reach the mid-point of his career, and in the meanwhile complete scholarly editions of his letters and his journal are under way.[88] Moreover, almost every modern historian of eminence has committed himself to an opinion on this man, encouraged by the commemoration of the centenary of his death in 1959. Unfortunately, this embarrassment of material does not necessarily make interpretation any easier.

It is tempting to regard Macaulay as a great Victorian. He had to an abundant degree all the less pleasing Victorian attributes, of complacency, self-satisfaction, personal *pudeur* and condescension. Yet, born as he was in 1800, he was very much a child of the revolutionary era, and all his basic opinions were formed long before Victoria came to the throne in 1837. The recently discovered fragment of his *History of France* reminds us, with something of a shock, that when he was in his early teens Napoleon I was still a world-embracing colossus; and twenty years later he still remembered him in no very charitable way: 'With talents for war and government not inferior to those of Julius Caesar, he united a violence of temper and an impatience of all opposition, such as Greek historians ascribe to Cambyses and Xerxes.'[89]

His father Zachary Macaulay was a man of strong Evangelical opinions, which were shared by his mother, Selina Mills, and he was noted in his generation as a crusader against slavery and the slave trade. His influence on his son's character and psychological make-up has been a matter for some speculation, largely fruitless; the best that can be said is that his parents' sublime confidence in their own rectitude, under God, may have given him his superb indifference to opinions which conflicted with his own. He was never himself a man of strong religious feelings.

His parents' decision to have him privately educated saved him from the moral and intellectual terrors of the contemporary public schools, and he enjoyed a happy and bookish childhood. As soon as he entered Trinity College, Cambridge, in 1818 his brilliance was manifest. His mastery of the classics was absolute, medals and prizes were showered upon him; and though his weakness in mathematics barred him from an honours degree he was elected to a fellowship in 1824. But at this stage his father's business collapsed, and he was faced with the prospect of providing not only for himself but for his idolized younger sisters, Hannah and Margaret. He was called to the Bar, but on the Northern Circuit he experienced one of the few failures of his career.

Fortunately for him, he did not have to persevere with the law. His essay on Milton in the *Edinburgh Review* for August 1825 brought him fame overnight. This kind of notoriety is something we associate with the media presentation of the twentieth century, but it had already happened to two men in his time: to Scott on the publication of *Waverley* and to Byron with the first instalment of *Childe Harold's Pilgrimage*. From then on Macaulay had these two literary giants constantly in mind.

Once made, his literary reputation varied very little. Looking back in after years, Gladstone wrote of him: 'It was an extraordinarily full life of sustained exertion – a high table land without depressions. If in its outer aspects there be anything wearisome, it is only the wearisomeness of re-iterated splendour, and of success so uniform as to be almost monotonous.'[90] Further brilliant essays followed in the *Edinburgh Review*, some of them sensational. His review of John Wilson Croker's edition of Boswell's Johnson in 1831 was a massacre, and made him an enemy for life; a similar review of Mackintosh's *History of the Revolution*, in 1835, nearly led to a duel with its editor, Wallace. In 1830 the Whig grandee Lord Lansdowne offered him a seat in the Commons for his pocket borough of Calne, in Wiltshire, and he made a second reputation as a parliamentary orator; after his speeches on the Reform Bill he was bracketed with Burke and Chatham. An eye-witness said of them: 'Never was a more extraordinary compound of deep philosophy, exalted sentiments and party bitterness, enunciated with a warmth, a vigour and rapidity inconceivable. . . . It is like the course of a meteor, never to be forgotten by those who have the fortune to see it.'[91]

He passionately believed in parliamentary reform as the only alternative to revolution, but he was also caught up in the historical drama of the proceedings. He exulted in the fact that he himself was experiencing a great moment in history, and the vivid letters he dashed off at the time foreshadow the style of his later writing. After the famous late-night division of 23 March 1831, when the Reform Bill passed by one vote in a crowded house, he said: 'It was like seeing Caesar stabbed in the Senate House, or seeing Oliver [Cromwell]

take the mace from the table.' He exulted at the Tories' dismay: 'The jaw of
Peel fell; and the face of Twiss was as the face of a damned soul, and Herries
looked like Judas taking his neckcloth off for the last operation.'[92]

Ironically, the Reform Act disfranchised Calne, but he stood successfully
for the new urban constituency of Leeds instead. He seemed destined for a
distinguished political career, with a seat in the Cabinet before he was forty.
But a political career was still hazardous without an assured income; journalism would not do. In 1834 he decided to sacrifice his immediate career in
return for financial independence; he accepted a seat on the Supreme Council
of India, reckoning that if he saved half his princely salary of £10,000 a year
for four years, the income from the capital would meet his needs. He already
had in mind a new history of England which would bring him another kind
of fame.

He was a success in India. His two great Minutes, on Education and the
Penal Code, fixed English as the official language of the subcontinent, for
good or ill, and the Common Law as the basis of the legal system. But he was
far from happy in exile. He found singularly little to interest him in India,
outside his work, and he refused to adapt himself to the Anglo-Indian way of
life; he lived very much as a recluse, reading omnivorously. He was plunged
into grief by the unexpected death back in England of his sister Margaret,
and taken aback by the defection of another. His prime favourite Hannah,
who had come out to India to keep house for him, now announced her
engagement to a young civil servant, Charles Trevelyan. Macaulay's affection
for his sisters had an element of the unhealthy in it – even contemporaries
realized this – and he took time to recover from this double blow.[93]

When he returned to England in 1838 it seemed that he might resume his
political career after all; in 1839 he was elected to parliament again, for
Edinburgh, and he was appointed Secretary at War in Melbourne's government. But only six weeks after his return, with his bags scarcely unpacked, he
had told his friend Napier that the following spring he would begin his history
of England since the Glorious Revolution:

'The first part, which I think will take up five octavo volumes, will extend
from the Revolution to the commencement of Sir Robert Walpole's long
administration – a period of three and thirty very eventful years. From the
commencement of Walpole's administration to the commencement of the
American War, events may be despatched more concisely. From the commencement of the American War it will again become necessary to be
copious. These are at least my present notions. How far I shall bring the
narrative down I have not determined. The death of George IV would
be the best halting place. The History would then be an entire view

of all the transactions which took place between the Revolution which brought the crown into harmony with parliament and the revolution which brought the parliament into harmony with the nation'.[94]

By March 1839, true to his word, he was on his way.

He lost his seat in the Whig debacle of 1841, and any lingering doubts he may have had were set at rest by the spectacular success of his *Lays of Ancient Rome*, published in 1842. It was not only an immediate bestseller, it earned him some literary acclaim. We may smile at its rocking-horse rhythms, but a second edition was called for inside the first year, and it stayed in print the rest of the century. By 1875 it had sold 100,000 copies, and even in the 1930s it was a rare English schoolboy who had not heard of Lars Porsena or Horatius at the Bridge. In 1843 he was also persuaded to publish his collected essays to date, in order to forestall a pirated American edition. Macaulay seemed genuinely reluctant to republish what he now regarded almost as juvenilia, but in their first ten years they sold an average of 1,230 copies a year; in the next decade this rose to 4,700, and after that 6,000.

Not startling figures, perhaps, by our standards, but books were relatively more expensive then, and the book-buying public much smaller. Free libraries were for the future. What is impressive is the sustained character of his sales, over ten, twenty, thirty years. But this was as nothing compared with the sales of the *History of England*. Longmans predicted it, and on 1 September 1848 they gave him a handsome contract – £500 a year for five years on a first edition of 6,000, and two thirds of the profit on subsequent editions.[95] The first two volumes were published on 7 November in an edition of 3,000, and that morning Ludgate Hill was jammed with booksellers' carriages trying to reach Longmans' offices in Paternoster Row. It was a complete reversal of Hume's experience. By early December another 3,000 copies were being run off, and Macaulay preened himself on a success as resounding as Sir Walter Scott's. 'Of "The Lay of the Last Minstrel"', he wrote, '2250 copies were sold in the first year, of "Marmion" 2000 copies in the first month; of my book 3000 copies in ten days.' By the end of December the first edition of 6,000 was exhausted and another edition of 5,000 was out; early in the New Year another 2,000 were in hand. Macaulay exulted: 'On the whole I remember no success so complete, and I remember all Byron's poems and all Scott's novels.' He triumphed indecently when he spotted a copy of Hume in a bookseller's window, reduced to two guineas, with a notice saying 'highly valuable as an introduction to Macaulay'. 'I laughed so convulsively', he said, 'that the other people who were staring at the books took me for a poor demented gentleman. Alas for poor David!'[96] Summoned to Buckingham Palace by the Prince Consort, he was astonished to be offered the regius chair of modern history at Cambridge, which he promptly refused. 'It would be strange', he wrote, 'if, having sacrificed for liberty a seat in the cabinet and £2500 a year, I should now sacrifice liberty for a chair at Cambridge and £400 a year.' The financial angle was never far from his mind.[97]

When the third and fourth volumes came out in December 1855 Longmans took advance orders for 25,000 copies. Macaulay, typically, was thrilled by the sheer magnitude of the whole enterprise. 'The stock lying at the book-binders', he said, 'is insured for £10,000. The whole weight is fifty-six tons. It seems that no such edition was ever published of any work of the same bulk.' Nor did he have any qualms about its quality. When his own copies arrived he at once re-read it, and he confided to his journal:

> 'I dawdled over my book most of the day, sometimes in good, sometimes in bad spirits about it. On the whole, I think it must do. The only competition which, as far as I perceive, it has to dread, is that of the other two volumes. Certainly no other history of William's reign is either so trustworthy or so readable'.[98]

The public certainly thought so. By March 1856 sales were such that Longmans, embarrassed at holding so much money, gave him a cheque for £20,000 (worth at least ten times that amount in modern currency) which was not due to him until December. Moreover, sales of the previous volumes rose in sympathy, from just under 1,200 in 1854-5 to nearly 5,000 the year following. He may well have been the first literary millionaire, and he was certainly the first literary peer; he went to the House of Lords as Lord Macaulay of Rothbury Temple in 1857.

But he was not destined to complete his *History*. A serious illness in 1852, probably a coronary thrombosis, slowed him down, and was at the same time a warning. He realized himself that he could never fulfil the ambitious plan he had made in 1858, especially since he had started not in 1689 but in 1685, so that the first four volumes only took him up to the Peace of Ryswick in 1697. In 1857 he told a correspondent: 'I now look forward to the accession of the house of Hanover as my extreme goal.'[99] He was possibly also influenced by the appearance between 1836 and 1854 of Viscount Mahon's seven-volume history of England from 1713 to 1783. Lord Mahon (later the 5th Earl Stanhope) was a thorough Whig, in history as in politics, and he understood the use of sources. His carefully structured account is now almost forgotten, but it was the first serious attempt to write a full history of the previous century, including the American Revolution. As a stylist Mahon was not in Macaulay's class, and Macaulay rather unkindly said so when he reviewed an earlier work of his, on the War of the Spanish Succession, in 1833; and in a letter he took him severely to task for an excess of party spirit.[100] However,

Mahon took it in good part, and the two men were on friendly terms thereafter.[101] Macaulay may possibly have felt less need to hurry on with his own task, now that the eighteenth century was at least adequately covered.

However, this is surmise. What is certain is that he died quite suddenly, in December 1859, leaving only a few draft chapters, including an account of the death of William III, which were published as a slim supplementary volume in 1861. Nor has anyone else come forward to complete it on the same scale, though in 1870 Mahon (now Earl Stanhope) published a history of Queen Anne's reign avowedly intended to bridge the gap between Macaulay's work and his own. Yet, unfinished as it was, Macaulay's *History* remained a bestseller. For instance, in the nine years 1848–57, while Macaulay was still alive, the first volume sold 30,478 copies; in the next nine years, up to 1866, 50,783; and from then up to 1875, 52,393. The whole work has never been out of print from that day to this, a unique record.[102]

Macaulay's success, in retrospect, is not surprising. His was not the first history, of course, to be conceived as a work of art, but it was the first to be conceived as a painting in full colour. (On this analogy Gibbon and Hume were essentially artists in monochrome.) Moreover, his wide reading in all the sources he could find, plus the fact that he was covering a much smaller area in much greater depth than any predecessor, enabled him to fill his canvas with pointilliste detail.

His vocabulary was rich and dense, redolent with the knowledge packed away in his eidetic memory. He thought nothing of committing a whole Shakespeare play to memory in the course of an evening, and he once solaced himself on a sleepless night packet boat trip to Ireland by reciting to himself the whole of Milton's *Paradise Lost*. This gift he took for granted, and he thought it strange that others could not recite the names and dates of all the archbishops of Canterbury backward to St Augustine, or the names of all the Senior Wranglers at Cambridge for the past hundred years. His reading covered all the ages and all the Western world, for in addition to his other attributes he was a natural linguist; he once read a Lapp New Testament with the aid of a Norwegian dictionary so that he could acquire a rough knowledge of both languages simultaneously. Coupled with this he had a strong sense of the dramatic, and a desire to make history live again which he inherited from Walter Scott; as we have seen, he was delighted to have exceeded Scott's popularity, but he never thought of him as anything but the Master.[103] He also had a strong sense of place and a gift for communicating it to the reader; he insisted on seeing all the places he had to describe – Londonderry, Sedgemoor, Glencoe, St Germain and the rest. He spent two whole days perambulating Derry, and made the circuit of the walls four times; he went twice to Glencoe and twice to Killiecrankie. 'He paid a second visit to Killiecrankie for the special purpose of walking up the old road which skirts the Garry, in order to verify the received accounts of the time spent by the English army in mounting the pass.'[104]

But this is not all. Not only is Macaulay's prose exceptionally vivid, it is unusually dynamic. I defy anyone who opens the book at random and reads a page not to read the next page, and the next page and the next. He was a master of what might be called 'pace' – a quality which was recognized from the beginning. Of the first two volumes the *Edinburgh Review* said rhapsodically:

> 'He has a singular felicity of style; and, as he moves along his path of narrative [he] spreads a halo around him, which beguiles the distance and dazzles his companions.... The tale, as we proceed, flows on faster and faster. Page after page vanishes under the entranced eye of the reader; and, whether we will or no, we are forced to follow as he leads – so light, and gay, and agreeable does the pathway appear'.

Gladstone described it more succinctly as 'the union of ease in movement with perspicuity of matter, of both with real splendour, and of all with immense rapidity, and striking force'.[105]

His great set-pieces, his battles or sieges, are justly celebrated. The *Edinburgh Review* gushingly called him 'our great magician of romance', and Lord Acton – never one of Macaulay's firmest admirers – acknowledged that he made scenes like the siege of Londonderry, the relief of Limerick, the victory and death of Lord Dundee at Killiecrankie, 'as vivid as anything in epic poetry'.[106] Sir John Seeley thought his influence on a later generation had been little short of pernicious, but he agreed that: 'It is most right and desirable that there should always be historians of the type of Macaulay. Noble deeds should be told in splendid language; great events should pass before us in swelling and stately narrative.'[107] He was always a noted raconteur, in society as well as in the family circle, and his constant habit of writing verse, whether for publication or not, gave him a sense of rhythm which he carried over into his prose. But this was not done instinctively. He worked hard on his prose, and his methods are a lesson to any writer. For instance, it took him from 22 March 1849 to 4 April to write his account of the Massacre of Glencoe. On 27 March he wrote in his journal: 'I am getting on fast with this most horrible story.' From 29 March to 2 April he was too exhausted at the end of the day to add anything except the single word 'Wrote'. On 3 April he added: 'This Glencoe business is infernal.' Next day: 'Wrote; walked round by London Bridge, and wrote again. Today I finished the Massacre.' Nor did he shrink from criticism, though it is not clear that he acted on it. On 11 April he had his old friend Thomas Flower Ellis to dinner:

'I read him Glencoe. He did not seem to like it very much, which vexed me, though I am partial to it. It is a good thing to find sincerity.'[108]

According to his nephew, he 'never allowed a sentence to pass muster until it was as good as he could make it. He thought little of recasting a chapter in order to obtain a more lucid arrangement, and nothing whatever of reconstructing a paragraph for the sake of one happy stroke or apt illustration.' This drudgery was followed up on the proofs, and 'he could not rest until the lines were level to a hair's breadth, and the punctuation [was] correct to a comma, until every paragraph concluded with a telling sentence, and every sentence flowed like running water'.[109] At a later stage he confided something of his technique to his journal. On 15 April 1850:

'After breakfast I fell to work on the conspiracy of the Jacobites in 1690. This is a tough chapter. To make the narrative flow along as it ought, every part naturally springing from that which precedes, to carry the reader backwards and forwards across St George's Channel without distracting his attention, is not easy. Yet it may be done. I believe that the art of transition is as important, or nearly so, to history as the art of narration'.

By 28 July he was in the Highlands:

'My account of the Highlands is getting into tolerable shape. Tomorrow I shall begin to transcribe again, and polish. What trouble these few pages will have cost me! The great object is that, after all this trouble, they may read as if they had been spoken off, and may seem to flow as easily as table talk. We shall see'.[110]

Moreover, this supreme literary craftsmanship was at the service of an awesome self-confidence; his judgment on men and measures was instant and unflinching. He was a master of antithesis, an art he developed early. Witness his dismissal of James Boswell, in an essay published in 1831: 'He had, indeed, a quick observation and a retentive memory. These qualities, if he had been a man of sense and virtue, would scarcely of themselves have sufficed to make him conspicuous; but because he was a dunce, a parasite and a coxcomb, they have made him immortal.'[111] This is clever but rather crude; by the end of his life he had softened his technique and brought it to perfection. Perhaps the best example (though everyone has a particular favourite) is his great philippic against Robert Harley, whom he cordially hated, perhaps because he had met men like him in the nineteenth-century House of Commons:

'His influence in parliament was indeed out of all proportion to his abilities. His intellect was both small and slow. He was unable to take a large view of any subject. He never acquired the art of expressing himself in public with fluency and perspicuity. To the end of his life he remained a tedious, hesitating and confused speaker. He had none of the external graces of an orator. His countenance was heavy, his figure mean and somewhat deformed, and his gestures uncouth. Yet he was heard with respect. For, such as his mind was, it had been assiduously cultivated. His youth had been studious; and to the last he continued to love books and the society of men of genius and learning ... His taste led him to plod amongst old records; and in that age it was only by plodding amongst old records that any man could obtain an accurate and extensive knowledge of the law of parliament. Having few rivals in this laborious and unattractive pursuit, he soon began to be regarded as an oracle on questions of form and privilege. His moral character added not a little to his influence. He had indeed great vices, but they were not of a scandalous kind. He was not to be corrupted by money. His private life was regular. No illicit amour was imputed to him even by satirists. Gambling he held in aversion, and ... his practice of flustering himself daily with claret was hardly considered as a fault by his contemporaries. His knowledge, his gravity and his independent position gained for him the ear of the House; and even his bad speaking was, in some sense, an advantage to him ... From the absence of show in Harley's discourses many people inferred that there must be much substance; and he was pronounced to be a deep read, deep thinking gentleman, not a fine talker, but fitter to direct affairs of state than all the fine talkers in the world. This character he long supported with that cunning which is frequently found in company with ambitious and unquiet mediocrity. He constantly had, even with his best friends, an air of mystery and reserve which seemed to indicate that he knew some momentous secret, and that his mind was labouring with some vast design. In this way he got and long kept a high reputation for wisdom. It was not until that reputation had made him an Earl, a Knight of the Garter, Lord High Treasurer of England, and master of Europe, that his admirers began to find out that he was really a dull, puzzle-headed man'.[112]

Macaulay also used a greater range of material than any previous English historian, though his virtuosity in this respect can be, and has been, exaggerated.* In many ways his approach was superficial and glancing. At the very beginning, in 1839, he told Lady Holland:

'My present object is to collect as many facts as I can to illustrate the internal arrangements of private families towards the close of the seventeenth century. I have got the household books of an old Leicestershire

---

* I discuss his sources more fully on pp. 85–6 below.

family with which I am connected; and there I find full accounts of their income, their expenses, what they gave Lord Rutland's cook when they dined at Belvoir, what the son at Cambridge and the son at Westminster cost them, and so forth. Lord Fitzwilliam promises me similar information about his own family, and some others in a much higher line of life. These are, in my opinion, the real materials of history. I have found more historical information in a small receipt book than in a folio of diplomatic correspondence. I hope to get at the very ancient books of one or two of the oldest banks in London. They will no doubt contain much curious information. Whether I shall succeed I cannot tell. But I shall do my best to place my readers in the England of the seventeenth century'.[113]

The result was his celebrated chapter iii, on the state of England in 1685. Unfortunately scarcely a sentence in this chapter still stands, and in many ways its distorted picture of English life, particularly the life of the wage-earning classes, has impeded subsequent research.[114] It was the first example of a kind of pictorial, sentimental social history which was to reach its apogee in Macaulay's great-nephew, G.M. Trevelyan, and was always subject to a certain degree of self-delusion. For instance, it is difficult to take seriously Macaulay's assertion that he had found 'more historical information in a small receipt book than in a folio of diplomatic correspondence'. However, this chapter iii was in its time a new intellectual venture which confirmed the huge success of volume one of the *History*, a pioneering effort which has considerable claims on our respect.

So much for Macaulay's style and methods. His content, and his views, are more difficult to assess. His contemporaries, with his public career in mind, took him to be a sanguine and uncritical Whig who was entirely satisfied with Britain and the British Constitution. As the *Edinburgh Review* put it:

'He has the honest, hearty pride of a lover of liberty in the fresh and free spirit of constitutional independence. With him there are no half-hearted, hollow words of freedom, with dislike hinted, and faults hesitated, while despotism is faintly condemned, and the crimes and caprices of tyrants are palliated and pitied. He rightly judges that to have fixed on a rocky basis this mighty sea-mark of the nations - this great retreat of the oppressed - where constitutional government has now sat enthroned for a century and a half, and has looked down unmoved on the turmoils and convulsion of Europe, is an achievement to be regarded with awe and recorded with reverence.'[115]

However, this is not the whole picture by any means. Though Macaulay's *History* covers such a short period it is possible to deduce some of his broader

views from earlier essays, particularly his review of Hallam's *Constitutional
History* in 1828. Of the Reformation in England he took much the same view
as Hallam: 'zeal was the tool of worldliness', he said, and Henry VIII was
'despotism itself personified'. His attitude to 'the imperial lioness', Elizabeth I,
was distinctly cool; in particular he blamed her ecclesiastical policy for the
intensification of Puritan aggression in the half-century after her death,
though he acknowledged that this was a revisionist view. He had little but
contempt for James I, 'one of those kings whom God seems to send for the
express purpose of hastening revolutions', and as for Charles I, he thought
that 'the fixed hatred of liberty which was the principle of [his] public conduct
... made him ... a more dangerous enemy to the constitution than a man of
far greater talents and resolution might have been'. He was 'a tyrant whose
whole life was a lie, who hated the constitution the more because he had been
compelled to feign respect for it, and to whom his own honour and the love
of his people were as nothing'. Strafford he denounced with equal violence;
he was 'this great, brave, bad man', 'the lost Archangel, the Satan of apostasy'.
Because his abilities were so much greater than his master's, on him lay the
heavier blame.[116]

In contrast, the econcomiums he heaped on the leaders of the Long Parliament were quite as extravagant as those of his namesake, Mrs Macaulay. 'We
never turn to the annals of those times', he said, 'without feeling increased
admiration of the patriotism, the energy, the decision, the consummate wisdom, which marked the measures of that great parliament.' As for John
Hampden, 'We can scarcely express the admiration which we feel for a mind
so great, and at the same time, so healthful and well-proportioned', for a man
who displayed 'the sobriety, the self-command, the perfect soundness of
judgment, the perfect rectitude of intention, to which the history of revolutions furnishes no parallel, or furnishes a parallel in Washington alone.'[117]
Like Hallam, he undertook an elaborate comparison between Cromwell and
Napoleon, but found emphatically in favour of Cromwell, who 'possessed, in
an eminent degree, that masculine and full-grown robustness of mind, that
equally diffused intellectual health, which, if our national partiality does not
mislead us, has peculiarly characterized the great men of England'. 'No sovereign', he added, 'ever carried to the throne so large a portion of the best
qualities of the middling orders, so strong a sympathy with the feelings and
interests of the people ... he had a high, stout, English heart', and he remarked, with some regret, that but for the incompetence of Richard Cromwell
'we might now be writing under the government of his Highness Oliver the
Fifth, or Richard the Fourth, Protector, by the grace of God, of the Commonwealth of England, Scotland and Ireland'.[118]

In contrast he regarded Charles II, and all his ministers, with unmeasured contempt. 'The inconstancy, perfidy and baseness, which the leaders constantly practised, which their followers defended, and which the great body of the people regarded, as it seems, with little disapprobation, appear in the present age almost incredible', or again: 'Vicissitudes so extraordinary as those which marked the reign of Charles the Second can only be explained by supposing an utter want of principle in the political world.'[119] But it is his verdict on the Revolution of 1688, again from his essay on Hallam, which is startling. No doubt, he said, England had derived great benefit from the Revolution:

'Yet that memorable event, in a great measure, took its character from the very vices which it was the means of reforming. It was assuredly a happy revolution, and a useful revolution; but it was not, what it has been called, a glorious revolution. William, and William alone, derived glory from it. The transaction was, in almost every part, discreditable to England. That a tyrant who had violated the fundamental laws of the country, who had attacked the rights of its greatest corporations, who had begun to persecute the established religion of the state, who had never respected the law either in his superstition or in his revenge, could not be pulled down without the aid of a foreign army, is a circumstance not very grateful to our national pride. Yet this is the least degrading part of the story. The shameless insincerity of the great and noble, the warm assurances of general support which James received, down to the moment of a general desertion, indicate a meanness of spirit and a looseness of morality most disgraceful to the age ... [Similarly,] in all the proceedings of the Convention, in the conferences particularly, we see the littleness of mind which is the chief characteristic of the times. The resolutions on which the two Houses agreed were as bad as any resolutions for so excellent a purpose could be. Their feeble and contradictory language was evidently intended to save the credit of the Tories, who were ashamed to name what they were not ashamed to do. Through the transaction no commanding talents were shown by any Englishman; no extraordinary risks were run, no sacrifices made for the delivery of the nation.'[120]

Everything in this swingeing paragraph is contained in the *History* he wrote in the 1840s, or can easily be deduced from it, yet the tone is radically different, and so is the viewpoint. This is surprising in a historian noted for adopting all his opinions early in life and thereafter never deviating from them. Can this be so? It used to be thought that Macaulay was deeply shaken by the French Revolution of 1830, which he witnessed at first hand on a visit to Paris, and the civil disorder of 1830 and 1831 in England itself, but that he was reassured by the passing of the Reform Act. But the latest student of

Macaulay, Joseph Hamburger, argues that even after the Reform Act he expected revolution to spread to England, and he was pleasantly surprised when he returned from India in 1838 to find a popular young queen on the throne, a Whig government still in power, and the Tory opposition converted, however reluctantly, to reform. One of his principal aims in writing the *History of England* was to consolidate this happy position, and to demonstrate by arguments drawn from the past that only voluntary reform could stave off violent revolution. Not until the Chartist Movement collapsed at the end of the 'Hungry Forties', and the Great Exhibition confirmed England's stability and wealth, did the tension in his work begin to diminish.[121]

In his early essays Macaulay seemed to be developing into a Whig in what Acton calls the 'Roundhead Tradition', believing that constitutionalism and democracy had been born in the Civil Wars, betrayed in 1660, and only partially and imperfectly restored by a sordid power transaction in 1688. But from 1832 or thereabouts he turned to the Whiggism of the grandees, of Holland House, Devonshire House, Woburn and Chatsworth, the Whiggism of broad acres and a balanced constitution, to whom 1688, and only 1688, was the Year I of Liberty. This is why, apart perhaps from King William, the heroes of the *History* are moderate, pragmatic constitutionalists like Halifax the Trimmer or the great Lord Chancellor Somers.

Moreover, much as he disliked Hume, his dynamic view of political history could not be gainsaid. The constitution was no longer a precious relic, to be jealously guarded and inviolably preserved by the heirs to the Whig tradition; it was subject to reform and improvement from generation to generation.[122] And while it might be interesting and edifying to trace it back to a Gothic past, this exercise had no direct purpose. 1688 was the real turning-point in English history; and it was a turning-point because the men who had made the Revolution had looked forward – not backward, like the men of the Great Rebellion. An enlightened ruling class had frustrated royal despotism, with considerable assistance, of course, from William, but he had been assisted by them, and substituted a benevolent and paternalistic oligarchy which had steadily broadened its power base, withstood the sordid anarchy of the French Revolution, pacified the Catholics, the Irish and the Nonconformists, and by a final act of statesmanship had secured the alliance of the middle classes in parliamentary reform. In the 1840s, however, with the Chartists angrily campaigning on behalf of the working classes, with Ireland gripped by famine, the landed classes at odds over the Corn Laws, and the capitals of Europe, Paris, Berlin and Vienna exploding again in red revolution, these truths were far from self-evident, and the easy confidence in the *rightness* of the British constitution so evident in the previous century had long since evaporated.

In the opening pages of his book he set out his stall. He began with the assumption that Britain was the greatest nation on earth; this was something which scarcely needed stating. This good fortune, he believed, stemmed from the Revolution of 1688, and he undertook to show:

'How under that settlement, the authority of law and the security of property were found to be compatible with a liberty of discussion and of individual action never before known; how, from the auspicious union of order and freedom, sprang a prosperity of which the annals of human affairs had furnished no example; how our country, from a state of ignominious vassalage, rapidly rose to the place of umpire among European powers; how her opulence and her martial glory grew together; how, by wise and resolute good faith, was gradually established a public credit fruitful of marvels which to the statesmen of any former age would have seemed incredible; how a gigantic commerce gave birth to a maritime power, compared with which every other maritime power, ancient or modern, sinks into insignificance . . .'

and so on.

He rejected, of course, any idea that Britain had fallen off from her former glory:

'Unless I greatly deceive myself, the general effect of this chequered narrative will be to excite thankfulness in all religious minds, and hope in the breasts of all patriots. For the history of our country during the last hundred and sixty years is eminently the history of physical, of moral, and of intellectual improvement. Those who compare the age on which their lot has fallen with a golden age which exists only in their imagination may talk of degeneracy and decay; but no man who is correctly informed as to the past will be disposed to take a morose or desponding view of the present.'[123]

Since the whole point of his work was to justify the Glorious Revolution his failure to complete it scarcely mattered. In fact, as the *History* stands the Revolution is at the centre of it, its status emphasized by that great paean of gratulation which greets the Declaration of Rights and the accession of William III:

'The highest eulogy which can be pronounced on the Revolution of 1688 is this, that it was our last revolution. Several generations have now passed away since any wise and patriotic Englishman has meditated resistance to the established government. In all honest and reflecting minds there is a conviction, daily strengthened by experience, that the means of effecting every improvement which the constitution requires may be found within the constitution itself.

'Now if ever', he went on, warming to his theme, 'we ought to be able to appreciate the whole importance of the stand which was made by our fore-fathers against the House of Stuart' – no mention now of 'meanness of spirit', 'looseness of morality', 'littleness of mind'. 'All around us the world is convulsed by the agonies of great nations. Governments which lately seemed likely to stand during ages have been on a sudden shaken and overthrown. The proudest capitals of Europe have streamed with civil blood.'

Socialism roused his worst passions, passions shared, no doubt, by most of his readers. He thundered as bitterly as any Bishop of Rome against:

'Doctrines [which are] hostile to all sciences, to all arts, to all domestic charities, doctrines which, if carried into effect, would, in thirty years, undo all that thirty centuries have done for mankind, and would make the fairest provinces of France and Germany as savage as Congo or Patagonia ... Europe has been threatened with subjugation by barbarians, compared with whom the barbarians who marched under Attila and Alboin were enlightened and humane.'

The contrast in England could not be more marked – 'In our island the regular course of government has never been for a day interrupted'. And why was this? The answer was obvious:

'It is because we had a preserving revolution in the seventeenth century that we had not a destroying revolution in the nineteenth. It is because we had freedom in the midst of servitude that we have order in the midst of anarchy. For the authority of law, for the security of property, for the peace of our streets, for the happiness of our homes, our gratitude is due, under Him who raises and pulls down nations at His pleasure, to the Long Parliament, to the Convention and to William of Orange'.[124]

A comforting message indeed, and one which was at once received and understood by those to whom it was directed. Lord Halifax wrote to congra-tulate Macaulay most heartily on behalf of 'all lovers of truth, all lovers of liberty, all lovers of order and civilized freedom'; in this year of 1848, its lessons were apposite to the state of Europe, and might influence its better educated leaders. 'But I fear', he said unctuously, 'that the long education in the working of a constitution such as ours is not to be supplied by any reading or meditation. Jameses we may find; but Europe shows no likeness to William.'[125]

However, Macaulay's triumph was not as complete as he thought. For instance, he had not really superseded Hume, whose *History of England* continued to be republished, with continuations by various hands, at regular intervals down the century, often in sumptuous editions. In 1891 it was even reissued in a popular edition by Ward Lock under the title 'The Imperial History of England'.[126] In fact, it had no serious rival until the appearance of J.R. Green's *Short History of the English People* in 1875, and even after that it probably retained its appeal for readers of conservative or conventional tastes. Nor was Macaulay's reception in academic circles rapturous. The great German master von Ranke once referred to Macaulay as an 'incomparable' historian, but that did not deter him from doing his work all over again, and the first volume of his *Englische Geschichte vornehmlich im Siebzehnten Jahrhundert* appeared in 1859, the year of Macaulay's death. (Their only meeting, at a literary breakfast in London in 1843, had been a fiasco. Ranke knew no English and his French was unintelligible; Macaulay, rather surprisingly, was 'indifferently skilled' in German, and had reviewed Ranke's 'History of the Papacy' from an English translation.)[127] In his own work Ranke eschewed Macaulayan high drama and provided a straight political and diplomatic narrative, in which the Revolution of 1688 was viewed as a European event. He extended Macaulay's sources, and subjected some of them to a more searching examination. Above all, he deplored Macaulay's disposition to sit in judgment on characters in history. Discussing the fall of James II, he sombrely remarked: 'We do not consider ourselves authorised to adopt the tone which English historians have borrowed from the proceedings of the criminal courts; we have only to do with the contemplation of the historical events.'[128] When the newly established School of Modern History at Oxford wanted a basic text on seventeenth-century history it was to Ranke they turned. Eight separate college tutors, encouraged by Stubbs, set about translating the eight volumes of his *Englische Geschichte*, which were published in six volumes in 1875 as *The History of England principally in the Seventeenth Century.*[129]

Acton, too, emerged as one of Macaulay's severest critics. In fact, he regarded his whole approach to English history as wrong, and thought 'he never mastered the real point at issue between the Whigs and all other parties', though he grudgingly admitted that he was 'preserved from many errors to which his superficial treatment of principles would have exposed him, by an unswerving admiration for the writings of Edmund Burke'. In his private notes he recorded that even he was staled by Macaulay's heavy-handed judicialism, and he called for 'a little abstinence from perpetual judging'. Yet he admitted in a letter to Mary Gladstone: 'He remains to me one of the greatest of all writers and masters, although I think him utterly base, contemptible and odious.' He was, in fact, like thousands of readers, a victim of

Macaulay's charm. The *History of England*, he told Mary Gladstone again, was 'wonderful':

> 'He knew nothing respectably before the seventeenth century, he knew nothing of foreign history, of religion, philosophy, science or art. His account of debates has been thrown into the shade by Ranke, his account of diplomatic affairs, by Klopp.* He is, I am persuaded, grossly, basely unfair. Read him therefore to find out how it comes that the most unsympathetic of critics can think him very nearly the greatest of English writers'.[130]

* Onno Klopp, *Der Fall des Hauses Stuart*, 14 vols, Vienna 1875–88.

Four

◆ ◆

The High Victorians

Archives and Sources

The bent of Macaulay's mind was essentially eighteenth-century; in fact, in the latest study of his work he is described as 'the most Augustan of the great Victorians'.[1] He was consciously writing to combat Hume, whose *History* has essentially been an extended philosophical essay with some reference to original sources, and this is reflected in his own work. Though he obviously devoted much time to the collection of original material he was using it to strengthen or flesh out conclusions he had already reached by the exercise of his intelligence and imagination. A note he made in his diary in 1849 is very typical: 'I am glad to find that whatever I now discover relating to the reign of James II confirms my general views.'[2] Notes in the opposite vein are not to be found. His technique was thus entirely divergent from that of his contemporary Ranke, who forcefully argued that the sources must be allowed to tell their own story; it was the historian's function to establish and evaluate these sources, which would then impose their own pattern on his narrative; in fact, the material would construct its own story. This ideal, which was never fully realized, even by Ranke himself, nevertheless dominated the historical thinking of the nineteenth century.

As his diary shows, Macaulay's research was vigorous but random.* He worked quite assiduously in the British Museum, only rarely in the 'State Paper Office', as he still called the Public Record Office. At the Museum it seems that he read mainly pamphlets, on which he set much store, perhaps too much; for books he used the libraries of the Athenaeum, the Royal Institution and the House of Commons. He never went to the Dutch archives, though he commissioned transcripts of the Dutch envoys' despatches in the reign of William III; and though he made seven recorded visits to Paris on holiday, only twice did he visit the archives there: for two days of an eleven-

---

* Unless otherwise stated, what follows is based on an inspection of Macaulay's MS Journal, Trinity College, Cambridge.

day visit in September 1849, and for a week in September 1854 which he spent in the War Office as well as the Foreign Office archives – perhaps studying Jacobite material; he does not say. For the period up to 1688, as he freely admits, he relied mainly on the French transcripts made by his friend the late Sir James Mackintosh, which are in themselves a selection. He showed unusual enterprise in searching out copies of discarded or defeated bills in the House of Lords Record Office, and used them to good effect, and he visited the muniment rooms of country houses like Althorp and Chevening, though not, it seems, on any organized basis. He combined this research with social visits to Whig peers he happened to know, and he apparently made no effort to see the important papers of the Duke of Portland or the Duke of Marlborough, to mention only the most obvious. He went to Oxford in October 1854, apparently his only visit, and spent two days working on Narcissus Luttrell's diary at All Souls'. He spent the next two days in the Bodleian Library, flicking through the Tanner MSS, the 'Wharton MSS' – he probably meant the Carte MSS – and the Nairne papers. On 5 October he remarked in his diary: 'I could amuse myself here ten years without a moment of ennui', but the following afternoon he left for London.

This casual, episodic approach to the records is evident also in the technique of Macaulay's contemporary John Lingard, whose *History of England*, published in eight volumes between 1819 and 1830, is now almost entirely forgotten, but in that generation and the next posed a serious challenge to Hume. He was a Roman Catholic priest who set out to provide an accurate history which would be acceptable to Protestants and at the same time correct the anti-Roman bias of previous accounts, whether by Hume or by the Whigs.

His approach is not to be admired, and there is something repugnant in his willingness initially to pander to Protestant prejudice, then alter his work in subsequent editions, when the 'enemy' was off his guard. In 1847 he warned a Catholic friend off the first edition in these words:

'I had then to acquire credit amongst Protestants, and was therefore extremely cautious – and I believe in that respect successful, for I was held by many to be a moderate, perhaps impartial writer; this made me bolder in the duodecimo edition'.

For nine years his agent in Madrid pursued the rumour that somewhere in the archives at Simancas were letters to Philip II from Queen Elizabeth's 'camerara mayor' (Groom of the Stole?) which proved her adultery with the Earl of Leicester, yet when his publisher expressed mild alarm at his characterization of Elizabeth, he received this remarkable reply:

'I have been careful to soften down what might have appeared too harsh to prejudiced minds, and not to let any worse expressions escape, that I may not be thought a partial writer. I should be sorry to hurt the sale of the book, and on that account have been particularly guarded in the conclusion, where I touch upon her character. However, if there be any expression which you think likely to prove prejudicial, I shall be ready to change it'.[3]

In fact, his insinuations against Elizabeth's chastity, with which he persisted to the end,[4] were the only part of the book which gave serious offence to Protestants, and his success is the more remarkable when we remember that it was published in the 1820s, when the Catholic Question was at the forefront of politics, and Lingard himself was deeply engaged in pamphlet disputes with Protestant divines. Initially he met with more criticism from his fellow Catholics, who were deeply shocked at his cavalier treatment of St Thomas Becket and St Joan of Arc.* John Milner, Vicar-Apostolic of the Midlands District, even denounced him to Rome in 1825 – 'It's a bad book,' he said, 'only calculated to confirm Protestants in their errors.'[5] However, Lingard was in high favour at Rome; he was offered a bishopric and the rectorship of the English College, Rome, and there was even a rumour that had Leo XII not died in 1831 he would have made him a cardinal. Though his obituary notices in the *Tablet* and the *Dublin Review* cautioned the faithful against his 'liberalism', his *History* received the ultimate seal of orthodoxy when it was abridged for use in Catholic church schools in England (1854) and even in Ireland (1867); in this form it was heartily endorsed by Cardinals Wiseman, Gibbons and Gasquet, and it was republished as late as 1915 with a continuation by Hilaire Belloc.[6] In its complete form it went through six editions between 1830 and 1852, and from the first two alone Lingard received royalties of £4133, some of which he used to endow scholarships at his old college, Ushaw. By the time of his death in 1851 it is estimated that it had earned him between £8000 and £9000. He was elected an honorary Fellow of the Society of Literature, and in 1839, at the instance of Lord and Lady Holland, he was awarded a grant of £300 from the Privy Purse. He was also on excellent terms with another notorious Whig, Lord Brougham.

Lingard's private letters reveal that he had nothing but contempt for the Hollands' other protégé, Macaulay. He dismissed his work as 'a string of critiques or essays', and as for his scholarship:

---

* His comment in the first edition (iv, 26) that St Joan was the victim of 'an enthusiasm which, while it deluded, yet moved and elevated the mind of this young and interesting female', was later removed; but in the sixth edition of 1852 he still says of her childhood (iv, 14) that 'in those day dreams the young enthusiast learned to invest with visible forms the creation of her own fancy', and of her trial (iv, 21) that 'an impartial observer would have pitied and respected the mental delusion with which she was afflicted'.

'One half of the quotations from him are of no authority. He has been fishing in cesspools and quagmires, and has filled his memory with all kinds of filth and falsehood, which he retails, mixed up with facts, as if they were facts also ... His work abounds in claptrap of every description'.

Carlyle, too, was 'a complete windbag, with his Anglo-German jargon and his pompous profundity', and in his swan song, the new preface he wrote for the edition of 1852, he said:

'Novelists, speculators and philosophists always assume the privilege of being acquainted with the secret motives of those whose conduct and characters they describe; but writers of history know nothing more respecting motives than the little which their authorities have disclosed, or the facts necessarily suggest'.[7]

Lingard himself always paraded his virtue as a writer who dealt entirely in original authorities, and this claim was largely accepted by his contemporaries; but it is quite ridiculous to describe him as 'The English Ranke', the title given him by his latest biographer – though he was in fact admitted to the French Academy on the same day as the great German, in 1838. In fact, most of his material was drawn from printed books; this is apparent in his famous public controversy with John Allen of the *Edinburgh Review* over the Massacre of St Bartholomew.[8] Certainly he was the master of an unusually wide range of languages, French, Spanish, Italian, Latin, Greek, Hebrew and Italian, and his command of the printed sources was absolute; when he spoke of composing his *History* 'entirely (or at least as far as may be) from the original letters and papers', he meant little more than that.[9] In fact, like many Victorians, he was largely rooted in one spot, and that not the most convenient. He was the parish priest of Hornby, in Lancashire, and apart from one visit to Italy, in 1817, he remained there all his working career. His correspondence shows that he relied heavily on the loan of books from wealthy co-religionists, friends and sympathizers, and this was a severe handicap, especially when he was trying to deal with subsequent criticisms. His great coup was the purchase, for five pounds, of the transcripts made by the French historian F.A.J. Mazure of the diplomatic correspondence between France and England in the reign of James II, which put him in a stronger position than Macaulay.[10] But it is not at all clear that he ever used the British Museum or the Public Record Office, vague assertions by his biographers notwithstanding.[11] In his preface to the edition of 1849 he reviewed the new material he had used, but this was in the form of printed books, except that he thanked Sir Robert Peel for procuring on his behalf transcripts of the Gunpowder Plot papers – from the Public Record Office. He used his one visit to Italy to good effect, and he must be given full credit for appreciating the importance of the Venetian *relazioni** even before Ranke did; he found some in the Barberini archives in Rome, and tried to get hold of more.[12] At the same time he obtained permission to take transcripts from the jealously-guarded Vatican archives – apparently the first scholar to do so. But the transcripts had to be made by his friend Robert Gradwell, rector of the English College, and in the absence of a catalogue this was a hit-or-miss affair, especially after his return to England.[13] This was even more so at the Simancas, where his amanuensis was not allowed to copy the documents at all; he had to memorize them as best he could and write them up later. The archbishop of Paris obtained copies from Besançon of the despatches of Simon Renard, the Imperial ambassador to Mary I, but in this lucky dip process he missed the equally important despatches of his predecessor Eustace Chapuys, at Vienna. In fact, he operated very much as Robertson had done, half a century before; he used only an accidental selection of manuscript material, and it came to him, not he to it.

Lingard and Macaulay, in fact, were transitional figures; their working careers spanned the period, roughly 1815 to 1850, during which government archives across Europe were progressively opened to scholars. On the Continent this development is usually associated with the successive revolutions of 1789, 1830 and 1848, which broke down the obsessive secretiveness of arbitrary governments. In England, however – and probably elsewhere, in fact – the main obstacle to open research was dirt, confusion and disorder. Records were stored higgledy-piggledy, and often inaccessibly; catalogues, where they existed at all, were quite inadequate; and there were no staff available to issue documents and monitor their use.

To this the English State Paper Office was at first an honourable exception, largely because it was a working library for the Privy Council and the Secretaries of State. It was founded in 1578 with the title 'The Office of her Majesty's Papers and Records for the business of State and Council', with a keeper who was usually a prominent second-rank civil servant. James I, who typically declared that 'he would make it the rarest office of that quality in Christendom', encouraged Thomas Wilson to sort the papers – it was he who first established the division between 'foreign' and 'domestic' – and move them to more commodious quarters in Whitehall. He also issued an order, renewed by succeeding sovereigns, that all ministers should deposit their papers at the Office when they resigned.[14]

This order was often ignored, but it was equally often complied with, and the complaints of successive keepers were principally directed at ministers

---

* On completion of his mission each Venetian envoy submitted to the Signoria a *relazione*, which was a comprehensive description and analysis of the court to which he had been accredited.

and ambassadors who borrowed papers and never bothered to bring them back. Subsequently the Office had the advantage of a series of diligent and long-serving keepers, notably Sir Joseph Williamson from 1661 to 1702, who was also Under Secretary of State until 1674 and Secretary of State 1674-9. It was Williamson who actively reassembled the state papers purloined or dispersed during the Interregnum, and commandeered the records of the Interregnum governments themselves, a task which took him most of Charles II's reign. However, the title of the crown to all government documents past and present was well recognized; in 1623 Wilson seized the papers of Queen Elizabeth's secretary, William Davison, which had been offered for sale privately, in 1633 Charles I confiscated the papers of John Wright, 'Clerk to the Parliament deceased', and as late as 1755, Henry Fox, as Secretary of State, issued a warrant for the seizure of 'twenty-two bags of ancient writings and records, belonging to his Majesty', concealed at the house of John Anstis garter king-at-arms, at Mortlake.

Access to these records was always limited, however, usually to those authorized by the Secretary of State, and the same applied to the only other state repository with a regular keeper, the Tower of London. Burnet confidently asserted that for the first volume of his *History of the Reformation* he had searched 'all public records and offices', but he had done no such thing. Such state papers as he had used he had found in the Cottonian Library, and even there, since it was a quasi-governmental institution, he had operated clandestinely.[15] Not until 1679 did Charles II allow him access to the State Paper Office. At the Tower Robert Brady, as befitted a defender of the royal cause, had unrestricted access, and the keeper, Lawrence Halstead, acted as his amanuensis. In 1684 Brady was even granted a pension of £300 a year 'for his care and pains in and about the records in the Tower of London'. On the other hand, we know that Brady's Whig opponent, William Petyt, also had access, because Halstead asked Brady if he should eject him.[16] Appropriately enough, Petyt displaced Halstead after the Revolution.

Thereafter admissions are difficult to monitor. Clearly Rymer and Sanderson had full access to all records in order to compile their *Foedera*, and a few private requests for access to the State Paper Office survive; Dalrymple's, for instance, in 1772, and one from the Earl of Shaftesbury in 1767, seeking information on his ancestor, the 1st Earl. But it is doubtful if all the records were usable in a systematic way, and as early as 1700 the government was expressing concern at their physical condition. In 1704 Petyt was given three clerks to help him 'digest' the Tower archives, and in 1705 the State Paper Office was transferred to the upper floor of the Lord Chamberlain's lodgings at Whitehall, now refurbished under the supervision of Sir Christopher Wren. (The Committee of the House of Lords which recommended this change noted that very few papers of any significance had been deposited there since the death of Charles II.) Wren also supervised the repair of the Chapter House, Westminster, which housed the Exchequer records. Money was voted for the Tower in 1723, to have 'the broken earth floor boarded over, the windows altered to keep out the wet, and the leads on the Wakefield Tower mended', which is a sufficient commentary on conditions previously. In 1727 John Lawton was appointed to 'methodise' the Chapter House records and index them, and in 1746 Henry Poole set about a similar task in the Tower. But in 1750, when part of the old Lord Chamberlain's lodgings were pulled down, the state papers were found to be much affected by damp and vermin. Half of them stayed at Whitehall, where in 1764 they were found to be infested with weevils, which could be swept up in large quantities from the floor; the other half were moved first to an old house in Scotland Yard, where they were still a prey to damp, and then in 1819 to another house on the corner of Great George Street and Duke Street. It is to be doubted how far they were available at all to historians at this stage, and the two halves of the archive were not reunited until 1833, when they ended up in a purpose-built office by St James's Park. Meanwhile in 1800 the Commons had appointed a Select Committee on the public records, whose work was continued by a series of Record Commissions, reporting back in 1812, 1819, and 1837.

The record commissioners found that the national archives were scattered across London in fifty-six separate repositories, usually uncatalogued and stored haphazardly, and often in far from ideal conditions. The Tower, the Rolls Chapel and the Chapter House at Westminster were the exceptions; they were open to the public in a regular and orderly way most of the year, with permanent staff in attendance. But the records of the Common Law courts, when they were available at all, could only be consulted during the law terms, and not easily then. They found that the rolls of King's bench, for instance, 'were shut up, and to secure the attendance of an officer for the purpose of searching, it was necessary to apply at certain offices in the Temple', and even when this officer was found, 'there was no convenience for searching, and the record rooms were very rarely cleaned, ventilated or warmed'. This last phrase recurs like a litany from archive to archive – 'no part of the building kept clean, ventilated or warmed'; 'never warmed or cleaned'; 'never cleaned, aired or warmed'; 'damp, ill-ventilated and offensive'. Some important records were not available at all; the records of the Equity side of Exchequer, for instance, at Carlton Ride, were simply locked away. Elsewhere, the official responsible had to be wooed away from his normal duties in the courts of law and tipped accordingly; especially one Mr Caley, of the First Fruits Office in Dean's Yard, Westminster, who had removed the records to his private house. At Somerset House the attendant was 'an inferior workman', but it is doubtful if his socially superior colleagues at other repositories knew any more about the manuscripts in their care, which were often in a deplorable condition. For instance:

> 'A search for any records in the roofs above the Augmentation Office, containing some of the King's Bench records, was a most uncomfortable and unsatisfactory operation. The person employed, officer or applicant, had to ascend the ladder and make the search by candlelight, the records being covered with soot and filth'.

Conversely, 'the records at Somerset House were in vaults two stories under ground, damp, extremely filthy, ill-lighted and worse ventilated; in fact, inaccessible except with candles.'[17] Spurred on perhaps by the disastrous fire at Westminster in 1834, which destroyed all the Commons records and some of the Treasury records in the Stone Tower, the Commissioners finally recommended that all the records of government be concentrated in one central, custom-built repository under a deputy keeper responsible to the Master of the Rolls, with a permanent staff, whose task it would be to catalogue the records and make them freely available to the public. This was carried out by the Public Record Office Act of 1838, backed up by an Order in Council of 1852 obliging all government departments to transfer their own papers to the Record Office as soon as they were no longer required for current use.[18]

The effects of this measure were far-reaching, and in particular the great leap forward in the study of medieval history in this century would have been virtually impossible without it. The move was completed by 1862 under the supervision of the first deputy keeper, Sir Francis Palgrave, who had some pretensions to being a historian himself.* The incoming documents were stored at first in houses along Chancery Lane, until the first stage of the present Record Office building was opened in 1856.† The sorting, cleaning, arrangement and preliminary cataloguing of the collections proceeded with remarkable speed, and in addition to the 'Lists and Indexes', primarily intended for use in the Search Room itself, the Public Record Office almost at once began the publication of its famous Calendars. The *Calendars of State Papers Domestic* began in 1856 with the first volume for Edward VI's reign, and this series was completed in 1872 with the death of James I. Meanwhile another series, beginning with Charles I's accession, had been launched in 1858, though it took until 1897 to reach his death. Charles II's reign took even

---

* Not to be confused with his son, Francis Turner Palgrave, who edited *The Golden Treasury of Songs and Lyrics*.

† Most of the later records were transferred to a new repository at Kew in 1977.

longer to cover, from 1860 to 1947. William III's reign took from 1895 to 1937, by which time the impetus provided by the Victorians had almost exhausted itself. James II's reign was only 'filled in' after the Second World War, and the Calendars for Anne's reign are still in progress, as are the *Calendars of State Papers Foreign* and the *Calendars of State Papers Colonial*, which began in 1861 and 1860 respectively. The cost of producing such calendars is now prohibitive, and the introduction of microfilming and xerography has made them largely redundant, but in their heyday they were a boon to historians. Perhaps the Record Office's greatest trumph in this respect was the encyclopedic *Letters and Papers of Henry VIII*, which broke the existing rules by printing documents from other archives. Begun by J.S. Brewer in 1862, it was finally completed by James Gairdner in 1910, in thirty-three volumes.

Meanwhile, investigations were proceeding into manuscripts in private hands. In 1869 the queen, being informed that there were various collections of papers, many of them state papers, in private hands, whose examination by scholars would 'tend to the elucidation of history and the illustration of constitutional law, science and literature', appointed a royal commission to locate such private archives, assess their significance, and make 'abstracts and catalogues', so that their existence and their whereabouts could be made known more widely. The Commissioners accordingly drew up a circular which they despatched to virtually all the nobility and landed gentry, to the Inns of Court, the borough corporations, the colleges of Oxford and Cambridge, and other owners or potential owners of manuscripts to the number of 120 or more. Their first report was submitted in 1870 and published in 1874.

They were delighted at the riches they had uncovered at the first cast, and the good nature with which owners had welcomed their inspectors. One of the most astounding finds, and the least expected, was at the House of Lords, which apart from its journals held 29,507 documents – the inspectors were always as precise as possible – which it knew little about. They included such treasures as the correspondence between Charles I and Queen Henrietta Maria during the first Civil War, intercepted by the Long Parliament.[19] While the work of sorting and recording the new material went on, the Commission was renewed from time to time, and indeed it has continued down to the present day.

The Commissioners also commented on the state of the documents they found. This was generally good, but many owners did not realize the importance of what they had, and most of them put too much emphasis on legal documents. The Hatton Papers were 'in a state of chaotic confusion', and 'documents of inestimable value were mixed up with papers comparatively worthless'. (This report no doubt prompted their presentation to the British Museum soon afterwards.) The Earl of Dalhousie had his title deeds well arranged in presses, but other material, of great historical importance, was jumbled together in tin boxes on the floor. Early medieval charters were mixed in with 'papers of all kinds and dates', and important Jacobite material, hitherto unknown, was unearthed in a box 'marked No. 4', in the corridor outside the muniment room.[20] As for the unfortunate inspector assigned to Hatfield House, he reported: 'The collection is so large and the papers so important that I was at a great loss how to begin and where to end.'[21]

In fact, by the time the second report was published, in 1874, some inspectors had already proceeded from mere lists to summaries of documents, others from summaries to full transcripts.[22] After the ninth report, in 1884, the reports were issued separately from the appendices of documents, and the number of collections covered in each appendix steadily decreased, eventually to one. Meanwhile the Commission undertook the task of publishing major collections *in toto*, and by 1900 these had entered upon a separate existence, independent of the annual reports. The first volume of the Salisbury Papers at Hatfield was published in 1883 (and the last in 1976); the House of Lords Papers began in 1887, and were later taken over by the House itself and are still in progress; the series of Ormonde Papers at Kilkenny began in 1875 and was completed in 1920; and so on.*

Finally, the high Victorian age saw the complete reordering of the British Museum's collections of printed books and manuscripts. The Museum had its origins in the decision of Sir Robert Cotton's grandson to give his library and collections to the nation in 1700. They were moved to a house in the Strand in 1712, and in 1730 to Ashburnham House, where they were severely damaged by fire the following year. In 1753, when Sir Hans Sloane bequeathed his scientific collections and his library to the nation also, the government was forced to act, and in 1757 their deliberations were hastened by George II, who presented them with the Royal Library. That year they passed the Copyright Act, obliging all publishers to deposit a copy of every book they published, and floated a lottery to provide for a suitable building and also to purchase the Harleian Library, assembled by Robert Harley, 1st Earl of Oxford, and his descendants, which was now on the market. All this material was transferred to Montagu House, fronting on Great Russell Street, which was purchased from the Duke of Bedford.

A rough catalogue of the Cottonian Library was issued in 1802, but no adequate catalogue was available, even at Montagu House, for the other

---

*This is a cursory view of a very complicated process, which is fully set out in the RHS publication *Texts and Calendars*, by E.L.C. Mullins (1958).

manuscript collections or the printed books, and conditions of access were highly unsatisfactory. George IV's decision to sell his father's personal library to the nation in 1823 again forced the pace, and in 1827 the present King's Library, designed by Robert Smirke, was built in the grounds of Montagu House. Montagu House itself was demolished in 1845, and the present front-age and forecourt to the Museum were built to the designs of Sidney Smirke between then and 1852. As early as 1831 Carlyle – a man not easily pleased – was delighted with the King's Library when he returned to London after a five-year absence. He found it 'in excellent order', which had not been the case before; 'I tried the place in my former sojourn, but found it useless, and had given it up.'[23]

The Museum was now taken in hand by that most colourful of great Victorians, Sir Anthony Panizzi. Panizzi's career as a lawyer was cut short in 1822, when he was exiled from his native Naples for political reasons. Arriving destitute in England, he rebuilt his career from rock bottom, first as a teacher of Italian – he was the first professor of Italian at London University – and then as a librarian. He was appointed an assistant librarian at the British Museum in 1831 under the aegis of the Whig Lord Chancellor, Brougham, and henceforward enjoyed the support and patronage of successive govern-ments. Riding on a whirlwind of contestation, culminating in the appointment of a Commons Select Committee, he rose to be Keeper of the Printed Books in 1837. From then on his influence was prodigious. He initiated the replace-ment of Montagu House, and insisted, in the teeth of considerable opposition, on instituting an alphabetical catalogue, which was made available to readers in a preliminary form in 1850; this paved the way for a full printed catalogue later in the century. He also braved the wrath of the London publishers by insisting on the strict enforcement of the Copyright Act, and in 1845 he secured a Treasury grant of £10,000 a year for further acquisitions. He also persuaded the millionaire bibliophile Thomas Grenville to bequeath to the Museum his library of over 20,000 volumes, valued at £50,000. Above all, Panizzi sponsored and designed in rough the great circular reading room, which was opened in 1857 and was one of the wonders of the age; by this time he was Principal Librarian, the equivalent of the present Director.[24] It is in the 1850s that we find Macaulay sitting at one of the oak tables in the King's Library (long since removed) and studying the Museum's pamphlet collec-tions at his ease. As a trustee of the Museum he also had the privilege of access to the closed shelves, without an attendant.[25]

The Manuscript Collections were never in the forefront of Panizzi's mind, but that does not mean that they were neglected, and at the very least they could now take advantage of the vacant space left by the rehousing of the books. As a result, and also because of the publicity given the Historical

Manuscripts Commission, an increasing number of manuscripts were being presented or bequeathed. In the 1850s a steady trickle became a flood, and in the 1870s a tidal wave. To take just a few examples: fifty-five volumes of Godolphin-Osborne papers arrived in 1869, overshadowed in 1872 by Warren Hastings's papers, in 263 volumes; two years later the Finch-Hatton MSS, in forty-nine volumes, provided invaluable background material to Charles II's reign; and in 1879 a comparatively slender collection (eight volumes) consisting of the papers of Sir Edward Nicholas, gave a new slant on Charles I's. Most splendid of all, in 1886 the Earl of Chichester handed over 522 volumes of family papers, mainly those of Thomas Pelham-Holles, Duke of Newcastle, and Philip Yorke, 1st Earl of Hardwicke. Cataloguing went ahead with remarkable vigour, but clearly the staff were swamped; before they could deal with what they already had, new acquisitions crashed in on them. Thus, the catalogue of manuscripts acquired between 1836 and 1840 was published in 1843, and that for 1841–5 in 1850, but the catalogue for 1846–7, a mere two years, did not appear until 1864, followed in 1868 by that for 1848–53. As for the earlier manuscripts, acquired between 1782 and 1835, an index was published in 1849, but the full catalogue did not appear until 1977. At the time of writing the published catalogues do not go beyond 1945.* Nor were the cataloguers the only ones to be swamped; so were the historians. For instance it was not until the 1920s that the vast bulk of the Newcastle Papers were thoroughly explored by Namier.

These overwhelming developments bespeak the gigantic energy, the intense curiosity and the sheer munificence of the Victorians. Their motivation is not as obvious as it might seem, but in an era of Reform it ill behoved them to fall behind Continental governments distinguished by corruption and arbitrary power in any respect, especially in access to information, and as their satisfaction with the virtues of the British constitution increased, so it became necessary to establish as accurately as possible how that constitution had evolved.

However, the opportunities offered were not immediately embraced. The failure of the universities to establish a professional discipline in history left the profession rootless and leaderless, in marked contrast to the situation in Germany. With the exception of Stubbs, all the English historians of the High Victorian era were amateurs, usually resident in or around London, and existing on private incomes or the proceeds of higher journalism. Their work often partook of the nature of literature or general reading; naturally, since a knowledge of history was regarded as part of the usual, though not compulsory equipment of a well-bred gentleman, together with a knowledge of

---

* I would stress the word 'published'. The typescript catalogues and indexes in the search room are kept up to date, of course.

poetry, drama, art and (after Darwin) some science. Carlyle is the prime example of a historian whose work is best classified under the heading of general literature.

Untrained and working largely alone, except for letters exchanged with kindred spirits, these men often spurned the use of archives, or even libraries. Freeman and Buckle are extreme examples of this trend, and J.R. Green another. Their connexion with their university, where they had taken degrees in classics, was tenuous or non-existent, though Freeman and Froude returned in a rather ambiguous glory late in life. With the exception, again, of Stubbs, and to some extent Froude, they were deaf to the dicta of Ranke and his German colleagues. Even Carlyle, who was easily the most receptive to German influences, was far from being record-conscious, or professional in his approach to evidence.

The Prophets: Carlyle and Buckle

Thomas Carlyle was Scotland's last great gift to English history, and he was the first of the great Victorian prophets – in the hebraic sense of that word, meaning self-styled gurus and teachers who denounced the sins of their generation and called for a return to older values or the substitution of new. Had he not lost his faith, and his vocation for the ministry, he would have emerged, no doubt, as one of the ayatollahs of Scottish Calvinism. (Strangely enough, he lost his faith after reading Gibbon's *Decline and Fall*, when he was a young schoolteacher at Kirkcaldy.) As it was, he eked out a penurious existence for many years on the fringes of London publishing, writing occasional articles for the reviews and translations from the German. One of these was Goethe's *Wilhelm Meister*, which gained the author's enthusiastic approval. At intervals he was forced to retreat to Scotland, to his father's farm near Dumfries, or that of his in-laws at Craigenputtock, East Lothian. It was not until 1834, when he was nearly forty, that he settled for good at 5 Cheyne Walk, Chelsea (now No. 24).

His difficulty in establishing himself is not surprising when we contemplate the impenetrability of Carlyle's writing – his bizarre vocabulary, his contorted syntax and rhetorical violence – not to mention the wild exaggeration with which most of his views were expressed. He was unique amongst nineteenth-century historians in that he rejected the Enlightenment and the Ancien Regime alike, and at the same time rejected Reform.[26] Nor was this violence confined to his published work. Here he responds to an invitation to visit a friend of his in Yorkshire in 1821: 'York to me is like a city of the mind. In my dreams, I have heard the Humber loud that bears the Scythian name, and seen the field of Marston Moor with the *iron bands* of Cromwell, when the genius of England awoke, descending like reapers to the harvest of death.'[27] Even so, this is clarity and balance itself compared with much of his later writing, which gives the impression, in the words of one modern critic (and admirer), that he was 'trying to discover what he wanted to say by the familiar process of writing it down first and then seeing what it meant'. (Monckton Milnes once commented that Carlyle's ideas might be 'dangerous if turned into the vernacular'.)[28] Nevertheless, his books are still read,* and he has commanded the respect of historians as diverse as James Anthony Froude, G.M. Trevelyan and Hugh Trevor-Roper. To ease the pangs of unrequited love, Trevelyan once spent a weekend at the Bush Hotel in Ecclefechan, Carlyle's birthplace, re-reading *Sartor Resartus*.[29]

This is loyalty indeed, for this was Carlyle's first book and his most difficult, a seething, heavily Germanized, philosophical semi-autobiography which – in the words of another modern admirer – presented a picture of the world 'in images of ingestion, digestion, fermentation, obstruction, explosion, dung'.[30] Not surprisingly, he had difficulty finding a publisher. It was serialized in *Frazer's Magazine* in 1833 and 1834, where according to the editor it 'excited the most unqualified disapprobation', and pirated in Boston the following year, but it was not published in England in book form until 1838, after the success of *The French Revolution* had established his reputation.

He began *The French Revolution* in 1834, when he settled in Chelsea, wrote half of it in five months, then lent the only copy to John Stuart Mill, whose maid accidentally burnt it. It took him nearly two years to rewrite it and bring it to completion, though the delay may have been salutary. He indulged in his usual rhodomontade, of course. When he started in 1834 he told his brother: 'It shall be such a book! Quite an epic poem of the Revolution, an apotheosis of Sansculottism', and when he had finished he trumpeted to his wife: 'I could tell the world: "You have not had for a hundred years any book that comes more direct and flamingly from the heart of a living man."' He told John Sterling: 'It has come hot out of my own soul, born in blackness, whirlwind and sorrow.'[31] Certainly it is quite unlike any other book, on the French Revolution or on anything else. Oppressed himself by chronic constipation and dyspepsia, he saw the Revolution as a cataclysmic explosion of violence

---

* I was rather surprised to find, in 1982, that not only was *The French Revolution* available in the Everyman series, but also *Sartor Resartus*, *Past and Present* and *Heroes and Hero-Worship*. There was even an abridged edition of *Frederick the Great* available under an American imprint.

pent up by the decadent obscurantism of eighteenth-century Europe – if you like, a gigantic fart. Violence, and exultation in violence, sways the whole book, and he positively glories in the coming of the Terror:

'Ye have roused her, then, ye Emigrants and Despots of the world; France is roused! Long have ye been lecturing and tutoring this poor Nation, like cruel, uncalled-for pedagogues, shaking over her your ferulas of fire and steel: it is long that you have pricked and filliped and affrighted her, there as she sat helpless in her dead cerements of a Constitution, you gathering in on her from all lands, with your armaments and plots, your invadings and truculent bullyings; – and lo now, ye have pricked her to the quick, and she is up, and her blood is up. The dead cerements are rent into cobwebs, and she fronts you in that terrible strength of Nature, which no man has measured, which goes down to Madness and Tophet: see now how you will deal with her.'[32]

The agonies of the Terror itself engendered an excitement verging on the unhealthy, and his account of the murder of the Princesse de Lamballe in September 1792 is regrettably typical:

'She too is led to the hell-gate; a manifest Queen's-Friend. She shivers at the sight of the bloody sabres; but there is no return: Onwards! That fair hind head is cleft with the axe; the neck is severed. That fair body is cut in fragments; with indignities, and obscene horrors of moustachio *grands-lèvres*, which human nature would fain find incredible, – which shall be read in the original language only. She was beautiful, she was good, she had known no happiness. Young hearts, generation after generation, will think with themselves: O worthy of worship, thou king-descended, god de-scended, and poor sister-woman! Why was not I there; and some Sword Balmung or Thor's Hammer in my hand?'[33]

When he came to the end of the book, with 13 Vendémiaire, he went 'right over the top', as we would say:

'Imposture is in flames, Imposture is burnt up; one red sea of fire, wild-bellowing, enwraps the World; with its fire-tongue licks at the very Stars. Thrones are hurled into it, and Dubois Mitres, and Prebendal Stalls that drop fatness, and – ha! what see I? – all the Gigs of Creation: all, all! Woe is me! Never since Pharaoh's Chariots, in the Red Sea of water, was there wreck of Wheel-vehicles like this in the Sea of Fire. Desolate as ashes, as gases, shall they wander in the wind. Higher, higher yet flames the Fire-Sea; crackling with new dislocated timber; hissing with leather and prunella. The metal Images are molten; the marble Images become mortar-lime; the

stone Mountains sulkily explode. RESPECTABILITY, with all her collected Gigs inflamed for funeral pyre, wailing, leaves the Earth, not to
return save under new Avatar. Imposture how it burns, through generations: how it is burnt up; for a time. The World is black ashes; – which, ah,
when will they grow green? The Images all run into amorphous Corinthian
brass; all Dwellings of men destroyed; the very mountains peeled and riven,
the valleys black and dead: it is in empty World! Woe to them that shall
be born then!——A King, a Queen (ah me!) were hurled in, did rustle
once; flew aloft, crackling like paper-scroll. Iscariot Egalité was hurled
in; thou grim de Launay, with thy grim Bastille; whole kindreds and
peoples; five millions of mutually destroying Men. For it is the End of the
dominion of IMPOSTURE (which is Darkness and opaque Firedamp);
and the burning up, with unquenchable fire, of all the Gigs that are in the
Earth'.[34]

This strange syntax and stranger punctuation, the meandering of the prose
from one thing to the next, these bewildering obsessions (with gigs, of all
things), are reminiscent of some modern American prose avowedly written
under the influence of drugs, and it may be that Carlyle's dyspepsia medicines
contained more than we know. But in his quieter moments he could be
mordantly compelling, as in this famous passage, which was a favourite of
G.M. Trevelyan's:

'The fireship is old France, the old French Form of Life; her crew a
Generation of men. Wild are their cries and their ragings there, like spirits
tormented in that flame. But, on the whole, are they not *gone*, O Reader?
Their Fireship and they, frightening the world, have sailed away; its flames
and its thunders quite away, into the Deep of Time. One thing therefore
History will do: pity them all; for it went hard with them all'.[35]

In any case, the public now seemed willing to swallow Carlyle, prose and
all, if only for the excitement he engendered. We tremble for Lily Dale when
she settles down with *The French Revolution* on a rainy afternoon at Allington;
but it is perhaps significant that Trollope thought it suitable reading for a
delicately bred young lady who had just been jilted.

It is doubtful if many people went to him for a factual account, and most
of them would have already read their 'Alison'. For it is salutary to remember
that Carlyle's *French Revolution* was competing in a market apparently dominated by a ten-volume history of the French Revolution and the Napoleonic
Wars by Sir Archibald Alison, a distinguished Scots lawyer and an unbending
Tory of the old school. His purpose was 'to show the corruption of human
nature, and the divine superintendence of human affairs'; indeed Mr Rigby is

found recommending it to the young Coningsby as 'a capital work, which proves that Providence was on the side of the Tories'. When he had completed his labours he wrote:

> 'If there is any one opinion which, more than another, is impressed on my mind by a minute examination of the changes of the French Revolution, it is the perilous nature of the current into which men are drawn, who commit themselves to the stream of political innovation'.[36]

Published over the years 1833 to 1842, it was a runaway success. It went through ten editions between 1842 and 1860; an abridged one-volume edition came out in 1845 and was reprinted several times; there was an epitome for use in schools in 1848, and another, for 'young persons', in 1852. In fact, so successful was it that Alison undertook a continuation up to 1848 and eventually 1852. Since over this same period Carlyle's *French Revolution* was selling well we must assume that the two books appealed to a different public or that they stimulated each other's sales. It is strange, too, that though Macaulay's whiggish history of England dominated the book market in the 1840s, recent European history was left to a Tory who thought all reform was dangerous and a radical maverick who thought the French Revolution a healthy phenomenon and in his later writings strongly hinted at the need for an English Revolution. Macaulay thought Carlyle mad, an opinion confirmed by his *Latter-Day Pamphlets* in 1850. He scribbled in his diary: 'At the Athenaeum I read Carlyle's trash – Latterday something or other – beneath criticism … Surely the world will not be duped for ever by such an empty-headed bombastic dunce.'[37] But he can have felt little sympathy, either, with Alison's view that the greatest blessing of the Revolution of 1688 was that 'it brought in a sovereign instructed in the art of overcoming the ignorant impatience of taxation which is the invariable characteristic of free communities'.[38]

It is difficult to assess the historical value of Carlyle's *French Revolution*. His sources were highly selective, and all of them printed; but it is reasonable to suppose that readers did not go to him for a connected account of events, and if they did they certainly did not get it. So clotted is his narrative that without some prior knowledge it is difficult to make sense even of the great set-pieces such as the storming of the Bastille or the death of Robespierre. Yet it sweeps us into the action, and makes us part of it in a way no other work of history quite does; Carlyle himself described the book as 'itself a kind of French Revolution', and we would perhaps call it a 'happening'. Acton said that' the vivid gleam, the mixture of the sublime with the grotesque, make [us] forget the impatient verdict and the poverty of settled fact in the volumes that delivered our fathers from thraldom to Burke'.[39] And what does so magnificently convey, too, is the irresistible impetus of the Revolution, different from anything that had gone before, the concept of revolution as something with an animal energy of its own, independent of the men involved in it, and greater than the sum of their individual energies:

'We are now, therefore, got to that black precipitous Abyss; whither all things have been tending; where, having now arrived on the giddy verge, they hurl down, in confused ruin; headlong, pellmell, down, down, – till Sansculottism have consummated itself; and in this wondrous French Revolution, as in a Doomsday, a World have been rapidly, if not born again, yet destroyed and engulfed. Terror has long been terrible: but to the actors themselves it has now become manifest that their appointed course is one of Terror; and they say, Be it so. *"Que la Terreur soit à l'ordre du jour".*'[40]

Even then, sales were slow at first, and Carlyle took to public lectures, on the Revolution and on 'Heroes'; the latter series was published in 1841 as *Heroes and Hero-Worship*. In 1840 the young Barclay Fox, a provincial intellectual from Devon, heard him lecture on 'The Hero as Priest', and found him as compelling in the flesh as in print – 'a black-haired, beetle-browed, wooden-faced, earnest genuine *Man*, the champion of Truth, the deadly foe of quackery, the defender of all sincere believers, be their belief what it may'; his delivery was 'eloquent, impressive, earnest, irresistible, sublime'.[41] Fox had been reading Carlyle's latest book, on *Chartism*, which was his first attempt to grapple, in his idiosyncratic way, with the problems of his time. In *Past and Present* (1843) he tried another tack, using an episode in the history of the medieval abbey of Bury St Edmunds, described in the chronicle of Jocelin of Brakelond, as a peg on which to hang a fierce attack on nineteenth-century England, which had lost all sense of the dignity of labour, the deference owed to superiors, the leadership owed by the nobility to the community; it was inferior to the Middle Ages even in its political forms. As one critic said: 'The brilliant picture of a fragment of medieval life helped the rather confused mass of gloomy rhetoric', but at the nadir of the Industrial Revolution the time was ripe for such a message, and *Past and Present* for many years rivalled *The French Revolution* in popularity. Rather surprisingly, Acton in his old age thought it 'the most remarkable piece of historical thinking in the language'.[42] Whether or not, Carlyle was now established as a leading historian, and in 1841 he refused to allow his name to go forward for the chair of modern history at Edinburgh. Three years later he rejected a similar overture from St Andrews.

But his next project was to prove a more significant and lasting contribution to history. Many of his early essays had been concerned with incidents in the reigns of James I and Charles I, and even in 1822 he was contemplating 'a kind of Essay on the Civil Wars, the Commonwealth of England – not to write a history of them – but to exhibit if I can some features of the national character as it was then displayed'.[43] Then over the next ten or fifteen years his ideas became increasingly focused on the theme of the Great Man in History, and it is not surprising that his lectures on heroes reached a climax with Oliver Cromwell, nor that by 1839 he had decided to attempt his biography. But for some reason he found the task beyond him, and what he eventually published in 1845 was a 'complete' collection of Cromwell's letters and speeches, with a running commentary.[44]

Carlyle always exaggerated the revisionist nature of his Cromwell; it was the burden of his tale that his greatness had never been appreciated by his fellow countrymen. At best this is only partly true. Even Clarendon, as we have seen, acknowledged Cromwell's transcendent ability, while he lamented his moral iniquity, and though the persistence of monarchy in England undoubtedly dimmed the reputation of the only man who had tried to suppress it, and though he had the misfortune to attract the hostility of David Hume and Catherine Macaulay alike, his fame was kept alive by a series of biographies and collections of original material published down the eighteenth century. His memory was revered by both sides in the political and social ferment of the early nineteenth century, hailed by working-class radicals as the spokesman of the people, he was also cited by the apprehensive middle classes, more accurately, as a strong man who had the right recipe for dealing with agitators. Interest quickened after 1840, as the two-hundredth anniversary of the Great Rebellion came round, and to some extent Carlyle was riding a new wave: certainly he did not 'rediscover' Cromwell, as he would have us believe.[45] But it is certainly true that in the eyes of historians Cromwell's reputation had suffered from a certain duality: to royalists, or conservatives, he was a violent radical, a king-killer who had plunged England into chaos; to republicans and would-be revolutionaries like Mrs Macaulay he had been a military dictator who had betrayed the Revolution, an interpretation which gained added point from the career of Napoleon. Moreover, Clarendon's principal charge against him, of hypocrisy, had stuck, and it seemed the best way of reconciling the successive phases of his career. As late as 1839 John Forster's biography of Cromwell embodied some of these ideas: up to 1647 or 1648 he had been a democrat and a disinterested patriot; then came the descent into tyranny. Carlyle would have none of this; he sought the clue to Cromwell's career in his sincere and possibly idiosyncratic Puritanism, which enabled him to portray him as a puzzled and entirely unfeigned seeker after truth. Forster was one of those who generously admitted the truth of this interpretation.[46]

According to Carlyle, it was Cromwell alone who had imposed discipline on Puritanism, and given it the driving force to accomplish a revolution. He failed in the end, but that he attempted it at all was a triumph. The ambiguity of his reputation was a disgrace to his countrymen; it was not so much that he was not famous, he was not famous enough. In his lecture on 'The Hero as King' Carlyle deplored the inflated reputation of Eliot, Pym and Hampden; these men were not heroes:

> 'They are very noble men, these; [they] step along in their stately way, with their measured euphemisms, philosophies, parliamentary eloquences, ship-moneys, *Monarchies of Men*;* a most constitutional, unblameable, dignified set of men. But the heart remains cold before them; the fancy alone endeavours to get up some worship of them. What man's heart does, in reality, break forth into any fire of brotherly love for these men? They are become dreadfully dull men!'[47]

Cromwell in contrast was the epic Carlylean hero, summoned from the plough, as it were, to combat the rampant evils of his day, whether they were embodied in the crown, parliament or his fellow Puritans:

> 'Oliver Cromwell quitted his farming; undertook a Hercules' Labour and lifelong wrestle with that Lernean Hydra-coil, wide as England, hissing heaven-high through its thousand crowned, coroneted, shovel-hatted quack-heads; and he did wrestle with it, the truest and terriblest wrestle I have heard of; and he wrestled it, and mowed it and cut it down a good many stages, so that its hissing is ever since pitiful in comparison, and one can walk abroad in comparative peace from it – and his wages, as I understand, were burial under the gallows-tree near Tyburn Turnpike, with his head on the gable of Westminster Hall, and two centuries now of mixed cursing and ridicule from all manner of men'.[48]

To Carlyle, this was, of course, a reflection on his own degenerate age, languishing under the rule of 'valets' and 'quacks' (two of his favourite epiphets), rattling their ridiculous ballot boxes. (The proposed secret ballot was another of his many pet hates.)

> 'Not a Hero only is needed, but a world fit for him; a world not of *Valets*; – the Hero comes almost in vain to do it otherwise! Yes, it is far from us: but it must come; thank God, it is visibly coming. Till it come, what have we? Ballot-boxes, suffrages, French Revolutions: – if we are as Valets, and do not know the Hero when we see him, what good are all these? A heroic Cromwell comes; and for a hundred-and-fifty years he cannot have a vote

* *The Monarchy of Man* was a political treatise written by Sir John Eliot during his imprisonment in the Tower, 1629–32.

from us. Why, the insincere, unbelieving world is the *natural property* of the Quack, and of the father of quacks and quackeries! Misery, confusion, unveracity are alone possible there. By ballot-boxes we alter the *figure* of our Quack; but the substance of him continues. The Valet-World *has* to be governed by the Sham-Hero, by the King merely *dressed* in King-Gear. It is his; he is its! In brief, one of two things: We shall either learn to know a Hero, a true Governor and Captain, somewhat better, when we see him; or else; or else go on to be ever governed by the Unheroic; - had we ballot-boxes clattering at every street corner, there were no remedy in these.

Cromwell had come, but Cromwell has been spurned:

'Poor Cromwell, - great Cromwell! The inarticulate prophet; Prophet who could not *speak*. Rude, confused, struggling to utter himself, with his savage depth, with his wild sincerity; and he looked so strange, among the elegant Euphemisms, dainty little Falklands, didactic Chillingworths, dip-lomatic Clarendons! Consider him. An outer hull of chaotic confusion, visions of the devil, nervous dreams, almost semi-madness; and yet such a clear determinate man's-energy working in the heart of that. A kind of chaotic man. The ray as pure starlight and fire, working in such an element of boundless hypochondria, *con*firmed black of darkness! And yet withal his hypochondria, what was it but the very greatness of the man? The depth and tenderness of his wild affections: the quantity of *sympathy* he had with things, - the quantity of insight he would yet get into the heart of things, the mastery he would yet get into the heart of things, the mastery he would yet get over things; this was his hypochondria. The man's misery, as man's misery always does, came of his greatness ... Sorrow-stricken, half-dis-tracted; the wide element of mournful *black* enveloping him, - wide as the world. It is the character of a prophetic man; a man with his whole soul *seeing*, and struggling to see'.[49]

When it appeared in 1845 *Oliver Cromwell's Letters and Speeches with Elucidations by Thomas Carlyle* was a positive sensation. He made many errors of transcription as well as fact, and accepted as genuine several docu-ments which even he, with his superficial knowledge of the period, should have recognized as spurious, but exact scholarship was never his strong point, and he was increasingly immersed in a struggle with the British Museum authorities which was a distinct impediment to research. When he was writing *The French Revolution* he was apparently quite happy with the Museum; he described it as 'an excellent library, where one *can read* [his italics]; a capital library'. He worked there two days a week, and his only complaint was that the walk from Chelsea took him through some rather insalubrious neighbourhoods. But in 1840 he set about founding the London Library, which would lend books to its members, and he was soon complaining of the crowded conditions in the British Museum Reading Room, which made it impossible to concentrate, and asking for a private room and direct access to the stacks, which was only allowed to Trustees, of whom Macaulay was one. He and Panizzi were both passionate men. Panizzi objected to being referred to as 'a respectable official', and 'declared that he would not allow the library to be pulled about by an unknown man of letters'. Carlyle, appearing before the Trustees, admitted that he was 'rather a thin-skinned type of student', to which Panizzi's reply was: 'I never felt the skin of any reader, and they are all treated alike.' By 1853, Carlyle had to admit defeat, though he magnanimously excused Panizzi himself:

> 'The blame is not in him, but in the prurient darkness and confused pedantry and ostentatious inanity of the world which put him there, and which I must own he very fairly represents and symbolizes there. Lords Lansdowne and Brougham put Panizzi in; and the world with its Hansards and ballot-boxes and sublime apparatus put in Lords Lansdowne and Brougham'.

He could comfort himself with the success of the London Library, though even there it is said that his membership was distinguished by 'his persistent failure to comply with practically all the Library's regulations'.[50]

By this time Carlyle was positively contemptuous of exact scholarship. In view of the fact that the great majority of the letters of Cromwell's he printed, and all the speeches, had been published before, it ill became him to denounce all his predecessors in a long introduction which was volcanic even by his standards, and which raises very serious doubts as to his sanity – or rather, confirms existing doubts. For instance, he described Thurloe's state papers, on which much of his account of the Protectorate is necessarily based, as 'shoreless lakes of ditchwater and bilgewater'. Mark Noble, whose *Memoirs of the Protectoral House of Cromwell* had done half his work for him, was 'a man of extreme imbecility; his judgment, for the most part, seeming to lie dead asleep'; as for his book, it was 'not properly a book, but an aggregate of bewildered jottings'.[51] Rushworth's *Historical Collections* were worth a long, sad, mad paragraph all to themselves:

> 'What is it, all this Rushworthian inarticulate rubbish-continent, in its ghastly dim twilight, with its haggard wrecks and pale shadows; what is it, but the common Kingdom of Death? This *is* what we call Death, this mouldering dumb wilderness of things once alive. Behold here the final evanescence of Formed human things; they had form, but they are changing

into sheer formlessness; – ancient human speech itself has sunk into unintelligible maundering. This is the collapse, – the etiolation of human features into mouldy blank; *dis*solution; progress towards utter silence and disappearance; disastrous every-deepening Dusk of Gods and Men! – Why has the living ventured thither, down from the cheerful light, across the Lethe-swamps and Tartarean Phlegethons, onwards to these baleful halls of Dis and the three-headed Dog? Some Destiny drives him. It is his sins, I suppose: – perhaps it is his love, strong as that of Orpheus for the lost Eurydice, and likely to have no better issue!'[52]

The tone of this outburst was fortunately not maintained throughout the book which followed, but Carlyle was right to describe it as a 'Cromwelliad'; it had much more passion in it than considered judgment. Yet his wild and disordered vocabulary often hits the mark with amazing felicity, and when he speaks of the 'fat, terrene mind' of Bulstrode Whitelocke, or of Clarendon's prose style as 'a clothed, nay sometimes even a *quilted* dialect'; he not only scores points but advances our understanding.[53] On the other hand he was much less successful than in *The French Revolution* in bringing the past to life before our eyes, and he is at his most effective (or least ineffective) when he is paraphrasing his authorities; as in his description of the funeral of the Leveller mutineer Roger Lockyer in 1649. However, Mrs Macaulay apart, he was the first to call attention to the Levellers and treat them as a serious political and social phenomenon,[54] and his belief that the events of 1648 and 1649 constituted a revolution as decisive as the French Revolution of 1789, though many pooh-poohed it at the time, is one which finds favour with several modern historians.

But his main achievement, of course, was to bring Cromwell before the public. The book was reprinted eleven times before the end of the century, and was almost immediately raised to the status of an historical classic, along with Macaulay's *History of England* and Gibbon's *Decline and Fall*. Wilbur Cortez Abbott, his twentieth-century successor as an editor of Cromwell's papers, found much to criticize, but acknowledged that: 'He collected a heap of valuable material in one place. He blew away much of the chaff and dust which had obscured it; he purified the rest; and danced, and sang, and shouted and objurgated over the result until the world came to see. Having seen, they believed'.[55] Interest in Cromwell mounted steadily as the bicentenary of his death in 1658 approached, and several paintings exhibiting him in a highly favourable light were shown at the Academy in 1859 – *Cromwell refusing the Crown of England*, for instance, and *The Night before Naseby*. Some municipalities began raising statues to Cromwell, a development which did not entirely please Carlyle.[56] On a more serious level, the documents he printed acted like a magnet, attracting to them others, hitherto unknown; these were included in appendices to successive editions. This was the hardrock basis for the great revival in Cromwell studies after Carlyle's death, and without him it is unlikely that Gardiner in 1900 would have been able to describe Cromwell as 'the national hero of the nineteenth century'. Ironically, by the time Mrs S.C. Lomas produced a definitive corrected edition of Carlyle's work in 1904 it was too late; Gardiner and Firth had, as it were, passed beyond it.

Carlyle lived on until 1881, growing madder and madder, shriller and shriller. His domestic life, incautiously publicized by Froude after his death, roused disgust and consternation. His huge life of Frederick the Great was a paean of praise for monarchical absolutism, his *Latter-Day Pamphlets* a rejection of representative institutions altogether. (Lecky described his politics as 'more fitted for the latitude of Russia than of England'.)[57] By 1860 he had been overtaken by the second great Victorian prophet, H.T. Buckle.

Henry Thomas Buckle was one of those authors who enjoyed instant and almost overwhelming fame for the shortest possible period. His brief life, from 1821 to 1862, was comfortably enclosed within Carlyle's, and his span of fame was not much more than ten years, though his unfinished masterwork, *The History of Civilisation*, went on selling into the present century. He was the first exponent of the scientific study of history, and could even be regarded as a predecessor of Arnold Toynbee, but he was almost at once overtaken by Darwin's theory of Evolution, which he did not live to assimilate into his own work, and the sharp decline in his reputation after his death is demonstrated by the patronizing notice he received from Leslie Stephen in the *Dictionary of National Biography* twenty-five years later – 'The extent of his knowledge and the command of all his resources are remarkable, and though his conclusions are neither very new nor valuable, they are put forward with a rhetorical power admirably adapted to impress the less cultivated reader'.[58]

As with most nineteenth-century historians, his life-style and his method of work were *sui generis*. His father was a wealthy businessman, a partner in the London shipping firm of Buckle, Bagster and Buckle, but the son was what we would call a 'drop-out'. He was a delicate child and a valetudinarian adult. He went to a small private school in Kentish Town, but insisted on leaving at the age of fourteen, and whatever he learned thereafter he learned by his own unassisted efforts. At the age of seventeen, after a confrontation with his father, he was forced to join the family firm, but two years later his father died, leaving him an income of £1500 which was more than sufficient for his needs provided he did not marry, which he never showed any sign of doing. He devoted the rest of his life to reading and writing,[59] and boasted of a reading knowledge of eighteen or nineteen languages, living and dead, and an ability to converse in seven.

Like many children of this type he was deeply attached to his mother, and in her widowhood they were inseparable. In 1840 he took her with him on a tour of Belgium, Holland, Germany, Italy and France, the beginning of an extended programme of foreign travel. However, in 1843, when he went back to Europe alone, he fell ill with rheumatic fever at Munich and his mother came out to him and brought him home; they were never separated again. They bought a house at 59 Oxford Terrace (now 115 Sussex Gardens) which was large enough to hold his growing library. His aversion to public libraries was even stronger than Carlyle's, and he would never use any book which was not his own; he spent £300–400 a year on books, over a quarter of his income, and at one stage owned 22,000 volumes, all catalogued and labelled; by then they had spread all over the house, even into the butler's pantry. He worked at a specially constructed desk, with more bookshelves incorporated in it.

He was a strange figure, almost childlike in his overweening self-confidence, and full of amiable eccentricities. It is remarkable that until the publication of the first volume of his *History* he had virtually no contact with any other writers or intellectuals. The universities he shunned, of course. Apart from a seven-mile walk each day his only recreation was chess. In fact, he was one of the great players of his generation, though he never owned a board of his own and usually played at Simpson's Chess Divan in the Strand. He defeated some of the greatest of the contemporary masters, including Kieseritzki and St Amant, though he only played a public match once, at the Great Exhibition of 1851, when he beat Anderssen and Lowenthal. In the same year he began work on his *History of Civilisation*.

At first he apparently planned to write a more or less conventional history of England. Amongst his papers is a long piece of continuous prose on the reign of Elizabeth I, and notes on the political history of England and the characters of her monarchs from Henry VIII to Anne.[60] But as his reading broadened out, so did the scope of his work. The progress made by mankind in his lifetime gave him an illusion of optimism, and he conceived the idea that the whole field of human history could be analysed on scientific principles. He was far from unique in this belief, but as one of his greatest admirers later admitted: 'None shared the illusions of that period more fondly than [he].'[61] His ideas are most lucidly set out in an unpublished paper he wrote at the beginning, called 'The Possibility of History', which sufficiently explains the structure of his work:

'I shall, in the first place, by a general survey of modern universal history, arrive at certain conclusions, which, although they cannot be looked upon as scientific truths, will constitute uniformities of succession or of coexistence which will be of the nature of empiric laws, increasing in value in proportion as we increase the extent of the surface from which they are collected. These laws I then propose to employ deductively, and, descending in a particular period of history, verify them by a special investigation ... If, for instance, I can show that a certain law which I have arrived at by a general consideration of history, is in any large period separately applicable to all the great classes of society, I shall have made out a case very analogous to that in which the general laws of natural philosophy are applied to mechanics, hydrostatics, acoustics and the like'.[62]

As for his detailed research technique, this is exposed in a quite remarkable fashion in the three stout volumes of his *Miscellaneous and Posthumous Works*, nearly 2000 pages in all, which were published by his friend and disciple Helen Taylor in 1872, ten years after his death.

The first volume, apart from a few essays published in his lifetime, contains 138 fragments of continuous prose, varying in length from a short paragraph to twenty pages. They cover a wide range and are in no sort of order: a discussion on the origins of the middle classes, for instance, is followed by a piece on Arminianism; then come 'Observations upon Suicide', 'Improvement of Morals' and 'Horses', in that order.[63] All the same, there are substantial fragments – on the Middle Ages in Europe, on France and England in the eighteenth century – which are obviously drafts made at a very late stage.

His Commonplace Books, which fill the second and third volumes, may well be in the wrong order. Volume II contains 1437 numbered items, usually a paragraph in length, each consisting of notes, quotations and references on the same theme, though again they are bewildering in their variety and in no sort of order. These are the headings of ten items taken at random (Nos 874–83): 'Notice of Buskins', 'Cherries in England in the Fifteenth Century', 'Custom of Women in Labour wearing Blessed Girdles', 'Notes respecting Maundy Thursday', 'Roses in England in 1521', 'Natural: used for a legitimate son', 'In the Fifteenth Century sheets did not extend the whole length of a Bed', 'Notices respecting Carps', 'Invention of the Telegraph', 'Origin of the Title of Dauphin'.[64] In the third volume these give way to individual quotations and references, usually of a line or two, sometimes roughly grouped according to subject, sometimes not, but all of them numbered. It is tempting to see this as Buckle's material in its raw state; volume II then demonstrates the assembly of such notes into groups, volume I their transposition into continuous prose. A close study of this material, in conjunction with the completed sections of the *History of Civilisation*, would no doubt tell us much more about his methods. As it is, Lord Acton found it an invaluable quarry, and his copy is liberally sprinkled with his neat little paper book-marks.[65]

So, we can almost see Henry Buckle at work, in his large, high study at the back of Oxford Gardens. He had a powerful memory, his commonplace books were fully indexed, and his library was so exactly catalogued that servants could bring him books he wanted from other parts of the house. His health obliged him to limit his hours of work, however; he went for frequent walks, and ate only fruit for lunch. He rationed himself to three cigars a day. He meticulously recorded his progress in his diary, thus:

'Saturday, May 19, 1855. Rose at 8.30. Walked half an hour, and then breakfasted. From 10.40 to 1.50 finished the chapter in which I pass from physical laws to enquire into metaphysical resources.* Walked one hour and a half, and from 5.30 to 7.10 finished Transactions of Asiatic Society, iii, pp. 138–585. Dined at 7.15. In bed at 10.40, and to 11.40 read Journal Asiatique, i., series, 82–335'.[66]

He took immense pains with his style, studying and comparing the best French and English authors, but he never wrote in sentences. He paced the room until he had composed a whole paragraph in his mind, then he sat down and wrote it out. If he was then dissatisfied with it he preferred to rewrite it *in toto* rather than tinker with it. Sentence by sentence construction, he thought, produced an abrupt and jerky style, traces of which, according to him, could even be found in Macaulay's prose. Unfortunately the result was never commensurate with his expectations. His style is unfailingly lucid, but rather laboured; it is streets ahead of that favoured by the fathers of modern sociology – amongst whom Buckle is often numbered – but even J.M. Robertson, one of his great admirers, admitted that; 'His diction is frequently commonplace, and not seldom turgid; often inexact; built on an old conventional type; energetic and lucid, certainly, but unoriginal, unsubtle, sometimes even juvenile.'[67]

These are hard words. Buckle's exposition of difficult and complex questions is usually as clear as day, and he maintained the progression of his argument from paragraph to paragraph, chapter to chapter. Unfortunately, he was subject to the fascination of one of the greatest of English prose stylists, whom he could only imitate at a distance. The terms in which he denounced Charles II, for instance – 'the miserable incompetence of the king, the idle profligacy of his court, the unblushing venality of his ministers, the constant conspiracies to which the country was exposed from within, and the unprecedented insults to which it was subjected from without' – or the reaction of the Church to the Royal Society – 'it is easy to imagine with what

* Chapter 3 of the *History of Civilisation.*

terror and disgust these things were viewed by those inordinate admirers of antiquity who, solely occupied in venerating past ages, are unable either to respect the present or hope for the future' – these are much too reminiscent of Gibbon to be comfortable.[68] But since he lacked Gibbon's great gift of varying his tone and pace, the result, in large doses, is monotonous.

All the same, the book he produced was remarkable for his time. Even Leslie Stephen complimented him on 'the honourable ambition, so rare amongst men of leisure, which stimulated him to concentrate many years of unremitting labour upon the execution of a single vast design'.[69] It began with six long chapters on the physical and intellectual factors governing history, culminating in a short review of the Middle Ages. He was criticized for the flimsiness of his medieval learning, but in his wide-ranging view of human history – in his disquisition on the influence of the potato on Irish history, for instance, or the effect of the Trade Winds on Latin America – he was breaking new ground, though it is ground familiar to us now through the efforts of mega-historians like Braudel and Toynbee.[70] His next great theme was that the emergence of civilization as we understand it depended on the overthrow of organized religion; to him 'religion' was synonymous with 'superstition', and 'scepticism' with 'culture'. Carlyle, of course, had attacked the bigotry of certain elements in Protestantism, Gibbon had argued that Christianity undid the Roman Empire, but Buckle denounced all forms of religion, at all times and in all places, with equal contempt and rigour.

His account of civilization proper begins with 'an Outline of the History of the British Intellect from the middle of the Sixteenth to the end of the Eighteenth Century' (ch. 7). The focus here is the reign of Charles II, where to Buckle's mind the decline of religion and the corresponding rise of science began; but his main point – the contrast between the advances made in science and literature and the vicious and lamentable politics of the period – had already been made more cogently by Henry Hallam. It is unfortunate that Buckle never returned to English history. Instead, he went on to devote six rather tedious chapters to 'A History of the French Intellect' from the Reformation to the Revolution, which were predictably a celebration of the decline of Faith and the rise of Scepticism; and the book as he left it ends with special studies of two nations – Scotland and Spain – at opposite ends of the political spectrum, but united in Buckle's mind by their enslavement to bigotry and superstition. His attempt at a sociological history of Scotland has never been entirely superseded, and it was reprinted in a slightly abridged form as recently as 1970.[71]

The first volume, in 1857, was received in no very charitable spirit by rival seers, to whom its sudden appearance out of nowhere must have been rather startling. Macaulay, who read it in a day, 'skipping a little', admitted that

Buckle was 'A man of talent and of a great deal of reading, but paradoxical and incoherent. He is eminently an anticipator, as Bacon would have said. He wants to make a system before he has got the materials.'[72] Charles Darwin liked the book immensely; he thought it 'wonderfully clever and original, and written with astonishing knowledge'; but he added: 'I doubt whether his generalizations are worth anything.'[73] (Unfortunately, two years later, when the publication of *Origin of Species* made Darwin an intellectual saint, only this afterthought was remembered.) The reaction of others was predictable. Carlyle could not be bothered to read it, but dismissed it all the same. 'People kept asking him, "Have you read Buckle's book?" but he answered that he had not, and was not at all likely to do so. He saw bits of it from time to time in reviews, and found nothing in them but shallow dogmatism and inordinate conceit.' (Though he went on to say, with characteristic generosity, that Buckle was no worse than a hundred others: 'English literature had got into such a condition of falsity and exaggeration that one may doubt if we should ever again get a genuine book.')[74] Lord Acton, in common with other church-men of all persuasions, was deeply affronted by Buckle's materialism and his hostility to religion. He devoted two long articles in successive issues of *The Rambler* to a studied attempt to kill the book, ending up: 'We may rejoice that the true character of an infidel philosophy has been brought to light by the monstrous and absurd results to which it has led this writer, who has succeeded in extending its principles to the history of civilisation only at the sacrifice of every quality which makes a history great'.[75] Some of his criticisms were distinctly unfair, and those which were acceptable were couched in a tone which was not. It is a piece of work which does Acton no credit.

Nevertheless, his first volume brought Henry Buckle instant fame. Think-ing it over a few years later, the young blue-stocking Suzie Wedgwood said, 'I never remember any other book occasioning quite the same stir of interest and discussion, at all events in my circle. *The Origin of Species* did not open so many subjects on which *everyone* had an opinion.' Buckle was the celebrity of the year, dining out incessantly, and positively courted by some of the greatest men of the day; for if Macaulay, Carlyle and Acton were scoffers, and Darwin a doubter, there was no lack of entire believers – Herbert Spencer, for instance, as well as Huxley, Thackeray, John Stuart Mill and many more. He was elected to the Athenaeum, and invited to give a lecture at the Royal Institution, for which he chose that very modern-sounding subject, 'The influence of Women on the Progress of Knowledge'. The *History* was re-printed in America, and translated into Czech, German and Russian; a French translation came later, after his death. In Germany it roused the greatest interest, and was treated with high seriousness; in Russia it became something of a cult, and Chekhov could introduce it into the dialogue of *The Cherry Orchard* without explanation.[76]

But this abrupt transition, from the life-style of an unknown recluse to that of a literary lion, took its toll. In 1859 he was also prostrated by his mother's death, shortly followed by that of his favourite nephew, whom he had made his heir. Also it was difficult to see quite where his *History* was going. He always described it as 'A History of Civilization in England', but the ample and leisurely approach of the first two volumes, and the extended treatment given to Scotland, Spain and France, rather suggest a history of the world. A few weeks before his death he remarked that it could not be completed in less than sixteen volumes.[77] As it was, he published the second volume early in 1861, to renewed acclaim, and left in the autumn for an extended tour of the Middle East, but he went down with typhoid fever at Damascus, where he died on 29 May 1862. He is buried in the Protestant Cemetery there, under a stone which bears the Arabic inscription: 'The writer is resting under the earth, but his works endure.' Almost his last words, in fact, were: 'Oh, my book, my book! I shall never finish my book.'[78] No publishable continuation was found amongst his papers, though he had let it be known that his next topic would be the history of North America.

The *History of Civilization* held its popularity for at least a generation after Buckle's death. It was reprinted in two volumes in 1864, and in a three-volume octavo edition two years later. This was reprinted six times in the next twelve years, and it then passed over, in two volumes, into the 'World's Classics' series, where it remained at least until 1914. However, what prestige it had acquired with the intelligentsia was not sustained, and in 1880 Leslie Stephen pronounced its requiem in a long article for the *Fortnightly Review*. J.M. Robertson's book on *Buckle and his Critics*, in 1895, in which he undertook a full defence of the Master, must be regarded as atypical – certainly it won no converts. Leslie Stephen pointed out that Buckle's greatest misfortune was that he had been taken too seriously too quickly. The 1850s had experienced two great intellectual sensations, one of them Buckle's *History*, the other Darwin's *Origin of Species*. The latter, said Stephen, was still 'a leaven affecting the whole development of modern thought'; the former was 'here and there pregnant with some useful hints, but yet has left behind it scarcely a residuum of real, sound, verifiable theory'. Buckle's whole attitude, to him, was typical of 'that curious tone of popular complacency which was prevalent some thirty years ago, when people held that the Devil had finally committed suicide upon seeing the Great Exhibition'. Sublime overconfidence had led him to undertake a task which was impossible by random experimentation, without some guiding principle, and ironically that principle could only be found in the theory of Evolution.[79]

The Moralists: Froude and Acton

If Buckle epitomizes the self-confidence and the optimism of the High Victorians, then James Anthony Froude stands witness to their agonizing self-doubt and inner turmoil. Born in 1818, the son of a Devon clergyman of the old school, he went up to Oxford in 1836 and was shipwrecked on the reef of the Oxford Movement. With his elder brother, Richard Hurrell Froude, he became a disciple of John Henry Newman. Hurrell's death in 1838 was a shock, but Newman's conversion to Rome in 1845 was an even greater one; it was a sudden kink in the universe, an offence against natural law. Froude reacted not by following Newman to Rome but by losing his faith altogether, but unfortunately not before he had been elected a fellow of Exeter College and taken deacon's orders, from which he could not obtain release until the passing of the Clerical Disabilities Act in 1870. He tried to purge his religious doubts – and obviously some of his sexual frustrations – in a storming novel called *The Nemesis of Faith*. The lovely Helen Leonard, with whom the hero has an illicit though unconsummated affair, was modelled on one Harriet Bush, with whom Froude fell in love at the age of twenty. Her father forbade the match, and Froude subsequently contracted two happy marriages, the second idyllically so; yet when he was an old man on holiday in Norway, and she long dead, he had a vision of Harriet rising out of the waters of the Sogne Fjord at evening.[80]

The Sub-Rector of Exeter burnt a copy of *Nemesis of Faith* in the college hall in front of the undergraduates, and Froude hastily resigned his fellowship to avoid expulsion. Already disowned by his father, he went up to London, where he supported himself initially by writing for the reviews, notably the *Westminster Review* and *Frazer's Magazine*; in fact he edited *Frazer's* for thirteen years. He had a facile pen and an agreeable style, and many of his longer essays were later collected and republished as *Short Studies in Great Subjects*, in successive volumes which were reprinted up to the end of the century.

In London in 1849 he also fell under the spell of Carlyle, and they remained close though unlikely friends for the rest of Carlyle's life. Yet not even the Seer of Ecclefechan could resolve the younger man's doubts:

'I was unable to admit the possibility that Christianity might be untrue. Newman had gone to Rome, shattering as he went the theory of the inspired authority of the English Church. I could not yet follow Carlyle when he shifted the ground, insisting that institutions were like other organized creations, that the question was not whether such things were true, but whether they were alive'.[81]

In fact, though his relationship with Carlyle was obviously important to both men, it is difficult to see what Froude got out of it. Certainly his style was not affected in the least by the Master's, nor was his historical technique.

Froude began his *History of England from the Fall of Cardinal Wolsey to the Defeat of the Spanish Armada* in 1854, and the first two volumes, covering the 1530s, were published in 1856, when he was thirty-eight. His financial reasons for embarking on this long enterprise are obvious enough, with the example of Carlyle and Macaulay before him. It was also another attempt, *Nemesis of Faith* being the first, to rationalize his own ideas on religion; he hoped to justify the existence of the Church of England on social and political grounds, rebutting the taunts of the eighteenth-century rationalists and the doubts of the Oxford Apostles. But as the work progressed, and with it the age, deeper motives came into play. When he told a Royal Institution audience in 1864: 'We live in times of disintegration', he was not only thinking of the Oxford Movement and the decline of faith, but of the great Darwinian controversy, which now seemed likely to undermine all previous belief not only in the nature of God but in the nature of Man. It was an age, too, of deep social divisions, and the denial of natural authority. As an old man looking back he remarked that: 'the principle of the nineteenth century, that the children are wiser than their fathers, was [then] working in all classes.'[82]

In such an age history could be a bedrock to the framework of society. It could not, of course, restore faith – 'It is not on historical lines, as we understand history, that the truth of Christianity can be established, or was ever designed to be established' – and Froude is the first historian of the Reformation who was not a wholly committed Christian. Yet on the other hand he rejected the view, for which he blamed Henry Buckle, that man was governed by self-interest alone. Some men, said Froude, had always been influenced by much higher considerations, and it was:

'in the struggle, ever failing, yet ever renewed, to carry truth and justice into the administration of human society; in the establishment of states and in the overthrow of tyrannies; in the rise and fall of creeds; in the world of ideas; in the character and deeds of the great actors in the drama of life; where good and evil fight out their everlasting battle, now ranged in opposite camps, now and more often in the heart, both of them, of each living man – that the true human interest of history resides'.

And more than mere interest, too, there was instruction, there were lessons to be learned:

'The address of history is less to the understanding than the higher emotions. We learn in it to sympathise with what is great and good; we learn to hate what is base. In the anomalies of fortune we feel the mystery of our mortal existence, and in the companionship of the illustrious natures who have shaped the fortunes of the world, we escape from the littlenesses which cling to the round of our common life, and our minds are tuned in a higher and nobler key'.[83]

To Froude, then, history was to emerge as a vast psychodrama, with profound moral implications. But in 1856 his aims were more modest, and the preface to the first volume is pitched at a lower key. He avowed his intention of defending the integrity of the Church of England, and though his basic line of argument was much the same as Burnet's, his revisionist picture of Henry VIII, as a ruler of almost limitless potential shipwrecked by circumstances not of his devising, was highly controversial. He painted a dazzling portrait of the young king, his intelligence, his learning, his physical strength and beauty and his capacity for rule, but he observed that his Plantagenet blood had endowed him with 'a most intense and imperious will', and his upbringing as a Renaissance prince had ill equipped him for compromise. Unfortunately, 'late in life, when his character was formed, he was forced into collision with difficulties with which the experience of discipline had not fitted him to contend.' Given a different upbringing, 'he had [the] capacity ... to be one of the greatest of men', and 'with all his faults about him, he was still perhaps the greatest of his contemporaries; and the man best able of all living Englishmen to govern England had been set to do it by the conditions of his birth.'[84]

This was too much for Goldwin Smith, who treated the first four volumes to a forty-six-page article in the *Edinburgh Review* for July 1858. (To rub salt into the wound, this was only a few months after he had been preferred to Froude as regius professor of modern history at Oxford.) He thought, and quite sincerely, that Froude's account of Henry VIII was too abrupt a reversal of all the accepted norms – though he did not make it clear what those norms were based on – and he urged him to think again. But even he admitted that the book had given his great pleasure: 'The interest of the new matter is extreme, and it is given for the most part in the most interesting manner.'[85] As for the public, they took to it at once, ignoring as they usually do the opinions of learned critics, and the sales of the first four volumes made Froude financially independent, and enabled him to extend the scope of his research.

For this disciple of Carlyle's was also an avowed disciple of Ranke, determined to extend the scope of his sources as far as he could. In writing these early volumes he had to be content with what he could find in the Public Record Office and the British Museum, though he claimed to have ransacked these repositories thoroughly and to have read every printed book on the subject. Now, in the 1860s, he made three separate visits to the Spanish archives at Simancas, which he found in an appalling disorder. He described the monastery as 'a pile of brown bricks with holes in them, where people live like rabbits in their warrens in the midst of a wilderness of brown sand in the worst climate in the world'.[86] Sir John Fortescue later remarked: 'I do not think that sufficient credit has ever been given to Froude for the manful industry that he showed in wrestling with the Spanish sixteenth-century archives at Simancas. No one who has not attempted a like task has any idea of the difficulties.'[87] He also went to Paris and Brussels, and later to Vienna to consult the despatches of Eustace Chapuys, which Lingard had missed. He did not, however, go to Rome; perhaps because he had never mastered Italian, more likely because he had no hope of gaining admission to the Vatican archives. His relentless technique is illustrated in a letter he wrote to Lady Salisbury in November 1864:

'I am slowly drawing to the end of my long journey through the records. By far the largest part of Burleigh's papers is here [in the Public Record Office], and not at Hatfield. I have been incessantly busy in the Record Office since my return to London. The more completely I examine the MSS elsewhere the better use I shall be able to make of yours'.[88]

He is, in fact, the first Englishman to heed Ranke's dictum that if all the evidence were arranged in proper order it would tell the story itself.

Nevertheless, many contemporary scholars had no confidence in his methods, and charges of slovenliness and inaccuracy persisted even after his death. They originated with the medievalist E.A. Freeman, who launched intemperate and destructive attacks on each successive volume of the *History* in the *Saturday Review*.* Freeman could never support his criticism in detail – not surprisingly, since he freely admitted that he had no specialized knowledge of the sixteenth century at all – and his reasons for hating Froude, as he so manifestly did, are obscure. As a High Churchman he no doubt held Froude's religious views in contempt, but the marginal annotations in his review copy of the *History*, which ended up in Manchester University Library, have a pathological tone to them. 'Beast!' he would scribble in the margin; 'Bah!'; 'May I live to disembowel James Anthony Froude'; 'Froude is certainly the vilest beast that ever wrote a book,' and so on.[89] He told John Richard Green: 'Froude has a negative use; when he has said a thing happened one way, you don't know how it did happen, but you know one way in which it did not happen.' Green shared his patron's views, of course, and so, more surprisingly, did Stubbs. In 1869, when Froude delivered a Rectoral address at St Andrews University on Calvinism, Stubbs composed some malicious

* For Freeman see p. 154 below

verses which embraced Froude's brother-in-law Charles Kingsley, at that time regius professor in modern history at Cambridge:

> 'Froude informs the Scottish youth
> That parsons do not care for truth.
> The Reverend Canon Kingsley cries,
> History is a pack of lies.
>
> What cause for judgments so malign?
> A brief reflection solves the mystery.
> Froude believes Kingsley a divine,
> And Kingsley goes to Froude for history'.*

This attitude seemed to infect the whole profession. For instance, when Mandell Creighton was drawing up a list of potential contributors to the *English Historical Review* in 1886 he anxiously enquired of the assistant editor, Lane Poole: 'Do we do well to omit Froude? I think not: let us be entirely catholic,' and he comforted himself with the thought that Froude would probably not wish to contribute anyway. But a week later he nervously returned to the same subject: 'I don't like asking Froude, but I feel one ought not to let one's personal prejudices stand in the way of catholicity'. He was clearly the bane of all the so-called Oxford liberals of that generation, and even Frederick York Powell, normally good-natured enough, could not bring himself to call on him during his brief term as regius professor. In an obituary notice he said: 'The demon of inaccuracy, of mistake, of reckless statement, stayed by him all his life in all that he wrote. His persistent half-avowed disregard of fact was an ingrained, constitutional and unmistakable characteristic of the man.' (On another occasion he said: 'He handles his authorities as a wilful baby uses her dolls.') He applauded Froude's conscientious performance of his professional duties at an advanced age, and he added a remark which would have been better applied to his own tenure of the regius chair after him: 'If he were not the ideal of a regius professor of history at Oxford, the blame must lie with those who appointed him. ... It is as a man of letters he made his mark, and it is as a man of letters he must ultimately be judged.'[90] Here we detect the envy of a man who never published anything but a few school primers and Icelandic texts for a highly productive and successful author; of a man who was described as 'the worst lecturer in Oxford, and very possibly in the world' for an accomplished and popular public speaker.

---

* But Stubbs, too, had his enemies, who produced the couplet:
    'See, ladling butter from alternate tubs,
    Stubbs butters Freeman, Freeman butters Stubbs'.

The strange thing is that the charge of inaccuracy was always made by men who were not competent to judge the matter anyway. A.F. Pollard, who was, later said: 'There is inadequate justification for the systematic destruction of Froude's *History*, which has become the fashion. He held strong views and he made some mistakes; but his mistakes were no greater than those of other historians, and there are not half a dozen histories in the language which have been based on so exhaustive a study of the original materials.' As for Freeman, Fortescue later remarked that he 'probably could not have read a Spanish sixteenth-century letter to save his life', which was true.[91] In his inaugural lecture at Oxford in 1892 Froude defended himself in measured terms:

'During the twenty years in which I was at work on my *History of England*, I must have read, made extracts from, or copied with my own hand tens of thousands of manuscripts, private letters, secret state documents, minutes of secret councils, often in cipher for which a key was not always at hand. I worked long in our own Record Office. I worked in the Archives at Paris, Brussels, Vienna and Simancas. The letters which were of most importance were in half-a-dozen languages and in the desperate handwriting of the period ... I had to cut my way through a jungle, for no one had opened the road for me. I have been turned into rooms piled to the window sill with bundles of dust-covered despatches, and told to make the best of it. Often I have found the sand glittering on the ink where it had been sprinkled when a page was turned. There the letter had lain, never looked at again since it was read and put away'.

He went on:

'I have been taunted sometimes with having mistaken a word. It is likely enough: with some materials an occasional mistake is not to be avoided. But I think I made fewer than a great many people would have done ... Be that as it may, I can say with confidence that I added many material facts to the history of the period, though they have been totally unrecognised by most of my critics ... Being omniscient already, I conclude they did not feel that they had more to learn'.[92]

Volumes v and vi of the *History*, up to 1560, were published in 1860, and met with the usual mixed reception: critical hostility and general popularity. Froude applied in 1861 for the new Chichele professorship of history at Oxford, but was again passed over, this time in favour of Montague Burrows, though he had by now made his peace with Exeter College, in 1858. Then an unlucky remark in a lecture he gave to the Royal Institution in 1864 delivered him into his enemies' hands – 'It often seems to me as if history is like a child's box of letters, with which we can spell any word we please. We have only to pick out such letters as we want, arrange them as we like, and say nothing about those which do not suit our purpose.'[93] Taken, as it was, as an exposé of his own methods, this was damning enough.

In fact *suppressio veri* was not one of Froude's faults, but religious prejudice arguably was. His attitude towards Catholicism was regarded as extreme, at a time when a certain mild ecumenism was in fashion amongst educated Protestants. After the bland neutrality of Lingard, his savage criticism of Mary Tudor came almost as a shock; it seemed to the cognoscenti a throwback to less enlightened days. However, he may have been in touch with a broader and lower public opinion, and a clue to his popularity can be found in the revived interest at this time in Foxe's 'Book of Martyrs'. This was reissued in eight volumes in 1837-41, the first complete edition since 1684, and reprinted in 1844-9 and 1877. An abridgement by John Milner was also published in 1837, and reprinted in 1848 and 1863. Thus there was a reading public well disposed towards Froude's account of this 'frightful' reign, which seemed to offer an independent, scholarly confirmation of Foxe. To Froude the Catholics under Mary were not only sadists and bigots, they were cowards. Thus they held back from the nobility and gentry, though they were as deeply infected with Protestantism as any other class. They 'dared not strike', he said, 'where there was danger that they might be struck in return. They went out into the highways and hedges; they gathered up the lame, the halt and the blind; they took the weaver from his loom, the carpenter from his workshop, the husbandman from his plough, ... old men tottering into the grave, and children whose lips could but just lisp the articles of their creed; and of these they made their burnt-offerings; with these they crowded their prisons; and when filth and famine killed them, they flung them out to rot.'[94]

This was righteous exaggeration. But at the same time he took a less than enchanted view of Mary's sister, Elizabeth. His regard for her was undermined by his minute study of Lord Burleigh's papers at Hatfield and the Public Record Office; as early as 1864 he told Lady Salisbury: 'The private letters which passed between [Burleigh] and Walsingham about Elizabeth have destroyed finally the prejudice that still clung to me that, notwithstanding her many faults, she was a woman of ability.'[95] Of course, it was a fascinating period – 'It is all action', he said, 'and I shall use my materials badly if I cannot make it as interesting as a novel.' He certainly gave it extended treatment. Volume VI ended in 1560, and it took him six further volumes to reach his goal in 1588: volumes VII and VIII were published in 1863, IX and X three years later, and the last two in 1870.

Nevertheless, his opinion of Elizabeth was unchanged throughout. In his preface to the collected edition he said that just as the facts had obliged him to undertake 'a qualified defence' of Henry VIII, so 'with equal reluctance I had to acknowledge that the wisdom of Elizabeth was the wisdom of her ministers'.[96] Of course, he found much to praise in her style of rule – 'The human character showing always through the royal robes, yet with the queenly dignity never so impaired that liberties could be ventured in return.' He sternly rejected any slur on her private conduct; in fact, he admired the way she retained her control over men without descending to sexual entice-ments.[97] But he was appalled at her vacillation, which had blunted the impact of England's foreign policy, turned Mary Queen of Scots (of whom Froude cordially disapproved) into a martyr, and prevented the evolution of a truly Protestant Church of England. (Here he echoed Macaulay's verdict in his earlier essays, and J.R. Green's.) 'She was without the intellectual emotions', he said, 'which give human character its consistency and power,' and at bottom her approach to religion was her father's:

> 'They believed generally in certain elementary truths lying at the base of all religions; and the difference in the outward expression of those truths, and the passionate animosities which those differences engendered, were only not contemptible to them from the practical mischief which they produced ... They had the statesman's temperament, to which all specific religions are equally fictions of the imagination'.

As a result, 'neither Elizabeth nor later politicians of Elizabeth's tempera-ment' – and here no doubt he had some of his own contemporaries in mind – 'desired the Church of England to become too genuine. It has been more convenient to leave an element of unsoundness at the heart of an institution, which if secure, might be dangerously powerful.'[98] Yet it was typical of Froude, who alternated between a fierce arrogance and a kind of offhand humility, that he should have ended with the remark that Elizabeth 'should be rather studied in her actions rather than in the opinion of the historian who relates them. Actions and words are carved upon eternity. Opinions are but forms of cloud created by the prevailing currents of the moral air.'[99]

He may have been as disingenuous as Lingard, but certainly not consciously so. Critical sniping pursued him to the end, but the steady progression of these pairs of volumes, shoulder to shoulder, through the 1860s, bore down the more general opposition to his methods. The words he used to defend his decision to. end in 1588, not 1603, could well have been applied to his own achievement: 'Chess players, when they have brought their game to a point at which the result can be foreseen with certainty, regard their contest as ended, and sweep the pieces from the board.'[100]

In fact, it is strange that Froude's *History* dropped from sight so soon after his death; by 1914 it was almost forgotten. Either Freeman's unscrupulous character assassination was more effective than we have allowed for, or Froude's churchmanlike approach was distasteful to a new generation. When the American E.P. Cheyney set out to complete Froude's history of Elizabeth's reign, publishing his first volume in 1914, he left out religion altogether![101]

Also, though Froude's *History* is a book easily read, it is not one which provokes thought. Despite his great learning, and the even gracefulness of his style, there is an elegant shallowness in his narrative. He told an interviewer late in life that 'he was very fond of Hume, who was the clearest of writers', and though he certainly achieved Hume's clarity he had none of his scornful power. Lytton Strachey hit it off when he wrote of him:

> 'The extraordinary succession of events assumes, as it flows through his pages, the thrilling lineaments of a great story, upon whose issue the most blasé reader is forced to hang entranced. Yet the supreme quality of style seems to be lacking. One is uneasily aware of a looseness in the texture, an absence of concentration in the presentment, a failure to fuse the *whole* material into organic life. Perhaps, after all, it is the intellect and the emotion which are at fault here, too; perhaps when one is hoping for genius it is only talent – only immense talent – that one finds'.[102]

Yet Froude scarcely deserves such neglect. His research descended to a depth never previously envisaged, and there is a sense in which all subsequent work on the Tudors rests on his shoulders. The standard bibliography still describes his *History* as 'the classic for the period, ... and one of the great masterpieces of English historical literature ...; not accurate in detail and coloured by a strong anti-Catholic bias, but invaluable'.[103] In his approach to the archives and his handling of evidence he showed himself a true disciple of Ranke; in fact, he was the only nineteenth-century Englishman who even approached the great German. At the same time his first chapter, on 'The Social Condition of England in the Sixteenth Century', is superior in accuracy and balance to Macaulay's Chapter III, and his sixth chapter, on 'The Protestants', is a sensitive and brilliant piece of analysis which Macaulay could never have attempted. Also, though he called his work a 'History of England', he conscientiously covered the history of Scotland and Ireland, too, and in this he was more of a pioneer than he is always given credit for. (He was very fond of Ireland, and visited it often.) But above all he was a pioneer in the field of maritime history, the creator of that cult of Elizabethan naval heroism which is with us yet in an attenuated form. He wrote three chapters on Elizabethan sea power: chapter 47 (vol. VIII), on 'England and the Sea', chapter 64 (vol. XI), on 'The Voyage of Sir Francis Drake', and chapter 81 (vol. XII), on 'The Armada'; which fixed this great saga of derring-do in the

public consciousness and paved the way for a host of imitators. At the very
end of his life one of his lecture courses at Oxford, later published as a small
book, was on 'English Seamen in the Sixteenth Century'.

But he published nothing of importance after 1870. *The English in Ireland
in the Eighteenth Century*, published in two volumes in 1872 and 1874, was a
patchwork job, and suffered accordingly at the hands of reviewers. He received even rougher treatment when he went on a lecture tour of America in
1872 to explain the Irish Problem. In a very modern-seeming episode he
suffered a fierce Irish-American reaction mobilized by the nationalist leader
Thomas Burke, and had to abandon the tour halfway.[104] In 1874 he went to
South Africa on an unofficial fact-finding tour at the request of his friend
Lord Caernarvon, Secretary of State for the Colonies. He came back a strong
advocate of federation, but the South Africans, British and Boer alike, rejected his 'meddling', and the incident only confirms that academic historians
do not necessarily make good politicians.

Indeed, Froude's closing years were contentious on all fronts, though as
always he rode out criticism with a maddening equanimity. On Carlyle's
death in 1881 he accepted a commission to publish his *Reminiscences* of his
old friend (1881) and edit the *Letters and Memorials* of his wife, Jane Welsh
Carlyle (1883). His picture of Carlyle and his relationship with his wife was
so frank that the storm it aroused reverberates yet. But Froude, never exactly
a modest man, had now acquired the abundant smugness of old age. He was,
in fact, something of a celebrity, and a very wealthy man. Strachey calls him
'one of the salient figures of mid-Victorian England', and reminds us that he
was 'a man of letters who was also a man of the world, an accomplished
gentleman, whose rich nature overflowed with abounding energy, a sports-
man, a yachtsman, a brilliant and magnificent talker' – even Edwardian,
perhaps, rather than Victorian.[105] His triumphal tour of Australia and New
Zealand in 1884–5 was uncontroversial, for once, but on a visit to the West
Indies in 1886–7 he could not resist dabbling in Caribbean politics, with
predictable results. He was unperturbed.

He then returned to his *History*, incorporating new material he had discovered since 1870 in two supportive monographs, *The Divorce of Catherine
of Aragon* (1891) and *The Spanish Story of the Armada* (1892). Then, on the
death of his old enemy Freeman in 1892, the unpredictable Lord Salisbury,
who had perhaps met him at Hatfield, offered him the regius chair at Oxford.
He was seventy-four, but since there was no retiring age, this did not signify.
After some hesitation he accepted, and he approached his duties conscientiously. He gave three lecture courses (more than would now be considered
appropriate), on 'English Seamen', 'Erasmus' and 'The Council of Trent',
which were well received. But at the end of his second academic year, in

June 1894, he fell ill; he died on 20 October at his house near Salcombe, in Devon.

There is a curious epilogue. At Oxford, though he was cold-shouldered by the college fellows, he acquired a research student, Percy Stafford Allen, whom he fired with an interest in Erasmus, and who went on to produce the definitive text of his letters, the *Opus Epistolarum Des. Erasmi Roterodami*, which has been called 'the most accurate book in the world'.[106]

The appointment of Freeman to Oxford, followed by Froude, both of them late in life, signalized the slow drift of the London literary world towards the universities. The founding of a School of English Language and Literature at Oxford in 1894 was a portent, so was the appointment of Lord Acton to the regius chair of modern history at Cambridge the following year.

For Acton was one of the last of the great Victorian seers. His published output in his lifetime would not, it is safe to say, raise him to a senior lectureship in a modern university – a few articles, rather general in tone, in the *EHR*, and a few others, even more general, for Catholic journals he owned or edited. Two series of lectures he delivered at Cambridge, apparently taken down in shorthand, were published after his death. Yet this exceedingly modest oeuvre has been the subject of much academic attention and prolonged discussion; at least two substantial monographs and two biographies have appeared since the Second World War; and historians like the late Sir Herbert Butterfield have undertaken arduous labours on his behalf. His muddled indexes, deposited in Cambridge University Library, his lists and notes, have been shuffled and reshuffled. His exiguous essays have been reprinted time and again in various permutations – ' Acton on Freedom and Power', 'Acton on Papal Power', 'Acton on Church and State', 'Acton on Freedom', and even 'Acton on History', *tout court*. Many selections from his correspondence have been published, beginning in 1906 with *Lord Acton and his Circle*, carefully tailored by Cardinal Gasquet to display him as a true son of the Church. He has his place in the Chicago University Press's series on 'Classic British Historians', and his remark that 'power tends to corrupt and absolute power corrupts absolutely', though as often misquoted as not, has become one of the most famous aphorisms of our time.* It is one of the paradoxes of fame that his reputation is more secure than those of many of his contemporaries who wrote ten times as much.

His origins were bizarre, even romantic. He was born in Naples in 1834, and christened John Edward Emerich Dalberg-Acton. His father, Sir Ferdinand Acton, 7th baronet, of Aldenham in Shropshire, was the son of that

---

* Advertisements for his latest biography (from America) read: 'You know the maxim: do you know the man?'

remarkable adventurer Sir John Acton, successively admiral, minister of marine, minister of finance, prime minister and, some said, lover to Queen Caroline of Naples. (There is still a Captain Acton in the Italian Navy.) Though the fact is often slurred over by Lord Acton's biographers, his grandfather, Sir John, was of a cadet branch of the family, the son of an expatriate physician in Besançon, and he only inherited the family estates and title when the main line of the Shropshire Actons died out in 1791. But Sir Ferdinand, who remained in the service of the Kingdom of Naples, improved the family fortunes still further by marrying Marie Louise Pelline de Dalberg, only child of the Duke of Dalberg, in the Rhineland. (The present Lord Acton is still hereditary Duke of Dalberg.)

The family had always been Roman Catholic – Acton's uncle was a cardinal – and he was educated privately in Paris, then at Oscott, the Catholic seminary near Birmingham. Rejected by Cambridge, he went to the university of Munich, where he fell under the lifelong influence of the great German theologian and historian, Johann Josef Ignatius von Döllinger. In 1865 he married into the old Bavarian noble family of Arco-Valley. By now he was fluently quadrilingual, in English, French, German and Italian – his letters to his German wife were mainly in French – and in early manhood he divided his time mainly between Aldenham and the castle of Herrnsheim in Bavaria. After 1879, when he was forced to sell Herrnsheim and let Aldenham for a time, he spent even less time in England; summer and autumn found him at his wife's family home at Tegernsee, and he wintered most years at Cannes.

He might well have lived all his life outside England, for his family was overwhelmingly Continental and his nationality nebulous (his son thought it prudent to have himself declared a British subject by private Act of Parliament in 1911). But his father died in 1835, and in 1840, when he was only six, his mother married George Leveson-Gower, Lord Leveson, heir to one of the great Whig families of England, and already Under Secretary of State for Foreign Affairs. Lord Leveson succeeded his father as 2nd Earl Granville in 1846 and served in all the Whig–Liberal governments of the century down to his death in 1891. He was Foreign Secretary 1851-2, 1870-74 and 1880-85. Through him the young Sir John Acton came into contact with all the leading Liberal statesmen of that generation, and notably with William Ewart Gladstone, who became his friend and mentor. His mother died in 1860, and five years later Granville married again, but by this time it was too late. Acton was an Englishman – a very strange Englishman, true, but an Englishman.

He got on well with his stepfather, and as he grew up Granville was relieved to find that 'although Johnny Acton is only a moderate Whig, he is also a very moderate Catholic' – in other words, he was politically viable. According to Granville, as early as 1857 there was a move to strengthen the Whig ranks in the House of Lords by giving him a peerage, but he had 'a yearning for public life', and was 'too sagacious to accept being more or less shelved'. Still, Granville thought: 'There is a great opening for him as soon as Pam [Palmerston] breaks down,' and he began looking round for a suitable seat – there was talk of his succeeding Macaulay at Edinburgh. However, Pam did not break down, and in April 1858 Granville remarked rather mysteriously: 'Johnny by putting himself too much forward has got into scrapes'; the following year he had to settle for an Irish seat, at Carlow.[107] He made no impact on the House of Commons, and no preferment came his way; and in the election of 1865 he even failed as a local candidate at Bridgenorth, in Shropshire. (He scraped home by one vote, and was unseated on a petition.) In 1869 Gladstone and Granville prevailed on the queen, with some difficulty, to raise him to the peerage as Baron Acton of Aldenham – the first Catholic so honoured since 1688 – but he made no great showing in the House of Lords either. The years passed, with his public career at a standstill. In 1884 Victoria, by now converted, wanted him as ambassador to Berlin, but even Granville argued that his stepson could not be promoted over the whole of the diplomatic corps. Gladstone, we are told, reposed great trust in him, and he was 'one of the chief makers of the policy of the Liberal Party', but he had to wait until 1892 for office, and then only as a Lord-in-Waiting.[108]

His middle life was dominated by the religious tensions of the century. He was supposedly a Liberal Catholic, but the truth is that at this time there was no such animal. The Revolutions of 1848 had even swung the Liberal Pope, Pius IX, over to reaction. At home the old Catholic families, broadminded and passively ecumenical, had been overwhelmed by an influx of working-class Irish, bringing with them a priesthood as narrowminded and bigoted as themselves. The uproar provoked by the re-establishment of the Catholic hierarchy in 1850 brought the Catholic Question back into politics, and at the same time put the Catholic community in a psychological state of siege.

Acton viewed these developments with distant contempt. In 1858 he bought his way into *The Rambler*, an established Catholic periodical, with a view to enlightening his co-religionists. In 1859 he took over as editor. In 1862 he refounded it as *The Home and Foreign Review*, which briefly emerged as a serious rival to the 'Edinburgh' and the 'Westminster'. But he closed it in 1864 to forestall a direct prohibition from Cardinal Wiseman, archbishop of Westminster, and later in the same year Pius IX's 'Syllabus Errorum', which denounced liberalism, socialism, even trade unionism, as activities inappropriate to a true Catholic man, further undermined his confidence in the Church, if not in its doctrines. Worse still, on Wiseman's death in 1865 he was succeeded by that remarkable convert Henry Edward Manning, who not only distrusted Acton but despised him. 'Such men', he said, 'are all vanity: they have the inflation of German professors, and the ruthless talk of under-graduates.'[109]

Nor was Manning very far wrong. Not only was Acton egocentric, he was Europocentric, and he had no real contact at all with the English Catholic community. In a scathing letter to his friend Richard Simpson, he dismissed them thus:

> '1°. The old school, not warmed up by the Cardinal into devotion to Rome, and not intellectual or progressive – descendants of Milner, Lingard, and even Butler, so far as they all refused, like chaos, to be converted. Their strength is in the north and in the midland counties.
> '2°. Ourselves.
> '3°. The zealous converts and those of the old set who are under the Cardinal's influence, the Romanists, lovers of authority, fearing knowledge much, progress more, freedom most, and essentially unhistoric and un-scientific'.[110]

The crunch came in 1870, when Pio Nono, with the enthusiastic support of ultramontane hard-liners like Manning, asked the Vatican Council to pro-mulgate the dogma of papal infallibility. Acton went to Rome with Döllinger and fought the decree all the way. Through Gladstone he tried to get the British Cabinet to intervene. He even planned to raid the Vatican archives and seize documents casting doubt on papal infallibility which he neurotically suspected the Pope of trying to suppress. (One of his friends secretly warned the French troops surrounding Rome, and they tactfully intercepted the aristocratic burglar.) Döllinger was excommunicated, and for several years Acton tottered on the brink; if he escaped it was largely because of his high rank and his connexions throughout Catholic Europe. As Robert Schuettin-ger puts it: 'When someone suggested that his old friend might be excom-municated, Gladstone reacted as though he were a young English captain staring down a thousand rebellious Afghans: "His work may be put on the Index, but that is all. They will never excommunicate an English peer." '[111] But henceforward his hatred of the papacy, inflamed by his historical studies, knew no bounds. In his famous dispute with Mandell Creighton in 1887 he told him:

> 'I cannot accept your canon that we are to judge pope and king unlike other men, with a favourable presumption that they did no wrong. If there is any presumption it is the other way, against the holders of power, increasing as the power increases'.

So, his famous maxim on absolute power was directed at the papacy, for he went on:

'Historical responsibility has to make up for the want of legal responsibility. Power tends to corrupt and absolute power corrupts absolutely. Great men are almost always bad men'.

He made no bones about admitting to Creighton, Anglican though he was, that Manning and the English Catholic hierarchy were steeped in this corruption. Their only excuse was that they were not alone in this. 'My dogma', said Acton, 'is not the special wickedness of my own spiritual superiors, but the general wickedness of men in authority,' and he instanced Luther, Zwingli, Calvin and Bossuet, as well as Cromwell and Louis xiv. 'Before this', he said, 'it is a mere detail that imperfect sincerity is a greater reproach in divines than in laymen, and that in our church priests are generally sacrilegious and sacrilege is a serious thing.'[112]

Yet Acton always regarded himself as a true Catholic, and he said later in life that he had never seen any reason to doubt any of the Church's pronouncements on matters of faith or morals. So his quarrel with the Catholic authorities only accentuated his isolation. He was an only child, orphaned in his twenties; his mother had no further children by Lord Granville. One of his most poignant remarks is: 'I never had any contemporaries.' In the early years of his marriage, at least, his relations with his wife were tender and affectionate, but there was no meeting of minds. He sent her interminable letters, giving her detailed analyses of the problems of Europe, the world and the Church; when he was with her he presumably lectured her on similar topics. Perhaps she could not cope. There is some evidence of a definite estrangement later, in a series of anguished letters which he tore up but preserved amongst his papers – they were *evidence*, after all, and he was a historian.[113] Born in 1841, she lived on until 1923, but she always refused to live permanently with him in England. His relations with his children are obscure; they were brought up on the Continent. We do know that his idea of a birthday present for his favourite daughter was the collected works of Newman. In 1883 he even quarrelled with his old friend and father figure, Döllinger, and told him ceremoniously that 'it was time for our conversations to cease, in this world' – though despite these heroics they continued to meet every year at Tegernsee. From 1879 he found a rather unlikely confidante and correspondent in Gladstone's daughter, Mary.

From the beginning he took refuge in books. The Victorians were great readers, but Acton outdid them all. He read and read and read. He bought copy after copy of books which interested him, with very slight variants from edition to edition. There was something obsessive in this. He read them all, annotating them lightly in the margin, sprinkling them with his thin bookmarks, strips neatly torn from booksellers' catalogues or newspapers. The historian H.A.L. Fisher later said that Acton 'probably read and annotated more printed matter than anyone who has ever lived'. His stepfather was rather appalled when he visited Aldenham in 1859. 'His library is becoming immense,' he wrote. 'He has remodelled the old library. He has entirely filled the hall, he has furnished his room with books, and he has bagged a bedroom for the same purpose.'[114] Like Buckle, or E.A. Freeman, he had no use for public libraries.

In the Acton Collection in Cambridge University Library all his erudition is suddenly frozen, as in a still from a moving film. How would the film have continued? Nothing is sadder than to pull out one of Acton's bookmarks and see the contrast between the radiant cleanliness of the bottom half and the sere and yellow condition of the top, exposed to the air of ninety years. What were Acton's thoughts when he put this bookmark in, or that? Did he really intend to do anything constructive with his vast knowledge?[115]

It is even sadder to comtemplate his famous index cards or slips; his tormented and halting conclusions on his reading, set down in no sort of order, sometimes jerky and erratic as if written in trains or carriages. All too often his thoughts were gnomic rather than lucid – 'Teach to look behind historians, especially famous historians' – sometimes there were flashes of insight: 'The eighteenth century, poor of character,' he scribbled once, 'neglected individuals and dealt with laws, etc. in history; its incapacity made it advance in the sciences as an invalid may devise ingenious contrivances.' On another card appears the first draft of that famous saying: 'Power, the greater it is, the more it demoralises.'[116]

Some historians have shown an unhealthy respect for these random musings, and to the modern mind the way in which his reputation grew of its own accord, even during his lifetime, is extraordinary. In December 1884 Mandell Creighton told his wife: 'Tomorrow I am going to London to meet at dinner Lord Acton, whom I have long been pining to see. He is a Roman Catholic and the most learned Englishman now alive, but he never writes anything.'[117] In 1886 he and Creighton helped found the *English Historical Review*, and it is presumably to this, and his high social position, that he owed his honorary doctorates from Oxford and Cambridge in 1888, and his honorary fellowship at All Souls' in 1891. He was embarked, so it was understood, on a History of Liberty, which once it was finished would be the greatest book that ever was: but the trouble was, he never finished it; nor so far as we can tell did he ever start it. The papers he left behind on his death contain no plan, not a chapter, not so much as a page of his History of Liberty. Döllinger, who knew him better than most, said once that if he did not write a book before he was forty he never would, and he told him to his face that he wished he would attempt books it was possible to write. On the other hand, it is fair to say that at the age of twenty he had decided 'to aim not at accomplishment but at learning'.

By 1880 it seemed that he had abandoned the whole vast plan, that he was reading now for the sake of reading. Mary Gladstone laughingly called his History of Liberty his 'Madonna of the Future', after the Henry James story of a painter who is always absorbed, according to him, in the production of one great masterpiece, only to leave behind on his death a blank canvas. It is a moving story in itself – more so in relation to Acton. 'Then at last', says the anonymous narrator, 'I understood the immensity of his illusion; how, one by one, the noiseless years had ebbed away, and left him brooding in charmed inaction, forever preparing for a work forever deferred.'[118] Nevertheless, he took it up as a wry joke, and played with it in a way which suggests that he was not half so concerned at his literary impotence as she was. In 1896, telling her of the invitation to edit the *Cambridge Modern History*, which would contain very little work from his own hand, he teasingly remarked that it would be 'a whole choir of Madonnas'.[119]

Meanwhile his financial circumstances had deteriorated. As early as 1879 he had to let his house at Aldenham, and for all intents and purposes abandon his working library. He spent much of the next ten years abroad.[120] In 1889 he decided to sell the library, which now numbered about 60,000 volumes; sale catalogues were prepared. Gladstone was horrified, and immediately persuaded the library-fixated Scots-American philanthropist Andrew Carnegie to buy it *en bloc* and lend it back to Acton for his lifetime. But to Gladstone's amazement Acton was quite uninterested: he could not even be persuaded to make a special journey from Munich to meet Carnegie. Nor was this a manifestation of lordly pride; Acton, it seems, felt he had exhausted the usefulness of this library, and he simply wanted to sell it to maintain his standard of living. He was not sentimental about books. (The transaction went through nevertheless. On Acton's death Carnegie turned the library over to John Morley, who gave it to Cambridge University.)[121]

Yet his reputation as a pundit was unquestioned. His conversation was brilliant, his judgments infallible, his authority overpowering. And when he spoke of his great History of Liberty, as he still did from time to time, the mantle of a seer fell upon him. All her life Mary Gladstone remembered Venice in the autumn of 1879, when she and Acton and her brother Herbert walked out from the hotel after dinner one night, and sat in the moonlight on a marble bench by the shore, with the Piazetta behind them. There Acton held them in thrall, talking 'magically, tingling to his fingers' ends ... of his dream of a great History of Liberty which was the heart of the history of man'.[122] James Bryce treasured a similar memory, of an evening in the 1890s in Acton's library at Cannes, when, says Bryce:

'He expounded to me his view of how such a history of liberty might be written, and in what wise it might be made the central thread of all history. He spoke for six or seven minutes only; but he spoke like a man inspired, seeming as if, from some mountain summit high in air, he saw beneath him the far-winding path of human progress from dim cimmerian shores of prehistoric shadow into the fuller yet broken and fitful light of the modern time. The eloquence was splendid, but greater than the eloquence was the penetrating vision which discerned through all events and in all ages the play of those moral forces, now creating, now destroying, always transmuting, which had moulded and remoulded institutions, and had given to the human spirit its ceaselessly-changing forms of energy. It was as if the whole landscape of history had been suddenly lit up by a burst of sunlight. I have never heard from any other lips any discourse like this, nor from his did I ever hear the like again'.[123]

But would this History of Liberty have been a great book, or even a good one? There is room for doubt. Acton was deeply concerned with the history of history, he was obsessed with the hidden motives of historians, including his own, he was acutely self-conscious and introspective. He seemed unable to make up his mind about other historians, particularly Ranke,[124] to whose influence his German upbringing exposed him more than any other English historian. He expressed the greatest respect for Ranke's teaching, but his attitude towards his work and example is curiously ambivalent, and this had implications for his own technique. For instance, although he applauded Ranke's insistence on the use of archive material, though he had an unrivalled knowledge himself of the contents of the major European archives and often went to great trouble to secure transcripts of papers which interested him, he rarely used original documents himself. He preferred printed collections, but above all he considered it his prime duty to compare, criticize and assess the work of other historians. In his inaugural lecture he remarked that 'a lifetime spent in the largest collection of printed books would not suffice to train a real master of modern history', and on another occasion, with reference to his own collection of transcripts, he said: 'For our purpose the main thing is not the art of accumulating material but the sublimer art of investigating it.'[125] This partly explains his penchant for the byways and back-alleys of history; he liked to test his method on limited problems, such as the existence of Charles II's supposed Jesuit son, James de la Cloche. In matters like this he was dismayingly gullible. Moreover, when he applied this method to more important episodes, like the Massacre of St Bartholomew or the Flight to Varennes, the result was a bewildering mosaic of minute fragments, culled from hundreds of sources, usually found in the works of other historians. The reconstruction of his technique is the more difficult in that most of his work was not annotated, and as Herbert Butterfield complained: 'When he used footnotes at all, he seemed not to know what they were for.' And the end result was usually platitudinous and often misguided.[126]

But his most important divergence from Ranke was on the question of judgment. Ranke argued that the historian must allow himself to be led by his sources, keeping himself always in the background. He could explore and assess men's motives, but he must refrain from moral judgment. In contrast Acton passionately believed that his role was not only to assess the work of men and nations but to pass moral judgment upon them. In fact his view of the historian's function was ridiculously high-flown. 'God in Nature', he noted on one of his ubiquitous cards, 'more manifest than God in History. Yet History leads to him and Nature away from him.'[127] The historian had to preserve his conscience from all stain, because it was his prime duty to pass moral judgment on the historical characters he described – judgment presumably on God's behalf. This came out most spectacularly in his famous quarrel with Mandell Creighton.

Acton had given the first two volumes of Creighton's *History of the Papacy from the Great Schism to the Sack of Rome* an excellent review in *The Academy* in 1882. It was a dull book (Creighton almost gloried in its dullness), but Acton admired its solid scholarship and found few faults in it and much to praise. A mutually congratulatory exchange of letters ensued. In 1885 Acton was one of those who suggested Creighton as the first editor of the *English Historical Review*, and persuaded him to accept. Acton wrote for the first number, watched over the infant periodical, though from a lordly distance, and was full of encouragement.* The storm broke, quite unexpectedly, with the publication in 1887 of Creighton's next two volumes, covering, amongst other things, the establishment of the Inquisition and the pontificate of the Borgia Alexander VI. Creighton's preface shows that he anticipated criticism for his indulgence towards the renaissance popes:

> 'I have tried to deal fairly with the moral delinquencies of the Popes, without, I trust, running the risk of lowering the standard of moral judgment. But it seems to me neither necessary to moralise at every turn in historical writing, nor becoming to adopt an attitude of lofty superiority over anyone who ever played a prominent part in European affairs, nor charitable to lavish undiscriminating censure on any man'.

But he did not expect criticism on this score from a Roman Catholic, and he sent out the book to Acton for review. In reply Acton sent the first draft of his celebrated tirade against Creighton, with a redundant covering

* See p. 191 below.

note announcing dramatically: 'You must understand, it is the work of an enemy.'

Even in the amended state in which it was eventually printed in the *EHR* it is an extraordinary performance. It opens with a sneer at Creighton's technique, which allowed the minimum of annotation or direct quotation: 'The author prefers the larger public that takes history in the shape of literature', said Acton, 'to scholars whose souls are vexed with the insolubility of problems, and who get their meals in the kitchen.' This meant, according to him, that Creighton could not press his theories home with the same authority and exactitude as a scholar who was prepared to give chapter and verse. However:

> 'It has cost Mr Creighton but little to accept this drawback on his method. He is not striving to prove a case, or burrowing towards a conclusion, but wishes to pass through scenes of raging controversy and passion with a serene curiosity, a suspended judgment, a divided jury, and a pair of white gloves'.

He took particular exception to Creighton's preface, and accused him of operating a kind of 'sliding scale' of ethics, thus committing himself to the malign thesis 'that power goes where power is due, that the will of Providence is made manifest by success, that the judgment of history is the judgment of heaven'. To Acton this was unforgivable:

> 'In this transition stage of struggling and straggling ethical science, the familiar tendency to employ mesology in history, to judge a man by his cause and the cause by its result, to obviate criticism by assuming the unity and wholeness of character, to conjure with great names and restore damaged reputations, not only serves to debase the moral standard, but aims at excluding it. And it is the office of historical science to maintain morality as the sole impartial criterion of men and things, and the only one on which honest minds can be made to agree'.[128]

Creighton was naturally irritated that Acton had not sent the book back, if necessary announcing that he would criticize it adversely somewhere else. But fortunately he had a very even temperament – an Oxford tutor once remarked of him: 'Creighton possesses common sense in a degree which amounts to genius' – and he saw the humour of the situation. 'It seems to me so funny', he told Lane Poole, 'that I shall be sorely tempted to add a note to the review, "The editor is not responsible for the opinions expressed in the above article."' Acknowledging receipt of Acton's review in a neutrally-phrased letter, he told him: 'I wish I could induce you some day to put forward your philosophy of history in a substantial form. I am often called upon to explain it, and can only dimly guess.' Since the whole review explained by implication Acton's philosophy of history this was a polite slap in the face, but Creighton always found Acton obscure, or affected to do so. He told Lane Poole: 'I can only guess what he means in many passages, and to the ordinary reader he will be quite unintelligible.'

At this stage Acton softened the review considerably; in fact he announced that he had 'altered every passage which could be construed or misconstrued into hostility'; but Creighton now wrote him a rather sharper letter. Unfortunately it has not survived, but something of its tone can be deduced from Acton's reply, which accepted 'the impropriety of Carlylese denunciations and Pharisaism in history'. But he still insisted that it was unethical for any historian to attempt to palliate the sins of popes and kings simply because of the responsibilities they bore. 'I would hang them higher than Haman', he said, 'for reasons of quite obvious justice, still more, still higher for the sake of historical science. The inflexible integrity of the moral code is to me the secret of the authority, the dignity, the utility of history.'

But Creighton was not to be bullied, nor was he in the least in awe of Acton. His long reply is pervaded by all the urbanity of a great prince of the Anglican Church, which he soon afterwards became. Referring to the Inquisition, he wrote:

'You judge the whole question of persecution more rigorously than I do. Society is an organism, and its laws are an expression of the conditions which it considers necessary for its own preservation ... Nowadays people are not agreed about what heresy is; they do not think it is a menace to society, hence they do not ask for its punishment; but the men who conscientiously thought heresy a crime may be accused of an intellectual mistake, not necessarily a moral crime'.

If every ruler who ever made a mistake, he went on, or even committed a crime of some kind, was to be unsparingly denounced, then the writing of history would be a dismal task indeed:

'I am hopelessly tempted to admit degrees of criminality, otherwise history becomes a dreary record of wickedness. I go so far with you that it supplies me with few heroes, and records few good actions; but the actors were men like myself, sorely tempted by the possession of power, trammelled by holding a representative position (none more trammelled than popes), and in the sixteenth century especially, looking at everything in a very abstract way. I suppose statesmen rarely regard questions in the concrete. I can rarely follow the actions of contemporary statesmen with much moral satisfaction. In the past I find myself regarding them with pity, who am I that I should condemn them?'

He concluded with a suggestion that Acton write an article for the *Review* on the ethics of history – 'I have no objection to finding myself among the shocking examples.' Acton, perhaps suspecting that his leg was being pulled, withdrew. Creighton told Lane Poole:

'I have had a long correspondence with Lord Acton, and now begin to understand him. He demands that history should be primarily a branch of the moral sciences, and should aim at proving the immutable righteousness of the ideas of modern Liberalism, tolerance and the supremacy of conscience ... He is revising his original remarks, but I do not expect that much clearness will ensue, though it will be very interesting'.[129]

On his part Acton was somewhat chastened; he was driven to acknowledge Creighton as an equal, and when he came to plan the *Cambridge Modern History* he was not above importuning his aid. In 1889 he even attempted a joking reference back to his notorious review; commenting on the latest issue of the *EHR* he said: 'Everything is interesting in no. 13 and the reviews seem to me particularly solid. Neubauer complained that you are too fond of white gloves, but there is more severity here than usual.'[130]

His own ethical severity softened with age, but only slightly. After all, it seems to have been this which was at the bottom of his quarrel with Döllinger. He was absolutely appalled at Döllinger's assumption that Tories might aspire to heaven in the next world. To him political differences, even more than religious differences, were moral issues, and therefore the Tories were irrevocably damned. He was even more suspicious of Ranke; the man's scholarship was beyond praise, but he was altogether too scientific; he did not *judge* readily enough. So, even in his praise of Ranke, in 1886, there was an element of reproach:

'As he writes history, not dogma, he never sorts men into black and white according to their bearing in vital controversies. His evil-doers escape the just rigour of the law, and he avoids hero-worship as the last ditch of prehistoric prejudice. He touches lightly on matters pertaining to the jurist and divine, but he has not their exclusiveness. His surface is more level than theirs, but his horizon is wider. The cup is not drained; part of the story is left untold; and the world is much better and very much worse than he chooses to say'.[131]

But Ranke went serenely on, as did Creighton, indifferent to Acton's strictures. Creighton even expanded his views in his Hulsean Lectures for

1893–4 on 'Persecution and Tolerance'. By the time Acton went to Cambridge in 1895 he was conscious of an increasing isolation. Other men seemed to have no difficulty in resolving ethical problems and for that matter practical problems which he found insuperable. In his inaugural lecture he related how he had last seen Ranke in 1877, 'when he was feeble, sunken and almost blind, and scarcely able to read or write':

> 'He uttered his farewell with kindly emotion, and I feared that the next I should hear of him would be the news of his death. Two years later he began a Universal History, which is not without traces of weakness, but which, composed after the age of eighty-three, and carried, in seventeen volumes, far into the Middle Ages, brings to a close the most astonishing career in literature'.

He must have been conscious now of his own inadequacies, his inability to emulate Ranke, or come anywhere near it. He was also acutely conscious of the fact that he was out of step with most of his colleagues. He told his audience:

> 'The weight of opinion is against me when I tell you never to debase the moral currency or to lower the standard of rectitude, but to try others by the maxim that governs your own lives, and to suffer no man and no cause to escape the undying penalty which history has the power to inflict on wrong'.[132]

He himself had no hesitation in proceeding to judgment, even if he had not heard all the evidence or done the hard work. This makes him an entertaining book reviewer, but a poor historian. The surprising thing is that his followers apparently did not recognize the superficiality of much of his work. H.A.L. Fisher admits that it contains 'no traces of the scholar's diffidence, no delicate blends of light and shade'; but he goes on: 'He abounds in superlatives, the supreme reward of an exhaustive induction, and he moves in a world of his own values.' Fisher reminds us that words like 'almost' or 'probably' scarcely feature in Acton's vocabulary at all: Solon was 'the most profound political genius of antiquity', Sixtus v was 'the ablest of modern popes', Thomas à Kempis was 'the greatest religious writer that ever lived', and Burke 'the author of the noblest political philosophy in the world'. (He could not very well describe George Eliot as the greatest writer who had ever lived, and in one of his rare compromises he relegated her to the comparatively lowly position of 'the most illustrious figure that has arisen in literature since Goethe died'.) Napoleon, rather surprisingly, was to him 'the most splendid genius that has appeared on earth'; or again, 'the most entirely known as well as the ablest of historic men'.[133] His positive worship of Napoleon, who was apparently immune to the dangers of absolute power, is an interesting phenomenon. Did it reflect the scholar's frustrated regard for men of action, or was it merely that Napoleon was the only temporal ruler who had ever thoroughly mastered the papacy?

His view of English history was that of an outsider, and apart from Burke – and then only in certain circumstances – he had no opinion of English statesmen. His close relations with Gladstone seem to have left no mark on his historical thinking. The lectures he gave at Cambridge on the French Revolution, culminating in the crisis of 18 Brumaire and the emergence of Napoleon, reveal his true commitment. In his parallel course on general European history he gave the Revolution of 1688 a magisterial nod; it was 'the greatest thing done by the English nation', and the more worthy in that it was achieved without bloodshed. But 'the Act itself' – the Bill of Rights – 'was narrow, spiritless, confused, tame and unsatisfactory'. 'It was perfectly compatible with the oppression of class by class, and of the country by the state, as the agent of a class.' He turned with relief elsewhere:

> 'The consequences [of 1688] ripened slowly, and a time came, under George III, when it seemed that they were exhausted. It was then that another and more glorious revolution, infinitely more definite and clear-cut, with a stronger grasp of principle, and depending less on conciliation and compromise, began to influence England and Europe'.[134]

His Cambridge lectures also suggest that he was expecting the imminent dawn of a new millennium in historical studies, which may be another explanation of his literary constipation. Reviewing the sources for the French Revolution, he pointed out that contemporary memoirs were now being superseded by the publication of the relevant state papers:

> 'In a few years, all these publications will be completed, and all will be known that ever can be known. In that golden age our historians will be sincere, and our history certain. The worst will be known, and then sentence need not be deferred. With the fullness of knowledge the pleader's occupation is gone, and the apologist is deprived of his bread. Mendacity depended on the concealment of evidence. When this is at an end, fable departs with it'.[135]

There is a pathetic naivety here, as well as an unbalanced delight in the language of the law court, which Ranke had always deplored. Yet he returned to the same theme, with even greater emphasis, in the instructions he drafted for contributors to the *Cambridge Modern History* in 1896. 'We approach the final stage in the conditions of historical learning,' he told them, 'the long conspiracy against the knowledge of truth has been practically abandoned, and competing scholars all over the civilised world are taking advantage of

the change.' (Always with Acton there is conspiracy; always there is competition.) 'No compilation at second hand from the best works', to his mind,
'would meet the scientific demand for completeness and certainty,' and he
was still ready to sick others onto tasks which had proved beyond him.
'Froude', he said, 'spoke of 100,000 papers consulted by him in manuscript,
abroad and at home; and that is still the price to be paid for mastery, beyond
the narrow areas of effective occupation.'[136]

Acton's beachhead on the shore of history – to sustain his own military
metaphors – was limited, and in 1892 his high political ambitions culminated,
rather pathetically, in the post of Lord-in-Waiting in Gladstone's last government. He needed the money, and could not refuse. He charmed the queen
with his fluent German and his virtuoso knowledge of the *Almanach de Gotha*,
and during his tours of duty at Windsor he read indefatigably on in the Royal
Library.[137] He was no longer writing for the reviews, but at some stage in the
1890s his interest in history was rekindled. Obviously he ought to be a
professor, and in those palmy days, when it was not expected that a professor
should work his way up from the bottom of the academic ladder, this was
comparatively easily arranged. In 1895 Lord Rosebery advised the queen to
appoint him to the regius chair at Cambridge, in succession to Sir John Seeley.

The news was greeted at Cambridge with general applause, but some
apprehension. As H.A.L. Fisher delicately puts it: 'Some predicted that a
man who had placed so strict an inhibition on unweighted utterance would
find continual and copious discourse an intolerable affliction.' They need not
have worried. Acton cancelled his winter sojourns at Cannes, took rooms in
Trinity, and threw himself into his new duties with enthusiasm. Young George
Trevelyan was amazed to find that this 'sage of immense and mysterious
distinction', this 'traveller from the antique lands of European statescraft,
religion and learning, with the brow of Plato above the reserved and epigrammatic lips of the diplomatist', was accessible to the lowliest undergraduate.
His lectures, delivered to large and enraptured audiences, were, we are told,
'charged with an austere and pregnant eloquence foreign to graduate practice
and undergraduate expectations'.[138] He was a social lion, and he loved it. In
fact according to his daughter: 'The years when he professed history at
Cambridge were the most contented time of his life. He found at last a home,
and a fulfilment of that academic vocation which was still so unnatural to
one of his social background, and therefore so hard for him to follow, but
which, though seldom recognized, was a necessity to his happiness.'[139]

Nor was the traffic, as it were, all one way. F.W. Maitland, of all men the
best qualified to judge, said later that the loss the university had incurred by
his death was 'irreparable'. He told Reginald Lane Poole: 'Within a few years
Acton did more [than any other man] to elevate the study of history here

towards the position that it has at Oxford. If we had had him here ten years earlier we might by this time be within measurable distance of you ... I learnt to admire [him] enormously – and on his merits, for I was not by any means prejudiced in his favour.' An anonymous obituary in the *Athenaeum* also spoke of his influence at Cambridge in terms which have a more general application:

> 'He represented to a world not altogether sympathetic the worth and dignity of historical studies. He showed their real importance for a right understanding of the destiny of man, however regarded. He demonstrated also in his own person that history was not at once the Cinderella of the sciences and the playmate of the arts, below scientific inquiry as a means of training the mind to exact thought, and behind classical studies as an instrument of culture; but that if properly and consistently pursued it was a mental gymnastic of the highest order, and a great trainer in patience, sympathy and refinement. He made history respectable'.[140]

But it was at Cambridge that Acton encountered the ultimate irony: the *Cambridge Modern History*. Scenting rich pickings from the new wave of undergraduates who were now studying history, not only at the ancient universities, but at the new foundations springing up all over the provinces, the Syndics of the University Press asked Acton to edit a new History of the World. In the discussions which followed this was narrowed down to 'modern history only, beginning with the Renaissance'. From then on Acton's proposals define pretty accurately what the 'Cambridge Modern' was not. For instance, faced with the question whether it was to be 'a serious compilation or original work', he and the Syndics chose 'original work'. He told the Syndics weightily: 'Universal history is not the sum of all particular histories, and ought to be contemplated, first, in its distinctive essence, as Renaissance, Reformation, Religious Wars, Absolute Monarchy, Revolution, &c. The several countries may or may not contribute to feed the main stream, and the distribution of matter must be made accordingly.' But he was definite that 'attention ought not to be dispersed, by putting Portugal, Transylvania, Iceland, side by side with France and Germany'. He told a potential contributor: 'My plan is to break through the mere juxtaposition of national histories, and to take in, as far as may be, what is extra-territorial and universal.' It would help towards this end 'to define chapters not by a limit of years, but by some salient point and catchword'. The plan he submitted to the Syndics ended with the brave words, 'Chart and compass for the coming century'.[141]

But the work weighed him down; arguably it killed him. His editorial labours were horrendous, and his papers present a vivid picture of the amount of drudgery involved in this kind of undertaking before the introduction of the typewriter. Some of his drafts and memoranda are in a secretarial hand, but he wrote all his own letters. He exchanged ninety-five letters over the years 1896-9 with one man alone, his assistant W.A.J. Archbold, of the Local Examinations Syndicate.[142] Contributors were awkward and refractory, of course, and often difficult to find. He sent an almost plaintive appeal to Creighton, now bishop of London, asking him to write the first chapter of the first volume, on 'the medieval roots of modern history' – 'They made me draw up a scheme, which they adopted, and they expect me to find the men, and then to ride on the whirlwind.' Creighton demurred – he was to die eighteen months before Acton, ulcerated by episcopal cares – but he was enthusiastic for the plan as a whole. 'It will indeed be a mighty work', he said, 'and what is still more important, it will bring under your influence and supervision all the men in England who are engaged in historical writing. The effect of this to raise the standard will be enormous. I envy you the opportunity, and still more the capacity to use it, as you alone can do.'[143]

But it was not to be. The Syndics insisted that Acton write the first chapter, which he never did, though Creighton did manage a short introductory note which seems to deny the very principles on which he had urged Acton to work:

'Elements of interest and suggestiveness, which are of vital importance to the specialist, disappear before the abstract system which the compiler must, whatever may be the scale of his undertaking, frame for his own guidance. The task is too large, its relations are too numerous and indefinite, for any one mind, however well stored, to appreciate them all. It is better to allow the subject matter to supply its own unifying principle than to create one which is inadequate or of mere temporary value'.[144]

Creighton died in January 1901. That summer Acton suffered a stroke, and retreated to Tegernsee, where he died a year later, on 19 June 1902. He is buried in the churchyard by the lake. *The Times* lamented that he 'should have vouchsafed us so little of his accumulated stores of learning, and left so few memorials of it behind him except his magnificent historical library and the vivid recollection which all who knew him must cherish of his brilliant conversational powers'.[145] Charles Oman, a fellow of All Souls' in his early forties who had already published three substantial books, went down to Aldenham to look at Acton's library shortly after his death. He was appalled at its nature and its extent:

'There were shelves on shelves of books on every conceivable subject – Renaissance Sorcery, the Fueros of Aragon, Scholastic Philosophy, the

Growth of the French Navy, American Exploration, Church Councils. The owner had read them all, and many of them were full in their margins with cross-references in pencil'.

He was baffled by Acton's famous indexes, which showed a zany catholicity of learning which rivalled Buckle's:

'There were pigeon-holed desks and cabinets with literally thousands of compartments, into each of which were sorted little white slips with references to some particular topic, so drawn up (so far as I could see) that no one but the compiler could easily make out the drift of the section. I turned over one or two from curiosity – one was on early instances of a sympathetic feeling for animals, from Ulysses' old dog in Homer downward. Another seemed to be devoted to a collection of hard words about stepmothers in all national literatures, a third seemed to be about tribal totems'.

Acton's ghost still seemed to hover in this sepulchre of learning:

'Arranged in the middle of the long, two-storied room was a sort of block or altar composed entirely of unopened parcels of new books from continental publishers. All had arrived since Lord Acton's health began to break up.* These volumes were apparently coming in at the rate of ten or so per week, and the purchaser had evidently intended to keep pace with the accumulation, to read them all, and to work them all into his vast thesis – whatever it was. For years, apparently, he had been trying to keep up with everything that was being written – a sisyphean task. Over all there were brown holland sheets, a thin coating of dust, the moths dancing in the pale September sun. There was a faint aroma of mustiness, proceeding from thousands of seventeenth- and eighteenth-century books in a room which had been locked since the owner's death. I never saw a sight that more impressed on me the vanity of human life and learning'.[146]

At the Cambridge University Press, meanwhile, everything was confusion. 'Admirable principles had been enunciated' – everyone hastened to admit that – but the lesser mortals who had taken over in November 1901, headed by Sir Adolphus William Ward, were disconcerted to find in the first volume of the *Cambridge Modern History*, which was almost ready for the press, 'not only great gaps, but considerable dangers of overlapping'. Ward, formerly professor of history at Owens College, Manchester, then Vice Chancellor of

---

*It is more likely that these parcels date from the sale of the library to Carnegie in 1889 (see p. 131 above), and it is difficult to decide what Oman precisely saw. Latterly Acton had a library at Cannes, and he kept a great many books at Trinity; it seems unlikely that he would have had new books sent to Aldenham.

the Victoria University, had begun a new career as Master of Peterhouse in 1900, at the age of sixty; he lived until 1924. Not content with the *Cambridge Modern*, he went on to edit the *Cambridge History of English Literature* (1907–27) and the *Cambridge History of British Foreign Policy* (1922–3). He had been helping Acton for some time, and Maitland was surprised to find that their relations were not always harmonious: 'I thought that [Ward] was dull', he said, 'but did not guess that he would be unruly.'[147]

Under Ward's direction as many of the gaps as possible were hastily and expeditiously filled, and the plan went ahead for a comprehensive compendium of the history of every known country in Europe, which was not what Acton had intended at all. The editors thought it a matter for smug gratulation, not modest apprehension, that they managed to rush out the whole twelve volumes in eight years.[148] Had Acton lived, no doubt the 'Cambridge Modern' would have been very different: the inspiration of his grandiose ideas, coupled with incoherent editing, would have produced a variegated, interesting, perhaps even an exciting work. The good Sir Adolphus and the men of like calibre he called to his aid, such as G.W. Prothero, produced a solid, reliable compendium of stodge; invaluable for teachers and students alike in the new universities, or for sixth-formers cramming for scholarships, but of no great interest to anyone else. It sold in its thousands and its tens of thousands.

◆ ◆

Five

The Professionalization of History

The Professors and the Universities

The appointment of Acton to the regius chair at Cambridge, and the launching of the *Cambridge Modern History*, were symbolic of the new union achieved in the late nineteenth century between the history written by the English intelligentsia, chiefly in London, and the history now studied and practised at the universities.

As the careers of men like Macaulay, Carlyle and Froude show, there was an enormous appetite for history in Victorian England, and a new belief in its importance. The movement for university reform in general at last forced modern history into the degree syallabus, and as the century progressed it was to make serious encroachments on the classics in the field of what we would now call 'liberal arts' studies, though well on into the twentieth century classics continued to dominate the curricula of the independent schools which provided most of the Oxford and Cambridge entry. In a broader field dogmatic assertions by men as diverse as Acton and Stubbs that their discipline was of paramount importance in the field of humane studies were accepted with remarkable docility by the educated public. In fact, the only scepticism expressed came from a few university tutors of the previous generation. This is in marked contrast, for instance, to the study of English Literature, which had an uphill struggle to establish itself as an intellectual pursuit.

It is difficult to say why this should be so. The example of Germany, where history had already established a firm footing in the universities early in the nineteenth century, was obviously important. The international reputation of Mommsen and Ranke drew attention to England's comparative backwardness. At the same time the French Revolution was a cataclysmic interruption of the orderly development of human history, calling for an explanation which presumably historians were best equipped to give; in mid-century the theories of Darwin held out the hope that social evolution would soon be as logically explicable as biological evolution; and the rise of nationalism made it imperative that every Englishman should be aware of the history of his own country; lastly, the proper reform of our national institutions called for some knowledge of how those institutions had come into being. Later in the century historians like Seeley even offered the study of history as a training in the techniques of current politics – a training which seemed the more desirable as the party battle at Westminster intensified. In particular, it was hoped that history would be a unifying influence on the new electorate, which was now subjected to compulsory literacy.

Unfortunately the universities took generations to catch up, and the process was not completed even by the end of the century. Written examinations were introduced at Oxford in 1800, and the honours classes of first, second and third in 1807, but the pass candidates remained in a large majority, and were not separated from the honours men until 1830. Moreover, these examinations were exclusively in mathematics and classics, and it was not until 1853, in the wake of a Royal Commission, that Oxford established a School of Jurisprudence and Modern History, together with a School of Natural Sciences. Even then, history was very much the junior partner in a school intended primarily for professional lawyers, and it did not gain its independence until 1872. At Cambridge reform was even more leisurely, though the end result was much the same. The Mathematical Tripos dates back to the mid-eighteenth century, perhaps as far back as 1748, but the Classical Tripos had to wait until 1824, and the transition from oral to written examinations was a piecemeal process; the practice of verbally dictating questions one by one to the candidates was only dropped in 1827. A Royal Commission ensured the introduction of Triposes in Natural Sciences and Moral Sciences in 1851, but for nearly twenty years history remained a subsidiary element in the moral sciences. A Tripos in Law and History was set up in 1870, in imitation of Oxford, but the two were separated in 1875. The Historical Tripos was divided into the present Part I and Part II in 1899.[1]

Initially, however, the introduction of these new disciplines created more problems than it solved. A new generation of tutors and lecturers in history had to be trained, and the centre of gravity of the profession was slow to move away from London; in some important respects it never has. Some of the most distinguished historians of the century – Macaulay, Froude, Acton, Green – never had any formal commitment to the universities, or only acquired one very late in life.

*

On the face of it history had an important initial advantage in the possession of a regius chair at each university, which ought to have provided bridges, as it were, between the literary world and the world of academe. Unfortunately the universities themselves could not provide historians of distinction, and the appointment of outsiders was a mid-nineteenth-century development. The efforts of George III* did bring some improvement. At Cambridge by the end of the eighteenth century it was accepted that the holder of the chair should give regular lectures, and William Smyth, who was appointed in 1807, excelled in this respect. He lectured vigorously and extensively, and published a detailed book-list, amounting to a bibliography, in 1817. This was followed by his *Lectures on Modern History*, in two volumes, which were reprinted more than once, and three volumes on the French Revolution, in 1840, which were regarded as an important contribution to the subject. The lectures as such were linked to a course of reading in set books, in quite the modern manner, and they seem to have been generally popular. One gentleman commoner, Lord Teignmouth, said: 'It would be difficult to overstate the debt of public gratitude due to Professor Smyth for his admirable lectures', and though he had gone down in 1816 he came up again in the Michaelmas term of 1823 to hear Smyth's revised series on modern history. Smyth tailed off towards the end, and in 1847 he left Cambridge for good; but since he was by then eighty-two years of age this may be forgiven him.[2]

When Smyth died in 1849 royalty again intervened, this time in the person of the Prince Consort, who was determined to appoint a historian of real eminence, if necessary from outside the university. His efforts over the next ten years, here and at Oxford, were to prove disastrous. In this case he approached Macaulay, who refused,† and in the end he had to fall back on Sir James Stephen, a supremely distinguished civil servant who had lately resigned from the Colonial Office because of ill-health; a man after the prince's own heart, of formidable *gravitas* and high intelligence. His pretensions to scholarship were slight, but he had published a collection of 'Essays in Ecclesiastical Biography', and for five or six years he delivered a series of well-prepared lectures on the history of France. But he was offended and disheartened by the small size of the audiences he attracted. He lectured intermittently up to his death in 1859, but he regarded residence at Cambridge as 'superfluous', and he told the Royal Commissioners in 1852 – in a letter from Paris – 'Of the actual state of historical studies in the university I know and can report nothing'.[3]

His successor was Charles Kingsley, clergyman, Christian socialist, popular

* P. 59 above.
† Pp. 71–2 above.

novelist and, rather surprisingly, a favourite of the queen and her husband. He had a superb delivery, he was a notorious public figure of Byronic fame, and his lectures attracted large audiences. His own idea of his function remains a trifle uncertain – his wife said complacently: 'Men all over the world have thanked God for the lessons of manliness, charity and godliness they learned in the room of the professor of modern history' – but he certainly publicized the subject, and the topics he offered were varied enough: from 1860 to 1862, 'Early Medieval Europe'; in 1862–3, 'The History of the United States'; in 1863–4, 'The Invasion of the Teutonic Races'; from 1864 to 1866, 'The Norman Conquest'; and in 1866–7, 'The Congress of Vienna'. He was also tutor to the Prince of Wales, who had private classes in British Constitutional History 1660–1832. His approach was too emotional for some, and his knowledge was certainly sketchy, but he was arguably too modest in his decision to resign in 1869.[4] By this time Prince Albert was, perhaps fortunately, dead, and Gladstone's choice fell on J.R. Seeley, with whose appointment the history of modern history at Cambridge may be said to have begun.

Oxford followed a similar pattern. George III's attempts to rehabilitate the regius chair were at first frustrated by the inertia of patronage, but they were resumed in 1813 by the prime minister, Lord Liverpool, though the king had by now succumbed to insanity. Liverpool even went to the length of drawing up regulations for the chair. The professor was to reside in Oxford at least ninety days a year, he was to give one public lecture on a fixed day each term, and a regular course of at least twenty ordinary lectures in one of the two winter terms. If he defaulted the Vice-Chancellor had the power to fine him or even suspend payment of his stipend. It is strange that after all this Liverpool's choice should have fallen on Edward Nares of Merton, a man who he knew very well had no qualifications at all in history – though he did have the advantage of being married to a daughter of the Duke of Marlborough.

Nevertheless, Nares approached his duties conscientiously. After eighteen months' preparation he began to lecture in 1816 to large audiences; this went to his head, and he rashly said that 'no former professor had had such success, and that it was to some degree the commencement of a new era'.[5] When his audiences fell to single figures the following year, and stayed there, his disillusionment was correspondingly great, and in the 1820s he gave up. In 1832 the Vice-Chancellor tried to enforce Lord Liverpool's rules; Nares put up a spirited defence, and after lecturing for another three years to audiences varying between two and six, he gave up for good. But he was far from being as negligible as his eighteenth-century predecessors, and his enormous *Life of*

Lord Burleigh (1828–32), though it was pilloried by Macaulay,* was an impressive performance for a self-taught historian.

Then the Prince Consort took a hand, appointing Thomas Arnold of Rugby to succeed Nares in 1841. In the short term he was a resounding success; his introductory course of lectures attracted audiences of 4–500, and on one occasion he reduced the Master of Balliol to tears.[6] Unhappily, he died within a year, and the post reverted to an old-fashioned Oxford careerist in John Anthony Cramer, tutor in rhetoric at Christ Church and Principal of New Inn Hall. The regius chair was just another string to his bow, and though he delivered an inaugural lecture, which was never published, he did nothing else. He was appointed dean of Carlisle in 1845, and died at Scarborough in 1848.

The Prince Consort's next attempt was an even greater disaster, especially on the eve of the appointment of a Royal Commission on the universities. Henry Halford Vaughan was a brilliant academic lawyer, but he was already a controversial figure in Oxford, where his conflict with the Newmanites had led to his well publicized ejection from an Oriel fellowship in 1842. His professorial career was equally stormy. He was an ardent supporter of reform, and he put before the Royal Commission of 1852 a scheme which would have given the professors, their numbers significantly enhanced, the ascendancy in teaching, and subordinated the colleges to the university.[7] He showed no interest in the new School of Jurisprudence and Modern History established in 1853, which fell far short of his expectations, and five years later he resigned. He settled at Upton Castle, Pembrokeshire, where he occupied himself with the over-elaborate annotation of Shakespeare's plays and a treatise on 'Man's Moral Nature' which he destroyed, unfinished, just before his death.

Nor was Prince Albert's next choice any better. If Halford Vaughan was roughly the equivalent of Sir James Stephen at Cambridge, then his successor Goldwin Smith may be regarded as Oxford's answer to Charles Kingsley. He was an ardent if rather rackety liberal, a member of the smart London intelligentsia, with a finger in every intellectual pie. The *DNB* succinctly describes him as a 'controversialist'; Disraeli dismissed him as 'an itinerant spouter of stale sedition'. He had served as Secretary to the Royal Commission of 1850–52, and was a member of the executive commission appointed

---

*Noting that the book contained 2,000 pages, in three volumes, that it was 1,500 cubic inches in size and weighed sixty pounds, Macaulay said: 'Compared with the labour of reading through these volumes all other labour, the labour of thieves on the treadmill, of children in factories, of negroes in the sugar plantation, is an agreeable recreation.' (*Essays*, Everyman edn., I, 77.)

to carry out the Oxford University Act of 1854. In other words, he was much too closely associated with the reform party to command general support. Not surprisingly his inaugural lectures – he gave two – were devoted to syllabus reform, and the range of his interests, and his overweening self-confidence, roused alarm in conservative circles even outside Oxford. As the *Westminster Review* said:

> 'We have in a pamphlet of nearly ninety pages nearly all the leading problems in theology, morals and metaphysics. Amongst the preliminary questions disposed of are the attributes of the Creator and the character of Christ, the origin of evil and a future state, the doctrine of Free Will and Necessity, the philosophy of the Absolute and the theory of the Inconceivable. Comte and Hegel, Mr Mansel and Mr Mill, Mr Buckle and Mr Darwin, are reflected [on] in successive paragraphs, or tossed upon the horns of a lively dilemma. And all this in two lectures upon the study of history! And *à propos* of a proposal to reduce that study to a method!'[8]

This aggressive eccentricity isolated the new professor, and he was frustrated by his inability to partake in the direct teaching of undergraduates. In 1866 he resigned and went to America, where he accepted the chair of history at the new university of Cornell two years later. In 1871 he moved on to Toronto, where he married a wealthy widow and lived happily ever after, until 1910. His successor in the regius chair was William Stubbs.

It was Stubbs who initiated the serious study of history at Oxford, or indeed, in the English universities.[9] He was also the first English historian of any weight to make a significant contribution to knowledge while he was a university teacher. In other words, he was the first 'professional historian' in England as that term is now understood. With 'The Norman Conquest' and 'Henry V' on the list of special subjects, and his *Select Charters*, first published in 1870, on the list of basic set books, his shadow still lies across the Oxford School of Modern History in 1980.*

Stubbs's career coincided with the revival of medieval studies in the nineteenth century. The writers of the Enlightenment had little patience with the Middle Ages, and as late as 1841 Thomas Arnold announced that his professorial lectures would go no farther back than the fourteenth century at the most. 'I could not bear,' he said, 'to plunge myself into the very depths of that

---

* At Oxford, as at Cambridge, 'modern' history begins with the Fall of Rome, which is why even in the twentieth century medievalists like Galbraith and Knowles have been appointed to regius chairs.

noisome cavern, and to toil through centuries of dirt and darkness.'[10] However, the success of parliamentary reform encouraged some scholars to delve back into the early history of the institution, partly in the hope of re-animating the idea of an Ancient Constitution. One of the pioneers was Francis Palgrave, later to be first Deputy Keeper of the Public Records. He published two volumes on *The Rise and Progress of the English Commonwealth* in 1832, and in 1851 *The History of Normandy in England*. He sought the origins of the constitution in France rather than in Germany. Meanwhile John Kemble had published a pioneering collection of Anglo-Saxon legal documents, the *Codex Diplomaticus*, and followed it up in 1849 with a learned but rather chaotic synthesis, *The Saxons in England*. But both men were somewhat outside the mainstream of English intellectual life; Palgrave was the son of a Jewish businessman (his real name was Cohen), and a lawyer by profession; Kemble came of a famous acting family – he was the son of Charles Kemble, and nephew to Mrs Siddons – and though he took his degree at Cambridge and studied under Jacob Grimm at Göttingen he was never a full-time scholar. They had no pupils, they founded no school. As Maitland said, of them and their like: 'We had our swallows, and beautiful birds they were; but there was spring in Germany.'[11]

However, the publication of basic medieval source material had begun in 1802 with the Record Commissioners appointed by parliament. Their work has been continued, in one way or another, down to the present day. The Camden Society began publishing a more modest series of records, mainly medieval, in 1838; in the provinces the Surtees Society, based on Durham, began in 1835, and the Chetham Society, based on Manchester, in 1844. There were many more. Moreover, in 1857 Lord Romilly, Master of the Rolls, was persuaded to sponsor the publication of medieval records still in private hands, under the title 'Chronicles and Memorials of Great Britain and Ireland during the Middle Ages' – rather confusingly called the 'Rolls Series', because of their sponsorship, not their content. To the modern eye the astonishing thing is the speed with which such projects were carried out in the last century. Here the decision was taken on 15 April 1857 and the first two volumes appeared in February 1858. Thirteen more followed before the end of the year, though after that the editors settled down to a steadier striking rate of three or four volumes a year.[12]

The scholarly standards of the Rolls Series were erratic, and it was only a crude imitation of the pioneering German project on which it was consciously modelled, the *Monumenta Germaniae Historica*, which began in 1826. To quote Maitland again: 'Chequered indeed were the books in which public money was invested; the scandalously bad elbowed the admirably good.'[13] This is not surprising, considering that the series was the work of private individuals, usually clergymen, often recruited by word of mouth, working alone and in their spare time, having very little contact with one another and none with the universities. Yet David Knowles has commented wrily on the sums of money, huge in the context of nineteenth-century taxation and living standards, which were paid to contributors, and which constituted an important government subsidy to scholarship.[14]

Stubbs's early career was set in a similar context of amateur zeal and scholarly isolation. He was born in 1825 at Knaresborough, in Yorkshire, the son of a country solicitor who died prematurely in 1843, leaving the family in straitened circumstances. But his brilliance had already attracted the notice of Thomas Longley, bishop of Ripon, who nominated him as a servitor (the lowest rank of scholarship boy) at Christ Church in 1844. In 1848 he took a first in classics and a third in mathematics, and was elected a Fellow of Trinity. (His servitorship banned him from a Studentship at Christ Church, then and later.) In 1850 he was ordained, and took the college living of Knavestock, in Essex, where he married the young village schoolmistress and stayed sixteen years.

In that time, though he functioned as a conscientious and respected parish priest, he also acquired by private study an astonishing grasp of the sources for English history up to 1216, and established a close relationship, chiefly epistolary, with other 'amateur' scholars like Freeman; he also kept in touch with his old patron Bishop Longley, who became archbishop of Canterbury in 1862 and at once appointed him Lambeth Librarian. His first book, *Registrum Sacrum Anglicanum*, establishing the course of succession to the English bishoprics in the Middle Ages, was published in 1858, but for some reason he could not break into the Rolls Series until 1863, though after that he edited a further eighteen volumes.

In the circumstances of the day his applications for Oxford chairs – the new Chichele chair of modern history in 1862, and the chair of ecclesiastical history in 1863 – were perfectly reasonable, and in both cases he was passed over in favour of candidates who even at the time were demonstrably inferior. He was fortunate that Goldwin Smith's resignation in 1866 coincided with the brief ministry of Derby and Disraeli, who were anxious to find a professor of sound conservative views. Reassured on this point, partly by Archbishop Longley, Derby offered him the regius chair, which was now combined with a fellowship at Oriel and carried a stipend of £650 a year. He joyfully accepted.[15]

Stubbs's scholarly activities were now redoubled. He lectured assiduously on Germany in the Middle Ages and on Early English History and held tutorials for undergraduates. His lecture audiences were small, but James Bryce records that 'by his mere presence in the university, and by the inexhaustible kindness with which he answered questions and gave advice, he rendered great services'.[16] In particular, on the founding of the independent School of Modern History in 1872 he was able to provide the specialized teaching for finals candidates which made it a real school of studies and not just an examination mill. Meanwhile he continued to publish a volume in the Rolls Series almost every year, and in 1870 there appeared his famous *Select Charters and other Illustrations of English Constitutional History* down to 1307, followed in 1874, 1875 and 1878 by the three stout volumes of his *Constitutional History of England*.

This brilliant synthesis has rightly been called 'one of the most astonishing achievements of the Victorian mind', and it is the more astonishing when we remember that Stubbs was working virtually alone; he was so far above all his contemporaries as a medieval scholar that he could only assist them, not they him. 'No other Englishman', said Maitland, 'has so completely displayed to the world the whole business of the historian, from the winning of the raw material to the narrating and generalising.'[17] It deserved the enormous prestige it immediately acquired, though that very prestige brought a predictable reaction against it after Stubbs's death. Its central section, from the Conquest to the death of Edward I, has been supplemented by later scholars, notably Maitland and Tout, and the sections before 1066 and after 1399 can now be discounted; nevertheless, it has held its own for nearly a hundred years as the Ur-text on English medieval history. Maitland remarked in 1904: 'The grand figure of William Stubbs seems to be destined to become grander and more solitary as the years roll by', and so it has proved. To Norman Cantor, writing in 1966, 'the *Constitutional History* remains the holistic work to which all subsequent research has had to be related'; and David Knowles said in 1968: 'Few historians would be the worse for reading Stubbs's introductions [to the Rolls Series] and volume II of the *Constitutional History* once every four or five years.'[18]

And this is despite the fact that Stubbs was very much of his age. This Tory churchman embraced with ease the Whig theory of the Ancient Constitution, with his own amendments and improvements. He started from the premise that England was a Teutonic nation – indeed, to him she was 'the country in which the Teutonic genius has most freely developed' – and in contrast to Palgrave before him and Maitland after, he rejected the notion of any significant Roman or Frankish influence on the developing constitution, except perhaps in the introduction of the jury. He accepted that parliament in a recognizable form had only existed since 1265, but he argued that England's Teutonic heritage had left her with a tradition of self-help, self-government and free consultation at local level which created, as it were, an 'atmosphere' of representation. This found a focus at national level in the Witenagemot of the Anglo-Saxons and the *curia regis* of the Norman kings. He did not take these institutions for proto-parliaments, as Coke and Petyt had so confidently done, but he did argue that however limited and restricted their membership, they were accepted by contemporaries as being representative of the whole nation, and therefore they paved the way for Simon de Montfort's brilliant innovation, later regularized by Edward I.

The Norman Conquest, he agreed, introduced a period of 'grinding despotism', but it was not comprehensive enough to grind the independence out of the English. It merely organized them and taught them the basic essentials of discipline and loyalty. Had feudalism developed naturally in England it would have ended in despotism; as it was the tension between the Normans and the English gave rise to the great reforms of the Angevins, culminating in Magna Carta. Stubbs had no doubt that the Charter was the expression of a great national movement; it was 'no selfish exaction of privilege [by the barons] for themselves', and 'the people for whom they acted were on their side'. The English Church, which according to Stubbs had already diverged significantly from the Roman model, joined the barons in defence of national aspirations. So by the end of the thirteenth century England was an organic nation, untainted by prejudices of race, tongue or class:

> We can scarcely doubt that Edward [I] had a definite idea of government before his eyes, or that that idea was successful because it approved itself to the genius and grew out of the habits of the people ... The nation, on whom and by whom he was working, had now become a consolidated people, roused by the lessons of his father's reign to an intelligent appreciation of their own condition'.

This nationalist interpretation of English history was a foundation on which others could readily build – on which Gardiner, for instance, was to build his picture of the seventeenth century as a defence of the balanced constitution. Also, Stubbs's concept of national liberty as the sum of individual liberties, and central government as the sum of local governments, was highly relevant in a period during which local government was being comprehensively reorganized.[19] It is this anachronistic view of medieval history, rather than the errors, omissions and misunderstandings which inevitably arose from the defects in his sources, which has aroused the furious wrath of some of his modern critics, and some of his most dubious assumptions are still at the roots of our historical thinking: 'Historians now eschew Stubbs's blatant nationalist and organic terminology, but they still work on the assumption that there was an identifiable constitution, of which the leaders of medieval society had at least a vague understanding.'[20]

However, in 1884 Stubbs left to be bishop of Chester, and though he returned as bishop of Oxford four years later, his episcopal duties left him no further time for research. (He died in 1901.) His successor in the regius chair was E.A. Freeman, a firm friend but a man of a very different stamp.

It is tempting to label Edward Augustus Freeman as one of the great Victorian eccentrics, but this is a category so crowded as to be almost meaningless. He had the greatest respect for Macaulay and nothing but contempt for Carlyle – 'I read a page of Carlyle when I was a scholar, and it seemed such unintelligible rant that I never read any more' – but in the violence of his animosities and the irrationality of his prejudices he resembled the latter much more than he did the former.[21] He was born in 1823, the son of a wealthy coal owner, and he always enjoyed a fairly comfortable private income. But he was left an orphan before he was two, he was raised by grandparents and educated mainly by private tutors, and in his make-up there was always a great deal of the spoiled child. 'The keynote of his character was the extraordinary warmth of his interest in the persons, things and places which he cared for, and the scarcely less conspicuous indifference to matters which lay outside the well-defined boundary line of his sympathies'.[22] He could never brook opposition or criticism, nor admit that he was wrong.

He won a scholarship to Trinity College, Oxford, in 1841, and though he only got a second in the Schools he was elected to a fellowship. However, he soon retired to a succession of houses in the West Country to devote himself to private study, ending up at Somerleaze, near Wells, in Somerset. This was in 1860, and he now embarked on a literary career which for sheer volume, irrespective of quality, has rarely been excelled. In the years from 1860 to 1869 he wrote 723 substantial articles and reviews for the *Saturday Review*, 'substantial' meaning at least 5000 words long and often nearer 10,000; he also wrote for other journals from time to time.[23] In the same decade he published the first volume of a *History of Federal Government*, and in December 1865 he started on his *History of the Norman Conquest*; the first large volume, of 770 pages, was published two years later. At that stage he thought he might complete it in two volumes, but it took six, the last being published in 1879. In 1882 he followed this up with two huge volumes on the reign of William Rufus. He told Goldwin Smith in 1888: 'As I get older, I seem to be planning greater schemes of work than I ever did, and in truth the mere power of work is constantly strengthening.'[24] By then he had embarked on a history of Sicily, three volumes of which appeared in 1891 and a fourth posthumously in 1894. He did not know the meaning of the words self-criticism and restraint, and all his literary projects developed 'on a scale so monstrous that only the demise of their author could achieve a closure'.[25] *Sicily* was left unfinished, and so was *Federal Government*.

His industry is the more surprising in that, like Buckle, he could not bear to work in a public library. 'I have never tried the British Museum', he once wrote, 'I never use Bodleian oftener than I can help … I must have my materials in my house or other place that acts as such for the time: a room in an inn or a friend's house will do.'[26] His failure to use manuscript material – he was in any case ignorant of palaeography – seems almost heretical to modern historians, and left him wide open to the criticism of men like John Horace Round. He was a man of violent and unattractive prejudices – against Jews, against Turks and, of course, against James Anthony Froude – and the respect in which he was generally held in his lifetime is difficult now to understand.

The sheer bulk of his *Norman Conquest* exacts a certain respect, it is true, nor did his basic ideas diverge significantly from those of Stubbs, whom he deeply admired. Those prepared to dig will unearth some gems of characterization and description, particularly of battles, which were his forte. But his rampant Teutonism, which he shared with many of the later Victorians, and his emotional romanticism, led him to see the Conquest as a much greater tragedy than Stubbs ever did: it marked the extinction of the golden civilization of the north by the vicious, swarthy, unscrupulous Franks. (Did he in his subconscious see the Franks as semitic?) His narrative was maimed by his confinement to printed sources, and his message was obscured by the complexities of his style, accentuated by a reluctance to use one Latin word where five Anglo-Saxon words could be made to fit. Much of his prose – 'Now the Landwaster of Norway was lowered before the victorious standard of the Fighting Man' – seems to foreshadow the modern fantasy epic, and such fads as his obstinate (and mistaken) determination to rechristen the battlefield of Hastings 'Senlac' were an irritation and an embarrassment. Thus he wrote only one article for the *DNB*, on King Alfred, then fell out with Leslie Stephen because he wanted to call 'Athelstan' '*Ae*thelstan', and so on. Stephen thought the first volume intimidating enough, without confronting the reader with a series of pedantic diphthongs. On top of this, his very eagerness to be understood, to convince, was an irritant. Mandell Creighton said: 'Freeman tries to make you understand each detail by isolating it, and surrounding it with nineteenth-century settings. He iterates and re-iterates, but you don't see it. His history is a series of tips.' Maitland, who contemptuously dubbed him 'The Arcadian Augustus', said that: 'just because [he] believed that history was past politics, he never succeeded in adding anything to our knowledge of medieval politics, but spoilt everything by inept comparisons'.[27] His fondness for the Saxons was innocent enough in itself, but the Aryanism and antisemitism which lay behind it were unattractive even in his own lifetime, when such attitudes were rather less disreputable than they are now. He called Liebermann, the great German medievalist, 'Stubbs's Jew'.

Horace Round accused Freeman of distorting history for party political ends, but his mind was more complex than that – 'It is history rather than politics which seems to have taken precedence; it would be truer to say that Freeman admired Gladstone because he admired Harold than vice-versa.'[28] Indeed, in contrast to Stubbs, who thought that the steady development of the English constitution down the centuries implied steady improvement, Freeman believed that progress could only be made by a regression to earlier forms. As he once put it, in typical Freemanese: 'We must recognise the spirit which dictated the Petition of Right as the same which gathered all England round the banners of the returning Godwin, and remember that the "Good Old Cause" was truly that for which Harold died on the field and Waltheof on the scaffold.'[29] A man of violent prejudices himself, with a strong disposition to view historical events in the light of present politics, he did not see how the objective study of history could be taken much beyond the Middle Ages. Faced by the first volumes of Gardiner's *History of England*, he commented that 'the nuisance of the seventeenth century' was that:

> 'One can't go unreservedly with any side, as one can with our friends in the thirteenth. My political and my religious sympathies are divided. I go with Parliament as Parliament, but I can get up no sympathy with the Puritan as Puritan.

Just before his death he read Gardiner's final volume on Charles I, and he was still decidely uneasy:

> 'Altogether the whole time is bothering, at least to me, as I can't go heartily in for any party. 'Tis a relief to fly to the thirteenth century, and shout for the Sword of the Lord and Earl Simon without any misgiving any way'.

As for Henry VIII, he was even more puzzled – 'Nobody has really got to the bottom of Henry VIII. I at least am many parasangs from understanding the man who refused all prayers for the preservation of Coventry minster, and sat down and wrote the statutes of Canterbury with his own hand as devoutly as if he had been St Lewis.'[30]

For this reason, as a distinterested outsider, he vigorously opposed the establishment of a School of Modern History at Oxford, even in conjunction with Law, and he even published a pamphlet to this effect, *Thoughts on the Study of History*, in 1849. He thought it was just possible for experienced scholars like himself to compare the Normans, say, with the Spartans, but 'any attempt to introduce the almost infinite field of modern history as a subject of ordinary study and examination on the same level as Grecian and Roman history must be utterly fruitless'. He repeated these views when he appeared as an expert witness before the Royal Commission of 1852, and it is not surprising that he was cold-shouldered for the regius chair in 1858 and

1866, and for the Camden chair of ancient history in 1861 and the Chichele chair of modern history in 1862. The strange thing is that he should have put forward his name each time with apparent confidence.[31] But it is even stranger that Gladstone's choice should have fallen on him at last in 1884. He had some reservations himself. He told Goldwin Smith: 'Leaving one's home for half the year to be in the whirl of Oxford, as Oxford is now, is a frightful prospect, besides the bondage of new and absurd rules.' Stubbs had forebodings, too. He told Mandell Creighton: 'My successor will be an older man than myself, and I heartily wish that he may have as peaceful a time as I have had.'[32]

Of course, he did not. For one thing, he never acclimatized himself to those 'new and absurd rules', and though the battle over history had been lost he was determined to halt the rout before it engulfed the whole university. For instance, though he supported the foundation of a new School of Modern Languages, his objection to the inclusion in it of English Literature found 'violent expression' in Congregation. 'What do they mean', he asked James Bryce, 'by "letters" and "literature" apart from language? I suppose, as I said, they want to chatter about Shelley. I told them that we did not want to discuss the "Harriet problem", having enough to do with Helen, Theodora and Mary Stuart.' (He obviously had some prejudice against Shelley; on another occasion he said that literature 'meant the study of great books, and not mere chatter about Shelley'.)[33] He was always on the alert, too, for any encroachment by the natural scientists:

> 'These physical science botherers do roar in the midst of our Congregations, and set up their ologies for endless tokens. No one knows what they are after, because no one can understand their jargon; the object, as far as it can be understood, seems to be to hinder any man from knowing more than one thing, and that thing must not be bigger than a bee's knee'.[34]

One of his most spectacular performances, however, was in the famous Vivisection Debate of 1885, which, as Oman says, was 'really a scandalous riot'. Freeman asserted with his usual intemperance that the practice of vivisection rivalled 'all the horrors perpetrated at the sack of Titus by Jerusalem – after which no more of his oration could be heard'.[35] (He was a great animal-lover, and had a notable public debate with Anthony Trollope over blood sports.)

Even so, history was not spared. He deplored the School of History, which he dismissed as an easy option for sporting men whose Latin was weak; it is typical of the man that his inaugural lecture contained a lavish encomium on the Cambridge Historical Tripos. Like most professors, he was upset by the tiny audiences his lectures attracted, but he was even more irritated by the attitude of the modern undergraduate. 'I once asked a man', he said, 'who came to my lectures on Gregory of Tours, whether he had brought a book, meaning, in my ignorance, a copy of the author whom we were going to read. "Yes, I have a notebook", was the reply.' Freeman was appalled that 'the result of forty years' tinkering with every part of the old system' was 'that instead of reading books with a tutor, men filled their notebooks with the tips of a crammer, to reproduce them in the examination schools'.[36] There was much in what he said, and Firth was to say it again in 1904, but his uncouthness told against him. Referring again to his course on Gregory of Tours, he said complacently that his audience, though small, had included 'scholars of high renown'; however, he added, 'amongst these classes professed teachers of history have supplied the smallest proportion. I merely state the fact; it is for them to explain it.' When he was invited to dine one night with the History Tutors' Association he entered the room saying loudly: 'I have come to see the crammers cram.' According to him the colleges had declined into mere hostels, 'companies of ushers with their pupils'. Many dismissed him as a buffoon, and good stories abound at his expense; but he also gave great offence. J.A.R. (later Sir John) Marriott, who was then tutor in history at Worcester College, found him 'rude, dogmatic and overbearing'.[37]

Strangely enough, Freeman was more seriously regarded in Cambridge, and his Rede Lecture in 1872 on 'The Unity of History' induced the Faculty Board to retain ancient history in the Historical Tripos, where it resides as an optional subject to this day.[38] But at Oxford he did permanent damage; Stubbs's relations with the college tutors had been delicate, but polite; Freeman's professorship marked a breach between them and the professors which persisted into the twentieth century and was to prove Firth's undoing.

Latterly, his lectures diverged farther and farther from the syllabus, and when he offered a detailed course on the history of Sicily his audience rapidly dwindled to a faithful four, one of whom, we are told, was 'a middle-aged clergyman from North Oxford with a taste for general information'.

> 'This cleric was compelled to break off his attendance in the middle of the term, but rose to explain to the professor that "to keep up the quorum" he must send his daughter, a very intelligent girl of fourteen. Freeman, who was growing more and more indignant as the term went on, and the hearers went off, broke off the series with an inarticulate groan'.[39]

Early in 1892 he departed for a holiday in Spain. It may well be, as Lytton Strachey insinuates, that the mounting attacks of John Horace Round on his veracity and his scholarly competence were beginning to wear him down; but in any case the stress of Oxford life, as he chose to live it, must have told on a man who was now in his late sixties. The weather in Spain was cold, wet and disagreeable. He fell ill with bronchitis at Alicante, and succumbed to smallpox on 16 March. He is buried in the Protestant cemetery there.[40] As we have seen, Lord Salisbury, sublimely indifferent to Oxford susceptibilities, now offered the regius chair to Froude, who accepted with some qualms. 'I must do the best I can', he said, 'and trust that I shall not be haunted by Freeman's ghost.'[41]

But, repulsive as he was in most respects, Freeman had a great gift for friendship, just as he had a great gift for enmity; and one of his more remarkable friendships was with John Richard Green.[42]

Green is one of the literary curiosities of a century full of such curiosities. His career was not unlike Buckle's. He was born in 1837, the son of an Oxford town councillor, and educated at Magdalen College School. He was orphaned at the age of twelve, however, and though he won a scholarship to Jesus College, Oxford, at the age of sixteen – too young to take up residence, he had to wait two years – once at university he just drifted. In the end he took a pass degree, not feeling himself sufficiently prepared for honours. However, whilst still an undergraduate he wrote a series of articles for the *Oxford Chronicle* entitled 'Oxford in the Eighteenth Century' which were remarkably mature pieces of writing; in fact, they were later published in book form.

In 1860, soon after graduation, he was ordained, and for the next nine years he served in some of the most poverty-stricken of the London slum parishes, in the districts of Hoxton and Stepney. There he probably contracted tuberculosis. From 1862 he supplemented his tiny income by turning out occasional articles and reviews, and at a meeting of the Somersetshire Archaeological Society he also struck up an unexpected friendship with Freeman which was to last his lifetime. Reading the correspondence of Green, Freeman and Stubbs we are struck by the importance of the growing network of local historical and literary societies to the isolated amateur scholar. We are also reminded of the important role of the London reviews, like the *Saturday Review* for which both Green and Freeman wrote, not only in forming public taste but in supplementing or even constituting the income of many scholars. In fact, at intervals between 1867 and 1876 Green and his friends discussed with Macmillans the introduction of a new review, which would be entirely devoted to history. But there was no agreement on its precise form, the others were encouraging but shied away from editing it, and Green's health was never up to it.[43]

Meanwhile Green's correspondence with Freeman was conducted with an alarming roguishness on both sides, and his habit of referring to his *Short History* as the 'Wee-Book' is distinctly unattractive. However, Freeman would stand things from 'Johnnikin' or 'Johnny' which he would stand from no one else; Green corrected his proofs with unsparing candour, and his reviews of his books were not always agreeable reading. He even tried to moderate the fury with which Freeman belaboured his opponents:

> 'I do wish, my dear Freeman, you would leave off poking at Kingsley and his Dietrich. Have you counted up the number of your references to that sad blunder? And ought there not to be some proportion between sin and punishment? "Blunders" was very good; but there are blunders of taste as well as blunders of fact'.[44]

Yet they were very cosy together and travelled extensively; Freeman intro-duced Green to Normandy, and Green showed Freeman round Italy. Luckily they shared a deep love of great architecture, but Freeman was indifferent to painting and literature to a remarkable degree. In fact, it was cited as proof of Green's hold over him that he had persuaded him to pay his one and only visit to an art gallery.[45]

It is a friendship the more remarkable in that their views on history were almost diametrically opposed. Freeman, after all, was one of the main expo-nents of the 'drum-and-trumpet' school of history Green most deplored; his only notable aphorism was: 'History is past politics, and politics is present history.' Green on the other hand was one of the pioneers of social history, and the whole of the preface to his *Short History of the English People* was an implied rejection of what Freeman stood for, a fact which did not go un-noticed, of course. In 1873, when Freeman asked him to write a short his-tory of France on similar lines for Macmillans, Green put his cards on the table:

> 'As you see in my own Wee-Book, I think moral and intellectual facts are as much facts for the historian as military or political facts; and if I deal with them at all (and deal with them I must if I write at all) I must deal with them much as I dealt with them in Little Book. That is to say, I can't muddle them in corners always ... but shall sometimes have to deal with them as of greater importance than anything else ... You mustn't groan over the "Poets" and so on, because the "Poets" and so on are sure to turn up'.

Freeman did groan, but almost uniquely he agreed to differ – 'You may bring in all that social and religious kind of thing, Johnny, but I can't.'[46]

In 1869 Green's health broke down and he had to resign his living, though Archbishop Tait, long a patron of his, at once appointed him to the sinecure librarianship at Lambeth. From then on he spent most winters abroad, at Mentone or San Remo, subsidized, we must suppose, by his literary earnings. It was in 1869 that he offered to write *A Short History of the English People* for Macmillans, for £350 down and another £100 if the first 2,000 copies were sold within six months.* He thought it 'might serve as an introduction to better things if I lived, and might stand for some work done if I didn't'.[47]

His pessimism was fortunate. The result was a brilliant piece of compression which only deteriorated as he tried to expand it. It was the first attempt to write a complete history of England on this scale – leaving aside the school or juvenile market – and it came at the last possible moment at which the amount of information available was still restricted enough to make it manageable. The skill involved was considerable, especially since he had no model to work from. He told his friend Boyd Dawkins: 'It was horrible to condense the English Conquest into five pages and the Conversion into six and yet be interesting, but I think I have managed pretty well.'[48] As indeed he had.

Moreover, apart from Macaulay on a much smaller canvas, he was the first historian of England who tried to give equal weight to social as well as political development, and to include art and literature. This alone gave the book an overwhelming novelty which it is difficult for us to appreciate today, when such things are commonplace. His preface reads like a manifesto:

'At the risk of sacrificing much that was interesting and attractive in itself, and which the constant usage of our historians has made familiar to English readers, I have preferred to pass lightly and briefly over the details of foreign wars and diplomacies, the personal adventures of kings and nobles, the pomp of courts or the intrigues of favourites, and to dwell at length on the incidents of that constitutional, intellectual and social advance in which we read the history of the nation itself'.

He affirmed his belief that 'in England, more than elsewhere, constitutional progress has been the result of social development', and went on to say:

'I have never shrunk from telling at length the triumphs of peace. I have restored to their place amongst the achievements of Englishmen the "Faerie Queene" and the "Novum Organum". I have set Shakespeare among the heroes of the Elizabethan Age, and placed the scientific discoveries of the Royal Society side by side with the victories of the New Model. If some of the conventional figures of military and political history occupy in my pages less than the space usually given them, it is because I have had to

* These were quite substantial sums, bearing in mind the fact that a private income of £600 a year maintained Freeman in some affluence even before he began to earn significant amounts by his pen. As late as 1909 an Oxford chair (the Chichele chair in military history) was established with a salary of £500 a year.

find a place for figures little heeded in common history – the figures of the missionary, the poet, the printer, the merchant or the philosopher'.⁴⁹

The *Short History* had a rather chilly reception from the intelligentsia, but the public loved it. Its initial success rivalled that of Macaulay's *History*, which is the more remarkable when we remember that Macaulay was already a public celebrity, which Green was not. Five impressions were exhausted in the first year, 1874, and it continued to sell in various editions, including an Everyman edition, well into the next century. This is partly because, for all Green's protestations, the book was not radically unconventional; it contrived to give a complete picture of national development, including politics, diplomacy and war. And despite its title, and despite the fact that Green was denounced by one critic as a dangerous left-winger, the *Short History* bears no resemblance to such modern pieces of special pleading as Cole and Postgate's *History of the Common People*. Indeed, it was essentially a patriotic and progressive piece of work, which told a success story: of the unification of England, the consolidation of her unique institutions and the reassertion of liberty in the seventeenth century culminating in great-power status in the eighteenth, and the overwhelming climax of Waterloo. (After that Green lost interest, or strength, and a seven-page epilogue carried the reader up to 1874.) The infusion of science, letters and poetry, of which Green was so proud, was skilfully managed, and it set the tone for a host of imitators, but it is not essential to the story, and it has long lost its capacity to surprise.

True, some of his conventionality is, as it were, retrospective. For instance, he seems to have been the first to use the hallowed term 'The New Monarchy' for the later Lancastrians and the early Tudors; in fact he pushes the term back to the death of Henry v in 1422. Similarly it was he apparently who first called the Puritans 'The People of the Book'. The terror of Henry VIII is conveyed in hints and touches, but the chapter headings of this section are the names of his ministers, and he is well in line with modern orthodoxy when he says of the 1530s: 'The history of this great revolution, for it is nothing less, is the history of a single man', Thomas Cromwell.⁵⁰ The section on the New Monarchy ends with Cromwell's execution in 1540, and the rest of Henry's reign is shuffled away in a page and a half.

His gloss on Magna Carta was essentially Stubbs's, though his sympathetic portrait of William I cannot have been pleasing to his friend Freeman. By a venerable Whig convention he dated his chapter on the Norman Conquest from 1068, not 1066. Though he never admitted it, his picture of Elizabeth I owed a great deal to Froude – ' As we track Elizabeth through her tortuous mazes of lying and intrigue, the sense of greatness is almost lost in a sense of contempt. But, wrapt as they were in a cloud of mystery, the aims of her policy were throughout temperate and simple, and they were pursued with singular tenacity'.[51] He acknowledged his debt to Gardiner, but in 1874 Gardiner's great history of early seventeenth-century England had only reached 1623. As we proceed, Pym and Strafford come through much more clearly in Green's narrative than Charles I; as with Henry VIII, he clearly preferred to approach a 'debatable' king indirectly. His eclecticism is everywhere apparent; his comment on the 'Eleven Years' Tyranny' of Charles I, for instance, is pure Hume: 'Vexatious indeed and illegal as were the proceedings of the Crown, there seems to have been little apprehension of any permanent danger to freedom in the country at large.'[52] It was a remarkable literary feat, but its historical value is doubtful; within a broad Whig framework it was an amalgam of other people's points of view.

As soon as the book was published an improvement in his health encouraged Green to expand it; he thus adopted the opposite tactic to most historians, proceeding from a summary towards a full exposition. Still rather confusingly known as *A Short History*, it was republished in four volumes, 1877–80, and he at once began to expand it again, this time, he said, 'for historians'. The first volume, *The Making of England*, which appeared in 1881, only proceeded as far as the reign of Egbert, in the ninth century, but it was praised for its pioneer use of archaeological material, and its success in imposing a coherent narrative on what had previously been confusion. How long this could have gone on it is difficult to say. He had married in 1877, and his wife, Alice Stopford, an intelligent and attractive Irishwoman, daughter of the archdeacon of Meath, was of considerable assistance to him. But the deeper he dug into English history, the greater the handicap imposed by his ignorance of foreign languages. His verbal memory was poor, and though he travelled so much in Italy and France, he scarcely knew enough of the native languages to order a dinner or buy a railway ticket.[53] He was also one of the last of the great independents who eschewed the use of manuscript material, and he was heavily dependent even on textbooks like Stubbs's *Charters*. Embarking on the reign of Edward II, for his *Short History*, he told Freeman that he felt like stating: 'All further remarks on the English Constitution are adjourned until Mr Stubbs issues more documents.' One of Green's coy little jokes, of course, but it had an element of truth. In his last days he talked of writing a history of the last seventy or eighty years, and this might have been a more practical proposition.[54]

However this may be, on an ill-advised visit to Egypt in 1881 he contracted an infection which he could not throw off. He died in March 1883, aged forty-six. Alice Stopford Green brought out his next volume, *The Conquest of England* (up to 1085), in December of that year, and went on in the course of a long widowhood – she died in 1929 – to establish an independent reputation as a historian, notably with her *Town Life in the Fifteenth Century* (1894), an extension of her husband's early work in urban history. In the 1890s she presided over one of the most distinguished salons in London, but early in the new century she became an ardent convert to Home Rule, and *The Making of Ireland* (1908) was not only a pioneer contribution to Irish history but a partisan statement in the great debate. She was a close friend of Casement's, and after the Easter Rebellion of 1916 she forsook London for Dublin, where she was one of the first of de Valera's nominees to the Irish Senate in 1922. She published her last book, *A History of the Irish State to 1014*, in 1925, at the age of seventy-eight.[55]

Meanwhile the fact that Green's *Short History*, avowedly written for a popular audience and by a man with no university connexions, should have been a recommended book for the Oxford School of Modern History in the 1880s demonstrates the weakness of history as an academic study. It was not an exclusively English problem. In 1876 we find Georges Monod lamenting that France had not adopted the German university system:

> 'We have gained perhaps in originality, and at least in literary form; but we have lost in scientific utility. Almost all our historians are auto-didacts; they have had no masters, and they have raised no pupils. They impose on history the stamp of their own temperament or personality; they are commonly – even the most learned of them – litterateurs before they are scholars'.[56]

Certainly this was true of contemporary England; in so far as 'professional historians' existed at all, they were gentlemen of private means, like Freeman, Stanhope and Acton, or working journalists like Froude and Green. All the regius professors up to the end of the century, with the exception of Seeley and possibly Stubbs, fell into one or the other of these categories. Indeed, the headquarters of the profession was in London; there the Royal Historical Society was founded in 1868 and the *English Historical Review* in 1886. (In the same way the Royal Institution was still the headquarters of experimental science.) It was not until 1922 that the universities produced an equivalent society and an equivalent periodical, in the shape of the Cambridge Historical Society and the *Cambridge Historical Journal*.

As for the teaching of history in the universities, there was in the beginning an acute shortage of teaching personnel, and young tutors educated in the classics had to be hastily retrained. This intensified the air of amateurism which prevailed, and made it difficult to establish standards. In the early years of the School of Jurisprudence and Modern History men like Stanhope, Freeman and even J.R. Green had to be called upon to act as external examiners.* The subject itself was impalpable. As R.W. Southern puts it: 'history had attained academic status on a wave of opposition to theological dogmatism and impatience with ancient restrictions, without anyone being clear whether the subject had a method, or a public, or indeed whether it was a recognised subject at all'. J.R. Green remarked at the time that: 'it was looked on as no special or definite study, but as part of that general mass of things, which every gentleman should know'.[57]

Initially the problems were disguised by the paucity of the numbers involved. For one thing, the pass degree retained its popularity at least for another generation; of all the students who matriculated at Cambridge between 1851 and 1906, one third took the pass degree and a quarter no degree at all. It was not until 1885 that the honours candidates overtook the 'pollmen' (or 'hoi polloi'), and in 1903 they still only comprised 53 per cent of the total number of graduates in all disciplines; in 1913, 62 per cent.[58] The History Tripos had a shaky start, with only ten graduates in 1875; by 1878 the total had risen to nineteen, but the following year it slumped to six, and it did not pass the nineteen mark again until 1884, when there twenty-five. Numbers continued to fluctuate quite arbitrarily; in 1899 there were still only forty-five graduands, and in 1900, for the first Part II, thirty-nine. However, by this time history was making steady inroads on the classics (mathematics now being the preserve of the natural scientists) as an appropriate discipline for those intending to make a career in the professions, the armed services, politics, business and sometimes the Church. With the new century numbers steadily rose, reaching three figures in 1910, with 101.†

At Oxford the figures were more promising; in 1872 only twelve men graduated in the new School of Modern History, but by 1900 there were 128 men and 17 women, considerably in advance of the equivalent numbers at Cambridge. But this only increased the strain on a tutorial system previously geared to classics and mathematics; men like Mandell Creighton took the final Schools one term and were teaching for it the next. On paper the situation was acceptable; the overall number of tutors increased by 25 per cent between 1877 and 1900, while over the same period matriculations only rose by 10 per cent. But much of this tutorial increase was in the natural sciences, and the institution in 1877 of the Common University Fund for the provision of teaching officers, financed by a levy on the colleges, merely meant

---

* This was before Freeman was appointed to a chair; he examined in 1857–8 and 1863–4, and in the single School of Modern History in 1873. J.R. Green was examiner in 1872.

† The striking thing about the Cambridge figures is the number of women enrolled. They were first admitted in 1881, when they numbered two out of eight; in 1899, the last year of the undivided Tripos, there were sixteen out of forty-five. Over the period between, the average percentage of women was 27.3.

a decrease in the amount of money available for college tutors at a time when the income of most colleges had been reduced by the Agricultural Depression. This even affected the income of endowed chairs; in 1894 York Powell found that Oriel College's inability to make its full contribution had reduced his stipend as regius professor from a notional £900 to about £600.[59]

Nor were the CUF appointments in history calculated to lighten the burden of day-to-day teaching. The first appointment was a reader in geography, in 1887, followed two years later by a reader in Russian (both allocated to modern history); and lectureships in medieval palaeography (1890) and diplomatic (1896) were of more interest to research students. A readership in Foreign (i.e., European) History in 1884 expired with the first holder four years later, and was not renewed until 1902, and then as a lectureship. The task of teaching for the Schools still fell mainly on the college tutors, a class whose status and expectations had changed dramatically now that they were allowed to marry and could therefore make a permanent career in academic life. Unfortunately, academic advancement was already to a great extent linked with research and writing, for which a tutor's teaching duties left him little time. The contrasting careers of A. L. Smith and Mandell Creighton exemplify the dilemma faced by able young historians in late Victorian Oxford.

Smith was appointed to a lectureship in modern history at Balliol in 1879 and a fellowship in 1882. He was one of the most successful teachers of his generation, and he must share with the great Benjamin Jowett the credit for Balliol's academic pre-eminence. But he never found the time for much research, so he could never compete for the professorship on which he had set his sights as a young man. Eventually, in 1916, he was elected Master of Balliol, which was to him no doubt a more than adequate compensation. He died in 1924.

In contrast the young Mandell Creighton, already senior tutor and dean of Merton, resigned in 1874 and took the college living of Embleton, in Northumberland. He had once been scathing enough with those of his colleagues – notably Mark Pattison of Lincoln – who had been converted by visits to Germany, and now wanted to make of Oxford an institution dedicated to learning and research:

'Mark Pattison is undoubtedly a researcher, so are we all; but one Essay and Review* and one edition of Pope's "Essay on Man" scarcely justify to the philistine a large endowment; nor can it be argued that abject poverty and hard work have prevented production. We live in days when we have to prove to our countrymen the value of knowledge, and we don't do it.

* The reference is to the controversial symposium *Essays and Reviews*, published in 1860.

The scientific men are always justifying their existence; but Jowett's crib to Plato and Fowler's *Deductive Logic* don't move the human heart very deeply'.

Brave words, but by 1874 he had come to realize that 'literary application and tutoring don't run side by side'. He no longer saw any prospect of writing anything of significance at Oxford, for all its research facilities. 'The tendency of Oxford', he wrote, 'is to make me a teaching drudge, and prevent me from being a literary student'; he felt that he was subject to 'mental dissipation'. The gamble payed off. At Embleton he wrote the first two volumes of his *History of the Papacy*, and in 1884 he was elected to a Cambridge chair. In 1890 he left for an episcopal career which was to take him to the see of London. He died prematurely in 1901, but alongside his career A. L. Smith's seems undistinguished and even parochial.[60]

The professors might have been expected to lend more assistance than they did, though they were barred from direct college teaching. But at Oxford they were viewed with suspicion from the beginning, especially by the tutors, who regarded them as invaders intent on taking control of the whole system, like their counterparts in Germany. The well-meaning intervention of Halford Vaughan and Goldwin Smith, and some of Stubbs's darker utterances, made things worse. The whole institution of the professoriate was regarded as un-English, and it is remarkable how rarely men like Stubbs and Creighton were addressed, or referred to, by their proper title; it was always 'Mr Creighton' or 'Dr Stubbs'. (Freeman in fact said that he did not care what people called him as long as they did not call him 'Professor Freeman'.) This is probably why the number of history professors increased so slowly, despite the recommendations of the Royal Commission of 1852, which by 1900 had boosted the overall number of professors in the university from 77 to 131. There was already a chair of ecclesiastical history, established in 1839, but it was located in the Faculty of Theology and combined with a canonry at Christ Church. The Chichele professorship of modern history was finally created in 1862, by the suppression of ten minor fellowships at All Souls', but the next chair, in colonial history, had to wait until 1909, and then it was privately endowed by the industrialist Alfred Beit. In the same year All Souls' was plundered again to finance a chair in military history, but that was all.

So, for much of the later nineteenth century there were only two professors of modern history, and they remained an excrescence on the Oxford teaching system, a fact emphasized by the habit of Freeman and Froude of lecturing on topics quite unconnected with the syllabus. Many believed on principle that this was right; a professor's function was not to teach but to write. This was very firmly Mandell Creighton's view as senior tutor of Merton, and his conduct as a Cambridge professor was consistent with it. He refused to lecture *for* the Tripos, though he was willing to offer courses which fell *within* the syllabus, and in his inaugural lecture he said: 'The most powerful influence that [a professor] can exert is the example of a life devoted to the pursuit of knowledge.'[61] But some professors were anxious to engage in direct teaching, and Goldwin Smith gave this as the main reason for his resignation. In 1868, on his appointment to Cornell, he wrote:

'The high education of all those who are to enter [the professions] is likely to promote learning and science much more than the books occasionally written by the holders of sinecure preferment. It is easy to exaggerate the service done by writing a single book as compared with that done by increasing the general intelligence through the effective discharge of educational duties'.[62]

This was all very well, but even Halford Vaughan, whose lectures, perhaps because of his contemporary notoriety, were quite popular, found it difficult to adapt them to what was at this stage a very elementary syllabus in English history, taught almost by rote. Very few of his audience were undergraduates, and still fewer went on to take honours. In 1861 the repeal of the regulation which required all graduands to produce a certificate of attendance at a minimum number of professorial lectures, though not necessarily in any relevant discipline, removed another important incentive to casual attendance.[63] Even Stubbs, who examined regularly in the Schools, and whose books during the latter part of his tenure were virtually set texts, found it difficult to attract an audience. He said himself:

'I have sometimes felt a little hurt that, after preparing and advertising a good course of lectures ... I have had to deliver them to two or three listless men; sometimes I have felt hurt that in the combined lecture list, when it appeared, I found the junior assistant tutor advertising a course on the same subject or at the very same hours as my own'.

Charles Mallett records that as a history student at Balliol in the 1870s he was never advised to attend Stubbs's lectures, though he rather ingenuously adds that those who did so on their own initiative included Horace Round, Tout, Firth and Lane Poole.[64]

Undoubtedly this reflected a certain jealousy and animosity on the part of the college tutors, exacerbated by Freeman's abrasive personality and Froude's dubious reputation. Charles Oman, rather cattily reviewing recent regius professors, says that Froude 'lectured brilliantly to a North Oxford audience, mainly ladies, so his case was exceptional'; but another tutor, Marriott, gratefully acknowledged that Froude 'gave every encouragement to us younger men', and he thought his lectures were 'models of their kind'.[65]

As for Stubbs, it may well be true that many of his lectures were above the heads of the normal undergraduate, but his obstracization is still puzzling. After all, he moulded the greater part of the Oxford history syllabus, almost single-handed, into the form it retained until the 1960s. His volume of charters, in the words of David Knowles, 'provided a textbook comparable, *mutatis mutandis*, to such classical works as Gratian's *Decretum*', and his *Constitutional History* was an orthodoxy in itself. Even in Cambridge its sacred volumes 'were approached in much the same spirit as that in which the youthful Brahmin draws near the Vedas':

> 'To read the first volume of Stubbs was necessary to salvation; to read the second was greatly to be desired; the third was reserved for the ambitious student who sought to accumulate merit by unnatural austerities – but between them they covered the whole ground. The lecturer lectured on Stubbs; the commentator elucidated him; the crammer boiled him down. Within those covers was to be found the final word on every controversy, and in this faith the student moved serene'.[66]

The trouble was, the greater the prestige the greater the potential power, and Stubbs in his prime posed a greater threat to the Oxford tutors than ever Firth did, because of his greater influence on what was actually being taught. It is easy to think of Stubbs as a blameless, almost saintly scholar, but he was as ambitious for power as any man – though always with the best of motives. He once said: 'We have much to do still before the History School at Oxford can take its place beside the historical schools of Paris, of Bonn, of Göttingen, or Munich, or Vienna', and it was a matter of keen regret to him that he was denied the authority freely granted to his colleagues in Europe. 'The German professors', he said, 'have the power and the right to direct the studies of their pupils, classes and individuals, to the specialised details of their own subject, not merely to general class examinations in which all the candidates are expected to show the same sort of knowledge derived from the same sort of books.' His admiration for Ranke was boundless; he was 'not only beyond all comparison the greatest historical scholar alive, but one of the very greatest historians that ever lived'.[67]

But he was making slow but sure progress, and if he had been succeeded by a scholar and an academic statesman of anything like his calibre, Oxford might well have possessed a professional school of history by the end of the century. As it was, Freeman's aggressive tactlessness and sheer political incompetence enabled the tutors to tighten their existing grip on the Oxford teaching system. About 1865 they had begun to make informal arrangements to pool their resources amongst the colleges. This was the genesis of the 'Combined Lecturing' system, and it was only natural that history should take the lead simply because its resources were so limited – at this stage there were only ten college lecturers or tutors in history across the university. The professors were soon admitted to the tutors' meetings at their own request, and when Boards of Studies were established in 1872 it was agreed that they should sit *ex officio*. However, it was also agreed that the History Board should include all professors in cognate subjects – such as Anglo-Saxon, Political Economy and International Law – and that these should be matched by an equal number of non-professors elected or coopted. Since the professors in cognate disciplines rarely attended meetings, the effect was to give the tutors a built-in majority. Nor were professors *ex officio* chairmen of the Board, as at Cambridge. Moreover, the 'Modern History Association', an informal body consisting of all the teachers of history in the university, continued to wield an unconstitutional but highly effective influence behind the scenes. An oligarchic situation was thus created which was, and is, unique in Western universities. Not only did professors not teach undergraduates except from the lecture platform, they had no natural or predetermined authority in the organization or administration of the discipline they professed.[68]

At Cambridge the tension between tutors and professors was never so acute, and the History Faculty owed much to the leadership provided by Sir John Seeley during his long tenure of the regius chair, from 1869 to 1895, followed by Lord Acton, with his tremendous extrinsic prestige.

Seeley was not an obvious choice, unless Gladstone was looking for a successor to Kingsley in Kingsley's own image. This may have been so; the prime minister greatly admired *Ecce Homo*, a controversial life of Christ which Seeley had published anonymously four years before. Otherwise Seeley was in appearance a classical scholar, a fellow of Christ's College, and since 1863 professor of Latin at King's College, London; he was currently engaged on a new edition of the First Decade of Titus Livy, published eventually in 1871.[69] When he was first offered the regius chair he demurred, saying: 'Though I have read discursively on modern history and have really given a good deal of thought to philosophies of history I have not studied a single period of modern history in the original authority'.[70]

However, once persuaded, he entered upon his new duties with vigour and decision. He at once took up residence in Cambridge all the year round – a sufficient innovation in itself – and assumed a keen interest in the teaching of his subject. His lectures were outstanding – 'Carefully prepared, epigrammatic in style, animated in delivery, attractive and stimulating from the originality, width and suggestiveness of their views' – an impression they give even in print. He held seminars for advanced students at his own home, and these too were a great success. One who attended them says:

'Seeley was witty, charming, sympathetic, entirely void of self-importance, never making ignorance an excuse for sarcasm, and under his presidency there was a great deal of serious thought given to politics in the higher sense; though pupils were often too shy to talk in the seminar itself, they did talk afterwards among themselves on the subjects there discussed'.

(Seeley himself said rather ruefully in 1884: 'As I grow older, my pupils have more respect for me, and do not question my authority as they did ten years ago, when to my delight they would hardily deny what I upheld.')[71]

Over his colleagues he wielded a similar influence, and he chaired the History Board from the inception of an independent Tripos in 1873 until his death twenty-two years later. It was rumoured later that he had not seen eye to eye with Mandell Creighton, the first incumbent of the Dixie chair in ecclesiastical history, founded in 1884. Creighton, a brilliant ex-Oxford don, an established historian and experienced academic politician, was certainly a potential rival, but his views on the teaching of history, and particularly on the importance of dissertations as against examinations, did not differ significantly from Seeley's. It was the younger tutors who opposed his rather idiosyncratic views on history, and particularly George Prothero, tutor of King's, with whom he had a public dispute in the *Cambridge Review* in 1885.

Like Freeman, Seeley regarded history as the handmaiden of politics; but unlike Freeman, he posited a direct connexion between them. His reputation as a scholar was established by his authoritative biography of Karl Stein, the brilliant statesman-administrator who rallied Prussia after her crushing defeat in 1806. He was disappointed, rather unreasonably, by its lukewarm public reception in 1878, but *The Expansion of England*, published in 1883, made him a public figure, and led eventually to a knighthood in 1894. In it he made an eloquent plea for the integration of the white colonies, or dominions, in a 'Greater Britain'; he also made one of the first attempts at an objective assessment of British rule in India. It was in fact only a transcript of two of his undergraduate lecture courses at Cambridge, but it was a runaway success. (Incidentally, it featured his most famous aphorism: 'We seem, as it were, to have conquered and peopled half the world in a fit of absence of mind.') It did not go out of print until 1956 – the year of Suez.[72] A similar course of lectures, *The Growth of British Policy*, was published shortly after his death.

Both books were working models to illustrate what he saw as the true function of history, which was 'to exhibit the general tendency of English affairs in such a way as to set us thinking about the future, and divining the destiny which is reserved for us'. To him history had no existence independently of politics, and he was very much in the business of educating an elite:

'Politics and history are only different aspects of the same study. There is a vulgar view of politics which sinks them into a mere struggle of interests and parties, and there is a foppish kind of history which aims only at literary display, which produces delightful books hovering between poetry and prose. These perversions, according to me, come from an unnatural division between the two subjects which belong to each other'.[73]

He had a particular animus against Carlyle and Macaulay, whom he tactlessly denounced as 'charlatans' in a famous encounter with the young George Trevelyan, a worshipper of the one and great-nephew to the other. In private correspondence he went further. Neither Carlyle nor Macaulay, he said, was primarily concerned with historical truth; instead they were 'bent upon producing an effect, upon interesting and thrilling the reader'. 'To my mind', he went on, 'these two men may be expected to be remembered some day as representing an extraordinary aberration in the English mind, an extraordinary misconception of the nature of history.'[74]

Nor did he have any patience with those who sought to recreate past conditions and assess historical events in relation to them. Since history's only proper function was to provide models for present conduct, it must be viewed strictly from the standpoint of the present day. 'It seems to be the ambition of our historians', he grumbled,

'to estimate the American Revolution just as they would have done had they been Members of Parliament at the time of the administration of Lord North. Instead of trying to give the philosophy of it and to assign to the event its due importance in the history of the world, they seem always to be making up their minds how it would have been their duty to vote at this stage of the proceedings or that ... I call this a newspaper view of affairs'.[75]

In particular he firmly rejected the idea of the continuity of English political parties; the idea that the present political situation was 'a transient phase of an eternal and necessary conflict between two different classes of men' could even be dangerous.[76] And he had even less patience with putative social historians like J. R. Green. He told his students categorically:

'History is not concerned with individuals except in their capacity as members of a state. That a man in England makes a scientific discovery or paints a picture is not in itself an event in the history of England. Individuals are important in history in proportion not to their intrinsic merit, but to their relation to the state. Socrates was a much greater man than Cleon, but Cleon has a much greater space in Thucydides. Newton was a greater man than Harley, yet it is Harley, not Newton, who fixes the attention of the historian of the reign of Queen Anne'.[77]

The first Tripos syllabus, drawn up in 1873, obviously reflected his views, and the intervention from Manchester of Adolphus William Ward was repulsed. (Cynics labelled Ward's scheme 'Facts without Thought', and Seeley's 'Thought without Facts'.) Candidates took 'Outlines of English History' (one paper), and a paper each on three 'special subjects', though these were more of the nature of 'special periods': in 1884, for instance, they were 'Greek History 510-404 B.C.', 'Italian History 1250-1494' and 'English History 1603-60' (taught by Seeley himself). The exam questions were almost entirely factual, and would be considered more appropriate today to GCE 'A'-level, or even 'O'-level.[78] But it was probably assumed that a candidate's powers of analysis and discussion would be tested in the remaining papers, which were 'Political Philosophy and Jurisprudence', 'Constitutional Law', 'Political Economy and Economic History' and 'International Law'. In contrast the Honours School at Oxford featured ten papers: four on the political and constitutional history of England up to 1848, two on a selected period of European history, two on a special subject studied through original sources, one on politics and economics and another on geography.[79]

But the shape of the Cambridge syllabus was not dictated by Seeley alone; Cambridge was slower than Oxford to divorce Law from History, and the Board which drew up the new Tripos regulations included the regius professor of civil law, the Whewell professor of international law and the professor of political economy; in 1888 they were joined by F.W. Maitland, as Downing professor of the laws of England. Moreover, another thing Seeley shared with Freeman was an indifference to, even a contempt for, public examinations. In 1885, in response to Prothero's proposals for Tripos reform, he wrote an article for the *Cambridge Review* pointing out that in more enlightened countries, like France and Germany, such competitive examinations were 'not much valued, or thought particularly appropriate to history'. 'I myself', he said grandly, 'have always regarded the Tripos as a thing which does not concern me and which might conceivably, though it has not actually done so, mar the effectiveness of my teaching.' The remedy was to introduce 'more vitality, not more artificial machinery':

> 'We should study to get the ablest lecturers, that these lecturers should lecture as well as possible, that they should produce more original work, and for this purpose should not allow themselves to be hampered by the Tripos, and that, further, the best students of each year should be encouraged to write dissertations involving original research'.[80]

He wanted to build up 'an aristocracy of students', who as graduates would support the professional historians, and he dreaded the emergence of a bastard history, 'wholly unprogressive, and loitering forever about the rudiments of the subject, which it would study to make palatable to the public by the relishes so well known to literary men'.[81]

Prothero was appalled – 'It is just because of Professor Seeley's influence and reputation that I most warmly regret the position he has taken up' – but the Tripos reforms of 1885 embodied many of his proposals, though Seeley did manage to frustrate his strange idea of subjecting students to two papers on 'Universal History'. The special subjects were deepened and strengthened, and tied to original sources, as at Oxford, though the introduction of under-graduate dissertations was delayed (until 1965). A candidate for honours had to take two papers on English constitutional history, one on English economic history, one on political science and two on his special subject. He then had the option of enrolling for a second special subject or for two further papers, on political economy and international law.[82] Acton on his arrival disowned any wish to change a syllabus with which he was not closely acquainted, but the introduction of three papers on European history in 1897 must have owed something to his influence or perhaps his very presence. (Oscar Browning of King's rather gratuitously observed that Seeley had always opposed the study of European history, which was best left to 'the École Normale, Victoria University [Manchester] and the inferior universities of Germany'.) The divi-sion of the Tripos into two parts was generally accepted; the only dispute was over which subjects should be allocated to each part.[83]

On Acton's death in 1902 the Conservative prime minister, Arthur Balfour, offered the regius chair to Maitland, who declined it; partly on grounds of ill-health, but partly because he was not prepared to 'profess' the subject in general.[84] Balfour's choice then fell on John Bagnell Bury, an alumnus of Trinity College, Dublin, where he was then professor of Greek. The two men had presumably met when Balfour was Chief Secretary in Ireland. Bury was the first professor of history in either university who was not a graduate of that university, and the first who was a specialist in ancient history, but it was a highly successful experiment. He pioneered the study of Byzantine history in this country, and wrote two authoritative studies of the Later Roman Empire; he also published, between 1896 and 1900, what is still the definitive, scholarly edition of Gibbon's *Decline and Fall*. He was one of the few regius professors apart from Acton ever to enjoy a European reputation, and he was not afraid to give leadership to the profession.

It is often supposed that his famous inaugural lecture on 'The Science of History', delivered on 26 January 1903, burst like a thunderclap on an astonished world. Yet even at Cambridge the feeling had been growing for at least twenty years that history was a science and ought to be taught in a scientific way. Seeley had taken it for granted – 'I need hardly say that it is as a department of science rather than a branch of poetry that we study history at Cambridge.' Creighton in his inaugural lecture in 1884 had also called for the encouragement of research: 'The highest result of a professor's labours would be the formation of a small class of those who were willing to prolong their university course, that they might study methods of research, that they might begin some work which would be capable of expansion into a worthy contribution to historical literature.' At Cambridge and at Oxford such postgraduate students were emerging, and in 1885 Creighton insisted that the major university prizes in history, the Prince Consort and the Thirlwall, should be awarded for a dissertation, which would be published by the University Press.[85] In 1895 Oxford and Cambridge had both discussed the introduction of research degrees; Cambridge hung back, but Oxford established the Bachelor of Letters (B.Litt.). York Powell, who was very far from being a radical, had spoken of the relationship between history, science and literature in much the same terms as Bury was to use,* and since 1899 Adolphus William Ward and George Prothero – no firebrands they – had been trying to persuade the Royal Historical Society to found a postgraduate training school in history. Prothero laboured this theme in his first presidential address to the Society in February 1902, and he may have faced apathy but certainly not opposition.[86]

Thus the furore roused by Bury's lecture must be taken as a reflection of his personal eminence, and the eminence of the chair he held after the tenure of Seeley and Acton. His central message was that historical research was not a luxury but a necessity; it was 'the highest duty of universities', and should be supported not only by generous private benefactions, as in England and America, but by public funds, as in Europe.[87] Unfortunately, this comparatively innocent recommendation was tainted by his abuse of the word 'science'. He began by arguing that history was not a branch of literature, it was 'a science, no less and no more', and he repeated this challenging phrase in his peroration – history, he said, might 'supply material for literary art or philosophical speculation', but in its essentials it was 'simply a science, no less and no more'.

Poor Bury, he did not express himself very well. All he seems to have meant was that history should be scientific in its approach to evidence and in its handling of sources, that it should employ the rigorous techniques in which he himself had been trained as a philologist and an ancient historian.[88] These rules observed, the subsequent presentation could be as literary as anyone could desire, provided the truth was not obscured, and he had a good word for Macaulay and even Treitschke. He freely admitted that if all the sources available to Tacitus were available to us, his *Annals* 'would remain to the furthest verge of time a monument of the highest significance, in its treatment,

* See p. 178 below.

its method and its outlook, for the history of the age in which he lived'.[89]
Moreover, on a visit to America the following year he clarified his position
further in an address he delivered to a Congress of Arts and Sciences at St
Louis. On this occasion he said:

> 'The interpretation of history that shall be more than a collection of
> plausible labels must grasp the vital process, perceive the breath and
> motion, detect the undercurrents, trace the windings, discern the fore-
> shadowings, see the ideas travelling underground, discover how the spiritual
> forces are poised and aimed, determine how the motives conspire and
> interact'.

This does not sound like a recipe for scientific history.[90]

The truth is, history had been bedevilled by scientific pretensions ever since
Buckle. By 1900 there is no doubt that spokesmen for the historical profession
like Bury were tempted to stress the scientific aspect of history, not only in
order to meet the intellectual challenge of the natural sciences, but to compete
with them for limited financial resources. In contemporary France such
competition was naked and unashamed. As Pierre Leguay sarcastically remarked: 'While the "barbarians" have no love for the humanities, they have
a superstitious respect for science. Hence, in order to save themselves, the
humanities will have to be disguised or transformed into sciences.'[91] It is this
which led to the spurious designation 'the social sciences', under which history
is still sometimes placed, especially in America. But even today these 'sciences'
are at a disadvantage in the face of a sceptical public because their methods
are often intuitional, their aims difficult to define and their achievements often
at variance with them. History has proved the stronger in the twentieth
century when it has disembarked from this dubious *galère*.

But it seems that it was Bury's attempt to divorce history from literature
which gave most offence. It provoked a celebrated riposte from G. M. Trevelyan in the *Independent Review*, subsequently republished in bowdlerized
form. It influenced Trevelyan's decision to resign his fellowship at Trinity in
the summer of 1903 and leave Cambridge, not to return until 1927, as Bury's
successor. Less well publicized, but equally cogent, was Prothero's last presidential address to the Royal Historical Society, in February 1905, in which
he said:

> 'A well-written book is a work of art; and the writing of history partakes at
> least as much of art as of science. If it is said that history is science, I reply
> that history is *not* science, and never can be science in the proper sense of
> that word – the sense that applies to astronomy, to physics or to biology –
> the sense that differentiates science from knowledge. I grant that the preli-

minary processes are scientific, or rather semi-scientific, for absolutely scientific they cannot be; . . . but in compacting these results into a finished whole, in laying them before the reader, we pass into another field – the field of art'.[92]

This reaction, perpetuated by Trevelyan, was to have unfortunate results. The idea was fostered in the public mind, and in the minds of many academics, that the history produced in universities was dull and dry, and no history was worthwhile which did not have pretensions to be considered as literature. This has put some of Trevelyan's devotees, who lack even his modest literary gifts, to peculiar straits.

However, at Cambridge itself Bury's inaugural was a nine days' wonder, and such dissension as it provoked was comparatively decorous. His leadership of the History Faculty was effortlessly maintained until his health broke down in the early 1920s. In contrast, Firth's inaugural at Oxford in 1904 provoked a public uproar which reverberated for years and weakened professorial authority still further.

The truth is, none of the nineteenth-century Oxford professors had provided the kind of leadership exerted at Cambridge by Seeley, Creighton, Acton and Bury. Stubbs had complained but done little; Freeman had offended by his eccentricity and appalling manners, Froude by his very presence; and the Chichele chair of modern history had been sterilized for more than a generation by a clownish first appointment in 1862. Montague Burrows, who was preferred to Freeman, Froude and Stubbs, was a career naval officer who forsook the sea at the age of thirty-three and came up to Oxford on half-pay. He took a first in classics in 1856, astonishing even himself, and went on to take another in jurisprudence and modern history the following year. (He was thus the first professor of history to hold a degree in that subject.) He was not elected to a fellowship, but he built up a considerable reputation as a private coach for the Schools, and his handbook to cramming, *Pass or Class*, was a bestseller. The electors were probably influenced by his proven capacity as a teacher and his conservative high churchmanship. He lectured conscientiously and published a few books, none of them of any academic distinction.[93] Unfortunately for the Oxford History School he lived to a great age, though Charles Oman was appointed his deputy and coadjutor in 1900.

However, Froude's successor in the regius chair in 1894 was only slightly less bizarre. Rosebery offered it to S.R. Gardiner, but he refused lest it impede his research. It appears that the university, informally consulted, then plumped for Frederick York Powell, a well-known Oxford 'character' who was universally liked, or at least, not disliked. So little was he expecting such an offer that he mistook the prime minister's letter for a tradesman's bill and parked it unopened behind the clock until the patronage secretary made discreet inquiries.[94] He was a tutor in law at Christ Church with strong literary interests, particularly in the Icelandic sagas; his publications in history consisted of a couple of school textbooks. Early in his career he had been given a trial as a history tutor at Trinity, but because of complaints from the undergraduates he had not been kept on; according to one student, he was 'the worst lecturer in Oxford, and quite possibly in the world'. Even his inaugural lecture, lasting only half an hour, baffled his audience; it was never printed, but Charles Oman described it as 'a sympathetic and suggestive torso'. His appointment was a disaster, and his only service to the university was to die comparatively young, aged fifty-four, in 1904. Even Oman, a stauch Oxford loyalist if ever there was one, could find nothing much to say in his favour. Powell, he said, spent most of his time 'browsing on miscellaneous literature'; he was a 'confirmed potterer', who was 'wont to indulge in casual talk' and call it 'informal instruction'. 'At weekends he vanished to London, where he had a wife whom no one had seen.'[95]

However, even this rather derisory figure was aware of the importance of research. In his truncated inaugural he called for the quicker and more efficient cataloguing of the state papers, and as a professor he gave intensive if rather eccentric classes on sources. In a preface he wrote for the English edition of Langlois and Seignobos's *Introduction to the Study of History* in 1898 he renewed his plea for the expansion of record facilities in England, and added: 'History must be worked at in a scientific spirit, as biology or chemistry is worked at.'[96] In fact, he went on record more than once to this effect, with a dogmatism equal to Bury's, but he was usually canny enough to make such pronouncements well away from Oxford. In an address at University College, Bangor, for instance, in June 1902, he used words which pre-echoed Bury's inaugural at Cambridge six months later: 'I confess I do not look on history as a branch of literature or as a province of ethics, but as a branch of science dealing with man under political and social and economic conditions, and my conception of history makes it the necessary complement to biology and anthropology'; and in an unpublished memoir on Gardiner written earlier in the same year he said: 'History is not a matter of beautiful expression but of absolute science, whose results are attained by careful observation, correct reasoning, and proper methods of investigation.'[97] So a new spirit was stirring, even in Oxford, and if Firth's inaugural lecture gave offence, as it clearly did, the fault lay in the occasion, the manner and the man.

Charles Harding Firth, it was once remarked, had only three disadvantages, 'bad health, a private income and a special subject'. His father was a director of the Sheffield armaments firm of Thomas Firth & Sons (later Thomas Firth & John Brown), and his uncle Mark Firth, the head of the firm, was the founder of Firth College, later the University of Sheffield. He went up to New College in 1875, won a Brackenbury scholarship to Balliol the following year, the Stanhope Essay Prize in 1877 and a first in modern history in 1878. He lectured at Firth College for a while, then settled privately at Oxford, where he became a disciple of S. R. Gardiner. He made his name with the publication of *Oliver Cromwell and the Rule of the Puritans in England* in 1900, and in 1901 he delivered a brilliant series of Ford Lectures, published the following year as *Cromwell's Army**. His ample private means made him independent of the university, and though he was elected to a history lectureship at Pembroke College in 1887 he resigned in 1893 on the plea of ill-health. Clearly he was regarded even in the 1890s as a leading spokesman of the 'research party' as against the 'teachers', and Balfour's decision to offer him the regius chair on York Powell's death was a calculated move.

In these circumstances his inaugural lecture, *A Plea for the Historical Teaching of History*, which he delivered on 9 November 1904, was even more tactless than Bury's. He declared that the history syllabus, as it stood, was 'an excellent training for journalists', and little else. Certainly it had nothing to offer those who wished to undertake research, and he doubted if the university had the staff capable of teaching them, though the training of such men was the most important function of any school of history. His remark that in the appointment of college tutors, 'after a man's place in the class list the social gift called "getting on with the men" is the qualification that counts most' gave great offence, and his subsequent attempts to reconstrue it were useless. The tutors organized a counter-manifesto, which was signed by highly reputable historians like H.A.L. Fisher, and though the public exchanges which followed were urbane enough, some colleges at least imposed a boycott on his lectures, which may have lasted into the 1920s.[98] The dispute became 'official' when Charles Oman, who had at last succeeded Burrows in the Chichele chair, used his own inaugural lecture, on 7 February 1906, to mount a considered reply.

It is a pity that Oman's inaugural has been overshadowed by Firth's. Oman was an old-fashioned, self-taught Oxford don, but he had an impressive record of research and publication, especially in the field of military history,

---

* The Ford Lectures have a curious, almost casual origin. In 1870 Revd James Ford, vicar of Knavestock (Stubbs's old parish), left the university £2000 in 3% annuities to endow a chair in English history. The income proving insufficient, the university secured leave from Chancery in 1894 to divert the bequest to a lectureship. The first Ford Lecturer, in 1896, was Gardiner, the second Maitland, the third Adolphus William Ward, and the high standard thus established and since maintained has made this lectureship one of the highest honours in the profession.

and he could not be accused of jealousy or special pleading. He began by pointing out, rather sharply, that none of the regius professors for the past forty years had had any significant experience of university teaching prior to their appointment, and many of them had been downright hostile to those who had. As for Firth, he had 'shared with Freeman and Froude the privilege of working when and how he pleased, except for the short time during which he took the history work of a college where history men are few and far between'.

But, these pleasantries apart, his answer to Firth is more cogent than is usually allowed. Because Firth backed research, and because research is usually assumed to be 'a good thing', we place him on the side of the angels. But at that time and in that place he was obviously wrong, and his conduct embarrassed even his friends, like Reginald Lane Poole, and his younger admirers, like J.C. Masterman and J.A.R. Marriott. Oman rebutted his argument that the School of Modern History did little for 'the exceptional man who wishes to study history for its own sake'; it had done a great deal for him, though under the old regulations he had only studied history for a year – and he could have added that it had presumably done a great deal for Firth, too. He reminded him that out of about 150 men reading history in any given year only ten or twelve had any intention of going on to do research; the rest would be embarking on careers of one kind or another for which a training in research technique was quite irrelevant. He agreed that the present syllabus was not perfect; too much attention, he said, was paid to 'early constitutional antiquities', and there was a need for more European history and more training in foreign languages. As for Firth's strictures on the college tutors, Oman did not entirely reject them, but he pointed out that research ability was not always associated with teaching ability, and in some instances they had been spectacularly disassociated.[99]

Firth continued to enjoy a career of the highest distinction, though after 1904 his published output was slight.* He was knighted in 1922 and resigned three years later at the age of sixty-eight, though he lived until 1936. He supervised many postgraduate students for the B.Litt. and later for the D.Phil., whose institution in 1917 he always regarded as his greatest triumph; if most of these research students had taken their first degrees elsewhere, this was a common, and healthy, Oxford phenomenon, and he was probably wrong to see it as a slight on him. However, it was said that none of his pupils, even the brilliant Godfrey Davies, could obtain a teaching post at Oxford. In 1908, on his insistence, the regulations were amended so as to allow a candidate for the Schools to submit a thesis bearing on his special subject, but since it was an optional extra it was understandably not very popular, nor were the

* See pp. 222ff below.

courses in palaeography and diplomatic, archaeology and source materials introduced in the same year. Firth had more hard words to say of his alma mater when he addressed the delegates to the International Historical Congress which met in London in April 1913. He blamed the failure of Oxford graduates to take advantage of the postgraduate training offered them on the fact that they did not need it in order to obtain college employment. He pointed out that at Cambridge 'the production of original historical work is usually required in order to obtain a Fellowship in History, and in this respect [she] is in advance of Oxford, which contents itself with a promise to undertake such work'.[100]

No doubt Firth was right. As J.C. Masterman artlessly remarks: 'In 1926 I was already thirty-five and had written nothing whatever ... Clearly I was earmarked as a college tutor and nothing else.' But it is difficult to see what Firth gained by pointing to faults which were inherent in the system and could only be rectified by persuasion, not force. Like too many previous professors, he had tried to bully the university, and the only effect was to reduce his influence, and that of his successors. For in 1908 the Modern History Association, which continued informally to control the teaching of history and the nature of the syllabus, split into two groups, the 'inner' and the 'larger'; from the former, which was the real seat of power and influence, professors were excluded. The informal authority of the 'inner' association of tutors easily survived the creation of a Faculty of History in 1913 – another reform backed by Firth, of course – and in 1932 and 1937 Sir Maurice Powicke, the then regius professor, had to come to them to argue his case for a reorganization of the School; meetings which were 'friendly and instructive' but produced no significant change. The 'larger' and the 'inner' Associations still survive, though only as 'an interesting fossil relic of ancient convulsions'.[101]

So Oman's view on the whole prevailed; 'that the Modern History curriculum must be drawn up rather with an eye to the vast majority of men who seek in it a general liberal education, than to the small minority to whom a technical training in historiography might conceivably be more profitable'. But he did not have it all his own way, and in particular his plea for more European history was ignored. In the comprehensive reforms of 1914 the 'Previous', or first-year examination, was for the first time made historical in character, and was devoted to either medieval or modern European history, with foreign set texts in the original languages. But this only led to an elementary pass/fail examination; the degree examinations proper at the end of the third year were still overwhelmingly devoted to English history, with one paper on the whole sweep of English constitutional history, another on English political history to 1885, a third on constitutional documents either up to or since 1485, and only one paper on a limited period of 'General' history.[102] Oman got his knighthood, like Firth, but he was unwise enough to hang on to his chair until his death in 1946, aged eighty-six. Like Firth, as a professor he was automatically excluded from the 'inner' History Association, and latterly he had to take some more of Firth's medicine, too. He 'often expressed disappointment at the unreadiness of college tutors to send their men to professorial lectures'.[103]

Nevertheless, the kind of history school which Firth and Bury envisaged had already been established at Manchester by Stubbs's greatest pupil, Thomas Frederick Tout. Tout left Oxford in 1881 to take the history chair at the moribund St David's College, Lampeter. Having pulled Lampeter round the corner, in 1890 he transferred his enormous energy and administrative gifts to Owens College, Manchester, where he succeeded Adolphus William Ward, who had been appointed Principal. He did not retire until 1925, at the age of seventy. He took over from Ward the idea of the 'special period', which he had imported from Cambridge, and used it as the basis of his new syllabus when Owens College achieved its independence, first as the Victoria University, then as the University of Manchester. By 1904 there were ten such periods on offer, from which the student chose three, and they were equally distributed across the field of ancient, modern and medieval history. In the third year the student went on to take not one but two special subjects, plus a dissertation related to one of them. (The special subjects were only reduced to one after his retirement.) He even argued that the Part I, which he also adopted from Cambridge, should be a pass/fail qualifying examination, and candidates should be classified for honours on their third-year work alone, for which 'the method of study was to be that of the laboratory, and the style a cross between the rigours of a German seminar and the urbanity of an English tutorial'. Through the department passed a remarkable succession of students and apprentice historians: James Tait, Ramsay Muir, George Unwin, H.W.C. Davis, W.A. Shaw and Maurice Powicke, to mention only a few. The department steadily expanded in size, too. In 1902 there were forty-six students in the final year, taught by Tout and two lecturers. By 1912 there were 104 students, three professors and seven lecturers; by 1922, 231 students, four professors, three readers and six lecturers. It was not only one of the largest history schools in the United Kingdom, it offered 'the best introduction to the work of the practising historian that then existed'.[104]

Nor was Tout the kind to leave the ancient universities in unenlightened darkness. He gave Firth's inaugural an enthusiastic review in the *Manchester Guardian*, and in January 1906 he read a paper at Newnham College, Cambridge, calling for a greater degree of professionalism in the study of history, along the lines laid down at Manchester. He placed the greatest emphasis on the proper training of staff, in research as well as teaching. 'We have slowly realised the truth', he said, 'that it is the function of the historical professor to write books, but many can write books who are not historical professors, and some books written by professors of history are not good.' He was quite as tactless as Firth about research standards in other places, and as tactless as Oman about Oxford's obsession with medieval history. 'It is a mistake', he said, 'to insist on everybody learning all the details of Stubbs, and much evil has, I am convinced, accrued in Stubbs's own university from the excessive cult of this great book.'[105] Calculating, no doubt, that a paper delivered in a women's college would not attract the attention he wanted, he had it printed, and circulated far and wide. The response from Oxford, still immersed in the Firth *affaire*, was rather muted, but at Cambridge Bury and his supporters were enthusiastic. In 1909 Bury steered through the most comprehensive reform of the Historical Tripos to date, which fixed its main outline up to 1948 and beyond. He could not introduce a dissertation, but he transferred the special subject from Part I to Part II and relegated English history to Part I. Candidates were obliged to study the whole field of European history, medieval in Part I, modern in Part II, or vice-versa; Part II featuring two papers. It was at least established now that the two parts of the Tripos were not of equal weight, and Part II demanded a more exacting and professional approach.[106]

The Expanding Field of Learning

The voice of Manchester could no longer be ignored, and it was no longer alone. Not all the civic universities founded in this generation were equally distinguished, but their emergence, almost *en bloc*, was a startling phenomenon.[107] The University of London was started in 1825 at Gower Street, boldly flaunting its indifference to religious tests. (In these early days it was not unlike the 'free universities' which sprang up for a while in the wake of the student revolts of 1968.) The Church of England's answer was King's College, in the Strand, three years later. In 1836 the two colleges were amalgamated by royal charter, the original university becoming University College. The dean and chapter of Durham, alarmed at the encroachment of ungodliness on higher education, and acutely conscious of the danger to their princely revenues in an age of reform, promptly founded Durham University in 1837 as a residential, strictly Anglican reinforcement for Oxford and Cambridge.

There followed a trio of eponymous colleges founded by local magnates: Owens College, Manchester (1851), Mason College, Birmingham (1870), and Firth College, Sheffield (1880). (Queen's College, Birmingham, was in fact the first, in 1831, but it went bankrupt in 1867.) Starting in a modest way, they were soon able to present candidates for external degrees at London University, as were further new colleges which sprang up at Leeds, Liverpool, Reading, Bristol and Nottingham. (Nottingham College, founded in 1877, was the only truly municipal college, financed from the local rates.)

In 1880 Owens College's application for university status was turned down; instead it was refounded as the federal Victoria University, in which Liverpool College was incorporated in 1884 and the Yorkshire College, Leeds, in 1887. Firth College was refused admission, but was refounded as University College, Sheffield, in 1897. The University College of Wales at Aberystwyth was founded in 1872, followed by Cardiff (1884) and Bangor (1885), and all three were merged in 1895 as the federal University of Wales. (University College, Swansea, followed much later, in 1920.) Manchester and Liverpool became independent universities in 1903, followed by Leeds in 1904 and Sheffield in 1905. University College, Bristol, founded in 1876, also became a university in 1909. At the same time an effort was made to raise London's status from that of a mere 'examining mill', chiefly by the founding or refounding of new teaching colleges like Westfield, Bedford, Holloway and Queen Mary (then the East London College). Meanwhile further university colleges were springing up; at Exeter and Reading in 1901, and at Southampton in 1902, all of which were raised to full university status after the war, when they were joined by still more university colleges, at Leicester (1922) and Hull (1928). Moreover, the principle that all such institutions, once they were officially 'recognized', were deserving of Treasury assistance, was acknowledged as early as 1889, when the University Grants Committee was established, though not as yet under that name.

Most of these colleges began with a strong scientific bias, and they were often based on existing provincial medical schools, which presented candidates for the examinations of the Society of Apothecaries. However, they also pandered to the Victorian craving for knowledge of all kinds, and it must not be forgotten that many Oxford teachers in the humanities were sympathetic to their early struggles. For instance, Bristol College owed a great deal to the famous Benjamin Jowett of Balliol, and York Powell took a keen interest in Liverpool, Bangor and Reading; at one stage he was offered the chair of literature at Liverpool. Moreover, as soon as an institution reached the status of a university or even a university college it was incumbent on it to offer a complete educational package. So they all speedily established faculties of arts, and departments of history, and in 1906 Tout reminded his Cambridge audience that: 'There is not a university, young or old, great or small, within the three kingdoms, which has not its chair of history.'[108]

Some had little else, of course. In an era in which there was no equalization of university salaries a professor need not be an expensive investment, and Arthur Taylor's study of the Leeds history department reminds us of the very modest beginnings of such institutions. But it also reminds us of the quality of the staff it attracted; the professor at Leeds from 1897 to 1927 was A.J. Grant, whose work in modern European history soon gave him a national reputation, and he was assisted for short periods by G.M. Young and H.W.V. Temperley; John Clapham was professor of economic history 1902-8. These men soon went on to win a wider fame elsewhere, but Alexander Hamilton Thompson stayed on, and was promoted to a second chair of history in 1924.[109] And from the beginning the new universities had a considerable attraction for candidates from the state schools; for one thing, though many of their history departments stressed the need for training in modern languages, few of them demanded a knowledge of Latin, which was still a requirement for entry to Oxford or Cambridge. The number of students entering such departments of history prior to the Great War was small, but there were so many universities now that the total began to assume significance; and since they were of a class or type of student who would not in the great majority of cases have been admitted to the ancient universities they represented a net gain. In fact, the numbers matriculating in history at Oxford and Cambridge steadily increased all the while.

This brought with it many problems, and not least a shortage of books. As early as 1884 the visiting Belgian professor Paul Frédéricq had commented on the hoary antiquity of some of the set or recommended books at Oxford and Cambridge. At Cambridge students were directed to Hallam's *Constitutional History* (1828), and for the medieval period Lingard was still in use as well as Stubbs. For the eighteenth century Macaulay and Stanhope were recommended, plus 'Massey's *George III*' (actually William Nathaniel Massey's *History of England*, vol. 1 (1855), now long forgotten). For the nineteenth century there was not much besides Harriet Martineau's *History of the Thirty Years' Peace* (1849). Lingard also featured in the Oxford book lists, together with J.R. Green's *Short History*. Freeman's *Norman Conquest* was there (in selected passages), presumably in deference to the regius professor, though the inclusion of.Froude for the sixteenth century cannot have pleased Freeman. But Lingard and Froude were ultra-modern compared with Burnet's 200-year-old *History of the Reformation*, or Hallam's *View of the State of Europe in the Middle Ages* (1818). Gibbon's *Decline and Fall* was recommended for the period of European history 1272-1519.[110]

Towards the end of the century there was some provision for special subjects, which had to be taught at least in part from original sources, and Stubbs's *Select Charters* was supplemented by Prothero's *Select Statutes and Constitutional Documents of the Reigns of Elizabeth and James I* (1894, 4th edition 1913) and Gardiner's *Constitutional Documents of the Puritan Revolution* (1889, 3rd edition 1906), two seminal and enduring collections. (Gardiner's is still in print, in paperback.) Most provincial universities adopted the special subject, and Grant at Leeds even introduced a dissertation, but library provision was slender, and not all had Manchester's good fortune in being able to buy the library of a man like Freeman after his death. In 1904 Leeds University Library had less than 14,500 books, 828 of them in history.[111] So, although Tout proclaimed outline courses and 'periods' as an academic orthodoxy, most syllabus planners were driven back on them out of necessity; yet if such outline courses were to have any pretensions to degree status they would have to be taught from textbooks of a much higher standard than had so far been achieved in such school series as 'Epochs in Modern History', in which Freeman, Gardiner, Creighton and York Powell were engaged, or 'The Story of the Nations'. The *Cambridge Modern History* was one of the earliest attempts to meet this need, on a grand scale, and so successful was it that one of J.B. Bury's first tasks as regius professor was to plan the *Cambridge Medieval History*, of which the first volume appeared in 1911 (and the last in 1936). But Cambridge had left aside the history of England, and commercial publishers were not slow to fill the gap. In 1905 Longmans launched the first of a twelve-volume 'Political History of England', and with an expedition typical of publishers and authors in that era they got eleven volumes out in five years, the twelfth following in 1913. In their prospectus the editors pointed out that Lingard was still the standard complete history of England, and that it badly needed extending, supplementing and enlarging, and despite the series title they assured the reader that 'notices of religious matters and of intellectual, social and economic progress will also find place in these volumes'. It was a sound production, edited by two leading Oxford tutors, William Hunt of Trinity, who died before the series was complete, and the distinguished medieval scholar Reginald Lane Poole of Magdalen, also editor of the *English Historical Review*. Its most notable contributors were Tout, who led off in 1905 with the volume for 1216–1377 – Longmans eschewed catchpenny titles – and A.F. Pollard on the later Tudors, 1547–1603 (1910).

Meanwhile Methuen were neck and neck with Longmans. In fact, they launched their eight-volume 'History of England' in 1904 with one of the most distinguished textbooks of the century, G.M. Trevelyan's *England under the Stuarts;* the rest of the series were not so memorable, but they were all out by 1910. Both these series were republished in the 1920s, and isolated volumes are in print to this day. There is no doubt that they made a great deal of money for their authors as well as the publishers, and such textbooks were and are an important form of patronage. Charles Oman scored heavily; he wrote the fourth volume in the Longmans series, on 1377–1485, published in 1906, and moved to the other end of the Middle Ages for the first volume in the Methuen series, *England before the Norman Conquest* (1910).

Rather surprisingly, Oxford University Press, next door to one of the largest history schools in Britain, was slow to rise to the bait. It did not launch its 'Oxford History of England', edited by Sir George Clark, until 1934, and by then the increasing complexity of historical knowledge called for fourteen volumes. Its rather stately progression was interrupted by the Second World War (only six volumes had been published by 1939), and by the usual accidents attending such long-drawn-out projects; two successive authors commissioned to write the volume on George III's reign, G.S. Veitch and Richard Pares, died in the process, and it had to be completed by Steven Watson in 1960. Even then, this was not the last volume to appear.* It remains on balance the most distinguished compilation of its kind, and some volumes, such as Sir Frank Stenton's *Anglo-Saxon England*, were an important contribution to scholarship – though others, notably Basil Williams's *The Whig Supremacy 1714–1760*, were out of date when they left the press.

As any student or teacher of history knows, the process still continues, and the increasing specialization of historical studies, the emulation of publishers and the ambition of authors seem to call for a reworking of textbooks every ten years. Methuen contented themselves with commissioning a new volume from G.R. Elton in 1955 on *England under the Tudors*, but otherwise they have left their old series alone. But Longmans decided to scrap their 'Political History of England' in 1959 and launch a new ten-volume series; it is still not complete (in 1982). In 1961 Thomas Nelson launched a new eight-volume series with Christopher Hill's *Century of Revolution 1603–1714*; the other volumes have not come up to this standard. In 1977 Edward Arnold began 'A New History of England' in ten volumes, beginning at the end of the Middle Ages; six have so far appeared. Meanwhile the first paperback history of England was published in eight volumes by Pelican Books in the remarkably short space of five years (1950–55), and in 1957 the *New Cambridge Modern History* began to appear, at a rather slower rate than its predecessor; the last volume, the Atlas, appeared in 1970.†

---

* This was by E.F. Jacob, on the controversial *Fifteenth Century*, in 1961. I have left out of account A.J.P. Taylor's *English History 1914–45* (1965), which was commissioned as a late addition to the series.

† I have left out of account the *Companion*, actually the penultimate volume, which appeared in 1979. In any case, it is very much an afterthought.

This tabulation is not purposeless. This continous series of textbooks has put a stamp on historical teaching and writing in this country which calls for a more detailed consideration than we can give it here. It has also encouraged 'periodicization': the chopping up of history into neat chronological sections, which are then assumed to be naturally separate. Of course, Hume and Lingard's volume divisions alone drove a furrow through dates like 1485 and 1603, and Hume in particular has been blamed for positing a sharp break between the Middle Ages and the Early Modern era. But since then the furrow has become a trench as book after book begins with one of a limited number of hallowed dates: 1485, 1603, 1660, 1714, 1760 and so on; creating what many historians regard as a positive distortion of the historical process, though it is strange that neither 1640 nor 1688 has been singled out for this purpose.* Of course, the arrangement of university syllabuses is at least partly to blame, and it is difficult to see which came first, the chicken or the egg. In the Cambridge Tripos, imitated by many other universities, English history was divided into three sections at 1485 and 1603; elsewhere it was divided into two sections at 1603.

Nevertheless, resolute attempts have been made to break the spell. For instance, Longmans inaugurated their 'New History of England' in 1959 with a volume by Asa Briggs on *The Age of Improvement* which apparently had neither beginning nor end, though on close scrutiny it seemed to run from about 1784 to about 1867. However, the remaining titles in this series bear such familiar titles as 'The Tudor Age', 'The Stuart Age' and 'Eighteenth-Century England', and drop into familiar pigeonholes. Similarly, Arnold's 'New History of England' asserts it novelty by ending the Middle Ages in 1450, but it chops off the remainder of English history at familiar points, or very near them – 1558, 1603, 1658, 1714 and so on. But the editor of the new Fontana 'Library of English History', Geoffrey Elton, has tackled the problem with a vigour amounting almost to violence, not only hacking down the hallowed chronological divisions wherever he can, but separating state, Church and society into individual volumes. It is too early to assess this bold experiment.

So much for books. At the other end of the teaching scale the boom in university history produced a new demand for expert staff. At first these new staff were recruited from the schools, or, like R.H. Tawney, from the adult education service; the emphasis was on teaching ability. But it was soon tacitly decided that university lecturers need not be brilliant teachers, because in contrast to schoolmasters they had a voluntary and presumably committed audience. Men like Firth and Tout argued that proficiency in

---

* Except for Mark Thomson's *Constitutional History of England 1642–1801*, published in 1939, which had an eccentric terminal date too.

research was the indispensable qualification, with teaching ability, where it existed, an added bonus. However, there was no objective means of testing ability in research, other than by publication. The Master of Arts degree was used in America and in some of the civic universities as a post-graduate research degree after one or two years, but the cachet it conferred was not enough; in any case it was a first degree in Scotland, and at Oxford and Cambridge it was conferred without examination. At all universities the existing doctorates, in Letters, Science and Law, were reserved for mature scholars of proven worth and usually of advanced age. But the German universities had long ago instituted a kind of intermediate doctorate, obtainable after three years' research and the submission of a substantial dissertation; the doctorate of philosophy, or Ph.D. This had been introduced in America in 1861, at Yale, and it had made rapid progress in the universities and colleges there.

The lack of such a degree in England was increasingly felt to be a disadvantage, and some young scholars even went to Germany to acquire one. Reginald Lane Poole, for instance, took a Ph.D. at Leipzig in 1882. It was also a matter for concern that graduates from the English-speaking colonies were now being drawn to America or Germany for postgraduate work, and Americans were deterred from coming to England. These points were put when the question was officially ventilated at Oxford and Cambridge in 1894, but there was strong opposition to any adulteration of the doctorate, and even stronger opposition to any ideas emanating from Germany. Oxford agreed to institute the B.Litt. (Bachelor of Letters), awarded on the submission of a dissertation after two years' research, but Cambridge would not even agree to this; the most it would offer was a 'Certificate of Research'. However, pressure was maintained, especially by the scientists, and discussion continued up to and into the Great War. By 1916 both Oxford and Cambridge were in danger of being outmanoeuvred. In 1912 the first Congress of the Association of Universities of the British Commonwealth, meeting in London, had pressed for the adoption of the Ph.D., with strong support from the Foreign Office. A working party was set up, with delegates from Manchester, Birmingham, Leeds, Liverpool and Sheffield, which in 1917 advised acceptance of the Association's proposals, and all the civic universities at once began to incorporate the Ph.D. into their degree structure. Oxford also bowed to the inevitable, though it used the abbreviation 'D.Phil.', in accordance with its practice with other doctorates, such as 'D.Sc.' and 'D.Litt.' Cambridge still balked at the fence, however, and it was only after three years' agonized debate that it accepted the Ph.D. in 1920. Then it found itself without a subsidiary research degree and had to bring in the M.Litt. the following year.[112]

The institution of the Ph.D. had a decisive effect on research. At first it was argued that it was a training in methods and technique, and the actual results did not matter. But this pretence was almost immediately abandoned, and it soon came to be expected that a doctoral dissertation would make an original contribution to knowledge, and in fact that it should be worthy of immediate publication more or less as it stood – a requirement which was not unreasonable in the 1920s but is a source of embarrassment and equivocation today. Whether in its English form it does offer a suitable training for a university teacher is in fact questionable. The institution in America of the graduate school, beginning with Johns Hopkins at Baltimore in 1870 and subsequently spreading to all the major universities, especially in the East, was never copied in England; Firth's Oxford History Seminar in the 1920s, and even the seminars held at the Institute of Historical Research by Pollard and his successors, were at best a pale imitation. Even Tout at Manchester thought that his research students would acquire the necessary skills 'by observation, osmosis and occasional words of advice'.[113] Nor does the British Ph.D. offer a broad training in university teaching, as it does at most American universities, where the candidate takes various supplementary written examinations and offers a special period covering several centuries, sometimes two such periods, on which he is subjected to a searching oral examination conducted by a large panel of professors. In England the 'viva' has degenerated into a private discussion of the dissertation between the candidate and two highly specialized examiners.

On the other hand, the Ph.D. has never become in England what it is in America, an essential 'union card', without which it is almost impossible to find employment in higher education. However, from the beginning it was popular enough to have a discernible effect on the nature of historical research. Required to display originality, and given only three years to deploy his resources, a candidate had to dig deeper and deeper into a narrower field. The result was the fragmentation of research. This was not peculiar to doctoral work, and it arose partly from the difficulty of the remaining unworked sources, but the Ph.D. encouraged it by offering a standard means of defining, limiting and assessing small-scale pieces of research. Gone were the days when a young historian might sit down to write a history of England, or even a history of the Norman Conquest. Maurice Powicke observed in 1933:

'The range of history which any single man or woman can hope to compass has narrowed very much. I doubt if any man, dealing with any period of European or world history since the eleventh century, could write a really great book which covered more than fifty years, or, if he attempted a complete history of one country or one important aspect of social life, more than a century'.[114]

Others would blame such overspecialization on the learned journals, which are open to the classic indictment that with every year they contrive to say more and more about less and less. But the evolution of the most important of such journals, the *English Historical Review*, suggests that it was a symptom of specialization rather than a cause. It was founded in 1886 on the urging of York Powell, though typically he never contributed to it. He approached James Bryce to act as editor, and then with Acton's assistance secured the services of Mandell Creighton. Acton also attended the dinner organized by Bryce in London to launch the journal, and wrote an article on 'The German Schools of History' for the first number.[115] It was probably he who insisted that it be modelled on its existing foreign counterparts, particularly the *Historische Zeitschrift*, founded in 1859, but it took several years for it to reach the same standard.

The trouble was, in England the well-established literary reviews had already absorbed much of the market for historical writing, and as we have seen, men like Freeman, Froude and Green published extensively in them, though much of their work was only semi-scholarly. Green had first toyed with the idea of a historical review in 1867, but his health was poor and no one else wanted to edit it, only write for it.* Moreover, Green feared that it would have to bid for popularity by accepting work from borderline historians; he told Freeman: 'I fancy one of the difficulties would be what to do with the Stanleys† and the Kingsleys. If they were shut out the thing would fail. And yet, would you let them in?'[116] Presumably not, for the matter was shelved until 1876, when Macmillans raised the question again, apparently prompted by James Bryce and Adolphus William Ward, then at Manchester. But Green was still pessimistic. A 'scientific' historical periodical of the kind envisaged would be a financial failure, he thought, even if it allowed a political bias, as Ward advised. On the other hand, if it admitted articles on current problems, even in a historical setting, or 'careful and philosophical biographies of persons of contemporary eminence', it would be compromising its position with its professional readership and entering upon a contest it could not win with the other reviews, which could cover natural science, travel and literature as well as history.[117]

This problem still troubled Creighton in 1886, and he was profusely grateful

* See p. 159 above.
† This was A.P. Stanley, dean of Westminster, and previously professor of ecclesiastical history at Oxford. A fairly respectable historian, but obviously out of favour in the Freeman-Green circle.

for Acton's offer of assistance. 'The assurance of your hearty co-operation', he wrote, 'gives me hope of the success of the Review which I had not felt before. We must confess that we are not strong in historical method in England. Our work has all the advantages and all the disadvantages of amateur work. Most of the well-known persons have already said all that they have to say. You are one of the very few persons who can add any novelty. You are the only person who has a knowledge of the general European literature of the subject.'[118]

In fact, Creighton felt unequal even to drafting a statement of aims, and James Bryce wrote a short preface to the first issue. He firmly rejected the view of Freeman and Seeley that history was solely concerned with politics; but on the other hand, if it were extended to include 'everything that man has either thought or wrought' it would be unmanageable. History should therefore be regarded as 'the record of human action', and the *Review*'s main concern would be with 'states and action' – which in fact seemed to bring it perilously near Seeley's and Freeman's definitions again. It would concern itself with theology, natural science, metaphysics, language or literature 'not as independent branches of inquiry, but only in their bearing on the acts of men'. Social history and sociology were passed over in silence.

Initially editorial standards were uncertain, except in one department. From the first the book reviews were very much as they have been ever since – tight, highly professional, accurate and frank – but too many of the articles were long, discursive and even shallow. In fact, this may have been deliberate. Bryce's preface shows that he and Creighton were still looking to the same public as the established literary periodicals, and he promised that 'an effort will be made to provide in every number some articles ... which an educated man, not specially conversant with history, may read with pleasure and profit'. This meant that apart from Acton's long article on 'The German Schools of History' the first issue featured an essay by Seeley on 'The House of Bourbon', another by A.W.Ward on 'The Electress Sophia and the Hanoverian Succession', and another by Nicholas Pocock on 'The Restoration Settlement in the Church of England'. Acton was approving, though a trifle condescending. 'I congratulate you very sincerely', he told Creighton; 'the Review is solid, various, comprehensive, very instructive and sufficiently entertaining ... At least half the great names are there, and I discern the makings of a sacred band of university workers.' However, 'It comes up to the level', he went on, 'but it makes no striking discovery and does not exhibit a great new force or open a new vista.' He placed it 'between' the *Revue Historique* and the *Historische Zeitschrift*; presumably above the former but below the latter.[119]

As indeed it was. Big, sprawling articles of a narrative or descriptive nature continued to set the tone. Volume II, in 1887, included Charles Mallett on 'The Empress Theodora', little more than a general essay, and Thomas Hodgkin on 'Visigothic Spain', though Gardiner contributed a tighter, more professional piece on 'Charles I and the Earl of Glamorgan'. Acton commented: 'There is variety, and there is solidity, and there are new lights, but there is not much in the way of stimulus or surprise.' Skipping to volume V (1890), we find a long, two-part article on 'Frederick Henry, Prince of Orange' by Revd George Stevenson, another on 'Provincial Concilia from Augustus to Diocletian' – which seems rather a long haul – by E.G. Hardy, and a very strange essay, superficial and highly literary, on 'The Seven Liberal Arts', by one H. Parker. At the other extreme Charles Langlois wrote on 'The Comparative History of England and France during the Middle Ages' in five pages, and J. Theodore Bent on 'The English in the Levant' in eleven. There was some compensation in a slight but perfectly executed article by Maitland on 'Northumbrian Tenures'.

This is not the place for a full analysis of the contents of the early *EHR*, but the impression is that Creighton's editorial standards were, to put it charitably, confused. We find him soliciting an article from Gladstone, which suggests that he still regarded the *Review* as a rival to the literary monthlies, and in fact Gladstone's contribution, on 'The History of 1852-60, and Greville's Latest Journals',[120] was just the kind of direct contemporary history, built round a book review, in which *Frazer's* or the *Westminster* excelled. In 1890 he cheerfully accepted another article from Acton, though he thought it far too abstruse for his readership – 'It is of course allusive and overweighted with learning in a way which makes it unintelligible to the uninitiated.'[121] There was an immediate improvement from July 1891, when Creighton resigned in favour of his assistant editor, Lane Poole, who now shared the editorship with S.R. Gardiner, though it must be admitted that under financial pressure Creighton had already taken the decisive step, in 1889, of ceasing to pay contributors even a nominal fee. There was now no pecuniary incentive to write long articles, and well-known authors who were to some extent dependent on their literary earnings departed elsewhere, leaving the field open to the professionals. New talent at once began to emerge, or find a place. J.H. Round's great pronouncement on the introduction of knight service into England appeared in volume VI, the first under the new editorship, and volume XII (1897) featured his essay on 'Military Tenure before the Conquest'. Also in volume XII appeared a pioneering article by Basil Williams on 'The Duke of Newcastle and the Election of 1734', which first drew attention to the immense riches to be found in the Newcastle papers now in the British Museum. Gardiner resigned in 1901, but Lane Poole continued as sole editor for another twenty years, and by the time he gave way to G.N. Clark in 1921 the pattern was set. The kind of discursive, biographical, descriptive essays which had clogged the early numbers of the *Review* were all but forgotten; the *EHR*, in its depressing pale-grey covers, was concerned with the strict examination of historiographical problems, conducted with reference usually to new evidence and offering a completely new interpretation. In other words, it had become what it remains today, a trade journal written by and for the historical profession. To some extent this may reflect a change in educated public taste – as the marked decline of the literary reviews also suggests – but a thoroughly professional historian, in Lane Poole, saw the demand from his profession, and moved to meet it.

Nor had the *EHR* any rivals in the field until the emergence of the *Bulletin of the Institute of Historical Research* and the *Cambridge Historical Journal* in the early 1920s, and even then they did not feature book reviews. As for the *Transactions* of the Royal Historical Society, which predated the *EHR* by several years, they reflect the dubious beginnings of the Society itself. It was founded in 1868 as a private venture by one Dr Charles Rogers, who is described as 'a Scots Presbyterian clergyman, journalist, hymnologist and genealogist'. Though it contrived to acquire the title 'Royal' in 1872 it had a continual struggle for membership, and only succeeded in attracting a miscellany of 'clergymen and physicians, army officers and civil servants, barristers and solicitors, bank managers, journalists, engineers, teachers', plus 'a sprinkling of peers and country gentlemen'. It also sustained a number of rather sordid crises; notably the forcible expulsion of Rogers from the secretaryship in 1881 and the suicide of his successor Patrick Dove in 1894 after embezzling most of its funds. In the 1880s it managed to recruit a number of eminent historians, including Acton, Seeley, Maitland and Creighton, but they were merely the icing on a very plain cake. The *Transactions* were published annually, but since they consisted of addresses given to the Society by members they remained for the most part on an amateur level, and a proposal to merge them with the *EHR* in 1887 came to nothing. Indeed, when Bryce wrote his Preface to the *EHR* in 1886 he seemed quite unaware of the infant Society and its doings; he twice lamented the absence of any English periodical devoted to history, and expressed some surprise that 'English historians have not yet, like those of other countries, associated themselves in the establishment of any academy or other organisation'. There was a slight improvement in the 1890s, when Hubert Hall became Director, and we have already seen how G.W. Prothero, as President of the Society 1903–5, was intervening in the higher politics of the profession.* But the full rehabilitation of the *Transactions* really began with the Fourth Series in 1918, after which the ranks of the membership began to close, and the Society underwent a

* See pp. 176–7 above.

decisive organizational change, which is obvious enough in outline but difficult to trace in detail. But over the period roughly from 1900 to 1925 the
Royal Historical Society changed from a semi-recreational society catering
for cultivated amateurs with a spare-time interest in history to a fully academic organization confined to university staff and those others who could
provide evidence of professional skills by publication.[122]

But it is typical of the development of history in England that the best training
in research and writing in the late nineteenth century was provided not at the
ancient universities, nor in the great libraries and museums, but in the offices
of a commercial publisher. That remarkable enterprise the *Dictionary of
National Biography* was the brainchild of the London businessman George
Smith, managing director of Smith, Elder and Company, a shipping agency
specializing in the India trade, who also ran a successful publishing business
under the same name. He published most of the great Victorian authors at
one time or another – Trollope, Thackeray, Ruskin, Browning, George Eliot
and Charlotte Brontë – and he was the founder of the *Cornhill Magazine* and
the *Pall Mall Gazette*. In 1882 he had the idea of commissioning a new
dictionary of universal biography; but when he consulted Leslie Stephen,
editor of the *Cornhill* at this time, he was advised to limit it to British history.
Stephen was promptly appointed editor of the project, and began what seems
in retrospect a mountainous task. With the assistance of Sidney Lee, who
eventually took over from him as editor, in 1895, he drew up lists of names
for inclusion and circulated them as widely as he could for comment; commissions were then issued, and the first volume appeared in January 1885.
Almost incredibly, the subsequent volumes appeared with clockwork punc-
tuality every three months thereafter until the sixty-third and last in the
summer of 1900. The finances of the operation are mysterious. Smith reckoned at the beginning that it would cost him £36,000, or £100,000 with
interest, but that was when only forty volumes were planned. He died in 1901,
leaving the copyright to his widow, and she gave it to Oxford University, who
reprinted it in twenty-two volumes in 1909–10, the edition most commonly
used.
　　This is not the place to discuss the remarkable nature of the *DNB*, which
still makes it, with its successive supplementary volumes, an indispensable
tool for literary and historical research. More important than the high quality
of the 'stock' entries – on Elizabeth I, for instance, Cromwell or Lord Byron
– is the depth of information it provides, often available nowhere else without
extensive research, on figures of the second, third or fourth rank. And though
it was directed by men who were in no sense professional historians – Leslie
Stephen had had a short spell as a tutor at Trinity Hall, Cambridge, but there

his fame rested on his reputation as a rowing coach – it provided a hard training school for the next generation of professional historians. The entries for the seventeenth century, for instance, were written largely by Firth, Gardiner and A.W. Ward; Firth wrote 222 articles, and his thirty-one-page article on Oliver Cromwell was the longest in the *Dictionary*; in fact, he was reckoned to have contributed the equivalent of a whole volume, and Ward two-thirds of a volume. Tout's contributions also made up a volume, and so did A.F. Pollard's. Though he was already a professor of history, Tout admitted later that the *Dictionary* gave him a training he had not acquired even at the feet of Stubbs:

'Like many Oxford men of my generation, I approached historical investigation without the least training or guidance in historical method, and felt very much at a loss how to set to work. The careful and stringent regulations which [Stephen] drew up, and the brusque but kindly way in which he enforced obedience to them, constituted for many of us our first training in anything like original investigation'.

Pollard felt and expressed a similar gratitude to Leslie Stephen and Sidney Lee. He deeply regretted the closure of the *DNB* office in 1901 and the dispersal of its reference library and files, and his subsequent creation of the Institute of Historical Research must be seen in part as an effort to replace it.[123]

Indeed, Albert Frederick Pollard was to go on from the *DNB* to contribute more than any other single man or single institution to the professionalization of history in the early twentieth century.[124] He took a first in history at Oxford in 1891, but he was advised not to stand for a fellowship; instead he came to London, where he supported himself for the next ten years or so by lecturing, coaching and writing for the *DNB*. In 1900 he published his first book, *England under Protector Somerset*, followed in 1902 by a short but influential biography of Henry VIII. In 1903 he was appointed to a part-time chair in English constitutional history at University College, London, made full-time in 1907, which he held until his retirement in 1931.

In his own inaugural lecture in 1904 he responded eagerly to the challenge recently issued by Firth and Bury. But he pointed out that even the undergraduate teaching of history at London was in a parlous state. There were only two professors and one assistant lecturer at University College, a professor and a lecturer at King's, and one lecturer each at Holloway, Bedford, East London and Westfield Colleges. Nor was this surprising, since only sixteen people had graduated in history at the University since the inception of a separate degree in 1896, and ten of these had been external candidates.

The recent attempt to found a chair in memory of Mandell Creighton had been a humiliating failure, only £300 being subscribed.* He lamented that 'a population many times more numerous than that which produced the art and the literature, the science and the statesmanship of ancient Athens, a population more numerous than that which made the Roman Empire', should be so ill-served in one of the basic disciplines of the humanities. He demanded that the schools of history in the university be properly staffed, so as to attract more students; if the staff were there, the students would appear. Berlin, he reminded his audience, had six professors of modern history, Chicago seven. Bolder still, he called for a permanent school of postgraduate historical research, which would not only offer professional training to graduates of any university, but would form a headquarters and a refuge for the foreign scholars who were now flocking to the rich archives of the British Museum and the Public Record Office.

He eventually forced the university to set up a Board of Studies in History, in 1910, and he chaired it until 1923. Within twenty years he had achieved all his aims, and largely by his own unaided efforts. Given the inertia and pettiness of the academic mind, the complexity of the federal structure of London University, the competing claims of other disciplines and the peculiar planning difficulties posed by the Bloomsbury site, this is a near incredible achievement. It displayed gifts of organization, a capacity for political manoeuvre, powers of leadership, a stamina and a boldness which have taken other men to the leadership of great nations. It is the more amazing when we remember that through it all Pollard was engaged in historical research and steady publication.†

Twenty years after his inaugural, in the year 1923-4, there were 250 resident internal students at London University reading history, and there were twelve professors, ten readers and twenty-two lecturers to teach them, distributed through the various colleges. The Institute of Historical Research was founded in 1920, with the assistance of a wealthy neighbour of Pollard's at Putney, John Cecil Power, who was persuaded to give £20,000 to endow it. Pollard ensured that all its staff were paid by the university, and in 1926 successfully resisted an attempt to evict it from the Gower Street site. A library was speedily built up, other universities began to register their research students as members, and to scholars from abroad, especially America, it became a haven. The teaching of research students was organized round the graduate seminar, under one or more professors.

Nor was Pollard content with this. In 1906 he was the driving force behind

* Though by 1907 enough had been collected to fund an annual Creighton Lecture, which still continues.
† See pp. 202-5 below.

the establishment of the Historical Association, which was designed through its nationwide branches to link all teachers of history, whether in schools, colleges or universities, with each other and with the educated public. In some respects it fulfilled the original intentions of the founders of the Royal Historical Society. He persuaded Firth to serve as its first president, then Tout, and in 1916 he bought up a moribund periodical, *History*, and refounded it as a serious but not exclusively professional journal. In 1921 he also founded the *Bulletin of the Institute of Historical Research*, on more austere lines.

The Institute remains the headquarters of the profession in England, in so far as it has one at all. It keeps a national register of research students, and their topics, and of university staff. It holds the only annual conference open to all British historians, and it has strong links with the great American graduate schools. It arranges British representation on international histori-cal conferences abroad; it houses, amongst other things, the organization for the Official History of Parliament and the Victoria County History. Oxford and Cambridge have nothing like it.

Yet compared with Oxford and Cambridge its hold on the profession remains tenuous. Even after the Royal Commissions of 1926 neither Oxford nor Cambridge acquired a physical base for history; apart, that is, from the Seeley Historical Library at Cambridge. The controversial faculty building on West Road, Cambridge, was built in the 1960s; Oxford now has some history offices and a small library on Merton Street. Research seminars are infrequent, and dependent on the initiative of individuals; the professors have remained, as they were in the nineteenth century, *primi inter pares*, though rather more *primi* at Cambridge than at Oxford. Nor are they very numerous, considering the size of their faculties. At Cambridge the regius professor and the Dixie professor reigned in solitary glory until 1919, when Lord Rother-mere endowed the Vere Harmsworth chair of naval history in memory of his son, killed in the Great War. Its scope was enlarged to 'imperial and naval' in February 1939 – rather late in the day, one feels – and in 1952 it was overlapped by the Smuts chair in the history of the British Commonwealth. Otherwise, a chair in economic history was specially created for Sir John Clapham in 1928, though it was not made permanent until 1936. A chair of modern history, equivalent to the Chichele chair of modern history at Oxford, was belatedly established in 1930, and the then General Board, conscious of a gap, pronounced that 'whilst the university had no professorship of medieval history, the title of the [modern] professorship is to be inter-preted as including medieval history'.[125] The creation of a medieval chair had to wait until 1937, but even then Cambridge was ahead of Oxford; it was not until 1948 that another chair of modern history was founded at

Oxford, the Chichele chair of modern history then being rather confusingly accepted as medieval.

Nevertheless, it was Oxford and Cambridge who provided the men to staff the new civic universities in their early years, and despite the rise of the Institute in London they have never relaxed their grip. In 1980 nearly 73 per cent (116 out of 159) of professors of history at United Kingdom universities, excluding Oxford and Cambridge, held a degree from one or the other, usually a doctorate. Only 17.6 per cent (37 out of 210) of all history professors, including those at Oxford and Cambridge, held a London degree.* Also, though in the 1920s almost everyone would have agreed that Tout at Manchester and Pollard at London were the most respected and influential professors of history in Britain, their teaching and their example had singularly little effect on the syllabuses of other university history departments. All universities acknowledged the importance of the third year special subject but very few felt able to introduce the undergraduate dissertation so prized at Manchester, and those which did did not always retain it. Scarcely any were prepared to increase their teaching of European history at the expense of British history, as Pollard did at London, nor did they abandon total coverage in favour of teaching by selected 'periods', as Tout did at Manchester. In fact up to the Second World War, at least, most provincial universities were remarkably loyal to the traditions of late Victorian Oxford: whatever the cost English history must be taught in its entirety, wherever possible with the aid of original documents, and overseas history, including European history, must find a place where it could. Sir Richard Lodge and George Prothero even imposed early English constitutional history, complete with Stubbs, on the hapless Scots at Glasgow and Edinburgh.[126] This bias was to have a significant effect not only on what history was taught but on what history was written.

---

* These figures, which do not claim to be 100 per cent accurate but are roughly correct, are drawn from the annual list of teachers of history in the universities issued by the Institute ('The Green Book'). I have excluded professors of ancient history and of political thought, but I have included economic and social history and American history, which if anything gives the figures a bias towards London, certainly away from Oxford and Cambridge.

Six

• •

The Fruits of Research

When we turn from the structure of the historical profession to its function, from what it is to what it does, we are confronted by problems which stem from the very degree of specialization which has taken place over the past hundred years. No one historian can hope to explain the activities of all his colleagues in other fields or come to any reasoned judgment on them.

Nowhere is this more evident than in medieval English history, where the comparatively simple construct erected by Stubbs had been subject to modifications and reinterpretations of increasing subtlety and sophistication. The question of the exact nature of feudalism was difficult enough when it was argued eighty or ninety years ago by John Horace Round, that meticulous scholar of independent means and unamiable disposition, who lived most of his life at Brighton, whence he bombarded the profession with a series of minutely researched articles and reviews overturning many of his colleagues' most treasured assumptions. It is twice as difficult today, as a glance at the latest pronouncements on the subject, such as *The Legal Framework of English Feudalism* by S.F.C. Milsom, will show. Even the splendid Frederic William Maitland, whose career was tragically cut short by diabetes in 1906, who revolutionized the history of English law in the Middle Ages, and who was the best loved as well as the most respected English historian of the last hundred years – even his achievement is not immediately and clearly explicable. I sympathize with the scholar who said quite recently: 'Historiographers often treat it as central to their theme that Maitland's historical technique, method and purpose were unique; however, they never tell us what this uniqueness consists of.'[1] The last great attempt at a synthesis of English medieval history was by J.E. Jolliffe in 1937, in his one-volume *Constitutional History of Medieval England*, and that was not without its critics.

If we seek enlightenment on how modern historians work, we must turn to the great proving grounds of early modern history, the sixteenth century, the seventeenth and the eighteenth, where new theories are tested every generation. Here not only are the minutiae of fact often in dispute, but the broad structure, the general ideas which hold these facts together. Yet at the same time the nature of the facts and the nature of the ideas are readily and widely comprehensible.

The Tudors: Creighton to Elton

As any publisher will tell you, the Tudor monarchs remain a firm favourite with the British reading public. Froude's success suggests that this preference goes back a long way; on the other hand, as Froude's career also shows, the Tudors posed serious ethical problems for the Victorians. The character and conduct of Henry VIII were obviously a sore embarrassment to those obliged to regard him as the founder of their Church, yet many Anglicans resisted as hypocritical any attempt to rehabilitate him. To an age more conscious than ever of a Catholic Problem and a Nonconformist Presence, Queen Elizabeth's treatment of religious minorities was another grey area. Arriving at Cambridge in 1884, Mandell Creighton found it difficult to prepare a course of lectures on Church history for his new audience. 'As for the Tudors', he exclaimed, 'they are awful! I really do not think anyone ought to read the history of the sixteenth century.' He had already written a school textbook on *The Age of Elizabeth* for the 'Epochs of Modern History' series, but the more he studied the great queen the less he liked her – or as his wife puts it: 'With an increasing appreciation of the extraordinary ability of Elizabeth, he had a constantly diminishing opinion of her morals.'[2] In the short biography which he wrote after he had left academic life he pleaded that he could do no more than 'sketch a rough outline of a very complex personality, which reflected only too faithfully the perplexities of a very difficult time'.

It was not a deep book, nor was it intended to be; he used no manuscript sources, and took most of his facts from Froude. On certain questions – notably Puritanism – he was by modern standards under-informed. But his very disenchantment with his subject gives him what Elton calls 'a powerful strain of distance and independence', and makes this 'still one of the best portraits of this difficult monarch ever painted'.[3] This is perhaps exaggerated; Creighton's *Elizabeth* is an interesting example of a subject gradually over-mastering the author, and after 1588, when the restraining arm of Froude fell away, his 'distance and independence' sharply declines. His view of Elizabeth as a woman of the future – 'Round her, with all her faults, the England which we know grew into the consciousness of its destiny' – is profoundly whiggish. He did his gallant best to rationalize her relations with men in a way which illustrates his hesitant but commonsense approach:

'She was surrounded by men representative of English life; they must be made to fall into line, and any method which served this purpose was good. Above all things she must impose her will equally on all. Personally, she was attracted by physical endowments, and let herself go in accordance with her feelings up to a certain point. But she was both intellectually and emotionally cold'.

Yet in his conclusion he abandoned all caution, and gave us that uncritical and adulatory picture which until a few years ago was to remain the twentieth-century norm:

'When it came to decisive action she fell back on her instinctive perception of what England wanted. As she could not explain this, she was driven to all sorts of devices to gain time. She could not, on the other hand, fully take her people into her confidence. It was the unconscious tendency of their capacities which she interpreted, not their actual demands. She was eliciting from them their meaning, and educating them to understand it themselves. For this purpose she must seem to govern more absolutely than she did, but on great occasions she took them into her confidence, and fired them with a high conception of the greatness of their national life'.[4]

Rather surprisingly, Creighton's unpretentious biography held the field for more than thirty years after his death, while research veered away to the earlier Tudors, under the pull of A.F. Pollard.* Deeply engaged as he was in teaching, administration and reform in the university of London, Pollard maintained an astonishing output of published work. His first book, *England under Protector Somerset*, in 1900, was a 'revisionist' interpretation of the policies of 'The Good Duke' which set him firmly in the centre of the Tudor period. This was followed in 1902 by a biography of *Henry VIII* for the Goupil series, which was reissued in 1905 with bibliography and notes and held its own for the next sixty years as the standard life. But his most popular book was *Factors in Modern History*, in 1907, though it now owes most of its fame to the splenetic attack launched against it by the American historian J.H. Hexter in 1961.[5] (Indeed, Hexter brought to mind a book long forgotten, although certainly in its time it had a powerful influence on our fathers' and grandfathers' thinking about the sixteenth century.) In 1910 came Pollard's volume in the Longmans 'Political History of England' series, for the period 1547–1603; a remarkable synthesis for its time, and one which held its own

* See pp. 196–8 above for Pollard's career.

into the 1930s as a teaching aid. Even Hexter, in 1961, described it as 'the best single treatment of the era it covers'.[6] In 1912 he published a brief *History of England* for the 'Home University Library' series, which encapsulated his historical philosophy; it is significant, perhaps, that he did not bring this up to date after the war, but instead produced *The Evolution of Parliament* (1920), on which he had been working for years. It was to prove the most controversial of his books, and his account of the Middle Ages was particularly roughly handled by his critics; but astonishingly enough it remains the only attempt to trace the continuous history of what most people regard as the most important of English institutions. His swan-song was a biography of *Wolsey* in 1929, based on his Ford Lectures the previous year.

The strange thing about Pollard is that although he spent all his working life in University College, London, in immediate proximity to the great national archives, and though he laboured hard and long for an institute which would provide a base for scholars using those archives, he used them very little himself. Most of his work, even to the detailed articles he wrote on the machinery of the Tudor Council and Star Chamber, was based on his virtuoso knowledge of the printed calendars, particularly the *Letters and Papers of Henry VIII*. He certainly argued that the importance of manuscripts as against printed transcripts had been exaggerated, and that a superstitious reverence for a manuscript *qua* manuscript was one of the less fortunate byproducts of the professionalization of history. There was some sense in this, but he carried the idea to extremes, and the deficiencies in the calendars, the concealed gaps, the misattributions, vitiated some of his best work. Only his life of *Henry VIII*, and to some extent *Wolsey*, survived him, and even his *Henry VIII* has now been displaced by J.J. Scarisbrick's definitive biography in 1968.[7]

Another striking thing about Pollard was his insularity, which was literal as well as metaphorical. Most of his predecessors, including those as chauvinistic as Freeman and J.R. Green, had been great Continental travellers; Stubbs, Creighton and Firth went abroad regularly, for research or recreation. But Pollard visited Europe rarely – it was not to his taste; nor was he deeply read in European history. He was even more nationalistic than the Victorians, and though he imposed on the public mind a new picture of the Reformation, it was one which was compatible with the Whig tradition, or with the 'historical Darwinism' of J.R. Green, who influenced him profoundly.

He played down the religious aspect of the Reformation, which had so much concerned the Victorians, and represented it as a social and political event and, what was more, a natural stage in England's rise to nationhood, not a decisive break with the past. In his view Henry VIII's marital misadventures were merely the proximate cause of the event, which would have taken place, one way or another, even if St Edward the Confessor had been on the throne. At the same time he took over J. R. Green's idea of a 'New Monarchy' and extended it. The policy of the Tudors was merely one aspect of a Europe-wide phenomenon, the rise of the new Renaissance princedoms, and the question was not whether the Reformation had created the nation-state but whether the emergence of the nation-state had provoked the Reformation. Stubbs's thesis that under the fifteenth-century Lancastrian kings parliament had enjoyed powers later suppressed by the Tudors was now rejected; on the contrary, the Tudors had nurtured a sickly parliament and unwittingly assisted its rise to power in the next century. The evolution of the constitution from Edward I to James I was one continuous process.

With the New Monarchy there rose the 'New Men'. Pollard perpetuated, if he did not create, the 'myth of the middle class': the idea that to replace the feudal baronage the crown cultivated a new, bourgeois managerial caste, of which Thomas Cromwell was only the most prominent representative. Yet valuable as they were, such men were only assistants to the prime mover, which remained the king. Caught he might have been in the groundswell of the New Wave, but Henry VIII had ridden it to triumphant success. For to Pollard this self-willed and vicious tyrant, the arch bogeyman of the Victorians, was a man of cosmic genius. His presence at this time was not necessary to the Reformation, but it was determinate; without his leadership it would have been a very different, perhaps a lesser thing. He was beyond criticism, even for this indiscriminate resort to the halter and the axe, and as Elton remarks: 'When Pollard roundly asserts that Henry was never capable of "a lust for superfluous butchery" we must wonder where for him superfluity had its beginning.'[8] For saying much less in Henry's favour Froude had been roasted, but the early twentieth century swallowed Pollard entire: the New Monarchy, the New Men, the idea of Henry as a sort of bravura Old King Cole, was the orthodoxy of school textbooks right up to the Second World War and beyond. Yet despite Henry VIII's 'imperial vision' – for Pollard's Henry, like Creighton's Elizabeth, sensed the future development of the nation centuries ahead – he was still subject to impersonal social and political forces; his genius lay in the skill with which he modified and controlled them.[9]

This certainly suggests a weakening of religious prejudice on the public's part, perhaps the onset of national self-doubt. As England's world status came increasingly under threat in that uneasy lull between the Boer War and the Great War the intensely nationalist picture presented by Pollard's books had increasing attractions. His portrayal of Elizabeth as a national symbol is a curious reversion to sixteenth-century iconography, and when he says: 'Elizabeth could bend the Tudor bow because her arm was strengthened by her people and lifted in their cause', he was raising a statue as much as making a phrase.[10] Now that the Reformation was flattened out, as it were, the separate works of Stubbs (judiciously amended), Pollard himself, Creighton, Gardiner and Macaulay could be laid end to end to form a panorama of England's irresistible rise to national greatness. It helps place Pollard in perspective if we realize that apart from his book on Wolsey all his major work was completed by the end of the Great War. (*The Evolution of Parliament*, though not published until 1920, was begun in 1911 or 1912 and finished by 1916.)

Yet it should not be thought that Pollard's veneration for parliament was a reflection of contemporary public opinion: rather the opposite. His attitude was in fact defensive – as was Gardiner's. They were not trying to augment parliament's existing prestige but seeking to recreate it. The wrecking tactics of the Irish Party, such apparently minor incidents as the Bradlaugh Case, the deep divisions on Home Rule and Tariff Reform, the negativism of the House of Lords, the rise of extra-parliamentary authorities like the trade unions, had now called in question the competence of parliament to govern the country. The attitude of unquestioning acceptance and approval which had characterized the middle-class attitude towards parliament in Macaulay's generation had undergone a 'Copernican revolution'. The remedy now, as Pollard saw it, was not the reinforcement of parliament itself, but the strengthening of the corporate state in which it was set. He pointed to the efficiency and forcefulness of Tudor government, and argued that this was the best guarantee of public order and individual liberty. Thus his emphasis on aspects of the Whig tradition which a man like Macaulay, who had come to manhood before the Reform era, took for granted. He argued his case most vigorously in his *History of England*, subtitled 'A Study in Political Evolution', which was reprinted eighteen times between 1912 and 1947:

'Whether this growth of power in the individual and in the state is a good or an evil thing depends on the conscience of those who wield it. The power of the overmighty subject has generally been a tyranny; and all power is distrusted by old-fashioned Liberals and philosophic Anarchists, because they have a traditional suspicion that it will fall into hostile or unscrupulous hands. But the forces of evil cannot be overcome by *laissez-faire*, and power is an indispensable weapon of progress. A powerless state means a helpless community ... Political liberty and religious freedom depend upon the power of the State, inspired, controlled and guided by the mind of the community ... The individual ... needs the strength of Union for his herculean tasks; and he has found that Union in the state. It is not an engine of tyranny, but the lever of social morality; and the function of the English government is not merely to embody the organised might and executive brain of England, but also to enforce its collective and co-ordinating conscience'.[11]

Pollard lived on until 1948, long after his retirement, though his last years were marred by a tragic quarrel which led him to resign from the Directorship of the Institute of Historical Research he had created. He left no school of historians behind. Great scholars, and especially great scholar-administrators, create an academic desert around them; pupils of initiative and independent thought withdraw from the influence, as C.H. Williams withdrew from Pollard and retreated into the fifteenth century. John Neale also moved forward into Elizabeth's reign, where Pollard's writ did not run.[12] Pollard – 'a shortish man, sturdily built and wearing pince-nez' – was pre-eminently the type who did not relish criticism or opposition, and his persona was intimidating. There was an occasion when one of his young pupils had to be physically led into his Tudor seminar at the Institute by 'a friend who found her downstairs, too nervous to force herself to attend it'.[13] In the end he left a solitary heir. Just as in seventeenth-century history the torch passed from individual to individual, from Gardiner to Firth and from Firth to Davies, so in the sixteenth century it passed from Pollard to Neale (and from Neale to Joel Hurstfield).

Born in Liverpool in 1890, John Ernest Neale had to overcome the initial handicap of a second in history at the new university there; not an auspicious beginning to an academic career, and one which he himself would never accept in aspirant pupils. However, strongly recommended by Ramsay Muir, he gravitated to University College, London, and after the Great War he returned as an Assistant in History to Pollard, and began his life's work on the parliamentary records of the sixteenth century. He displayed his quality in a number of important contributions to the *EHR*, and a revisionist article on the Commons' right of free speech in a *festschrift* for Pollard in 1924. In 1925 he left for a chair at Manchester, but returned only two years later to succeed Pollard at University College, Pollard having reverted to a part-time appointment so as to give himself more scope as Director of the Institute. He was knighted in 1955, a year before his retirement, and died in 1975.[14]

The work for which Neale is still universally known is his biography of *Queen Elizabeth*, published in 1934, which enjoyed overwhelming and sustained success. It was unusual in that it earned equal praise from the literary reviewers and the academic profession, despite Neale's controversial decision to dispense with the scholarly apparatus of footnotes and bibliography. In fact, his wisdom was questionable; he only encouraged a host of gimcrack amateurs to invoke his illustrious example, and present their 'findings' without the support of detailed references, which in most cases they would have been at a loss to provide. Neale himself was complacently satisfied with his large sales, and he fell into the trap – to which historians seem more vulnerable than other scholars – of regarding them in themselves as a sign of excellence. (By the same argument the *Sun* would be a better newspaper than *The Times*, and *Airport* a better novel than *Middlemarch*.) Someone said to the medieval historian Eileen Power: 'He has sold the pass.' Power, another one who ought to have known better, replied: 'He has also sold 20,000 copies.'

Nevertheless, it was the major definitive biography which a monarch of Elizabeth's historical stature obviously deserved, based on all the available sources, printed or otherwise; for Neale was very far from sharing Pollard's aversion to manuscript work; rather the opposite. Its solidity is such that Neale never felt it necessary to revise it, and it has defied all subsequent competition. It owed its success not only to its style and scholarship, but also to its glorification of England's past greatness, its mood of nationalist euphoria, which the public found comforting in a decade of disillusion, depression and fear. They continued to draw comfort from it during the Second World War and on into the austerity-ridden era of the Welfare State; at the dawn of a much-trumpeted 'Second Elizabethan Age' in 1952 the book's title was changed accordingly.

The only serious defect in Neale's interpretation – but it is basic – is that he is too indulgent to the queen. Froude took the view that she owed most of her success to her ministers, whom she only frustrated and hampered. Creighton did not go so far as this, of course, but he was only intermittently enchanted by her, and he saw flaws in Elizabeth's policy and in her character to which Neale was blind. To Neale Elizabeth could do no wrong, her indecisiveness was masterly temporization, her aversion to novelty a laudable desire for stability, her vanity self-confidence, her mistakes compromises forced on her by others; in any difference of opinion between her and her ministers she was invariably right. Her outrageous bad manners, her aggressive bullying, her personal unpleasantness, her sexist behaviour, the ruthless authoritarianism which Hume had noticed and stressed, were either ignored or glossed over as symptoms of strain. In addition Neale was as insular in his attitudes as Pollard, and his knowledge of European affairs no better grounded; the Dutch, for instance, are viewed exclusively through the queen's eyes, and so is Philip II of Spain. Almost alone amongst English historians in the 1920s and 1930s he never wrote a general textbook, and his grasp of the century as a whole was a trifle suspect.[15] His sanguine view of Elizabeth, his attitude of 'Gloriana, Right or Wrong', was exuberantly maintained by A.L. Rowse, whose *England under Elizabeth* was published in 1950; and Conyers Read was another disciple. Read's two ponderous volumes on William Cecil, Lord Burleigh, showed the extent of Elizabeth's debt to him very clearly, but he still tried to insist that she did it all herself.[16] Neale's thesis is still paramount, but it has taken some knocks, and will no doubt take more; it is surprising that there has not already been a bluntly revisionist biography. Neale himself in later years sounded a healthier note of caution, even pessimism, notably in his Raleigh Lecture in 1948 on 'The Elizabethan Political Scene'.[17]

Meanwhile Neale's research on the history of parliament never stopped, and the first fruits came with a brilliant analysis of *The Elizabethan House of Commons*, in 1949, based on his Ford Lectures in 1941–2. He followed this up with a two-volume narrative history of *Elizabeth I and her Parliaments*, in 1955 and 1957. This time he used footnotes, though not lavishly.

Taken together, these three volumes were a splendid addition to our knowledge of the period. The first is likely to retain its value longest, because a static analysis demands less emotional involvement. His confirmation that by Elizabeth's reign the landed gentry had taken over most of the borough seats theoretically allocated to townsmen was of crucial importance – not least in buttressing Tawney's thesis on the rise of the gentry. His narrative volumes provided a much fuller account than any previous historian had managed, and he brought to life a number of notable sixteenth-century MPs, particularly that voluble defender of parliamentary privilege, Peter Wentworth. Building on earlier work of his own, he also elucidated the passing of some crucial statutes, notably those establishing the religious settlement in the first parliament of the reign. Yet his work was very much of its time, and after only twenty or twenty-five years it is now in some ways as dated as Creighton's or Froude's. His purpose was evident in the opening of *The Elizabethan House of Commons*, which reads: 'In these days of institutional malaise, a historical study of our English parliament ... cannot be entirely remote from our interests. The past explains the present, and the historical process, so far as it emerges from such a study, has its bearing upon our understanding of contemporary life'; and his repeated comparisons between the 'cold war' of the 1950s and the struggle between England and the Counter-Reformation were a trifle jarring even at the time.[18] Moreover, despite certain criticisms of his attitude towards Elizabeth, and joking speculations that he was in love with her, which clearly nettled him, his portrait of the Virgin Queen was grander than ever. It can best be studied in the concluding chapter to each book. Here the royal headmistress, all-wise and all-seeing, hindered as often as not by her squabbling staff, always in the end gets the better of her mettlesome and aggressive pupils. Her affectionate condescension never wavers as she adroitly sidesteps their premature demands for partnership in government, and even in the worst crises she recognizes in them the seeds of future greatness – and so on. It is a familiar script.

Indeed in Neale the present is always before our eyes as we consider the past, and he is much more of a Whig historian than many who are branded as such. His Whiggish belief that parliament's authority steadily increased over the reign owed something to the Darwinian theories of Pollard, perhaps even more to a seminal paper read to the British Academy in 1924 by Wallace Notestein of Yale, on 'The Winning of the Initiative by the House of Commons' over Elizabeth's reign and James I's. A detailed scrutiny of this famous thesis shows that it was not so starkly expressed as some of its imitators assumed, but it provided a bridge between Pollard and Gardiner, a bridge now strengthened by Neale. Taking Pollard, Neale, Notestein and Gardiner together, the history of parliament from 1529 through 1641 could now be expressed as a steady upward curve. Many historians now question whether parliament under Elizabeth made the advances claimed for it by Neale, or whether it even wanted to. Others have questioned whether the Puritans in the Commons were so militant and well-organized a force as he suggests.[19] But it is a more serious defect in Neale's work that because of the standpoint he adopted and the nature of the material he used, his account of affairs always stresses confrontation or disagreement between crown and parliament, at the expense of agreement and cooperation, which was less exciting but nonetheless quite as important – some would say more important. Neale saw parliament in 1601 as poised for the great challenge to the monarchy in the seventeenth century; it is a difficult thing for a sixteenth-century historian to put the Great Rebellion out of his mind, but there is no sign that Neale even tried. The fact is, however, that opposition activity fell off as the reign progressed, enjoying only a brief revival in 1601 on the restricted issue of monopolies, and Neale's successors, Conrad Russell and Geoffrey Elton, now see the reign as a period of overall consensus, punctuated by minority demonstrations which ended in futility.[20]

Geoffrey Rudolph Elton is now, of course, the prime moving force in Tudor history, and is likely to remain so. By dint of his enormous output, his scholarly rigour, his forceful personality and his unflagging vigour in debate he has imposed his own reconstruction on much of the period, and certainly on the earlier half of it.

He is one of two brilliant sons born to Victor Ehrenberg, professor of ancient history in the University of Prague, who fled to England in 1939 and settled at Oxford. (The other is the nuclear physicist Lewis Elton, professor at the University of Surrey.) Elton's career was largely self-made; he worked for a London external degree during the earlier part of the war while he supported himself by schoolteaching, then he took his Ph.D. at University College, London, in two years, after army service in occupied Germany, during which period he changed his name. It was a casual meeting with John Neale which directed his attention to the papers for Henry VIII's reign, still largely neglected in the original. After a year at Glasgow University he was appointed an assistant lecturer at Cambridge in 1949, to stand in for Kenneth Pickthorn, the university's resident authority on early sixteenth century history, who had entered parliament and taken up a political career.

Pickthorn never came back, but Cambridge was stuffy, and it was five years before the young Elton was elected to a fellowship at his adopted college, Clare. (Another exiled central European, Walter Ullmann, had similar difficulty at Trinity, though he ended up as professor of medieval history.) But his reputation was resoundingly established with his first book, in 1953, *The Tudor Revolution in Government*. This set the tone for all his subsequent work, and though he has modified some of his conclusions since he has not fundamentally altered them.

The Tudor Revolution was based on an intensive re-examination of all the documentary material for the 1530s, of which Elton is still the master; much of it difficult to date, to interpret or even read, and often only loosely calendared. Elton's approach has been described as teutonic; it has been said that of all English historians his attitude is most akin to that of the great German nineteenth-century masters. In fact it probably owes as much to his early training by his father in the handling of the textual evidence for ancient history. On the basis of his intense documentary research Elton argued that modern methods of government had their beginning not under Edward IV or Henry VII but Henry VIII, and even then they were not the creation of the king but of his secretary, Thomas Cromwell, later his Vice-gerent in Spirituals and Lord Privy Seal. J.R. Green had given Cromwell his due, but otherwise it has been customary to dismiss him as a doctrinaire hack, the unscrupulous agent of a despotic master. He was now emphatically reinstated as the presiding genius who, beginning with the bare fact of Henry's breach with Rome, invented the statutory instruments and the administrative processes which made the Reformation a reality. The translation of the royal supremacy into legislative terms, the creation of new organs of government to administer the wealth of the Church, the comprehensive and thorough demedievalization of the central administration, were all Cromwell's work, and it constituted a revolution in method, largely unseen, whose effects were felt over the next two centuries.

The immediate effect was to 'depose' Henry VIII from his position as leader of the Reformation in England; with him went the concept of a 'New Monarchy', and indeed much of the previously accepted synthesis of early Tudor history. Particularly deplorable was the fate of J.D. Mackie's volume of the Oxford History of England on *The Earlier Tudors 1485–1558*, which had been published only the year before but was now outmoded. Reviewing it, Elton made this inexorable pronouncement: 'What has to be grasped is that there is no question of just correcting points of detail or of discovering a few new facts. A whole complex of underlying ideas, a whole frame of references, is being discarded.'[21]

Since then the machine has ground relentlessly on, and those who have thrown themselves in the path of the juggernaut have been crushed or swept aside. Elton admits that his original contention that Cromwell's Revolution was as significant as the Revolution of 1688 was overstated, but a slight retreat on that front has only enabled him to advance on others. He has emerged substantially unscathed from a full-scale confrontation with two of his leading critics, Penry Williams and G.L. Harries, arranged by the periodical *Past & Present*, while engaging in subsidiary contests with two of the most formidable of modern controversialists, J.P. Cooper and Lawrence Stone. He has upheld his view of Henry VIII as a skilful, intelligent but entirely unconstructive ruler even against his own pupil J.J. Scarisbrick, whose definitive biography of Henry was published in 1968.[22] Stone admits: 'He has failed to persuade more than a minority of his colleagues in the profession that the changes that took place at that time can reasonably be described as a "revolution in government", but it is an idea with which every serious student of the period must henceforth grapple.'[23]

Indeed, such students have little choice. Elton's power and authority rest on his unflinching self-confidence and his terrifying industry. He writes whole articles while others are labouring over paragraphs, books while they are completing articles. His *England under the Tudors* in 1955 established his views in a major textbook for sixth forms and universities, backed up in 1960 by *The Tudor Constitution: Documents and Commentary*. Those who opposed his interpretation now did so in the consciousness of radicalism. His Ford Lectures at Oxford in 1972 were at once published under the title *Policy and Police*, an account of government measures against dissent in the 1530s, largely by Cromwell, of course. The Wiles Trust lectures in Belfast a year later produced *Reform and Renewal*, a discussion of Cromwell's broader views on the Commonwealth. His shorter publications on all these topics and more were reprinted in 1974 as *Studies in Tudor and Stuart Government and Politics*, filling two large volumes.

Personally a very kind man, of some charm, in public he is impatient with naivety or error, which unfortunately surround him everywhere. He did not endear himself to some of his colleagues by a candid review of English historical writing since the war, which was published in 1969 as a supplement to the *Historische Zeitschrift*. He obligingly translated and republished it in 1970 as *Modern Historians on British History 1945–1969*. Since then by mere repetition his power accumulates. His volume on *Reformation Europe 1517–1559* (1963) for the Fontana History of Europe set the Continental record straight for English readers; he is the general editor of the influential 'Historical Problems' series for Allen & Unwin, and the potentially even more influential 'Fontana Library of English History'. He is also general editor of the bibliographical series 'Sources of History; Studies in the Use of Historical Evidence', to which he has contributed a volume on the period 1200–1640. He is a watchful and stringent reviewer. In 1977 he patiently ground across his territory again in another major textbook, *Reform and Reformation 1509–1558* (volume two in Arnold's 'New History of England'). 'I should like to make it clear', he says in the preface, 'that this book neither recants nor denounces, though it often (and I hope humbly) reconsiders.' Dissension continues to rumble, but it has recently been remarked that Elton's most influential critic is now Elton himself.[24]

He distrusts abstract theories of history and historical writing, as he has pointedly said in *The Practice of History* (1967) and *Political History: its Principles and Practice* (1970).* This is part of a general aversion to intellectual history which he is too intelligent to carry to extremes. Nor does religion feature largely in his many accounts of the Reformation, and his long and contentious attempt to deflate the posthumous reputation of Sir Thomas More, while to some extent justified by the uncritical attitude of hagiographers Catholic and otherwise, betrays a certain lack of sympathy with religious experience. Fortunately the history of the Reformation as a religious movement has been taken over by Geoffrey Dickens, whose *English Reformation* (1964) is written with great style, relentless historical accuracy and a genuine though dispassionate religious commitment – surprisingly rare amongst English historians writing on religion.

In many ways Elton is similar to Namier, though he has none of Namier's disabling psychological complexes. They were both central European Jews, and both suffered a certain amount of ostracization because of it – Namier much more than Elton, as we shall see. Both of them have remained staunch admirers of English institutions, more so than many who were born under them, but with none of the flag-waving sentimentality which mars the work of 'patriotic' historians like Trevelyan. Both are natural conservatives; both have a marked distrust of socialism and similar theoretical abstractions. Their attitude to British government is much the same, though Elton's belief in the strong state as the best guarantee of liberty is not so far adrift from Pollard's either. His first book, on *The Tudor Revolution*, opens like this:

'English government has a special claim to be studied. It developed in comparative freedom from outside interference, producing a curious blend of decentralised and popular freedom with strong, efficient and centralised

* See pp. 278–80 below.

administration. Of these two ingredients neither ought to be ignored, though the first has always struck observers as the more important. In truth, English history has been as remarkable for good government as for free and constitutional government, though the two have not always co-incided. Nevertheless, either by itself will fail to explain the peculiar de-velopment of a country the whole structure of whose politics is so different from that of any other. Neither freedom nor order has ever had the field exclusively to itself. The desire for constitutional guarantees has never altogether swept away the sense that government must be strong to be worth having, nor have governments ever for long tried to turn strength into abuse of strength. The interaction of these two principles is at the root of England's exceptional constitutional history and her exceptional stabil-ity, never more clearly seen than in times of revolution ... The sanctions of that stability – the safeguards against despotism – have long been under-stood and often described; the other side of the matter – strong rule preventing anarchy and preserving order – requires still more exploration. Our history is still much written by whigs, the champions of political freedom; to stress the need for controlling that freedom may even today seem not only not liberal but even illiberal'.

Elton is very much a historian's historian, writing within the profession, and though his influence on the teaching of early modern history at schools and universities has been more profound that that of any other man of his generation, he is not so well known to the general public as some of his colleagues, like Hugh Trevor-Roper and J.H. Plumb. But he is now en-trenched, at the comparatively tender age of sixty, at the top of the profession. Reader in Tudor Studies at Cambridge in 1963, and later chairman of the Faculty Board of History, he was appointed to a personal chair in 1967. He served as president of the Royal Historical Society from 1972 to 1976. Friends and enemies alike were dumbfounded when he was passed over for the regius chair at Cambridge in 1968, but it can still, and surely must, come his way. After some alarming incursions into seventeenth-century history he has now settled down to a thorough re-examination of all the records for Elizabeth's parliaments. Many historians have produced some of their best work in their sixties and seventies, and prodigious as Elton's output has so far been we have probably only seen half of it, or at most two thirds.[25]

The Stuarts: Gardiner to Trevelyan

The neo-Whig interpretation of the sixteenth century put forward by Pollard and Neale was preceded in time by a neo-Whig interpretation of the seventeenth century which will always be associated with the name of Samuel Rawson Gardiner.[26]

Gardiner is a strange, reclusive figure; it is no accident that his name was scarcely mentioned in my earlier account of the professionalization of history in the late nineteenth century. His eccentric religious affiliations removed him at an early stage from conventional academic life, and he only rejoined it in old age. By then he was devoted to, almost obsessed with, research. Born in 1829, he matriculated at Christ Church, Oxford, in 1847 and took a first in classics in 1851. However, he was then converted to the millenarian Catholic Apostolic Church founded in 1832 by Edward Irving; he was a deacon in the 'Irvingite' Church from 1851 to 1866, and in 1856 he even married Irving's daughter, Isabella. Unable to comply with the religious tests still imposed on university teachers, he had to resign his fellowship at Christ Church after less than a year and retire to London, where he earned his living mainly by teaching. In 1872 he was appointed a lecturer in history at King's College, London, and in 1877, a professor. (He lapsed from the Irvingite Church in 1872, though his first wife did not die until 1878.) His exclusion from Oxford probably hurt him more than he would admit. On the title pages of his books he continued to describe himself as 'Sometime Student of Christ Church, Oxford', even after he had gained a London chair.

The few who knew him at all well spoke of his sweetness of temper, his bountiful good nature and his generosity, but his personality, and his private life, remain shadowy. His only important recreation was cycling, but as often as not this led him to the sites of Civil War battlefields. He travelled extensively abroad in search of material, but he left no account of his visits, and they left no trace of his work – apart from the new evidence he brought back, of course. For instance, to read his account of Prince Charles and Buckingham's visit to Madrid in 1623 you would not suspect that the author had visited the city. On London society he made no impact at all, even after he had achieved a modest fame. This was the London of Froude, Green and Freeman, but it does not appear that he knew them more than casually. It is significant that no one, in public at least, ever referred to him by his first name – he was always '*S. R.* Gardiner'. He had no known enemies, and at the same time no known friends, though latterly a close working relationship developed between him and the young Charles Firth, and after his death some of the tributes paid him have a warm, personal touch; York Powell's is more than that of a professional colleague.

But of him it can be said, as of few men, that his life was research, and vice-versa. He registered as a reader at the British Museum in 1856 and the Public Record Office in 1858, and until his death in 1901 he rarely strayed from one or the other of these two repositories, except to visit other archives at home and abroad. At first he lived at 22 Gordon Street, near the Museum, and kept regular office hours, 9 to 5, and he kept this up as well as he could when he moved successively to Bromley, Bedford and Sevenoaks. Very early he decided to write a full narrative history of seventeenth-century England. What brought him to this decision, or what led him to history at all, no one can say, but from then on he worked steadily through all the original material he could find, in manuscript or in print, extending his scope gradually to cover the archives at Paris, Madrid, Venice, Brussels and Stockholm. From all this he laboriously constructed a detailed month-by-month, week-by-week, sometimes almost day-to-day account of his chosen period, beginning in 1863 with *A History of England from the Accession of James I to the Disgrace of Chief Justice Coke 1603–16*, in two volumes. This was followed in 1869 by *Prince Charles and the Spanish Marriage 1617–23*, in 1875 by *The Duke of Buckingham and Charles I 1624–28*, and in 1877 by *The Personal Government of Charles I 1629–37*, each in two volumes. *The Fall of the Monarchy of Charles I 1638–42* (1882) was intended to launch a new section, up to 1649, though eventually Gardiner decided to start afresh with the Great Rebellion.

For sheer bulk of exposition this is a work which has never been equalled, and it is doubtful now if any modern historian would undertake a similar task – though E.H. Carr's history of Bolshevik Russia, in ten volumes to date, rivals it in size and scope. It is still an indispensable work of reference for any student of the seventeenth century, and it first opened up a period which ever since has been a field of active research. Reviewing Gardiner's achievement after his death, Charles Firth said it was difficult to assess its value without taking into account the state of seventeenth-century studies before he wrote – 'It is like comparing an eighteenth-century map of Africa with a modern one. The outline of the country is the same in both; but we know now where the great rivers rise, and can follow their windings.'[27]

Unfortunately, it is far from being a lively work; some would say that it is not even agreeable to read. Gardiner's style was lucid and workmanlike, and it improved slightly as he progressed, but to a generation whose standards in such matters had been set by Macaulay or even Froude it was dull stuff indeed. He took literally the strictures of Ranke, his acknowledged master, and not only did he reconstruct each episode from as wide a range of material as possible, allowing the evidence to tell the story, eschewing the work of previous scholars and avoiding so far as he could subjective characterization, he also worked in strict chronological order. He was determined to read history forwards not backwards, and he carried this worthy resolve to extremes. It was said that if he was working on the events of, say, 1653, he would decline the offer of material for 1654, with the remark: 'I am not ready for that yet.' Many pages were drafted at his desk in the British Museum, and it was afterwards said that he sometimes despatched them straight to the printers from there. Certainly his technique never made for lively prose.

As a result the first two volumes, up to 1616, were a total failure; their critical reception was lukewarm, and most of the edition was pulped. (Though it is only fair to say that Gardiner himself looked upon this section with disfavour, and it was the only part he completely rewrote for the collected edition.) The second instalment, up to 1623, only sold 500 copies, and made a loss. The third instalment broke even, the fourth and fifth made a small profit, and the whole work was reissued in ten octavo volumes in 1883-4, the edition now generally used. Even then, and despite the schoolbooks he contributed to Longmans's 'Epochs of Modern History' and 'Epochs of English History' series, on *The Thirty Years' War* (1874) and *The Puritan Revolution* (1876), and despite his *Outline of English History for Children* (1881), his *Students' History of England* (1890), and his *Constitutional Documents of the Puritan Revolution*, published in 1889 as a set book for the Oxford History School and continuously in print to this day – despite all this hack work he was never affluent, and Pollard was later to cite his case as an example of the poor financial standing of the historian.[28] In 1882 Acton persuaded Gladstone to give him a civil list pension of £150 a year to subsidize his further research, and in 1884 All Souls' elected him to a non-resident research fellowship worth £200. Even then, his widow – his second wife, Bertha Cordery – was awarded a civil list pension of £75 a year in 1903.

However, the historical value of his work came to be generally recognized in the 1870s and 1880s, and the reviews swung to the other point of the compass, heaping uncritical adulation upon him. Indifferent apparently to praise or blame, he ground relentlessly on past 1642 and through the Civil Wars. His *History of the Great Civil War 1642-1649* appeared in three volumes, in 1886, 1889 and 1891, and was reissued in four volumes octavo in 1893. He published three further volumes on the *History of the Commonwealth and Protectorate* in 1895, 1897, and 1901. In these last years honours began to accrue, and he renewed his contacts with academic life. As we have seen, he took over the editorship of the *EHR* in 1890 and when his All Souls' fellowship expired in 1892 he was at once elected to another at Merton. He received honorary degrees at Oxford, Cambridge, Göttingen and Edinburgh, and an honorary studentship at Christ Church. In 1894 he declined the offer of the regius chair at Oxford, but he agreed to launch the Ford Lectures two years later.

He had originally intended to take his account up to the Restoration, perhaps further, but he had now lowered his sights to the death of Cromwell, in 1658. He might have reached this goal, too, had he not been deflected onto two books on Cromwell himself: *Cromwell's Place in History*, which was his Ford Lectures, and a biography for the Goupil series.* Of the latter he remarked, rather touchingly: 'I am half sorry I ever undertook it; the pictures were so good, I felt obliged to try after a better style than I usually write, and it interrupted me sadly.' But his descent from the Protector through his daughter Bridget, wife of Henry Ireton, was one of the few things in which he took a strong personal pride, though he was chary of talking about it. In 1897 he was also regrettably embroiled in a time-wasting public dispute with Fr John Gerard SJ, who argued that the Gunpowder Plot of 1605 was a government fabrication.† As a result, when he died in 1901 he had only reached 1656, and he left it to Charles Firth to complete the task. Firth got as far as 1658 in *The Last Years of the Protectorate 1656-8*, studiously modelled on Gardiner. This was in 1909, but he went no further, though he lived another twenty-seven years, and it was left to his own pupil, Godfrey Davies, to plug the final gap as late as 1955, with *The Restoration of Charles II 1658-60*.

Meanwhile for nearly twenty years after his death Gardiner's *History* was accepted at his own valuation, as a dispasssionate, almost Rankean account of events 'as they really happened'. There is no doubt that he himself firmly believed this. In the long preface he wrote in 1884 for the octavo edition he heartily agreed with Seeley that 'the way in which Macaulay and Forster regarded the development of the past – that is to say, the constant and avowed comparison of it with the present – is altogether destructive of real historical knowledge'.‡ 'He who studies the society of the past', he went on, 'will be of greater service to the society of the present in proportion as he leaves it out of account.'[29]

---

* In the 1890s Goupil et Cie commissioned a series of biographies of English rulers, sumptuously printed and illustrated, which are now collectors' items. Pollard's *Henry VIII* and Creighton's *Elizabeth* were first published in this form.

† The Society of Jesus, which never dies, has not given up on this point. See Francis Edwards SJ, *Guy Fawkes: the Real Story of the Gunpowder Plot?* (1969).

‡ J.E. Forster published several extremely whiggish monographs on the reign of Charles I, including an absurdly laudatory biography of Sir John Eliot (1865). The truth is, Gardiner used Forster extensively, and appropriated his view of Eliot as a great patriot-democrat with scarcely any amendment.

He considered himself almost entirely impartial. In 1875 he wrote:

'We have had historians in plenty, but they have been Whig historians or Tory historians. The one class has thought it unnecessary to take trouble to understand how matters looked in the eyes of the King and his friends; the other class has thought it unnecessary to take trouble to understand how matters looked in the eyes of the leaders of the House of Commons. I am not so vain as to suppose that I have always succeeded in doing justice to both parties, but I have, at least, done my best not to misrepresent either.'

He was also a determined foe of the analytical method. 'Much confusion', he said, 'has been caused by the habit which prevails where it would be least expected, of clarifying events rather according to their nature than according to their chronological order, so that the sequence of the history is lost.'[30]

It was always obvious that Gardiner's books on Cromwell scarcely approached this elevated ideal: to him Cromwell was the great liberal author-itarian who had 'saved' the Revolution and brought order out of chaos; he was even 'the typical Englishman of the modern world'. But Cromwell had a special place in Gardiner's mind, nor was he singular in this; a wave of approval swept over the literary world of the late 1880s and 1890s as the tercentenary of Cromwell's birth, in 1599, drew near.[31] This reflected the current disillusion with parliamentary institutions, and it is part of what might be called the 'Direct-Liberal' approach to biography. Another example is Hilda Foxcroft's biography of George Savile, Marquess of Halifax, 'The Trimmer', in 1898. In her hands Halifax emerges as a distinctly Gladstonian figure, as does John Morley's *Walpole*, published at much the same time. But this apart, it was supposed that Gardiner had always been true to his own exacting rules. This idea was ruthlessly denied by the eminent American historian Roland G. Usher, but the news was slow to percolate because Usher published his findings in the American Mid-West at the height of the European War.

In *A Critical Study of the Historical Method of Samuel Rawson Gardiner*, published by Washington University, St Louis, in 1915, Usher drew attention to several faults, some of which had been noticed by early reviewers, whose voices had been drowned in the subsequent storm of praise. For one thing, Gardiner's final judgment on men and events did not always accord with his own facts; he discovered new material, displayed it, then did not use it. Moreover, his manner of work, one year at a time, had led to astonishing inconsistencies; he offered at least three different views of Charles I, barely reconcilable one with another, he could not make up his mind about the Earl of Stafford, and he even wavered in his view of John Pym. And though he constantly referred back to 'the Elizabethan Constitution' as the touchstone of political orthodoxy, he never explained what he meant by that term. Most serious of all, Usher showed that for all his protestations to the contrary Gardiner had approached the period with his mind made up, and tailored his narrative accordingly.

An anonymous correspondent calling himself 'HISTORIAN' drew attention to Usher's book in the *Times Literary Supplement* for 25 September 1919, and heartily endorsed his verdict, adding examples of his own. The first reaction, from A.P. Newton, was highly emotional and uncritical – 'It is an ungrateful act', he trumpeted, 'to kick down the ladder whereby you have climbed.'[32] (Newton was Rhodes Professor of Imperial History at London University, but his magnum opus, *The Colonising Activities of the English Puritans*, had given him a vested interest in the Whig view of the 1630s.) Pollard wrote in on 16 October to point out that 'HISTORIAN' was much more severe on Gardiner than Usher had been, a point taken up by Charles Firth on 6 November, when he returned from abroad. The correspondence then settled down to the usual *TLS* jogtrot, with nothing much settled but a great deal of bad feeling fairly harmlessly ventilated.*

Much time was wasted discussing Gardiner's methods of work. Firth rebutted Usher's charge, based on anonymous reminiscences in *The Athenaeum* for 1902, that he sent copy direct to the printers from his desk in the British Museum Reading Room, and he was vigorously seconded by Bertha Gardiner.[33] But since Firth was only six years old when Gardiner began publishing the *History*, and Bertha Cordery did not marry him until 1882, by which time he had reached 1642, none of their evidence was relevant to that part of the *History* against which Usher's criticism was principally directed. Nor did anyone answer Usher's pertinent query: why had Gardiner not taken the opportunity to revise the whole work for the octavo edition of 1884? Instead, Firth and 'HISTORIAN' soon became locked in a fierce, detailed argument on one specific point, the shipment of Scots prisoners to Guyana after the battle of Worcester in 1651.

None of this met the real gravamen of Usher's case, either. Usher pointed out that for all the protestations of Gardiner and his admirers there was nothing at all novel in the *History* up to 1649, except in depth of detail; his general interpretation was much the same as Hume's, or for that matter Clarendon's.[34] Moreover, in spite of his elaborate precautions his whiggish bent was obvious enough: 'Gardiner has done exactly what he blamed Macaulay for doing; he has decided a great issue in history, which was by

---

* As Bernard Levin has recently remarked: 'the letters in the *TLS* constitute the very last stronghold of absolutely unrestrained and unqualified authorial, academic and critical pedantry, vanity, obstinacy and malice' (*The Times*, 27 Nov. 1980).

no means clear to men at the time, by applying to it his later knowledge.'[35] As a result he wrote his history backwards, like any common-or-garden Whig: the king was always wrong, even if he was legally and morally right; his opponents were always right, even if they were legally and morally wrong. Moreover, every incident in the struggle between them, beginning with the parliamentary session of 1604, pointed in the same direction; it was part of an inevitable and irresistible process leading straight to the grand confrontation in 1642. In his unguarded moments Gardiner even admitted this: in his account of the debates of 1610 he describes the opposition arguments as defining 'the system upon which the constitution was finally moulded after the conclusion of the struggle, and towards which, during its continuance, every step taken in advance was constantly tending'.[36] Usher could have added, too, that his textbooks, written far ahead of the main narrative, made nonsense of his claim to chronological objectivity. He published *The Puritan Revolution*, with its question-begging title, in 1876, when the *History of England* had only reached 1628.

Usher was particularly critical of Gardiner's free use of the term 'nation', and every historian could profitably study his mordant words on this issue. Gardiner enthusiastically adopted the convention that an English 'nation' existed in the early seventeenth century, its size unspecified but clearly comprehending a majority of the people – a nation, in Usher's words, 'intelligent, alert, trained in political thinking by the parliamentary struggles of centuries, and believing that its liberties can be secured only through parliamentary legislation'.[37] This 'nation', according to Gardiner, feared Charles I, hated Stafford, rallied behind Pym, and so on, apparently as a corporate object. Sometimes this reached ridiculous heights, as when he said that through Sir John Eliot in 1626 'spoke the voice of a mighty nation, conscious of its power and impatient of the tutelage under which it had been thrust'.[38]

Usher reminds us that it was scarcely possible to speak of an articulate, informed 'nation' even in the 1870s, and in the seventeenth century the evidence for its existence boiled down to a hundred or so letters, 'the work of some score or two of gentlemen, mostly on the parliamentary side'.[39] It was, in fact, a construct of Gardiner's imagination. On the other hand, said Usher, there was a body of perfectly consistent evidence, in the words of the king and his ministers, that the great majority of the English people at this time were ill-informed, apathetic and trusting; incapable of mature judgment or decision, and needing to be told how to act and what to do by a paternalistic government. In Charles I this was denounced as authoritarian, but when Cromwell as Lord Protector adopted the same attitude it was deemed inevitable and even praiseworthy.[40]

He was particularly hard on Gardiner's account of Charles I's 'personal' rule, from 1629 to 1637, and indeed this is much the worst part of the *History*, largely because chronology is of less importance here, and Gardiner even had to fall back at times on analysis. A concomitant of his belief in a cohesive political nation in the early seventeenth century was his belief in that nation's universal displeasure with Charles I's policy. He again and again asserted that the issue of new patents of monopoly, the enforcement of forest law, the levy of ship money, even the draining of the Fens, were universally resented.[41] His treatment of ship money was particularly important, because his assertions on this point were extensive and unequivocal, and they have had a marked effect on the treatment of the subject ever since. A host of lesser writers, aping Gardiner, have told us that this tax was 'universally unpopular', or some such words, and that John Hampden's resistance to it 'set the nation aflame'. Up to a few years ago this was one of the accepted verities of seventeenth-century history; only then was it noticed that there was no evidence for this prior to 1638, when the tax had been successfully levied for four years. But Usher, checking over Gardiner's footnotes, pointed all this out in 1915:

'On its face, the case of ship money proves merely that Hampden and his friends disbelieved Charles's claim that ship money could legally be collected. That it sounded the tocsin for national revolt is not proved by describing the lawyers' arguments, by saying that England stood behind Hampden, and then by admitting that the vast majority paid the money.'[42]

Gardiner's aim – probably unconscious – was to fit the 1630s into a preconceived picture of escalation. A lull in the 1630s, a plateau, would never do. This continuous and inevitable escalation from 1603 to 1642 was in conformity with the best Whig-Liberal thinking, and subsequent 'revisionist' accounts of the Tudors, particularly Neale's, slotted readily into it. Because of Gardiner's acknowledged supremacy in matters of fact, and because of the exaggerated praise he received – Usher particularly deplored York Powell's remark that 'he found the Stuart period legend and left it history', as being grossly unfair to Hume – his general view of the seventeenth century was not seriously questioned until the 1950s or 1960s, when historians like Conrad Russell, taking each parliament in turn, found a distinct lack of continuity, and quite often a marked regression from one parliament, even one session, to the next.[43] As early as the 1920s, it is true, the economic historians were beginning to turn up new causes for the Great Rebellion, but they were seen as supplementing Gardiner's account, or perhaps displacing it, not *altering* it. If politics and the constitution were admitted to be a serious issue between king and parliament, then Gardiner had it right; one could perhaps dismiss the whole idea, but not amend it.

Religion, too, was a sphere peculiarly Gardiner's own, but here Usher did not tackle him head-on, which is strange, for Gardiner's view of Puritanism was extreme, highly influential and almost certainly wrong, and Usher was a noted ecclesiastical historian. When Gardiner forsook the Irvingite Church for Liberalism and Positivism, it is reasonable to assume that he retained a certain sympathy for persecuted minorities; at the same time his new liberalism made him deplore the bad press which the opponents of Archbishop Laud and Charles I had experienced in his lifetime. He remarked in 1882: 'A dislike of agitation and disturbance has in some quarters taken the place of a dislike of arbitrary power, whilst reverence for culture has often left little room for reverence for liberty.'[44] As early as 1875, when he published the section of the History for 1624–8, he had decided that Puritanism, only halted by Elizabeth, had resumed its irresistible expansion in step with the constitutional opposition in parliament and had provided much of its motive force.

In fact, he painted so violent and aggressive a picture of Puritanism that it requires a conscious effort of will to remember that most of his 'Puritans' were loyal members of the Church of England and so remained; and his failure clearly to distinguish between the Puritan reformers and the sectaries who broke away from the Church altogether – Cromwell's 'Puritans' – has been the cause of much confusion ever since. In the political sphere he also propounded an undistributed middle, and got away with it: all Puritans were opponents of the crown, therefore all opponents of the crown were Puritans. He clinched this by arguing that the split over the Grand Remonstrance in November 1641, and the very outbreak of Civil War in the autumn of 1642, occurred because of the dispute over religion, though in the latter case this is patently untrue and in the former arguably. He personally coined the term 'Puritan Revolution' to cover the whole period, and gave it currency by using it in the titles of two of his most popular textbooks. We find him using it in 1882, in the preface to *The Fall of the Monarchy of Charles I*.[45] After his death the concept became if anything stronger, and extended itself back into Elizabeth's reign. Even Gardiner had by implication accepted that there was a lull in the religious struggle under James I, and he dated the resurgence of Puritanism from the failure of the Spanish Marriage negotiations in 1623,[46] but his followers would have none of it.

Gardiner's earliest disciple, his friend in later years, literary executor and designated successor, was Charles Harding Firth.[47] He was not, however, Gardiner's pupil in any real sense, and it is significant that though he set out to complete Gardiner's *History* he abandoned the task halfway.

Firth was an ardent bibliophile, and something of a dilettante; his considerable private means meant that he lacked the drive to undertake work which did not interest him. He had a deep feeling for literature, which Gardiner lacked, and an unrivalled knowledge of seventeenth-century paintings and prints, which he displayed to the full in his illustrated 'coffee-table' edition of Macaulay's *History* (1913-15). In his early years he also edited a number of rather peripheral seventeenth-century texts, like the *Memoirs of Lucy Hutchinson* (1885), the *Life of William Cavendish Duke of Newcastle* by his wife (1886) and *Ludlow's Memoirs* (1894), on which he lavished a knowledge and an expertise which other men might have preferred to devote to books of their own devising. However, it is arguable that his greatest service to seventeenth-century history was in this role of editor and historiographer. His discovery at Worcester College, Oxford, of the papers of William Clarke, Secretary to the New Model Army 1647-9 and to General Monck 1651-60, enormously enlarged our knowledge of politics during the Great Rebellion and may be said to have created an entirely new sub-school of history.* But his edition of the *Acts and Ordinances of the Interregnum*, with Sir Robert Rait (1911), was an equally important contribution to scholarship. His talents as a historiographer are best displayed in three articles he wrote for the *EHR* in 1904, in which he traced the successive stages in the composition of Clarendon's *History of the Rebellion*. The lectures he gave at Oxford on Macaulay were posthumously published in 1938 as *A Commentary on Macaulay's History of England*; unfortunately the similar lectures he delivered on Gardiner in the 1920s have not survived.

He always venerated Gardiner, and defended his ideas and his approach to history, though not necessarily his technique and style. For instance, he did not entirely approve of Gardiner's rigid adherence to chronological narrative, or his reluctance to indulge in characterization.[48] He also admired Macaulay, as one who had produced great literature without sacrificing scholarly standards as he understood them. 'It is better not to try to draw the bow of Macaulay', he once said, 'for few men have his rare power of visualising the knowledge they have gained from books.'[49]

But the most obvious difference between master and pupil was in religion. Firth's religious commitment was 'faint even in youth and with the passage of time seems wholly to have faded'.[50] But he remained entirely loyal to Gardiner's concept of the 'Puritan Revolution', and he even reproved Clarendon for giving it insufficient weight: 'Just as he fails to understand the nature of the Puritans, so he fails to understand Puritanism in general, and his *History of the Rebellion* has the fundamental defect, that it is a history of a religious revolution in which the religious element is omitted.'[51] It is commonly said that Firth was more conscious of social and economic factors than Gardiner, and much less expert in foreign policy, but an objective scrutiny of

*Chiefly via A.S.P. Woodhouse's *Puritanism and Liberty* (1938), containing selected extracts from the four volumes of Clarke Papers published by Firth for the Camden Society 1891-1901.

their work lends no support to this notion. They both seem equally indifferent to economic trends, and though Gardiner devoted more time to diplomacy and foreign policy his weight of learning was such that he often made his narrative laboured and tedious; he obviously found it difficult to leave out any of the material he had found abroad. Where Firth had the clear super-iority was in military history, which would arguably have been his *métier* if he had had to work for his living. *Cromwell's Army* (1902), based on his Ford Lectures the previous year, is far and away his best book; in fact it is still the best study of any army in English history. These military studies gave him a much keener sense of realism than Gardiner; as he said in the preface to *Cromwell's Army:* 'A civil war is not only the conflict of opposing principles, but the shock of material forces.'

The two historians came together with their biographies of Cromwell, published almost simultaneously in 1900 (with another by John Morley). They reviewed each other's work, not uncritically, in the *EHR* a few months apart.[52] Both books were *pièces d'occasion*, one for Goupil and the other for the 'Heroes of the Nations' series, and neither was presented in a scholarly format. It is Firth's *Cromwell* which has survived, and not unreasonably so. It was reprinted in 1934, not long before his death, and was translated to the 'World's Classics' series in 1953. Despite its understandably old-fashioned air, it is still the standard biography, largely because the more details ac-cumulate round this man the more difficult it becomes to give an overall view of him. It was undue modesty which led Firth to represent it merely as a summary of Gardiner; Gardiner himself clearly did not think so.

Firth's assessment of Cromwell was distinguished by a healthy temperance. He criticized the Protector severely for attempting to impose on the nation the views of a religious minority, especially a minority whose cohesion as a party or class was steadily weakening in the 1650s. (Firth was, and still is, unusual, in that he recognized the *fall* as well as the rise of Puritanism.) Cromwell, he said, was 'too much the champion of a party to be accepted as a national hero by later generations'; which did not please Gardiner. All the same, he acknowledged his pre-eminent services to the nation, and it was natural that he should place more stress on Cromwell as a general than Cromwell as a politician. 'Thanks to his sword absolute monarchy failed to take root in English soil. Thanks to his sword Great Britain emerged from the chaos of the civil wars one strong state ... No English ruler did more to shape the future of the land he governed.'[53]

Nevertheless, the ambiguities remain, and after Carlyle no entirely whole-hearted advocate of Cromwell has emerged. From 1845 periodic proposals to erect a statue of Cromwell at public expense in the precincts of Westminster were defeated, and even when Lord Rosebery commissioned one at his own expense in 1899 it provoked furious opposition. It had to be unveiled by an anonymous workman early in the morning of 3 September. King George V in the First World War refused to let Churchill name a new battleship after Cromwell, and he had to be content with a Second World War tank.[54]

Unfortunately, as we have seen,* after his appointment to the regius chair at Oxford in 1904 Firth degenerated into an academic statesman, deeply involved not only in schemes of reform at Oxford, but also with the Royal Commission on the Public Records, the Historical Manuscripts Commission, the Royal Historical Society and the Historical Association, an involvement rewarded by a knighthood in 1922. He even served on an Admiralty Committee set up to investigate the battle of Trafalgar. His only major book thereafter, *The House of Lords during the Civil War*, was published in 1910 as a contribution to the contemporary debate over the Parliament Bill, and the research on which it was based had been undertaken twenty years before. Subsequently his energies were principally devoted to a detailed analysis of the New Model Army, regiment by regiment, which he wrote in conjunction with Godfrey Davies, though it was not published until after his death in 1936. At Oxford his influence was mainly exerted through postgraduate seminars, but even then he never built up a 'school' of followers or disciples, any more than Gardiner did, who had no strong university connexions.

This was probably because his own research was sterile; the reason often given at the time, not least by him, was that his pupils continued to be black-listed by the Oxford colleges in appointments to teaching posts. Certainly this is the reason given for the emigration of his one substantial pupil, Godfrey Davies. Davies was his research assistant at Oxford from 1914 onwards, and a fellow and tutor at Pembroke College. But in 1925 he left for Chicago, transferring in 1930 to the Huntington Library, California. In 1939, when he married the daughter of Edwin Gay, the distinguished economic historian, he became an American citizen. He taught occasionally at various Californian universities, but the remainder of his life was large devoted to research. His greatest achievement was his comprehensive *Bibliography of British History: Stuart Period*, published in 1928 under the joint auspices of the Royal Historical Society and the American Historical Association, which had first been suggested by Prothero as long ago as 1903 and had been in gestation ever since. It was the model for a series of similar bibliographies for other periods which followed.[55] In 1940 he published *The Regimental History of Cromwell's Army*, which he had planned with Firth, and in 1955 he at last completed the great task undertaken by Gardiner nearly a hundred years before with a densely factual volume on *The Restoration of Charles II 1658–60*. His volume in the 'Oxford History of England' on *The Early Stuarts*

*See p. 179ff. above.

(1937) was another bleak factual narrative along accepted lines laid down by Firth and Gardiner, though he jibbed at the use of the term 'Puritan Revolution' to describe what he saw as 'a revolt against authority' in all its aspects.[56] When he died, in 1957, *The Times* sombrely noted that he was 'an accurate and insatiable student of the original authorities on British seventeenth-century history', who 'did much to maintain the central tradition regarding it against eccentric revisions from writers of the left and the (clerical) right'.*

Firth's work, rooted as it was in the late nineteenth century, was palpably old-fashioned by the time he died. Even Godfrey Davies was not abreast of new developments in historiography. But G.M. Trevelyan, whose career overlapped theirs, made a virtue and a triumph out of being old-fashioned.

Like Firth he was born to independent wealth, but this time with a distinctly patrician tinge. He was inordinately proud of the Trevelyans' descent from the gentry of Devon and Northumberland, as well as of the intellectual achievements of his immediate forebears. His was an old Whig-Liberal family with a strong tradition of public service; he was the grandson of that great civil servant Sir Charles Trevelyan, who had married Macaulay's sister Hannah. His father, Sir George Trevelyan, was an active Liberal MP and a historian of no mean gifts. Apart from his classic biography of his uncle, Lord Macaulay, he wrote an account of the early life of Charles James Fox and a full-scale history of the American Revolution; books now forgotten, but well received in their day and rightly so. In particular George Macaulay Trevelyan was always conscious of the great-uncle from whom he derived his middle name. The legacy, of course, was double-edged. In 1926 or 1927, when he began work on Queen Anne's reign, he admitted that: 'the idea of taking up the tale where my great-uncle's history had broken off was perhaps a fancy at the back of my consciousness'. But in his youth he was conscious of the dangers of Macaulay's magnetic style; he told his brother in 1900: 'I always read Ruskin while I am writing to prevent falling into Macaulayese.'[57]

An able if rather priggish young man, he initially found life in the Cambridge of the 1890s almost entirely congenial. He took a first in history in 1898 and was elected to a fellowship at Trinity – the first fellowship in history at that college. He rewrote his fellowship dissertation and published it in 1899 as *England in the Age of Wycliffe*; a raw work, perhaps, but one of rare distinction for a man of his age and experience.

But Cambridge was not all honey and roses. Even as an undergraduate he was disproportionately dismayed by an interview he had with Sir John Seeley, who curtly told him that Macaulay and Carlyle (whom Trevelyan idolized, and read and reread all his life) were both charlatans. Lord Acton himself

*30 May 1957. Who the obituarist had in mind when he wrote of 'the clerical right' is unfortunately not clear.

soothed the well-connected youth, assuring him (rather ambiguously) that 'for all his faults [Macaulay] was on the whole the greatest of historians'. No doubt Trevelyan soon realized that Seeley was then dying of cancer, and may not even have realized who this undergraduate was; but he was not appeased. In 1949 he said: 'I still resent his words', and a close friend says he even remembered them on the day of his death, in 1962. This sensitivity to the family honour – for this is what it was – tells us a great deal about him.[58]

But worse was to come with Bury's famous inaugural on the science of history in 1903. Trevelyan's published riposte setting forth the claims of history to be considered as literature placed him in the forefront of Bury's opponents, and in 1904 he resigned his fellowship at Trinity and retired to London.* There were, of course, other reasons for this move. To judge by his later career, he found teaching uncongenial, and something he was not particularly good at. He was attracted by the literary life of London, and found a certain fulfilment in Liberal politics, even if it meant associating with radicals like Tawney and the Hammonds.[59] He probably overestimated Bury's authority at Cambridge, just as he misunderstood his message, and he may have feared changes which it was not in the power of a regius professor to make. He always insisted that he had no personal animus against Bury, and at his own inaugural lecture in 1927 he paid his predecessor some handsome and probably genuine compliments. But in the interval he was curiously distanced from academic life. Happening to meet Warden Smith of New College, he was astonished when Smith launched into a furious tirade against his own regius professor; he was quite ignorant of the furore provoked by Firth's inaugural, and it all had to be explained to him. He referred to Firth's successor, H.W.C. Davis, as 'the excellent Davis', and to the British Academy as 'the fatuous dons who compose the so-called "British Academy"'.[60] Not until he was over fifty did he undertake anything like detailed archival work, and he never wrote an article or a paper for a learned journal. In fact he was the antithesis of many modern historians, who seem able to write articles but not books. Trevelyan could only write books, which he did with extraordinary flair and rapidity.

England under the Stuarts, published in November 1904 as the first volume in Methuen's new 'History of England' series, was one of his most successful books, and it set the tone for all the others. Out of date as it obviously is, it is still in print today. (It was lightly revised in 1925.) Bearing in mind that this was the first essay in what is now an overcrowded genre – one-volume textbooks on the seventeenth century – it was a remarkable synthesis, a blend of shrewdness and romanticism, the romanticism coming through especially in his accounts of warfare, where he displayed an unerring sense of place he

*See p. 176 above.

never lost. Here he describes the dreary manœuvres and counter-manœuvres of the Civil War armies in the Thames Valley in 1643:

> 'Sometimes Hampden and his troopers pounced down from his wooded Chilterns into the plain below; or Essex wound down in slow pomp of horse, foot and artillery over the uplands south of the Thames. More often Rupert, issuing from the fortress of Magdalen College at the bridgehead, where he was quartered with the hardest riders of the army, could be seen at first light of morning high on Shotover Hill, galloping towards glory and thunder afar.'

Or Rupert again, at Marston Moor in 1644:

> 'The sun was falling low, the Puritans had struck up the evening psalm, Rupert had retired to supper, and Newcastle to his coach to smoke, when suddenly the three Roundhead armies rolled down off the high cornlands where they stood, onto the moor, where the strength of monarchy in England had been gathered to a head and exposed at one stroke to ruin.'[61]

He always had a deep love of the countryside, later carried to bucolic excess. To him all seventeenth-century England was a garden, except where industry had already pushed out its 'iron claws', and he had a marked distaste for towns (except market towns, of course), which was part of a general distaste for the times in which he lived, which in the nature of things could only grow worse to him as life advanced. 'One condition of modern life', he wrote in 1904, 'is that what pays best is generally ugly, and that whatever man now touches for a purely economic reason he mars.'[62] He once told A.L. Rowse that 'he disliked practically everything since the Industrial Revolution'. 'Even I', says Rowse, 'thought that that was going a bit far.'[63]

He saw the emergence of religious toleration as the pre-eminent triumph of seventeenth-century Englishmen, amongst many other triumphs of that chosen race. 'At a time', he wrote, 'when the Continent was falling a prey to despots, the English under the Stuarts had achieved their emancipation from monarchical tyranny by the act of national will; in an age of bigotry, their own divisions had forced them into religious toleration against their real wish.'[64] He was as ready as Gardiner had been to assume the existence of a nation acting and speaking as one, but he was realistic about Puritanism in a way which Gardiner was not. He saw it as 'a social and spiritual influence inside the pale of the Church', and it was only persecution that made it 'a sect in religion and politics'. Even then, Trevelyan knew the Puritans were always a minority, though 'when at last the Puritan idealists rode out to battle against the King, they were followed by neighbours Pliable and Worldly-Wiseman, who had come to imagine by force of long political sympathy that they themselves were Puritans'.[65]

As for Cromwell, to Trevelyan he was a flawed hero, but a hero nonetheless. He was above all a man of circumstance. After the death of Charles I 'he took upon his massive shoulders the load of obloquy inherent in a situation created chiefly by the faults of others. Those Herculean shoulders are broad enough to bear also the blame for a deed pre-eminently his own, inscribed like a gigantic note of interrogation across the page of English history.'[66] Yet his muse was at the service, too, of that Divine Right which ultimately destroyed the great Protector's work:

'Obedience to the King was still in the age of Pym, as the worship of the Saints had still been in the age of Latimer, an instinct inborn in every child of the race at that stage of its evolution, wrapped in a thousand mysterious associations with a remote and still unbroken past, transmitted from father to son through thirty generations, since the kings of the Heptarchy had crushed their rebel thanes in ages which, though long forgotten, still had their influence on ideas unconsciously inherited.'[67]

No economic tension, no social jealousy, was allowed to mar this idealistic picture; and he persisted in this denial in his *History of England* in 1926, and even as late as 1940 in *English Social History*. It was to England's glory that her civil war had been a political war, a clash of parties. 'The French Revolution', he said, 'was a war of two societies; the American Civil War was a war of two regions; but the Great Rebellion was a war of two parties.'[68] To Trevelyan the two-party system was not an *ad hoc* political mechanism arising by chance, but a deliberate expression of all that was best in the English character, a theme he elaborated in his Romanes Lecture at Oxford in 1926.

This patriotic, romantic view of English history was well attuned to the mood of the post-Boer-War generation in England, the same generation which was entranced by Rupert Brooke's poetry, and departed to Flanders in 1914 and 1915 as to a crusade. Trevelyan's argument was that:

'Revolution is the historian's touchstone, by which to try the quality of a race or age. It may succeed or fail, pass or stay; but it will in any case reveal the worth or vileness of the soil whence it springs. That most rare of human events, a revolution loftily enacting lofty ideals, can occur only in a state where wealth is well distributed, classes fairly balanced and kindly related, the common intellectual food wholesome, the imagination alive and the moral standard high.'[69]

By the 1920s this approach had become mildly embarrassing, particularly in academic circles, though many others were plucking the same lyre, even if they did not make the same music – notably the Oxford historian and Conservative MP, J.A.R. (later Sir John) Marriott. Trevelyan's trilogy on Garibaldi and the Unification of Italy, published between 1909 and 1911, was different; it was recognizably an epic story which called for epic treatment, and it was safely distanced from England and set in a more romantic, even passionate venue. A certain excitement was understandable when dealing with Italian themes. Though it was always superficial and is now out of date, this trilogy was written with burning conviction and infused with Trevelyan's deep love of Italy; of all his works it seems the most likely to survive, if only as a piece of historical literature. However, by the 1920s his general popularity was enormous; he was the people's historian, and those in authority gladly bowed to the public will. Baldwin sent him back to Cambridge in 1927, ironically to succeed Bury as regius professor. George V admitted him to the Order of Merit in 1930, though he refused a knighthood, and in 1940 Winston Churchill appointed him Master of Trinity. Like Churchill, he was one of the very few non-scientists in this century to be elected a Fellow of the Royal Society.

To some his return to academe was not entirely welcome. Four years later, in 1931, a young Peterhouse historian, Herbert Butterfield, published a mildly sensational and highly influential essay on *The Whig Interpretation of History*. Butterfield was a tough and highly serious Yorkshire Methodist, with an intense, elusive style which was later to become famous, and an obliquity unusual in a Yorkshireman. (He attained the regius chair himself in 1963.) He politely but ruthlessly attacked historians whose interpretation of the past was influenced by their view of the present; the less they and their readers were aware of this predisposition the more dangerous it was. Some of his criticisms seemed to be directed at Acton, who, apart from one reference to Hallam, was the only historian mentioned by name, but it was generally assumed when the book was first published that it was directed chiefly at Trevelyan, together with his Whig predecessors Gardiner and Stubbs. Butterfield denied this more than once, but Trevelyan himself said it must refer to him, because he was 'the last Whig historian in the world', and certainly Butterfield must have been singularly obtuse not to realize that most of his strictures were immediately applicable to his own regius professor.[70] For instance, in his preface he said:

'What is discussed [in this book] is the tendency in many historians to write on the side of Protestants and Whigs, to praise revolutions provided they have been successful, to emphasise certain principles of progress in the past and to produce a story which is a ratification if not the glorification of the present'.

Later he remarked: 'It is astonishing to what an extent the historian has been Protestant, progressive and Whig, and the very model of the nineteenth-century gentleman', which sounds much more like Trevelyan than Acton, who Butterfield pretended was his prime target; and in the following passage he may well have been drawing a contrast between Trevelyan and Macaulay:

'It is not a sin in a historian to introduce a personal bias that can be recognised and discounted. The sin of historical composition is the organisation of the story in such a way that bias cannot be recognised, and the reader is locked along with the writer in what is really a treacherous argument in a circle'.

And finally, he was severe on that 'alarmism' which is the peculiar disease of English constitutional history, but which particularly infects the seventeenth century:

'The whig historian is apt to imagine the British constitution as coming down to us safely at last, in spite of so many vicissitudes, when in reality it is the result of those very vicissitudes of which he seems to complain. If there had never been a danger to our constitution there never would have been a constitution to be in danger'.[71]

Whether or not they were intended, there is no doubt that Butterfield's criticisms had a lowering effect on Trevelyan's reputation in a profession now becoming increasingly professionalized and unsentimental. Yet his return to academic life implied obligations which he was very ready to accept. He was an awful lecturer, reading from a script and reading badly, and he only ever had one officially accredited research student – the young J.H. Plumb, who gained his Ph.D. in 1936 with a dissertation on the parliaments of William III. But he considered research to be his most important professorial duty, and it was fortunate that in 1927 he was already embarked on a new history of Queen Anne's reign.[72] This was the only book for which he undertook detailed and rigorous work into sources, but even then it was completed with his usual speed, and published in three volumes between 1930 and 1934 as *England under Queen Anne*.

As we have seen, he had vague ideas of continuing his great-uncle's *History*, and at the same time doing justice to Marlborough, whom Macaulay had most spitefully used; but to him this reign also marked the heroic culmination of English seventeenth-century history, when a nation which had solved her own problems went on to solve Scotland's and win the hegemony of Europe. It remains his greatest achievement in the field of English history. He rose magnificently to the great heroic set-pieces – Blenheim, Ramillies, Gibraltar, Minorca and Oudenarde – and his sensitivity to literature also stood him in good stead when he came to deal with Swift, Defoe, Steele and Prior; but he also covered with unexpected skill the minutiae of parliamentary negotiation and cabinet intrigue, for which Keith Feiling's *History of the Tory Party* in 1924 had given him a taste. Even his rigid adherence to the two-party interpretation of the politics of the reign, after passing through a period in which it seemed hopelessly out of date, has now swung back into fashion.

England under Queen Anne did much to bolster his reputation, and at Cambridge there has always been a Trevelyan claque; its latest manifestation was Owen Chadwick's inaugural lecture as regius professor in 1968, on 'Freedom and the Historian'. On his retirement the Trevelyan Lectures were founded by the History Faculty in conscious emulation of the Ford Lectures at Oxford. But it is strange how many of Trevelyan's disciples are moved to defend him by comparing him with his great professional contemporary, Namier, as if one necessarily excludes the other.[73]

Trevelyan has not been without his descendants, though some of them have been much less intellectual than he. C.V. Wedgwood, for instance, has gone on her way without a qualm, writing readable history for mass consumption without once asking, let alone answering, any question which modern scholarship would think relevant. (Trevelyan himself said to Rowse: 'You and I know that Veronica is a historian of the second rank.')[74] Unfortunately, with direct encouragement from historians like Rowse and Neale – though not Trevelyan himself – the standards of the market-place have become clamant. It has somehow become accepted that no work of history can be called great which does not sell to more than 20,000 persons, most of them half-educated, and be read by them with instant and uncritical enjoyment. But J.H. Plumb, naturally, is the historian most directly affected by Trevelyan, especially in his earlier work: each volume of his biography of Robert Walpole begins, or will begin, with a semi-social survey or panorama on the lines of the opening chapters of Trevelyan's *England under Queen Anne* or Macaulay's Chapter III: volume I, 'Walpole's World', volume II, 'Walpole's Europe', and volume III, 'Walpole's Empire'. But apart from this, Plumb's deep concern for the future of the discipline, expressed in *The Crisis of the Humanities* (1964) and *The Death of the Past* (1969), has its roots in the old dispute between Trevelyan and Bury. 'The knowledge of the mechanics of historical change', he says, 'is far more profound than it was two generations back. But much of the professionalism of history remains professional; in spite of the huge output of paperback histories, the results of history are not conveyed with the emphasis and cogency that society needs.'[75]

This bespeaks Trevelyan's powerful influence on those who met him face to face. It is not something obviously apparent to posterity, and some of the memoirs which have appeared since his death, even that by his daughter,

Mary Moorman, present a somewhat unattractive picture. George Kitson Clark, who was his Vice-Master at Trinity and knew him well, acknowledged that 'there remained curiously abrupt and complete limits to his understanding of those ways of thought which lay outside his experience'.[76] Towards the end of his life he was perfectly well aware that the verdict of the profession on his status as a historian was at variance with that of the public. As Kitson Clark said:

'Though working historians did not attack his books, though they did not cease to honour him as a man who, without lowering his standards, had interested thousands of men and women in history, they came increasingly to disregard his work, as that of a man who had not learned to ask the questions which it was now clear that historians must ask, or to use the techniques which alone could provide satisfactory answers to any questions of any sort.'

By 1950 his social attitudes were not so much old-fashioned as retrograde, especially when we glance aside at the work done by his contemporary R.H. Tawney and his followers in the field of economic history. Even Plumb admitted that in *England under Queen Anne*: 'He lays major stress on the ease, virtue and sweetness of life for the possessing classes, and glosses somewhat the brutality and suffering which were the lot of the common man.' (Though Plumb adds robustly: 'Perhaps this is right, for the quality of an age is not the work of common men, they but labour namelessly to support it.')[77]

His historical approach had always been governed by his social setting, which in Northumberland was as much as a generation behind the south; thus his outlook was not so much Victorian as early Victorian. His beau ideal was that great Northumbrian aristocrat Lord Grey of Fallodon, whose biography he wrote almost as an act of piety. All his adult life the world that had spawned him, the world he loved, was passing: a whole society of liberal, independent landowners and liberal London intelligentsia. Of this he was only too well aware. He had retreated on London in 1904, but the *Independent Review* he founded folded in a year or two, and in the next decade or so all the great reviews which had done so much to mould nineteenth-century opinion closed or shrank, losing not only their readership and their influence but the men of distinction who had thought it a privilege to write for them as well as a source of income. George Prothero resigned the chair of history at Edinburgh in 1899 to take the editorship of the great *Quarterly Review*, but by 1905 he was campaigning (without success) for the Provostship of King's Cambridge. 'To go on as a hireling of John Murray', he said, 'running an obsolete magazine and patching up other people's work, is a poor sort of business compared with governing a great institution like King's.'[78]

Trevelyan also lived long enough to realize that his long defence of the English countryside as he knew it, his devoted service to the National Trust, had been largely in vain; the motor car had won. The decline of the Liberal Party, the rise of Italian fascism, warned him of the passing of other landmarks. As early as 1911 he was saddened that the Italian bombardment of Tripoli, which utterly disgusted him, should be led by the battleship *Garibaldi*. The Great War was bad enough, but the Second World War numbed him. He told his brother in October 1939: 'One half of me suffers horribly. The other half is detached, because the world that is threatened is not my world, which died years ago. I am a mere survival. Life has been a great gift, for which I am grateful, though I would gladly give it back now.'[79]

But even in 1904 he was writing with nostalgia of a former England, not just the England of the seventeenth century, but the England of his father and grandfather. That nostalgia returned with redoubled force in old age, and dominated his last book, *English Social History: a Survey of Six Centuries*. He had begun to write it in the 1930s, after finishing with Queen Anne's reign; it was intended as a complete social history of England, a companion to the short political and constitutional history he had published ten years before. But apart perhaps from a slightly intensified patriotic verve it was a book which might easily have been written in the 1890s or the early 1900s. In 1940 he decided to leave the first part unwritten, and begin with Chaucer; it was natural for him to end with Victoria's death. He regarded it as a contribution to the war effort, which in its way it was. It was published in America in 1942, in England two years later, and its flag-waving patriotism, its intense nostalgia for the English past, its chauvinistic assumption that England had always been great and England had always been right, catered to an obvious public need in the weary closing stages of the war, and the disillusioning postwar years of continued austerity and imperial decline. Academic historians might sneer at its romantic and sentimental presentation, its misplaced fondness for a bygone 'Merrie England' which was really an era of squalor, disease and human degradation, its simpleminded assumption that there was nothing to social history but 'history with the politics left out', but the public adored it, and it is still one of the best-selling history books of all time. By 1949 it had sold 400,000 copies in Britain alone; after that Longmans issued an illustrated four-volume edition 1949–52, later taken into paperback by Pelican. As late as 1978 it was republished in one volume with new illustrations, and with a title, *Trevelyan's English Social History*, which assumed for it a classic status.

This is a striking example of the way in which popular taste diverges so often from the academic, and ignores social trends. In the era of the new Welfare State the public sought out an author who was not only old-fashioned in almost every respect but a profound snob; a spokesman for the nobility and gentry, the squires and yeomen, 'owners of wealth, great and small', 'classes with which he was instinctively familiar, and from which he derived his own ancestry'. In *English Social History*, in fact, he sang their elegy, responding to 'their aspirations and to the beauty of the material civilisation which they created', and accepting, 'if uneasily, the poverty and suffering upon which it was, of necessity, based'.[80] But historians had long ago emerged behind Trevelyan who were not acceptive of poverty or suffering, even in the distant past, whose burning sense of social injustice, whether in the past or in the present, was to overwhelm his mandarin complacency.

Tawney and Social History

Richard Henry Tawney was born in 1880 at Calcutta, where his father, a noted Sanskrit scholar, was Principal of the Residency College. His was a distinguished upper-middle-class family and his forebears in the eighteenth century had been bankers, a fact which he took no pains to conceal but which he was not prepared to discuss in later life. He went to Rugby and in 1899 to Balliol. At Rugby he made a lifelong friend in William Temple, later archbishop of Canterbury, and at Oxford he also came under the influence of Canon Charles Gore, later bishop of Birmingham; both inspired him with a belief in the social and political mission of the Church of England. In fact, Tawney remained all his life a sincere Anglo-Catholic; as an old man it was said of him: 'He would frequently but not regularly go to church, often taking his dog, less frequently his wife.'[81]

At Balliol he was regarded as an undergraduate of surpassing brilliance, and there was consternation when he only took a second in Greats. (His father asked him: 'How do you propose to wipe out this disgrace?') It was probably a decisive turning-point: a first would have brought him a college fellowship, and held him in Oxford academic life. His second sent him to London, where he was soon engaged in slum missions like that run from Toynbee Hall, and work for the Children's Country Holiday Fund. Like the Hammonds, who soon became his friends, he was appalled by the squalor and starvation, the abysmal relationship between master and man, which lay beneath the pompous and vulgar glitter of Edwardian England. He joined the Independent Labour Party, but like Trevelyan he was soon aware that his most effective role lay in teaching and writing. The economic history of the past would expose the futility of the present and prepare the ground for reform.

The study of economic history in Britain had begun at much the same time as the serious study of constitutional history. There was an obvious need to explain the Industrial Revolution, and still more so the failure of the momentum of that Revolution in the 1880s and 1890s and the accompanying agricultural depression. The new discipline also drew inspiration from the great German school of economic theorists of which the most significant, though not the most scholarly, was Karl Marx, and from the post-classical economists nearer home, led by Alfred Marshall.[82]

In 1860 Thorold Rogers began that minute study of Oxford college accounts and estate documents which bore fruit in his *History of Agriculture and Prices in England* (8 vols, 1866-1902). In 1888 Rowland Prothero, younger brother of George (and later to become Lord Ernle), published *The Pioneers and Progress of English Farming*, which went through several revisions before achieving its final form in 1912 as *English Farming Past and Present*. Meanwhile at Oxford Arnold Toynbee,* of Balliol, was one of the first tutors to devote himself to the new subject, and his pioneering lectures on the Industrial Revolution, though they were cut short by his premature death in 1883, roused considerable attention. They were later published from his notes. It was typical of the proselytizing tone of economic and social history at this time that these lectures were also delivered to large audiences of managers and workers in some of the major industrial towns.

Toynbee deeply influenced a young Balliol postgraduate student, W.J. Ashley, who took a first in modern history in 1881 and also began to teach economic history; in 1885 he was elected a fellow of Lincoln College. In 1888 he published *An Introduction to English Economic History and Theory*, and in the same year he was appointed professor of political economy at Toronto. In 1892 he went on to Harvard, to the first chair in economic history in the English-speaking world, though he returned to England in 1901 as professor of commerce at Birmingham. The first full chair of economic history in England, or indeed the Empire, was established at Manchester in 1910 for the remarkable George Unwin, the son of a railway clerk at Stockport, who left school at the age of thirteen and later proceeded by scholarships first to University College, Cardiff, then to Lincoln, Oxford, where he took a first in philosophy in 1897. His major works, on *Industrial Organisation in the Sixteenth and Seventeenth Centuries* (1904) and *The Gilds and Companies of London* (1908), were written while he was working as secretary to the Liberal MP Leonard Courtney.

In the Oxford School of Modern History the new subject was regarded

* Not to be confused with his nephew and namesake, the mega-historian.

with polite indifference, and though it gained a foothold in 1884 in the paper on 'Political Science and Political Economy', it was not until 1902 that the words 'with economic history' were shyly added to the title. In 1916 it broke away in a separate paper under the title 'Economic History with Economic Theory', but the very rise of economics proper tended to overshadow its subsidiary, and in the reform of 1936 it was broken up and distributed amongst the three papers on English political and constitutional history, divided at 1307 and 1660.[83] The Chichele chair in economic history was not established until 1937.

At Cambridge the picture was much the same, though with less excuse, for here the subject was infused by the remarkable energies of Archdeacon William Cunningham, still regarded in his old university as the veritable founder of economic history in Britain generally if not the world.[84] Born at Edinburgh in 1849, he was educated at Edinburgh University, Göttingen and Cambridge, where he was bracketed equal top of the Moral Sciences Tripos in 1872 with F. W. Maitland. He was ordained in 1873, but spent the next five years organizing a scheme of university extension lectures, first in Yorkshire, then in Lancashire. He returned in 1878 as chaplain of Trinity and Secretary of the Local Examinations Syndicate. Finding that no one else would accept responsibility for teaching the second half of the new Tripos paper 'Political Economy and Economic History', he took it upon himself, and as soon as he found that his students had no textbook to fall back on he wrote one.

This book, *The Growth of English Industry and Commerce*, first published in 1882, is his chief memorial. What started as a comparatively small volume went through six subsequent editions, swelling all the time, and did not reach finality, or as near finality as Cunningham was prepared to take it, until 1910. It was always as much a work of continuing research as of compilation or even synthesis. Thus the first volume of the second edition, in 1890, only covered the Middle Ages, the second volume following in 1892. In 1903 this second volume split into two, and substantial revisions and alterations were made to all three volumes in 1905, 1907 and 1910. In the meanwhile Cunningham served as vicar of Great St Mary's, the university church, from 1887 to 1908, and as archdeacon of Ely from 1907; he published extensively on ethical and spiritual questions, especially in relation to capitalism, and travelled widely; at one time or another he visited India, Palestine, France, Germany and Sweden, as well as lecturing twice at Harvard by invitation, in 1899 and 1914. Incredibly, he also served as Tooke professor of economics and statistics at King's College, London, from 1891 to 1897. Though he lived until 1919, active almost to the end, he was a figure in the heroic Victorian mould.

Nevertheless Cambridge, like Oxford, was slow to adjust to the new subject. Cunningham, in the Victorian absolutist way, acted as though it would come to an end with his death. In 1885, to his considerable chagrin, Alfred Marshall was preferred to him as professor of political economy, and subsequently there was a certain personal antagonism as well as a divergence of views between the two men. It was left for Marshall to provide for the future of economic history at Cambridge by poaching from Acton one of his most brilliant students, the young John Henry Clapham of King's. In 1897 he asked Acton to release Clapham from his research into the French Revolution, and in 1898 he was elected a fellow of King's.[85] After a short spell as professor of economics at Leeds from 1902 to 1908, Clapham duly returned to King's as tutor in history. He was soon engaged in teaching for the new paper in 'English Economic History', added to the Tripos in 1909, and a chair of economic history was created for him eventually in 1928. But in 1934, as at Oxford two years later, economic history was distributed across the three basic papers in English history, divided at 1485 and 1689 (later 1760).[86]

Up to the turn of the century, moreover, the trend in economic history at the universities was decidedly whiggish – the counterpart in the economic field to Stubbs and Gardiner. Cunningham's emphasis, and Clapham's, was always on 'growth', on 'achievement', even on Britain's 'imperial destiny'. It was focused on banking, trade and business, fields in which England's success had been as striking as in politics and law, and it was implicitly if not avowedly acceptive of capitalism. The Industrial Revolution was presented as an almost unqualified success story. Nor was this entirely accidental. W.J. Ashley saw it as the first function of his department at Birmingham to train those who would 'ultimately guide the business activity of the country'.[87] He and Unwin were both strongly influenced by the German economic theorists, and saw it as their chief purpose to bring history and theory together. Even Unwin, despite his working-class origins and experience, was more interested in the organization of industry from the top.

The opposite thrust came from LSE, the London School of Economics and Political Science, founded in 1895 by a benefaction from Henry Hunt Hutchinson, with Sidney Webb as chairman of the board of governors. Then as now, it is a vulgar error to suppose that LSE was manned by advanced socialists. It numbered amongst its early lecturers Charles Firth, the legal historian A.V. Dicey, and the antiquary and records specialist Hubert Hall. It also received important benefactions from the great Edwardian industrialist Sir Ernest Cassel, as well as from the Rockefeller Foundation.[88] One of the conundrums of twentieth-century English historiography is that it has been so little influenced by Marxism, and in fact the principal English Marxist historian of this century, Maurice Dobb, was based at King's College, Cambridge. The stance adopted by the Webbs, the Hammonds, Tawney and other associates of LSE in its early days can best be described as left-wing Liberal; for a time Trevelyan himself was one of their number.

The Hammonds were typical of this middle-class coterie devoted to practical philanthropy and higher thought. John Lawrence Le Breton Hammond was a clergyman's son. Like Tawney he read Greats at Oxford and got a second; after that he earned a precarious living as a political journalist in London. In 1901 he married Barbara Bradby, daughter of a famous headmaster of Haileybury, who had given up a fellowship at Lady Margaret Hall and the prospect of an Oxford academic career the better 'to wrestle with the evils of the world'.[89] Their joint labours produced two huge studies of working-class conditions before and during the Industrial Revolution, *The Village Labourer* (1911) and *The Town Labourer* (1917). These were works of serious and painstaking research, but they were equally tracts for the time, provoked by the rural destitution which was the concern of all Liberal governments from the 1890s onwards, as well as the violent industrial unrest which reached a climax in 1911–12. In fact, it has been said that these books 'can not unfairly be regarded as historical prefaces to the Rural and Urban Reports of Lloyd George's Land Enquiry Committee, published in October 1913 and April 1914'. In more general terms, to Gilbert Murray they were 'books that made a permanent difference to one's outlook'.[90]

The Hammonds did not take it upon themselves to judge capitalism; like Tawney at this stage they accepted it, for good or ill, as the prevailing economic system, though they were hopeful of reforming it. Their argument was that the sordid and inhumane origins of the present system had left a mark on it which was still evident in current practice. In *The Village Labourer* they argued that the enclosure movement of the eighteenth century had unfeelingly destroyed the seigneurial, paternal relationship between lord and man which was the basis of the old agricultural society, and had put nothing in its place. Many villagers had been driven from the land altogether into the towns, and those who remained had had to accept a lower standard of life. They were still, in 1911, virtually helots.

The Town Labourer was even more damning, and here the Hammonds had the backing of a large section of early Victorian opinion, not least Frederick Engels's. They argued that the working class had never participated in the huge profits accruing from the Industrial Revolution; not only had their living standards fallen disastrously in the new slums of the factory towns, but the amount of real money at their disposal had also declined. They did not suggest that this was the result of a conscious policy on the part of the managerial classes, but they did indict them for moral blindness and a crying lack of social responsibility.

After the war the Hammonds went on to publish *The Skilled Labourer* (1919) and *The Rise of Modern Industry* (1925). But their whole thesis, in so far as it affected the factory worker, was vigorously rebutted by John Clapham in the first volume of a comprehensive *Economic History of Modern Britain*, published in 1926. Clapham reacted strongly against what he regarded as left-wing denigration of the achievements of the Industrial Revolution, and though he admitted that the comparatively sudden concentration of large numbers of families in the new towns had placed them in sub-standard living conditions, he brought statistical evidence to bear which showed that their standard of living in terms of purchasing power and real wages had markedly increased. This was the beginning of the great 'Standard of Living' debate, which raged to and fro, from generation to generation, over the next forty years and beyond, until the original combatants, Clapham and the Hammonds, were almost forgotten.[91] On the whole, in the profession the 'optimistic' or 'acceptive' school of thought may be said to have prevailed, but the general public have been left with the idea that the Industrial Revolution was a period of callous exploitation – a thesis transmitted to a wider public still in socialist histories like *The Common People 1746-1938* by G.D.H. Cole and Raymond Postgate, and *A People's History of England*, by A.L. Morton, both published in 1938, the latter by the Left Book Club. This was part of a conscious attempt to provide a historical background for the Labour Party, and led in addition to an increasing preoccupation with the Levellers; the Tories could keep Pitt and Burke, Labour had Lilburne (and Wat Tyler). The Hammonds' work, in popular translation, had an important role to play. A popular summary published in 1930, *The Age of the Chartists*, was abridged again and emerged with the evocative title *The Bleak Age* in 1934. This enjoyed even wider success in 1947, when it was reissued as a Pelican paperback.

There is no doubt where Tawney's sympathies lay, at any stage. In 1912 he wrote: 'The supreme interest of economic history lies, it seems to me, in the clue which it offers to the development of those dimly conceived presuppositions as to social expediency which influence the actions not only of statesmen, but of humble individuals and classes, and influence, perhaps, most decisively those who are least conscious of any theoretical bias.' Congratulating the Hammonds on *The Town Labourer*, he told them that they had succeeded 'in destroying the historical assumptions of which our modern slavery is based, unknown both to the slaves and the masters'.[92] Though he numbered George Unwin amongst his closest friends, he could never bring himself to regard economics as a science. 'We all respect economics,' he said casually in later years, 'it is a body of occasionally useful truisms.' As a young man his tone was sharper. 'There is no such thing as a science of economics', he wrote in

1912, 'nor ever will be. It is just cant, and Marshall's talk as to the need for social problems to be studied "by the same order of mind which tests the stability of a battleship" is twaddle.' (He always reacted badly to Alfred Marshall – 'the worthy Marshall', he called him.)[93] To his mind there could never be an exact science of human relations, for:

'In the infinite complexity of human relationships, with their interplay of law with economics, and of economics with politics, and of all with the shifting hopes and fears, baseless anticipations and futile regrets of countless individuals, a change which to the statistician concerned with quantities seems insignificant, may turn a wheel whose motion sets a world of unseen forces grinding painfully round into a new equilibrium'.[94]

In 1903 Tawney helped found the Workers' Educational Association; he served on its executive from 1905 to 1947, and was president 1928–44. In 1906 he was appointed to an assistant lectureship in economics at Glasgow, but in 1908 he left to organize evening tutorial classes for working men in Lancashire and the Potteries under the Oxford University Extension Scheme. In 1909 he married Annette Beveridge, the sister of William, the future Lord Beveridge, and for the time being settled in Manchester. He enjoyed his work immensely, and cared deeply for his pupils. This was why in a period of intense class antagonism he was able to win the confidence and the affection of the potters, weavers and miners he taught, even though it is said of him that he 'preserved throughout his life the outward manners – not only the tone of voice, but also the *façon d'agir* – of an Edwardian and even Victorian gentleman with family roots in the English countryside, the Church and the Indian Civil Service'. The relationship comes through in the commonplace book he kept from 1912 to 1914, when industrial unrest was at its height, and some of his remarks have not entirely lost their relevance now. For instance:

'Workmen are regarded as servants, and when they strike they are said to be "disloyal", to be "rebelling", to be "treacherous". Now this attitude is really a public menace. It lowers the whole tone of national morality. It encourages the idea that the mass of the people are productive tools. One of the first lessons we need to impress on the rich is that they have got to be *disciplined* into being servants of the public. We must recover the idea of the position of the landlord and employer being a *post*, an *office*.'[95]

His first contribution to the class struggle was his book on *The Agrarian Problem of the Sixteenth Century*, in 1912, which supplemented the Hammonds' work by showing that the enclosure movement of the sixteenth century, like that of the eighteenth, was a tale of exploitation and greed, the exploitation of the peasantry by the yeomanry, the yeomanry by the gentry.

It was a remarkable piece of scholarship, considering the conditions under which it was written. Tawney realized its limitations better than some of his admirers, and, unable to find the time to revise it, he would not allow it to be reprinted in his lifetime. Much of it has now been disproved, or shown to be exaggerated. But at the time it carried great conviction, not least because it was written with a burning power which distinguishes all Tawney's best work. His hatred of privilege comes through most strongly in passages like this, on the English 'county set':

> 'That blind, selfish, indomitable aristocracy of county families, which made the British Empire and ruined a considerable proportion of the English nation. From the galleries of their great mansions and the walls of their old inns their calm, proud faces, set off with an occasional drunkard, stare down on us with the unshakable assurance of men who are untroubled by regrets or perplexities, men who have deserved well of their order and their descendants, and await with confidence an eternity where preserves will be closer, family settlements stricter, dependents more respectful, cards more reliable, than in this imperfect world they well can be'.[96]

His rejection of his own class was total. He was once pressed to admit middle-class people to his WEA tutorials – after all, it was argued, God made the middle classes, just like anyone else. 'Are you sure?' said Tawney quizzically.[97]

The Great War interrupted his career, but it did not pose the agonizing problems of conscience it did for many socialists. As a Christian he believed that England's cause was just and right, and he never lost that conviction, though he was critical later of the way the war was conducted. He enlisted in December 1914, rose to the rank of sergeant, and was severely wounded at Fricourt in 1916 and invalided out. Strangely enough, it was in the trenches that he first met Lieutenant Clement Attlee. He was now well known as a historian and a Christian socialist. While still convalescent he helped Charles Gore prepare a report on 'Christianity and Industrial Relations', and in 1919 he joined the Sankey Commission on the coal industry, where he acquired plenty of fresh evidence of the iniquity of economic privilege. He also served on the Consultative Committee of the Board of Education which in 1926 produced the epochal Hadow Report on 'The Education of the Adolescent'.

Meanwhile his professional stature was confirmed by his election to a Balliol fellowship in 1918, but he transferred to LSE the following year as a reader in economics, at the request of his brother-in-law, William Beveridge, now director of the School. He was impressed by the new social unity and spirit of inter-class cooperation evident during the war, and slower than most to admit that it was a temporary phenomenon. But in *The Acquisitive Society*, in 1921, he advocated the nationalization of industry on a large scale, the abolition of unearned dividends, and the sweeping away of what he called 'functionless property'. He castigated the Church of England for abdicating its social responsibilities, and making religion 'the ornament of leisure, instead of the banner of a crusade'. The clergy, he said, 'acquiesced in the popular assumption that the acquisition of riches was the main end of man, and confined themselves to preaching such personal virtues as did not conflict with its achievement'. This and *Equality*, published at the height of the Depression in 1931, are two of the most brilliant political tracts published this century, and foreshadow the creation of the Welfare State which will always be associated with the name of his brother-in-law, Beveridge.

His distaste for the Church of England as an institution, and his rage against the possessing classes, spilled out into his most important and influential work, *Religion and the Rise of Capitalism*, published in 1926. It was a critique of the thesis advanced by the great German sociologist Max Weber, that Protestantism, by its emphasis on the work ethic and its approval of worldly success, had made possible the emergence of capitalism. In reply Tawney argued that capitalism emerged independently and irresistibly, and that Protestantism had merely adapted itself to it, though in a way which he himself found manifestly deplorable. It was a strange performance, its urbane and civilized argument suddenly illumined by great bursts of rococo description and flashes of sheer violence – as when he described the dissolution of the monasteries as 'a sweeping redistribution of wealth, carried out by an unscrupulous minority using the weapons of violence, intimidation and fraud, and succeeded by an orgy of interested misgovernment on the part of its principal beneficiaries'.[98] He lamented the disappearance of Christian morality from politics in the eighteenth century, and he closed with a great philippic against modern society:

'The quality in modern societies which is most sharply opposed to the teaching ascribed to the Founder of the Christian Faith lies deeper than the exceptional failures and abnormal follies against which criticism is most commonly directed. It consists in the assumption, accepted by most reformers with hardly less *naïveté* than by the defenders of the established order, that the attainment of material riches is the supreme object of human endeavour and the final criterion of human success. Such a philosophy, plausible, militant, and not indisposed, when hard pressed, to silence criticism by persecution, may triumph or may decline. What is certain is that it is the negation of any system of thought or morals which can, except by a metaphor, be described as Christian. Compromise is as impossible between the Church of Christ and the idolatry of wealth, which is the practical religion of capitalist societies, as it was between the Church and the state idolatry of the Roman Empire'.[99]

The book's influence was enormous, and sustained, and it was transferred early to paperback, in 1938. It is the main charge in the indictment drawn up against Tawney by conservative historians like Geoffrey Elton. According to Elton: 'it has greatly assisted in the decline of Protestant self-confidence and the consequent revival of Roman Catholicism, in the reaction against capitalism as an economic system, and even perhaps in the West's increasing inclination to relinquish world leadership'.[100] In the mainstream of seventeenth-century English history his near-hysterical magnification of Puritanism reinforced the views of Gardiner and Firth, and encouraged that school of thought, typified in this generation by Christopher Hill, which sees Puritanism as an all-embracing movement of overwhelming political force:

> 'On a world heaving with expanding energies, and on a Church uncertain of itself, rose, after two generations of premonitory mutterings, the tremendous storm of the Puritan movement. The forest bent; the oaks snapped; the dry leaves were driven before a gale, neither all of winter nor all of spring, but violent and life-giving, pitiless and tender, sounding strange notes of yearning and contrition, as of voices wrung from a people dwelling in Meshoc, which signifies Prolonging, in Kedar, which signifies Blackness, while amid the blare of trumpets, and the clash of arms, and the rending of the carved work of the Temple, humble to God and haughty to man, the soldier-saints swept over battlefield and scaffold their garments rolled in blood'.[101]

The main secondary influence on the neo-Puritan school was William Haller, whose study of *The Rise of Puritanism*, in 1938, was intended as the prologue to a thorough re-examination of John Milton's thought. It was an elegant and convincing book, which rapidly became a standard authority, but as its name implies it embraced the pseudo-Gardinerian assumption that the power and authority of Puritanism steadily increased from 1558 through 1640. Unfortunately, like most such books – though this time with some excuse – it rested its case almost entirely on 'literary' evidence found in sermons and works of theology or devotion. The voice of the lay Puritans was always muted, and it is difficult to assess their attitude even during parliamentary sessions. This has not prevented the establishment of this thriving sub-genre of historical thought which sees Puritanism as the guiding force behind all opposition to the crown in the early seventeenth century, a view most notably expressed in Christopher Hill's *Society and Puritanism in Pre-revolutionary England* (1964). Michael Walzer went even further: in *The*

Revolution of the Saints (1965) he argued that Puritanism was a revolutionary creed *per se*, like communism, though here he was to some extent building on the work of A.S.P. Woodhouse, in *Puritanism and Liberty* (1938). This takes no account of the revived interest in the Levellers, as precocious forerunners of nineteenth- and twentieth-century democratic ideas, and possibly founding fathers of the Labour Party.[102]

However, since the Second World War the pendulum of research has swung back. Doubts are now expressed as to whether there was any difference between 'Puritans' and 'Anglicans' at all, and there is a marked tendency to restrict the numbers of the Puritans and narrow the definition, to question the value of the term 'Puritanism' altogether, and to treat it as a source of confusion rather than enlightenment. Though Lawrence Stone, for instance, still regards Puritanism as a powerful political irritant, he is content to define it as 'no more than a generalised conviction of the need for independent judgment based on conscience and bible reading'.[103]

Meanwhile in 1926 Tawney helped to found the Economic History Society, and for seven years he was joint editor of its influential journal, *The Economic History Review*. During those years, however, much of his time was devoted to politics. He was one of that select group of academics and intellectuals – the others included Harold Laski, G.D.H. Cole, John Strachey and the Webbs – who guided and advised the leaders of the Labour Party. His influence on Stafford Cripps, whose religious views approximated to his own, was particularly strong. In those years of depression, distraction and stress he began to despair of parliament, and in the Labour Party manifesto of 1928, 'Labour and the Nation', which was largely his composition, he called for a concerted socialist attack on all fronts, and not just at Westminster. In 1932, when Ramsay MacDonald formed a National Government with Baldwin, Tawney joined Cripps, Bevan and Attlee in the Socialist League, which also envisaged direct action outside parliament.

But soon afterwards he began to withdraw from direct participation in politics. He was disillusioned by Labour's failure to establish itself as an alternative government, and by the apparent inability of any government to solve the problem of unemployment. Also, in 1931 he had been promoted to a chair at LSE, and he may well have decided that he was better employed moulding the minds of the students who flocked from abroad to what was now one of the most prestigious and influential schools of economics in the world.

At Houghton Street he was regarded with awe and affection, and the quality of his teaching and his example is indicated by the fact that almost all the leading professors of economic history in the next generation were at one time or another his pupils. He never suffered fools gladly, and one of his abiding upper-class traits was a lack of inhibition about saying so – Trevelyan was much the same. But his habitual aloofness was tempered by geniality, and his public persona was enhanced by the fact that by now he had acquired most of the attributes of the absent-minded professor, leaving half-eaten sandwiches to moulder among his papers, setting his jacket on fire with his pipe, emptying his pipe into his turn-ups. Much of his wardrobe would have disgraced a tramp, and his favourite black hat was so moth-eaten that he looked like nothing so much as 'a street musician caught by gunfire'.

He was now collecting material for a new book on the economic history of Tudor England. It never appeared, but in 1941 he published a thirty-page article in the *Economic History Review* which sparked off one of the most celebrated academic controversies of the century. It bore the innocent title, 'The Rise of the Gentry 1558-1640'.[104] Here he simply argued that the huge estates released onto the market by the Dissolution of the Monasteries in the 1530s had descended in that generation from the crown to the aristocracy, but in another generation or two they had again descended from the aristocracy to the gentry, and while the one declined sharply in economic power and authority as a result, the other made spectacular gains. The attempt of the crown to check this process created a tension which finally snapped in 1640, leading directly to the Great Rebellion, which was therefore what modern sociologists would call 'a revolution of rising expectations'.

It was a theory which won immediate acceptance. The article was beautifully written, lucidly argued, and buttressed by plausible statistics and references which no one had the time or the opportunity to check in the middle of the war. More important, it offered a satisfying and convincing explanation in economic terms of that established fact, the rise of the House of Commons over the same period. Neale's first book on the Elizabethan parliaments, in 1949, fitted it like a glove. It even accommodated Marxist dogma by positing a 'bourgeois revolution', preceding the 'revolution of the proletariat', which last was vaguely associated with the Leveller movement. Older, liberal explanations – 'love of liberty', 'hatred of privilege', 'devotion to the sanctity of law' – could now be abandoned without much regret, and 'The Rise of the Gentry' became the catchword of a new orthodoxy.

The first sign of trouble came as late as 1951. In 1945 a young Christ Church historian, Hugh Trevor-Roper, had returned from war service and published a bestseller on *The Last Days of Hitler*. He then began to probe Tawney's famous thesis on the gentry. He was still engaged in this task when another young Oxford don, Lawrence Stone, published a short paper on 'The Anatomy of the Elizabethan Aristocracy', which lent support to Tawney by exposing the extravagance and financial irresponsibility of many sixteenth-century English noblemen.[105] It was witty, entertaining and elegant, it seemed to reinforce Tawney's work at a crucial point, and tutors and lecturers hastened to press it on their persevering students.

But not for long. For in 1951 Trevor-Roper demolished Stone's paper in one of the most vitriolic attacks ever made by one historian on another: 'The Elizabethan Aristocracy: an Anatomy Re-anatomised'.[106] Stone's own description of the proceedings, that Trevor-Roper 'pointed out the extravagance of the language used, the very serious mistakes made in interpreting the statistical evidence for debt, and the unscholarly treatment of much of the ancillary evidence', is understandably restrained; it has also been called 'a magnificent if terrifying work of destruction'.[107] And when the pupil had been mugged the master could not expect to walk unscathed. In 1953 there duly appeared Trevor-Roper's full-scale demolition of Tawney's original thesis, in a lengthy supplement to the *Economic History Review* simply entitled *The Gentry 1540–1640*. He was not so brutal with Tawney as with Stone, but his axe was just as sharp, his club just as heavy. He showed that most of Tawney's statistics were wildly misleading – largely because they were based on a unit of measurement, the manor, which varied widely in size – and the casual contemporary evidence he had used to support his arguments could be matched by an equal amount of evidence pointing in precisely the opposite direction. In general Trevor-Roper concluded that the whole theory 'is not only unsupported by such evidence as has been adduced, but is positively repugnant to it'. He admitted that some elements in the landowning middle class were 'rising' in this period, but they were rising because of their access to court office or their involvement in trade or industry. The 'mere gentry', small landowners and nothing else, did not rise at all; on the contrary, they were remorselessly squeezed by the mounting inflation which was an admitted feature of the period. It was their desperation, not their ambition, which provoked the Great Rebellion and later radicalized it; in fact, in so far as Trevor-Roper's argument could be summed up in a phrase, he was arguing for 'The Decline of the Gentry'.

Tawney was now an old man. There is no doubt that the controversy pained him deeply, coming as it did at a time when he was more accustomed to an attitude of dazed respect. He made a brief, restrained reply, re-establishing some minor points; but on a broader front his professional judgment and competence had been impugned in the most public manner. Generous as always, be particularly regretted the tone Trevor-Roper had adopted towards Stone – 'An erring colleague', he said, 'is not an Amalekite, to be smitten hip and thigh'.[108] His last book, published in 1958, was muted and cautious, and it was received with an acclaim which was respectful rather than hearty. His choice of subject was unexpected – Lionel Cranfield, the London merchant and financier who rose to be James I's Lord Treasurer – but it was even more surprising that he found so little to criticize in a man whose career was a case study in capitalist exploitation.

Since his death in 1962 the decline in his reputation has continued. The statistical and evidential basis of one of his theories had already been destroyed; in 1967 Eric Kerridge, in a massive work on *The Agricultural Revolution*, undermined the other: his thesis that agrarian England under the Tudors was, to quote Kerridge, 'a giant manifestation of the exploitation of man by man', the operation of 'a relentless and remorseless agrarian capitalism which impiously rode down a wretched peasantry without any let or hindrance from the common law'. Kerridge's conclusion was particularly severe:

'Tawney the politician barred the way to Tawney the scholar. Time which he might have given to studying history was devoted instead to the Fabian Society and the Labour Party, and he tended to see the world past and present in terms of socialist dogma. Hence his wholly untrue picture of early capitalism as cruel and greedy, destructive alike of social welfare and true spiritual values. No one would wish to deny that Tawney was a great man, but his greatness caused him to lead generations of history students into grievous error'.[109]

As we have seen, G. R. Elton is another who believes that Tawney, probably unwittingly, was a malign influence on the younger generation. In his inaugural lecture at Cambridge in 1968 he said: 'With great regret I am coming to think increasingly that there is not a single word which that very good man Richard Tawney wrote which can be trusted. In all his work he was so dominated by his preconceptions that everything he wrote was unconsciously written to a propaganda purpose.' And he returned to the attack in 1977 in a splenetic correspondence in the *Times Literary Supplement*, where he again made the point that *Religion and the Rise of Capitalism* was 'one of the most harmful books written in the period between the wars'. Elton complained:

'At least one generation, and that a crucial one, was given grounds for believing that everything that contributed to the greatness and success of their country derived from sinful selfishness and money-grubbing wickedness. But this was not a truth demonstrated by Tawney's scholarship; it was a revelation from which he started and which directed the whole tenor of his argument. Tawney's example persuaded a powerfully influential school of historians that they may employ a method which involves selective study designed to document a previous conviction and neglectful of the changed setting in time, and that they are justified in doing so if their purpose is to serve a progressive cause'.[110]

There is no doubt that the asperity of such attacks was heightened by the uncritical hero-worship accorded Tawney in 'progressive' circles. Michael Postan, his contemporary and counterpart at Cambridge, said that he was 'simply the greatest living Englishman' – a phrase echoed by other worshippers. Even in 1980, on the centenary of Tawney's birth, Canon Eric James gushingly proclaimed in *The Times*: 'Tawney! Thou shouldst be living at this hour!'[111]

In fact, the saintliness of a man's character is irrelevant to considerations of scholarship, and there is considerable truth in Elton and Kerridge's criticism of Tawney's earlier work; it was influenced by his political beliefs, and the only palliation that can be offered is that he was perfectly well aware of it. The more circumspect of his defenders are driven back on the argument that if he misled a generation then his readers were at fault; his political bent was as well advertised as Macaulay's. But in defending his later work they are on firmer ground, and his theory of the rise of the gentry, however mistaken it might or might not be, exposed an area of genuine doubt, and generated a prolonged controversy which, while it reached no definite conclusions, produced substantial additions to our knowledge of seventeenth-century society and important extensions of theory.

It its initial stages the controversy generated more heat than light. Looking back on it all in 1965, Lawrence Stone austerely concluded that the episode had revealed 'the shoddy basis of much historical methodology'. 'Plausible rational grounds were found for quite contradictory hypotheses, since the proponent of each theory was free to choose his own evidence, and since there were too many individual facts pointing in too many different ways, this theorising could not – and here demonstrably was not – being controlled by facts.'[112] This is fair comment: the protagonists were like a group of card sharpers, shuffling and reshuffling the same greasy pack of facts and dealing them out in different patterns each time. But this was no longer so in the later stages of the controversy. A number of younger historians were inspired to write a series of detailed monographs on selected areas – Yorkshire, East Anglia, South Wales, Northamptonshire, Kent, and so on – which, while they demonstrated the complexity of the problem, at least extended the range of the evidence. Indeed, working from specialist studies of Kent and Cheshire respectively, Alan Everitt and John Morrill concluded that the tensions of local politics at county levels were a prime factor in the outbreak of the Great Rebellion, though this is still under debate.[113] In general, local history has been a growth area over the past thirty years, partly because of the tendency since the war for landed families to deposit their papers in county record offices, which have themselves been increasingly extended, restaffed and professionalized.

Meanwhile, Trevor-Roper had extended the basis of the controversy in another direction, to cover the contemporaneous revolts in Europe, notably in Spain, France and Italy. He posited a 'General Crisis of the Seventeenth Century', which he attributed to the undue weight of the bureaucracies which had been evolved by the post-renaissance monarchies and the difficulty of financing them.[114] In 1965 Stone, who had now left for Princeton, published the most important byproduct of the whole controversy in the form of a blockbusting 900-page study of *The Crisis of the Aristocracy 1558-1641*. He was still dogged by criticism of his methods, particularly his use of statistics, but the magnitude of his achievement was never in doubt.

Stone then went on to examine the general causes of the Great Rebellion, a task which, rather surprisingly, no one had attempted before. In *The Causes of the English Revolution*, in 1972, he sought the root causes in the Reformation, in a number of 'preconditions' over the century 1529-1629 which bred an atmosphere of chronic instability – or 'multiple dysfunction', as Stone called it – which was made still more unstable by the 'precipitants' which emerged during the Personal Rule of Charles I from 1629 to 1640, the Rebellion being finally set off by a number of 'triggers' in the last two years, 1640-42. In a notable review Elton pointed out that this was essentially a Gardinerian interpretation, that these voguish 'preconditions', 'precipitants' and 'triggers' were simply 'our old friends, circumstances and long-term causes', plus immediate friction.[115] Stone was displeased with the carping of those he calls 'antiquarian empiricists', but in his latest findings he has drastically shortened the time scale, and instead of 'multiple dysfunction' extending back to 1529 he now talks of a 'seismic rift' opening in 1621.[116] But even here he was pre-empted by Gardiner, as long ago as 1869. Writing of the Spanish Marriage project, which spanned the years 1618 to 1623, Gardiner said:

'When the marriage was first agitated, the leading minds of the age were tending in a direction adverse to Puritanism, and were casting about in search of some system of belief which would soften down the asperities which were the sad legacy of the second generation. When it was broken off, the leading minds of the age were tending in a precisely opposite direction, and that period of our history commenced which led up to the anti-episcopalian fervour of the Long Parliament, to the Puritan Monarchy of Cromwell, and in general to the re-invigoration of that which Mr Matthew Arnold has called the Hebrew element in our civilisation'.[117]

So there is no song but what it is an old song. But it is certainly strange, and an impressive tribute to the resilience of the topic, that the causes of the Great Rebellion are still the subject of intensive research and active debate.

Namier and the Eighteenth Century

The study of eighteenth-century history developed late. Much of the important documentation was not published until the 1830s and beyond, and when
it was it did not enhance the low regard in which the Hanoverian kings and
most of their ministers were held. Seeley said irritably in 1881:

> 'About the time of the accession of the House of Brunswick a change is
> supposed to have passed over affairs. A kind of winding-up took place, it
> is thought; all questions were settled, and history came to an end. Life
> settled down into uniform, comfortable prose; and from that time, though
> there is still politics such as one reads in the newspapers, there is no more
> history. There are indeed certain occurrences, events which it is useful to
> know, but nothing grand and classical – nothing the knowledge of which
> is learning, the acquiring of which is education'.[118]

There was certainly nothing 'grand and classical' about the eighteenth
century; it was dominated retrospectively by the loss of America, which
seemed the culmination of generations of sordid misgovernment. How Macaulay would have handled this period, had he reached it, is not entirely clear,
though he did not plan to extend himself on it – 'from the commencement of
Walpole's administration to the commencement of the American War, events
may be despatched more concisely', was what he said.* Some clues can be
gleaned from his essays, however. There he praised Sir Robert Walpole and
defended his use of corruption (which he much exaggerated), on the grounds
that it was inevitable in this generation. 'Walpole governed by corruption
because in his time it was impossible to govern otherwise ... We might as well
accuse the poor Lowland farmers who paid blackmail to Rob Roy of corrupting the virtue of the Highlanders, as accuse [him] of corrupting the virtue
of Parliament.' Walpole's rival Carteret was perhaps purer, but he was flawed:
'His measures were strong, prompt and daring, his oratory animated and
glowing. His spirits were constantly high. No misfortune, public or private,
could depress him. He was at once the most unlucky and the happiest public
man of his time.'[119] The Duke of Newcastle, of course, was a buffoon. 'No
man was so unmercifully satirised; but in truth he was himself a satire ready
made. All that the art of the satirist does for other men, nature had done for
him. Whatever was absurd about him stood out with grotesque prominence
from the rest of his character. He was a living, moving, walking caricature.'
Yet, said Macaulay, he was a dangerous buffoon: 'Under the guise of levity

* P. 70 above.

he was false beyond all example of political falsehood. All the able men of his time ridiculed him as a dunce, a driveller, a child who never knew his own mind for an hour together; and he overreached them all round.' Henry Fox was worse. He was a man of transcendent ability, but 'he had been trained in a bad political school, in a school, the doctrines of which were, that political virtue is the mere coquetry of political prostitution, that every patriot has his price, that government can be carried on only by means of corruption, and that the state is given as a prey to statesmen.' In fact, the only notable exception to the rule was the Elder Pitt. Under his 'Great Ministry', from 1757 to 1761, 'the filth of all the noisome and pestilential sewers of government was poured into one channel [via Newcastle, that is]; through the other passed only what was bright and stainless'. He admitted that Pitt was not without his faults, far from it; he was unstable, erratic and often insincere; but 'in an age of low and dirty prostitution ... it was something to have a man who might perhaps, under some strong excitement, have been tempted to ruin his country, but who never would have stooped to pilfer from her, a man whose errors arose, not from a sordid desire of gain, but from a fierce thirst for power, for glory and for vengeance'.[120]

This picture of eighteenth-century politics as a seething pool of corruption, with Pitt, the patriot minister, the only important politician not immersed in it, was entirely typical of nineteenth-century opinion. Direct bribery of MPs, which no modern historian has been able to detect, was very much taken for granted. According to Hallam, 'No one seriously called in question the reality of a systematic distribution of money by the Crown to the representatives of the people; nor did the corrupters themselves, in whom the crime always seems to be deemed less heinous, disguise it in private.' Macaulay remarks that it was 'to the lasting honour of Lord Rockingham, that his administration [in 1765] was the first which, during a long course of years, had the courage and the virtue to refrain from bribing Members of Parliament'.[121] Lord Stanhope thought that some of the charges of this nature brought against Walpole were inspired by party spite, but he admitted that he 'sometimes swerved from the straight path, and altogether lowered the tone of public morals'. William Hartpole Lecky, whose history of eighteenth-century England was published in 1879, took a more moderate view of the century as a whole, but he still seemed to assume that Walpole was guilty of gross bribery.[122] John Morley, whose short biography of Walpole was published in 1889, adopted substantially the same view as Macaulay, that his corruption was a symptom of a corrupt age:

'That Walpole practised what would now be regarded as political corruption is undeniable. But political conduct must be judged in the light of political history, [and] to say, with some modern writers, that Walpole organised corruption as a system, that he made corruption the normal process of parliamentary government, that he governed by means of an assembly which was saturated with corruption, is to use language enormously in excess of any producible evidence and of all legitimate inference.'[123]

The arrival in the British Museum in 1886 of the voluminous papers of the Duke of Newcastle and Lord Hardwicke had little immediate effect. Their bulk made them unmanageable. Basil Williams was the first to put them to effective use, in an article in the *EHR* for 1897 on 'The Duke of Newcastle and the Elections of 1734'. In some ways this article looked forward to the detailed techniques of Namier, but the new evidence for Newcastle's rather lurid electioneering only confirmed Williams's existing prejudice against the Pelhams, and it was not followed up. His deeply researched life of the Elder Pitt, published in 1913 and at once accepted as the standard biography, painted an almost entirely uncritical and laudatory picture of the man at the expense of most of his contemporaries, and particularly his fellow ministers. This was reinforced a generation later in his volume in the Oxford History of England, in 1939, *The Whig Supremacy 1714–1760*, and even more strongly in a joint study of *Carteret and Newcastle* in 1943, which was a sustained assault on the Augustan political system. The other standard history of the period, *England under the Hanoverians* by Sir Charles Grant Robertson, first published in Methuen's History of England series in 1911 and revised in 1930, conveyed much the same message.

But the great bone of contention was the opening years of George III's reign. All historians were agreed that in 1760 or 1762 George had initiated a momentous change, but they were not agreed what. What we loosely call the Tory interpretation of this episode held that George had simply set out to break the power of the Whig oligarchs who had kept his grandfather George II in thrall, and had called upon the Earl of Bute to form a new alignment of 'King's Friends'. This new system of management had nothing scandalous about it, it permitted the free play of Whig versus Tory politics for the first time in half a century, if anything it lessened political corruption, and it was entirely constitutional and was so regarded by all honest and disinterested contemporaries.

The Whig view had some contemporary support of a more decisive nature, in Edmund Burke's pamphlets and speeches, and in *The Letters of Junius*, but it was otherwise a mirror image of the other. George III had concealed his real policy from his accredited ministers by a system of 'double cabinet', and had set out to destroy the hallowed balance of the constitution, and even erect an arbitrary government, by enlisting a helot army of placemen and pensioners in the Commons. This was decidedly unconstitutional, and was so regarded, etc.[124]

The issues were befogged – as were most issues – by the explosive conduct of John Wilkes, his resistance to General Warrants in 1761, and the refusal of the Commons to accept his election for Middlesex in 1768. To Tory historians Wilkes was a debauched and unscrupulous demagogue who threatened the very fabric of good order; to the Whigs he was a gallant tribune of the people, championing their rights against the odious tyranny of an arbitrary monarch and his corrupt and incompetent minions. In the end the fiasco of the American Revolution gave the Whigs an obvious lever, though it was difficult to conceal the fact that Lord North's policy towards the colonies had had overwhelming bipartisan backing at the time. However, all arguments about George III's intentions were truncated, as it were, by his subsequent insanity and by the long wars against France beginning in 1792. Whatever he may have planned to do with the constitution or against it, he had obviously been thwarted, if not by the Americans, then by the French and his own malady. No one could trace a direct continuity between 1760 and 1820, so that moral arguments lost much of their force, and the 1760s could be viewed almost academically, and in isolation. In the early twentieth century the balance of debate swung towards the Whig interpretation because of the liberal historians' idolatry of Chatham; nothing could excuse the forced resignation of their idol in 1761, on the very crest of victory, or the 'shameful' Peace of Paris in 1763. To compound his villainy and obtuseness George had then ignored Chatham's sage advice on America. Yet no major historian, of the stature of Gardiner or Stubbs, or even Firth, had tackled the period at all until 1929, when an unknown newcomer called L. B. Namier published *The Structure of Politics at the Accession of George III.*

Despite the frank and affectionate biography written by his widow, there is much that is still obscure in the origins and early life of Lewis Bernstein Namier.[125] Nor is his own account of himself entirely to be trusted. However, he was born in 1888 in Austrian Galicia, one of the partitioned provinces of Poland, of a family of wealthy Jewish landowners who had renounced their faith and race in favour of Roman Catholicism. His name was Ludwik Bernatstyn, and he was known as Lewis Bernstein when he first arrived in the West. The 'Niemirowski' which he adopted, and anglicized to 'Namier' when he took out naturalization papers, merely signifies 'of the town of Niemirow'. The discovery at the age of nine that he was in fact a Jew administered a traumatic shock, which was to have endless repercussions in later years – in his sensitivity to antisemitism, his Zionism, his snobbery and his general neurosis.

He was sent abroad to be educated, and after false starts at Lausanne and

LSE he arrived in 1909 at Balliol, Oxford, on the invitation of A.L. Smith. Here he found all he sought, and more. He left in 1913 with a first in modern history, a deep and abiding love of England, focused particularly on Oxford and even more narrowly on Balliol, and a determination to be a professional historian. He had already taken steps to have himself naturalized. The war intervened, of course, and he rushed to join the Army, but his expertise in East European affairs, coupled with poor eyesight, led to his speedy transfer to the Political Intelligence Unit of the Foreign Office, where he stayed until after the Peace Conference of 1919. He then accepted a temporary lectureship at Balliol, but this expired in 1921.

His subsequent ostracization by Oxford hurt him deeply, and it has never been fully explained. There is firm evidence that blatant antisemitism denied him an All Souls' fellowship in 1911, but this was just one college, and in the interwar years many Jews of foreign birth were made welcome at Oxford, even before the Nazi persecution. Many other explanations have been put forward, even his relations with women, which may have infringed the rather rigid sexual *mores* of Oxford at that time. His thick guttural accent, and broken English, which made him at first hearing almost incomprehensible, may also have been considered an impediment in college teaching, though he made a deep impression on many Balliol undergraduates in 1920 and 1921, and Lord Boothby testifies to his willingness to persevere even with the most unpromising material.[126] The explanation probably lies in his granitic seriousness, and the monomaniacal way in which he would impose his thoughts on others, often at inordinate length. Sir Isaiah Berlin and Arnold Toynbee are important witnesses to this side of his character. Toynbee tells us how his wife once caught a chill standing in a howling draught for twenty minutes while Namier recited to her the original Slav names of all the towns in East Germany. (She calculated that if she interrupted him by moving to close the window he would start at the beginning again.)[127] She took this well enough, but few Oxford dons would have matched her stoicism, and such habits could have been murderous in the small, enclosed world of an Oxford college at breakfast, lunch and dinner. As J.H. Plumb tactfully remarks: 'Namier was blessed, or cursed, by an enormous weight of temperament.' To the vulgar he was 'Constipation Namier – the big shit we can't get rid of'.[128]

Nevertheless, he pressed on with his research alone. The family fortunes had been much reduced in the break-up of the Austrian Empire and the establishment of an independent Poland, and in any case his father had cut him off from his inheritance, apparently because of his espousal of Zionism. Until 1924 he scraped a living by journalism, partly abroad, and also by playing the stock market. He was always a trifle evasive about this period of his life, which was marred by a disastrous marriage. His exploration of psychoanalysis, beginning in 1922, encouraged his exaggerated conception of his own faults, and his strange lack of self-confidence, disguised by arrogance.

Meanwhile the perspectives of his research had changed. He had taken as his subject 'The Imperial Problem in the Age of the American Revolution', but the American Charles Andrews persuaded him that if he wanted to understand the Revolution he must first establish the home background. This fell in with his own inclinations. The vast resources of the Newcastle Papers were waiting, and his experience at Oxford and in the Foreign Office had given him a deep respect, almost a reverence, for the English upper classes. He was a profound snob and an inveterate name-dropper – traits his friends found endearing, his enemies less so. His closest friend was 'Baffy' Dugdale – Mrs Edgar Dugdale, a niece of A.J. Balfour's, whom he had met at the Foreign Office – and he found contact with the English aristocracy exciting. This he projected back into the eighteenth century.

But it was not mere snobbery. The tribulations of his race, the convulsions of Eastern Europe, had given him a fanatic belief in the sanctity of land, and an awed respect for stable societies based on landholding. He spelled this out in the preface to one of his major books:

> 'The relations of groups of men to plots of land, of organised communities to units of territory, form the basic content of political history. The con-flicting territorial claims of communities constitute the greater part of conscious international history; social stratifications and convulsions, pri-marily arising from the relationship of men to land, make the greater, not always fully conscious part of the domestic history of nations – and even under urban and industrial conditions ownership of land counts for more than is usually supposed. To every man, as to Brutus, the native land is his life-giving Mother, and the State raised upon the land his law-giving Father ... There is some well-nigh mystic power in the ownership of space – for it is not the command of resources alone which makes the strength of the landowner, but that he has a place in the world which he can call his own, from which he can ward off strangers, and in which he himself is rooted – the superiority of a tree to a log. In land alone can there be real patrimony, and he who as freeman holds a share in his native land – the freeholder – is, and must be, a citizen.'[129]

So it is not so bizarre as at first it seems that a Polish-Jewish immigrant should emerge as one of the most distinguished interpreters of English political history.

Although in 1924 he had enough money saved to make a start, in 1926 he had to apply for a grant from the Rhodes Trustees, and he even accepted loans from friends. But Baffy Dugdale now found him a publisher, and a lifelong friend, in Harold Macmillan, and in 1927 she persuaded the Chicago millionaire Julius Rosenwald to endow his work anonymously.

The result was *The Structure of Politics*, a detailed analysis of the political machine as it existed in 1760, which made his name in the profession over-night. It displayed an awesome knowledge of the minutiae of eighteenth-century politics and deployed manuscript as well as printed sources on a scale not hitherto envisaged, certainly not in English history and in such a tiny sector of the field. His procedure for elucidating history by prosopography, by a 'grass roots' study of individuals, added a new word to the language, the verb 'to namierize', with its attendant noun, 'namierization'. Not many historians have been thus honoured.

With its sequel, *England in the Age of the American Revolution*, in 1930, *The Structure of Politics* also aimed a sidelong but wounding blow at the Whig theory of eighteenth-century history, enshrined in the writings of men like Grant Robertson and Basil Williams. Namier showed conclusively that, given the complex and unstable nature of the political system at this time, its operation depended on unstinting hard work by men like Newcastle, whose sense of public duty and whose political ability, at least in the tactical sense, had been seriously underrated for too long. The extent of the corruption practised by such men had been flamboyantly exaggerated, too, if not in-vented, and when it was practised it was not on their initiative. 'Corruption', said Namier, 'was not a shower bath from above, constructed by Walpole, the Pelhams or George III, but a waterspout springing from the rock of freedom to meet the demands of the people.'[130] Above all he questioned the integrity of party in this era. A similar political vocabulary, he said, disguised the fundamental differences between late eighteenth- and late nineteenth-century political parties. The use of 'Whig' and 'Tory' in the 1760s was an empty convention which concealed the real machinery of politics, small groups of MPs and peers held together by loyalty to a patron or respect for the king. He went so far as to say that 'the political life of the time could be fully described without ever using a party denomination', though this was a position from which he later retreated; in fact, he began to retreat from it in the last sentence of *England in the Age of the American Revolution*, which reads: 'My next book, if ever written, will be on "The Rise of Party".' In this political atmosphere there was no doubting the constitutional propriety of George III's actions, and the effect of Namier's work – thought it may have been unintentional – was to revise the king's reputation upwards.[131]

However, he received no immediate offers of employment, and in 1931 he was thinking of retreating again into business or journalism when he was suddenly offered the chair of modern history at Manchester. The offer is supposed to have been inspired by G.M. Trevelyan, to whom Namier was ever afterwards grateful, though he later said that he had discharged much of his debt by declining to review any of Trevelyan's books. (This may be one of Namier's obscure witticisms, but it is difficult to be sure.)

He remained at Manchester, apart from the war years, until his retirement in 1953. He was apparently never considered good enough for one of the many chairs which fell vacant over these twenty years at Oxford, Cambridge or London. He himself never gave up hope, and though he punctiliously fulfilled his duties at Manchester he took little part in the affairs of the university, retained his flat in London, and on his trips north always stayed at a hotel in Buxton. During the Second World War he was seconded to the Jewish Agency in London, and in 1943 he told Mrs Dugdale that he had removed his books to his office, 'where certainly the greater part will rest till I go [back] to Manchester, or if fate is kind to me, till I move to Oxford or Cambridge, or *faute de mieux*, to London University'.[132] But his commitment to Zionism increased the coolness of an Arab-orientated upper class; this is the reason given for Attlee's refusal to offer him a regius chair. He was also monumentally tactless with those who might have helped him – witness his fair but bleakly discouraging analysis of the first volume of Winston Churchill's *Marlborough*, which Churchill sent him personally in 1934 for his opinion; witness, too, his butchery in 1937 of the edition of George III's correspondence prepared by that archetypal establishment figure Sir John Fortescue, Librarian of Windsor Castle'.[133] 'No one', said Trevelyan, 'should write about a man like Sir John Fortescue as Mr [sic] Namier has done.' In fact, Trevelyan, now the great panjandrum of English history, had increasing reservations about Namier; Manchester yes, Cambridge no. 'He's a good historical researcher', he confided to Leslie Rowse, 'but I don't think he's a good historian. He has no sense of the past.'[134]

In the profession he was certainly regarded as a great innovator, and even at this stage there was talk of the 'Namier Revolution', something he half encouraged himself. In the preface to *The Structure of Politics* he wrote: 'A system of non-Euclidean geometry can be built up by taking a curve for basis instead of the straight line, but it is not easy for our minds to think consistently in unwonted terms, parliamentary politics not based on parties are to us a non-Euclidean system, and similarly require a fundamental re-adjustment of ideas and, what is more, of mental habits.' Yet he was curiously uncontroversial. His work was not decisively challenged, but it was little known outside academic circles. Certainly he had not created the same stir in 1929 and 1930 as Elton did in 1953, or as Ronald Syme did in 1939, when he applied the new science of 'prosopography' to *The Roman Revolution*.[135] A surprising number simply ignored it all. Keith Feiling, for instance, took as the subject of his Ford Lectures for 1931 'The Second Tory Party 1714–1832', and published them in 1938, but he showed no signs of having read Namier's work, let alone used it. The same can be said of Basil Williams's volume for 1714-60 in the Oxford History of England, in 1939, and his *Carteret and Newcastle* in 1943. Those who did try and apply Namier's lessons, like Brian Tunstall, in a revisionist life of Chatham published in 1938, seemed to sink almost immediately into oblivion. This was partly Namier's own fault. In 1929 he had assumed that his second volume would reach 1765; he had already collected the material for a third volume, on the Rockingham Administration of 1765-6, and he was meditating a series of volumes up to 1784.[136] But *England in the Age of the American Revolution*, published in 1930, only reached August 1762 (in 450 pages), and after that, as the Zionist cause absorbed more and more of his time and energy, in the 1930s and right through the war, he fell silent. His Ford Lectures in 1934, on 'King, Cabinet and Parliament in the early years of George III', were well received, but he never published them, and after his death only fragments could be found.[137]

He reacted to the Nazi persecution of the Jews with devouring personal intensity, and his psychoanalyst even attributed the crippling paralysis of his right hand from which he suffered for the last twenty years of his life to a suppressed urge to kill Adolf Hitler. On the public as on the personal plane he was a bitterly tormented man, often on the verge of a nervous breakdown, on at least one occasion seriously contemplating suicide. Immediately after the war he began to analyse, with what materials were then available, the disaster of the 1930s. His findings were published in three books, *Diplomatic Prelude 1938-9* (1948), *Europe in Decay 1936-40* (1950) and *In the Nazi Era* (1952), which were welcomed as important pioneering work. His extended essay on *1848: the Revolution of the Intellectuals* (1946) also expressed in concentrated form his impatience with political ideas and at the same time confirmed that his attention was now fixed on modern European history. His books on eighteenth-century England were long out of print, and indeed difficult to come by. His findings on the early 1760s were rather limply accepted, but he had no important followers, unless we count Romney Sedgwick and Richard Pares, who were both independent scholars of much the same age as he.

Paradoxically, controversy rose to surround him as his personal life became stabilized, and at the same time the British Establishment moved to do him belated justice. In wartime London he met and found happiness with a Russian émigrée, Julia de Beausobre, whom he married on the death of his first wife in 1947. Her insistence that he enter the Russian Orthodox Church severed his close relationship with the Zionist leadership, though he had never been a Jew by religion. In 1944 he was belatedly elected to the British Academy, and in 1948 he was delighted to be made an honorary fellow of Balliol. In

1952 he was invited to give the prestigious Romanes lecture at Oxford, and in the same year was knighted. A drizzle of honorary degrees from various universities reached its climax in 1960 with the award of an Oxford doctorate at the hands of the new chancellor, his old friend Harold Macmillan.

By this time he had returned to the eighteenth century, and his Romanes lecture was on 'Monarchy and the Party System'. In 1951, two years before his retirement from Manchester, he accepted an appointment to the newly revived Trust set up to produce an official History of Parliament. (He had in fact been associated with the first such venture in 1929, which had petered out in the 1930s.) He was not, as is often thought, in charge of the whole project, only of the section for 1754–1790, but his prominence made him the target for much of the criticism of the Official History from within the profession, to the effect that it was a waste of money and an unjustified commitment of historical talent.

Meanwhile something like a Namier renaissance was under way. Richard Pares, afflicted by a terminal illness, resigned his chair of history at Edinburgh in 1954 and returned to Oxford. Commissioned to write the volume of the reign of George III for the Oxford History of England, but aware that he would not live to complete it, he poured his accumulated knowledge into his Ford lectures in 1952 on 'King George III and the Politicians', which were published the following year as a densely argued and densely footnoted book. (Namier said that it should be read twice; first the text, then the notes.) The important thing is that though Pares differed from Namier in some details his general approach was much the same; he confirmed Namier's findings and extended them to cover much of the reign. Next, followers began to arise from a new generation. In 1956 John Brooke, his chief assistant in the History of Parliament Trust, published a namierite volume on *The Chatham Administration 1766–68*, with a preface by Namier announcing that this was a new volume in the series 'England in the Age of the American Revolution', in which his own volume of that name would take its place under the title 'Newcastle and Bute'.* The following year he republished *The Structure of Politics*, and in 1958 this was followed by another volume in the planned series, *The End of North's Ministry 1780–82*, by I.R. Christie. *The Rise of the Pelhams 1742–49* (1957), by John Owen of Lincoln College, Oxford, was another avowedly namierite book, and so was Robert Walcott's *English Politics in the Early Eighteenth Century*, which appeared in 1956, though the original paper on which it was based had been published as long ago as 1941.

It is significant that the critics pounced first on those who were not members of Namier's immediate coterie in London. Owen was roughly handled, but

---

* In fact it was not reprinted until 1961, after his death, and then under its original title.

the American Robert Walcott was hammered. True, the weakness of his thesis – that political parties had no more meaning in the reign of Anne than in the reign of George III – was only equalled by his exaggerated and dogmatic assertion of it, and it was contradicted by most of the available evidence. All the same, there are signs that the attack on Walcott was an indirect attack on his Svengali, Namier, who was now supposed to be corrupting young historians in other fields. Amongst many damning reviews was one in the *TLS* for 9 March 1956, and it was also the subject of a majestic editorial in the same issue, headed 'Riders from the Tower'.

The editor painted a romantic picture indeed of Sir Lewis Namier, the 'great captain', 'clothed in the armour of proof, and armed with powerful cutting weapons of analysis', ensconced in his 'strong tower', from which he despatched expeditions under his trusted lieutenants into the surrounding countryside, to the terror of the inhabitants:

> 'The dwellers in the tufted brake, till recently living out their happy lives without being able to distinguish the wood from the trees, have seen fearful clearances. Peeping at the passing men-at-arms from what remains of the undergrowth, they complain, though faintly, that the impending peace and order in their jungle will make life less interesting than before.'

He went on to argue that there was more than one kind of historical writing, and Namier's methods of analysis were not applicable to all fields of history. He closed with a stern and pompous warning:

> 'However men may bind themselves in parties they retain their individual ambitions, interests and partialities. It is this that the analytic historian can demonstrate so effectively wherever he takes his section. But for the historian whose eye ranges over the continuum this is secondary. As he looks down the broad avenue he sees that, let the individuals be as free as they will, their general movement makes a series of continually developing patterns. He is more likely to be wrong, perhaps, but more likely to be interesting, and more likely, in the words of Burckhardt, to make us "wiser for ever".'

This was the burden of the much more severe, indeed savage attack launched by Herbert Butterfield the following year.

This is the same Butterfield who as a young man had put a curb on the Whig historians. Now, despite a modest and rather random output of published work, he was professor of modern history at Cambridge and Master of Peterhouse, soon to be regius professor. He specialized in elegant, teasing essays, full of ideas, but often rather tortuously expressed. He was supposed to be writing a life of Charles James Fox – a man who epitomized everything in politics which Namier held in contempt – but he had not finished it, and now he never would. He was a man with a reputation rather like an inverted cone, his wide-ranging prestige balanced on a tiny platform of achievement. But he had always had a well cultivated moral tone, and he had grown more righteous with the years. The Second World War affected him almost as deeply as it did Namier, and afterwards he became obsessed with the Bomb. He gave a series of public lectures in 1949, at Cambridge and on the BBC, which he published the following year as *Christianity and History*, the first of several such exhortations.[138] They were sombre, not to say apocalyptic in tone, and full of passages like this:

> 'I think it not too much to say that if Germany is under judgment so are all of us – the whole of the existing order and the very fabric of our civilisation. If once we admit that the moral factor operates in this way in history at all, then we today must feel ourselves to be living in one of those remarkable periods when judgment stalks generally through the world, and it becomes a question whether the orders and system to which we have been long attached can survive the day of reckoning'.

With iron fortitude he contemplated the fall of civilization, not because of the inadequacy of its state systems, which were all in themselves morally neutral – 'virtuous enough in themselves' was his actual phrase – no, 'At bottom', he said, 'it is an inadequacy in human nature itself which comes under judgment: for in the course of time it is human nature which finds out the holes in the structure, and turns the good thing into an abuse.' Yet, he went on, it is the systems which will fall, not man:

> 'Though the judgment is always upon us – upon man's universal sin – the sentence falls on great human systems, on nations, civilisations, institutions, indeed, on all the schematised patterns into which human life ranges itself in various periods. The systems break, the organisations crumble, though man himself goes on; and for this amongst other reasons we must never regard these systems and organisations as being the actual end of life, the ultimate purpose of history.'[139]

It was not to be expected that this austere but mischievous guru would look with favour on the 'structuralist' school of history, as he called it, and his sudden assault on Namier in 1956 gives the impression of long-bottled-up resentment breaking forth. Presumably he was roused to action by the great heretic's new and unholy fame, and the news that disciples had begun to gather.

The formal attack was launched with a short article in *Encounter* for April 1957 under the title 'George III and the Namier School', which was the outline of a substantial book, *George III and the Historians*, published later the same year. In 1958 he consolidated his arguments and slightly extended them in an article in the periodical *History* entitled 'George III and the Constitution'. Meanwhile he had launched a furious campaign against John Brooke's *Chatham Administration*, and in the two years following its publication in 1956 he reviewed it in four separate publications – apart from anything else, a flagrant breach of academic and literary etiquette. He was rather kinder to John Owen, though he used a review of his *Rise of the Pelhams* to intensify his attack on the 'Namier School' in general.[140] As John Brooke perceptively remarks: 'Butterfield set out to burn us at the intellectual stake, without passion or ill-feeling, solely for the good of our souls, and to prevent future historians from being contaminated'.[141]

In an interview he gave years later, Butterfield admitted that his main concern had been educational. There was much to admire in Namier:

'He was a historian's historian, because his research was all-embracing and flawless, his artistry imposing. He took a certain view of the eighteenth century, and I agree with him. But as a *teacher*, and a master of the college, I have to deplore his method. If I were to teach history by Namier's method, if we were to train students to do research and try to write history as Namier did, then history as a part of education would cease to exist … As far as I am concerned, the point of teaching history to undergraduates is to turn them into public servants and statesmen, in which case they had better believe in ideals, and not shrink from having ideas and policies and from carrying their policies through. We mustn't cut the ground from under them by teaching that all ideas are rationalisations. In brief, we must take a *statesmanlike* view of the subject. No doubt Namier would smile at this – I know it sounds priggish – but I happen to think history is a school of wisdom and statesmanship.'[142]

In other words, it was really a repeat of the clash between Firth and Oman long ago.

But whatever he said after Namier's death, at the time Butterfield certainly did not accept all his findings. He flatly argued that his interpretation of the opening years of George III's reign was wrong; that while it might be true that the king was acting within the letter of the constitution, Burke was right to argue that he was acting against its spirit. This remains a debatable point, and probably always will be. Much depends on the value we place on men's words and the implications we detect in them. Namier's grasp of the appropriate documentation was both wider and deeper than Butterfield's, but it was open to Butterfield to argue that Namier was temperamentally and ideologically unfitted to interpret it correctly. Butterfield also challenged the originality of the Namier School. Here he went to absurd lengths to show that obscure authors of the last century had here and there anticipated some of the Namierites' conclusions. He even resurrected what he himself called 'a racy chapter' by Harold Temperley (an old Peterhouse man) in the original *Cambridge Modern History*, volume VI, which anticipated in the course of a few pages some of John Owen's carefully documented findings in *The Rise of the Pelhams*. Understandably irritated, Owen replied that Temperley's essay contained 'many inaccuracies and errors of judgment, as well as some very shrewd observations, which are, however, unsubstantiated by any shred of evidence. It is not always easy to distinguish between genuine insight and lucky guesswork.'[143]

A more serious criticism, and one which gained Butterfield most support from other historians, was his contention that in abandoning narrative history Namier and his followers were allowing important questions of political principle to be obscured or ignored. Even Owen's book, of which he more than half approved, 'could bear a more dramatic treatment'. 'Those problems of political mechanics', he said, 'which have caught the interest of the present day ... cannot be properly understood without a more adequate picture of the dramatic events in diplomacy and war which were taking place at that time.'[144] As for Namier and Brooke, they had simply decided that 'after the accession of George III story telling must be over and done with', and 'the narrative method had been rendered obsolete'. 'Because the Whig historians took ideological pretensions too much at their face value, the modern school tend to drain the intellectual content out of the things that politicians do. The dramatis personae are portrayed without that outer framework of ideas and purposes which affects political conduct.' They had no interest 'in the springs of policy and the origins of important decisions, in the actual content of the political controversies of the time, in the attitude of the public to measures and men; and in the thrust and counter-thrust of parliamentary debate'. Problems of statesmanship and policy – such as Wilkes, the Peace of Paris, India, America – appeared only incidentally in their books, 'and since the fundamental theme, even in this narrative side of history, concerns rather the interplay of factions and the manipulative side of politics, even the topics that belong to statesmanship tend to be reduced to just such terms as these'. He accused them of studying only 'the underside of the piece of embroidery'; they were reducing history to 'a tale told by an idiot'. Research, he said with some passion, 'should not leave us desolate and bewildered in a land entirely without shapes and contours – leave us with the feeling that in fact there is no larger course of history, no theme that can turn one way or another'.[145]

The reception accorded Butterfield was mixed. Some leading historians, notably Alan Taylor and Hugh Trevor-Roper, endorsed his criticisms in general terms without taking the matter further. Those who had already voiced their discontent with the History of Parliament project were comforted and encouraged. But the general tone was one of amused incomprehension, summed up by one reviewer who said: 'It is perhaps the strangest thing of all to find so impressive a controversy reared on the insoluble and to some extent uninteresting question of what exactly were the relationships between George III, the Duke of Newcastle and Lord Bute.'[146] And though *George III and the Historians* was larded with compliments to Namier's own work so excessive that in any one else but Butterfield they would have been dismissed as hypocritical – he spoke of Namier's 'remarkable precision', his 'solid contribution to scholarship', the 'massiveness of his detailed researches', 'a type of achievement scarcely paralleled in the historiography of our time' – his attitude to the great man's followers was much less bland.[147] Indeed, the *TLS* remarked that Butterfield, like others before him, seemed to regard Namier 'in an almost magical light', and his followers as bewitched. These followers, according to Butterfield, were distinguished by 'cliqueish arrogance' and 'vulgar contentiousness'; they 'taunted and condemned' all their predecessors in the field. 'There can hardly ever have been another school of history', he said, 'so severe on its predecessors'; or again: 'It seems to be the habit of this school to recognise no debt to any forerunners, and to make acknowledgments only to one another.' Worse still, it was a school which had become 'so formidable an orthodoxy as to check the free play of criticism'; it was 'the most powerfully organised squadron in our historical world at the present time, the disciples relating the ideas of the master with closer fidelity than I remember to have been the case in any other branch of historical study since it became a serious form of scholarship'.[148]

This was quite hysterical. After all, the so-called Namierites numbered only four – Romney Sedgwick, Owen, Brooke and possibly Christie – and of these only Brooke was in any way attached to Namier. But it is significant that Owen, the non-Londoner, was the only one who replied to Butterfield publicly, which he did at considerable length in the *Cambridge Review* in May 1958.[149] John Brooke had to wait until after Namier's death. Namier's sole pronouncement on the matter was a letter to the *TLS* on 6 December 1957, in which he said: 'My work and that of other historians to whom [Professor Butterfield] refers will have to speak for itself, and for me to engage in controversies, or to deal with figments of imagination or nightmarish visions, seems a wrong use of time which at my age I must try to employ in a more constructive manner.'

John Brooke says: 'I have met people who imagine that Namier and Butterfield quarrelled. This was not so. There was disagreement, as there must be between two scholars who see history from entirely different points of view, but no quarrel or personal ill feeling.' Later Butterfield accepted an invitation to Gower Street, to view Namier's 'empire' in the Institute of Historical Research, and the occasion was cordial. Butterfield never retracted his criticisms, but he did not press them, and he was apparently not eager to review Ian Christie's book on Lord North's ministry, which appeared in 1958. His own book was allowed to go out of print, and a year after Namier's death he delivered on the Third Programme a memorable summing-up on his life work. It was a typical Butterfield performance, each paragraph cancelling out the one before, but on the whole he found much more to praise than to blame. It ended: 'He was a man whom many things in life had hurt, and sometimes he wanted to be formidable, not realising that he was the master of us all when he looked on the world with love.'[150]

But paradoxically the whole affair made Namier a top celebrity, worthy even of the attention of the *Daily Mail*, and the resulting debate on his extraordinary personality and the nature of his achievement continued up to his death in 1960 and well beyond. He has attracted a publicity which no other English scholar of this century, except Bertrand Russell, has even remotely attained; and this publicity, on the whole, has been favourable. A year after his death a feeble attempt by Norman Hunt (now Lord Crowther Hunt) to 'debunk' him on the Third Programme was simply swept aside with contempt; but this was an uncharacteristic episode.[151] The new American periodical *Journal of British Studies* published in its first issue, in 1961, an article on Namier by Jacob Price which was distinctly critical of Butterfield, stimulating a learned debate, in article and counter-article, which continued into 1964.[152] Meanwhile the tongues of the Namierites were at last unlocked, and they came forward to bear witness. John Brooke published a solid and valuable paper on 'Namier and Namierism' in 1963, as well as some shorter pieces; John Owen gave his own summing-up on the matter.[153] Sir Isaiah Berlin offered some detailed impressions of Namier the man, and so did another friend of long standing, J.L. Talmon; these were reinforced in 1971 by Lady Namier's biography.

Controversy continues, and will no doubt continue as long as there are people alive who knew Namier. Witness after witness testifies (as I can myself) to the overwhelming impact of his person and his personality. His physique itself was impressive to a degree: the guttural, rather toneless voice, intense and implacable; the broad shoulders, the beaked nose, the fathomless eyes; above all, his absolute stillness, the stillness, one felt, of a flywheel revolving too fast for the human eye. Even men whom he taught as undergraduates in the early 1920s felt his continuing domination over the next forty years. 'I think', wrote one of them to his widow, 'he was probably the only truly great man I have ever known personally.' Another said: 'Even in 1921 we knew he was a man of destiny.' The *TLS* once described him as 'History's Towering Outsider', and in his obituary *The Times* agreed that 'many found Namier overwhelming, in print and still more so in person'.

His reputation seems to be rising still, as the liberal-socialist school of historiography continues to decline. J.H. Plumb, who admired Namier but found his 'veneration for monarchy, aristocracy and tradition' distasteful, said rather sourly in 1969:

'He will remain a cult hero of conservative historians, and that means the bulk of the historical profession. His animus towards altruism, his cynicism towards human motivation, his reverence for inherited status, his belief in the authority of possessions, his near-idolatry for the English landed classes and for parliamentary monarchy will ensure a respectful and laudatory public within the establishment'.[154]

Elton's comment is:

'English historians have in the main been 'progressive' – whig, liberal, radical, socialist. The occasional conservative among them – an Oman or a Marriott – was clearly so devoid of a mind that he contributed nothing to the tradition, and the violence provoked by Namier owed much to the astonishment felt in conventional circles at the uncalled-for appearance of a historian with tory predilections who clearly outranked the liberals intellectually'.[155]

As a matter of fact, in his closing years Namier shared many of the doubts expressed by his critics. He did not accept their criticism of his approach – 'What matters in history', he said, 'is the great outline and the significant detail: what must be avoided is the deadly mass of irrelevant detail', and he told John Brooke that a searchlight concentrated at the focal point would give more light than rows of candles.[156] But latterly he began to doubt 'whether we shall ever know anything which is worth knowing'. 'Shall we', he said, 'get any nearer to explaining the senseless irrelevancy of so-called human thought and action?', and one of his favourite stories likened the historian to a man who sold anti-earthquake pills, because there was nothing to take their place. In fact there had always been a streak of pessimism in his attitude towards his work.[157] He sought an answer in psychoanalysis, to which he was increasingly devoted, and as a vehicle for psychological investigation he even turned to biography, a form of writing he rather despised. His biography of Charles Townshend, completed and posthumously published by Brooke, blames Townshend's bullying policy towards the American colonies on his early upbringing by a domineering father.

However, as Brooke remarks, much of the criticism of Namier's work in

English history falls away if we remember that he was a historian of parliament, not of Britain or of British policy. Nor was his interest in parliament entirely objective. His widow points out that he was a man entirely without social gifts, and this was why he was concerned to discover how the House of Commons worked. 'He never hunted in a pack', she says, 'he was always an outsider. Because he never learnt how to consort with people, he wanted to find out the principles by which people consort with each other.'[158] By August 1960 he and Brooke had at last completed the main body of *The History of Parliament 1754–1790* – the analysis of general elections, the studies of constituencies, the biographical dictionary of MPs. It only remained for Namier to write a long, introductory survey to the volume, which would be a justification of all his work and at the same time its summation, for he did not flatter himself that he had a long time to live. In fact, he had less time than he thought. When he collapsed on 19 August not a word was written.

As he lay waiting for the ambulance it was typical that he should talk to his wife about *The History of Parliament*. He sensed now that he would never see it published, but he still hoped to write the introduction, his 'Survey', which would complete the circle back to those far-off Balliol days and his original vision of the Imperial Idea. 'Since the *History* could no longer be a living skyscraper but had to be a mausoleum, his Survey would make of it a Testament projected towards future generations, unaware perhaps of the grand English effort to rule by consorting together – the greatest achievement of the time called the Second British Empire.'* But a few hours later he was dead.

On the death of the emperor it seemed that his empire would dissolve with him. Just as Namier did not live to see his own section of the History of Parliament appear, neither did Romney Sedgwick. Namier's section, with the Survey written by Brooke, appeared in 1964; Sedgwick's, for 1715–1754 with a Survey by Eveline Cruickshanks, in 1970. Opinion as to their value, except as works of reference, is decidedly mixed. John Brooke subsequently joined the Historical Manuscripts Commission, though in 1972 he published a revisionist biography of George III, and the fact that it had an introduction by the present Prince of Wales would have delighted Namier. Ian Christie gravitated into European history and foreign policy and John Owen emigrated to Canada, whence he has only recently returned. Brooke said despairingly in 1965: 'There are no disciples to carry on the work.'

But even in Namier's lifetime this was manifestly not true. Whatever Butterfield thought, Namier never set out to organize a school of historians,

---

* Julia Namier, *Lewis Namier*, pp. 332–3. She told Ved Mehta in 1961: 'He looked up, radiant, and said, "What a pity! Yesterday was the first time I saw in my mind's eye the Survey of Parliament as a whole"' (*Fly and the Fly Bottle*, p. 213).

but his technique lives on. He spawned many imitators. Douglas Brunton and D.H. Pennington's *Members of the Long Parliament*, in 1954, was widely regarded as an offshoot of his work; so was Mary Frear Keeler's biographical dictionary of the Long Parliament in the same year. Lucy Sutherland was deeply influenced by Namier, as her book on *The East India Company in Eighteenth-Century Politics* (1952) shows. *Politics in the Age of Peel*, by Norman Gash (1953), and *Elections and Party Management in the Age of Gladstone*, by H.J. Hanham (1959), tell the same tale. For that matter Neale's account of the parliaments of Elizabeth I, defective though it was because he lacked Namier's objectivity and analytical power, owed much to Namierian techniques, and he assumed responsibility for the appropriate section of the Official History. And since Namier's death there has been a rush of books by a younger generation of historians applying those techniques to further sections of George III's long reign: by Austin Mitchell and L.G. Mitchell, by E.A. Smith, Frank O'Gorman, John Derry, John Cannon and Paul Langford. Langford's *The First Rockingham Administration 1765–6* (Oxford 1973) and Cannon's *The Fox-North Coalition 1782–4* (Cambridge 1969) could even be regarded as parts of Namier's master scheme for a history of English politics from 1754 to 1784.

But perhaps the most surprising spin-off has been in the late seventeenth and early eighteenth centuries. Once Robert Walcott had been repulsed in 1956 and 1957, a new generation of scholars began to demonstrate that the parties of Queen Anne's reign were much more like modern parties than anyone save Trevelyan had hitherto supposed. The crowning achievement of this new school, and the only work of political history in this century which can stand alongside Namier's *Structure of Politics*, is Geoffrey Holmes's *British Politics in the Age of Anne*, in 1967. However, efforts to trace party as a living organism into the Age of Walpole have so far failed. Richard Pares's wise words on the office of prime minister apply with equal force to the history of parties:

'The development of this institution, as of all others which are affected by personal ascendancies or deficiencies in this quarter or that, must not be thought of as continuous – as when we perceive, in the heart of a fog, a whitish blob which curdles into a tram and advances along the lines, growing larger and more distinct, until it stops obediently at our feet. [Its] history . . . is more like that of the Cheshire Cat: sometimes there is a whole cat, sometimes no more than a grin, and it is not always the same end that appears first'.[159]

Seven

◆ ◆

Conclusion: History in the Twentieth Century

Notwithstanding the public fame of modern historians like Trevelyan, Neale and Namier, in the first half of the twentieth century the study of history at British universities was still dominated by the traditions of Oxford, and Stubbs. Degree syllabuses – even in Scotland – continued to be focused on English history, and especially medieval constitutional history studied with reference to original documents. Moreover the dominant figures in the profession between the wars were for the most part medievalists. At Oxford Firth was succeeded by H.W.C. Davis (1925–28), who died prematurely before he could complete his transition into modern history, then F.M. (later Sir Maurice) Powicke (1928–47) and V.H. Galbraith (1947–57), all three of them pupils or close associates of Tout at Manchester. In fact, Hugh Trevor-Roper began his inaugural lecture as the next regius professor in 1957 with the remark:

'I am, I fear, a somewhat eccentric occupant of this chair. It is now thirty-two years since it was last occupied by anyone whose interest was not medieval, whose Oxford education had not been at Balliol College, and whose historical training had not been at Manchester'.[1]

Other medievalists of power in these years include F.M. (later Sir Frank) Stenton, professor of history at Reading 1912–46 and vice-chancellor 1946–50, and J.G. (later Sir Goronwy) Edwards. Edwards was another protégé of Tout's, who was a research student at Manchester 1913–15, but after the war returned to Jesus College, Oxford, where he rose to be senior tutor and vice-principal. But in 1948 he answered the call to be director of the Institute of Research, in succession to Galbraith, and he stayed until his retirement in 1950. Even at Cambridge under Trevelyan, Bury's work was consolidated by Z.N. Brooke and C.W. Previte-Orton, successive professors of medieval history, and in 1954 Trevelyan was succeeded in the regius chair, somewhat to his surprise, by the Benedictine monk Dom David Knowles, an authority on medieval monasticism. In 1958, when the *Cambridge Historical Journal* dropped the 'Cambridge' from its title, it was announced that it would mainly be devoted to modern and contemporary history, since the *EHR* was virtually a medieval periodical.

The work of these great medievalists, brilliant though it was, was for the most part too technical for the man in the street, even the educated man in the street, nor did it alter in substance the picture of medieval history such a man had imbibed from Stubbs or from Stubbs-based textbooks. There were exceptions, but even a work of passion and imagination like Powicke's *Henry III and the Lord Edward* was published in a format and at a price which were alike intimidating. The profession retained an air of mystery, and its obscure activities were punctuated by enormous rows. The one historian of the interwar period who commanded a large popular following, perhaps even a household name, was Trevelyan, and it was tempting to ascribe his rather dubious and grudging reputation in the profession to mean-spirited jealousy.

In fact, it was in these interwar years that tension began to rise between the professional historians and their lay or 'amateur' colleagues.* At the end of the nineteenth century the gap between the two was easily bridgeable, but now it was steadily widening. The Royal Historical Society, which might have held them together, had developed into a professional, university-dominated body; the Historical Association united to a limited extent all teachers of history, whether at schools or universities, but the introduction of the Ph.D. was markedly divisive. There was, and still is, a distinct difference between those who have undertaken full-time postgraduate research in history and those who have not.[2] Meanwhile the attitude of Trevelyan, and the example of Neale, gave the impression that academic historical writing was not only unacceptably limited in scope – and here Nicholas Murray Butler's celebrated gibe that 'an expert is one who knows more and more about less and less' had a telling effect – but virtually unreadable.

Here it is worth noticing in passing that a premium is put on readability in history which is not imposed on any other subject, not even on literary criticism, which now seems to glory in its own obscurity. But it is not clear why an academic monograph on, say, *Politics and the Appointment of Justices of Peace 1675-1720* should be any more readable than one on *The Interferometry of Reversed and Non-Reversed Spectra.* True, history and politics

---

* The application of the term 'professional' to those who work in universities is itself questionable, and no satisfactory name for those who do not, but still write history, has been found. Philip Guedalla argued that he was a true 'professional' in the literal sense, in that his sole occupation and sole source of income was writing.

involve the human factor, but the importance of the human factor is often exaggerated, and in popular biography dangerously so. As Seeley once said: 'Public affairs naturally proceed, and ought to proceed, in a manner not at all romantic. They are governed, and ought to be governed, by a ponderous routine, by close adherence to precedent in action, and to conventional phraseology in speech, which is most wearisome to read.'[3] Nor is it clear why the *English Historical Review* should come under fire because it can only be understood by a minority of professionals, and not, say, the *Journal of Endocrinology*.

However, in the 1930s it seemed to some that professional historians were making no contribution to the great debate between Democracy and Fascism, nor indeed to any other current controversy, and in 1942 C.V. Wedgwood, one of Trevelyan's most distinguished disciples, took up the cudgels in terms reminiscent of Lord Acton. Professional historians, she said, were deluded by 'the groundless faith that there is an absolute standard outside the praise and agreement of the public', and they disparaged historians like Macaulay – and herself, she could have added – who had attracted such praise. In the interwar years, therefore:

> 'The greater number of historical writers failed entirely to understand what was expected of them. They turned their faces away from their audience and towards their subject, turned deliberately from the present to the past'.

As a result their contribution to the intellectual civilization of their own era was nil:

> 'They are no more concerned with the ultimate outcome of their studies than is the research scientist with the use of poison gas in warfare. The final results arise not from the nature of the material but from the depravity of human beings; and historical research of the truly scholastic kind is not connected with human beings at all. It is a pure study, like higher mathematics'.[4]

Reviewing the matter later, and more temperately, she still insisted that history had lost much of its relevance for the twentieth century:

> 'When the new disciplines and techniques of historical research were turned upon the various agreed fables which had served men well enough for several generations, these fables naturally disintegrated. They were replaced not by new, better and more truthful fables, but by furious arguments. Over almost the whole field of history – especially modern history – the increase in knowledge has brought a decrease of certainty; too many perspectives and too few principles. The accepted designs were shattered, the recognisable forms and figures would no longer do, and history, like other forms of art, entered on a period of abstraction'.[5]

Moreover, the two greatest historians of the postwar era, Elton and Namier, were foreign by birth, they were strongly conservative at a time when it was chic for academics to be left-wing, and though they were both passionately devoted to their adopted country, they sought to elucidate its history by a minute study of institutions in the far past. This was particularly marked in Namier, who was ready to make sweeping generalizations about European history, and scrutinize European diplomacy right up to 1939, but in English history confined himself to an in-depth investigation of parliamentary politics in the 1760s.

The granitic conservatism, the austere professionalism of these two men produced its own reaction. Trevor-Roper chose as the title of his inaugural lecture in 1957 'History: Professional and Lay', and made it a call for the relaxation of professionalism. 'History that is not useful,' he said, 'that has not some lay appeal, is mere antiquarianism', and he characterized much of the historical research going on in his own university as 'a private backwater in which those who have a taste for it may harmlessly fish' – sentiments for which he was sternly reproved by Elton.[6] In the same year Herbert Butterfield launched his major assault on Namier. The essence of Butterfield's criticism is significant. He who had belaboured the Whig historians in 1931 for mythologizing history now attacked Namier for undermining national myths, for destroying the continuity of history and the idea of progress without putting anything in their place.* However, it is true that his conversion to Whiggism had already been signalled in *The Englishman and his History*, in 1944.

Yet at this stage, roughly over the years 1955–70, the profession had to face its most severe challenge, and the scope and methodology of conventional historical writing and teaching were reassessed and found wanting.

First came the challenge of 'world history', which seemed to mock the parochialism of most university syllabuses. As Arnold Toynbee's monumental *Study of History* in ten volumes neared completion – the first three volumes appeared in 1934, the next three in 1938, and the rest in 1954 – respect for his achievement turned in some quarters to veneration, especially amongst the rising generation. Toynbee's thesis on the rise and fall of civilizations – and he seemed to have reviewed them all with equal erudition – pandered to the common desire to find a pattern in history, and the common expectation that the historian should essay prophecy. The sheer sweep of his work was intoxicating, and his habit of putting the abbreviation 'AD' in front of commonplace dates like 1912 or 1939 was suggestive of a vast sweep of time beyond the ken of most historians. A scale of values in which modern English-speaking society was a mere appendage to a civilization neither greater nor less than the Hittite, the Syrian or the Babylonian was a salutary shock, yet

* See pp. 262–4 above.

at the same time it offered some sort of reassurance to a generation bewildered by the seismic upheavals of recent years – the Second World War, the collapse of the British Empire, and above all, the Bomb. Lewis Mumford, himself a man with a world vision, declared that:

> 'No book that deals with human affairs has been more free from the blatant parochialism of our age and society: the obsessions of nationalism, our excessive pride in material conquests and mechanical productivity, our naive submission to the one-eyed methodology of the physical sciences, the notion that our age is the climax of human existence and that its ephemeral values are eternal'.[7]

It received no such accolades from the historical profession. The *English Historical Review*, the *Journal of Modern History* and the *American Historical Review* treated successive sections of *A Study of History* to reviews which ranged from the markedly cool to the hotly destructive. It was denounced by some of the leading historians of our time: by Charles A. Beard, Richard Pares, A.J.P. Taylor, Lawrence Stone, H.R. Trevor-Roper (twice) and Pieter Geyl (constantly). They not only questioned Toynbee's basic conclusions, but argued that he had manifestly reached those conclusions before assessing the evidence. Geyl and Trevor-Roper found his teaching not only wrong but perniciously wrong, and liable to undermine the values upon which Western civilization rested. Trevor-Roper accused him of 'a masochistic desire to be conquered':

> 'Toynbee destests Western Civilisation because it is basically liberal and rational. Detesting it, he wishes to see it destroyed, and he does not care who destroys it'.[8]

But the impact of academic disapproval did not undermine Toynbee's prestige in the public eye, or lessen his general influence. In particular, his assumption that Britain and Western Europe were very far from being the necessary focus of civilization or world history offered intellectual justification for the preoccupation with the 'Third World' which was a distinguishing feature of the 1950s and 1960s. In 1955 a prominent historian of medieval Germany, Geoffrey Barraclough, announced his conversion to wider views in a book called *History in a Changing World*. After a now almost conventional avowal of perplexity – 'We are beset by a sense of uncertainty because we feel ourselves on the threshold of a new age, to which previous experience offers no sure guide' – he went on to argue that European history was finished, in the sense that ancient history was 'finished', and the major bent of research and teaching should be towards world history. The influence of Toynbee was even more apparent in *An Introduction to Contemporary History*, in 1964, though Barraclough was never an enthusiastic disciple. According to Barraclough, the preoccupation of British professional historians, and through them their students, with the history of their own country and a limited portion of Europe, with an occasional canter through North America, was tantamount to navel-watching. Their attention should be focused instead on the history of China, Japan, India and so on; not only because of their importance for the modern world, but in order to redress a long-standing imbalance in academic studies. Such views chimed in with the prevailing mood in some circles, and in 1956 Barraclough was translated from the chair of medieval history at Liverpool to the Stevenson professorship in international relations at the Royal Institute of International Affairs. In 1961 the government also accepted the recommendations of the Hayter Commission, and centres for 'Third World' studies were sprinkled over the universities – Chinese studies at Leeds, Japanese at Sheffield, South-East Asian at Hull (and later Kent), South Asian at Cambridge – to train English graduates in the history, languages and culture of the East, though unfortunately most of the traffic has been the other way.

However, not everyone believed that history, on whatever part of the world it was directed, could meet contemporary needs, and there was a marked inclination towards newer, more voguish disciplines. The attractions of sociology, particularly to a younger generation which preferred not to study school subjects at university, and reacted sharply against the admittedly antique syllabuses still offered by many history departments, were obvious. As it happened, this threat was short-lived. Sociology had never established itself as firmly in Britain as it had done in Germany, France and America, though it is not easy to see exactly why, and the attempt to expand an infant discipline to full adulthood in response to this new demand resulted in a dramatic fall in academic standards. The decline in sociology was as rapid as its rise, and was accelerated by the student riots of 1968, in which sociology students, and often their lecturers, took a prominent part. Employers began to look askance at sociology graduates, notices sprang up alongside the toilet rolls in student union lavatories reading, 'Those wanting a degree in sociology help themselves'; the darker side of the discipline was explored in Malcolm Bradbury's influential novel *The History Man*, in 1975. Nevertheless, history as it was commonly written and taught had been weighed and in the minds of many had been found wanting, and just because sociology had not, after all, proved an acceptable replacement it did not mean that the rival discipline had been given a clean bill of health.

Far from it. The prestigious *Annales* school, centred on the École Pratique des Hautes Études at the Sorbonne, and led by men of the calibre of Fernand Braudel, Lucien Febvre and Emmanuel Le Roy Ladurie, had declared the death of 'l'histoire événementielle', the old concept of factual, narrative history, particularly political and constitutional history. They proclaimed instead the supremacy of economic and social history, and enlisted the aid of anthropology, climatology, psychology, geography and any other relevant sister discipline; such unaccustomed subjects for historical research as death, witchcraft, menstruation, marriage, childhood, were now very much in vogue. On the other hand, there were Toynbeean elements in the *annalistes*' doctrine, particularly in their insistence that economic and social history – and there was no other – could only be studied over long sweeps of time, the famous 'longue durée'. Above all, the *annalistes*, with enthusiastic support from America, invoked the aid of the new technology; the computer was solemnly crowned as the new queen of historical studies.[9]

Outside France, this assault on 'structural history' was only a limited success; in Britain a great many historians and a great many universities simply ignored it. But it captured the imagination of many younger scholars, enslaved a few leaders of the profession in America, and led others to make propitiatory gestures, and even meditate reform. The profession was not conscious of its strength, rather the opposite, and in Britain in the 1960s it even seemed that it had failed in one of its primary purposes, of training more historians. This is surprising, bearing in mind the huge increase in doctoral research over the previous thirty years. For instance, in 1932, when the Institute of Historical Research first tried to establish the number of research students in history over the whole country, there were forty-five reading for the Ph.D. or D.Phil. In 1964 there were 148, and numbers have continued to rise.* One of the reasons offered for the postwar boom in English local history is that it offered a multitude of self-contained subjects for new research students, the national archives having been combed ragged.[10] However, when the huge expansion of university arts faculties in response to the Robbins Report on High Education in 1965, plus the retirement of a cohort of lecturers dating from the early 1930s which had not been supplemented to any significant degree in the lean years 1930-50, faced chairmen of departments with the pleasant task of recruiting additional members of staff every year, they often found that their short-lists rapidly dwindled to one acceptable candidate, and sometimes disappeared altogether. Research ability of a high order was found to be rarer than had been thought, and it was not always combined with teaching ability – as Firth's critics at Oxford had been quick to point out. A less deferential generation of students began to question and even deride the performance of their tutors, and for a few years the question of formal teacher training for new university lecturers was much in the air.

---

*These figures do not include a large number of students enrolled for the two-year sub-doctoral research degrees, such as B.Litt., M.Litt. and M.A.

Standards of research supervision were also anxiously discussed, though with little result; it was too late now to found the postgraduate schools proposed earlier in the century.

The combined impact of a new generation of university teachers and students, and (not the least important) schoolteachers, made for change in the history curricula of many British universities, and powerfully influenced the syllabuses of the new universities founded in the 1960s. This 'revolution' has not yet been thoroughly analysed, and a superficial inspection suggests that it was not as far-reaching as either its supporters or its opponents supposed. Many of the older 'civics', like Sheffield, Leicester, Nottingham and Leeds, kept their heads well above the tide; so did Liverpool and Exeter, despite a mild infestation of African history.[11] But certainly there was a demand that courses should be more 'relevant', or, to use an epiphet popularized by George Watson, 'central', and the domination of British history was successfully challenged. Medieval history was also undermined by the abrupt decline of Latin as a school subject, to which universities were slow to adjust. But the history syllabuses of the new universities, totally exposed to change and usually welcoming it, revealed certain broad trends: 'the decline of medievalism, the pressure for contemporaneity, the growth of "world" history, and the fragmentation of history as a monolithic discipline'.[12] This last meant the proliferation of 'combined degrees', often with sociology or politics or economics but sometimes with geography or even biology, a process which reached its apogee in the degree in the 'History of Resource Management' offered by the New University of Ulster.* Nine out of twelve of the new universities offered no medieval history at all, and where British history continued to be offered as a main subject it was not compulsory – a trend which even spread to Cambridge. Degree syllabuses were studded now with courses in African history, Indonesian, Chinese and Japanese history, academically immaculate in theory, perhaps, but lacking the necessary back-up in tutorial competence and availability of books. They were also studded, particularly in the first year, with vague, semi-sociological topics such as 'Aristocracy and Elites', 'Revolution', 'Conservatism and Reaction', 'Comparative Imperialism' and the like; even Manchester, one of the most professional schools of history in the country, surrendered to a freshman course on 'Themes in Modern History'. This was the era, too, in which many degrees, and some departments, shyly added the word 'studies' to their title, so that 'French' became 'French Studies', 'Politics' 'Political Studies', and so on, with the implication that they were not really exclusively concerned with the subject, or that they were working round its periphery.

* Of course, joint honours courses had been common enough for years, but in such courses each subject had been kept separate.

Faced with this combined assault on their subject-matter, their techniques and their very ethos, some of the older generation crumbled, making propitiatory gestures to the new deity of youth, announcing their instant conversion, and making promises of amends. Barraclough is a prominent example, but in 1964 J.H. Plumb also edited a doom-laden compendium entitled *Crisis in the Humanities*, in which leading spokesmen for the various arts disciplines paraded in sackcloth and ashes. As an apologist for history, Plumb himself took up the threnody with gusto:

'Placed against the obvious power and effectiveness of scientific inquiry, or even economic analysis, historical generalisations must seem hopelessly tentative and jejune. And this natural inferiority has been strengthened not only by the anarchy of professional activity but the spiritual nihilism which pervades the subject ... Between the professional scholar and the [literary] historian is a chasm, unbridgeable but profound – the scholar pre-occupied with the *why*, the historian with the *how*. Professional analytical history is outside general culture, can never be part of it'.[13]

In his Trevelyan lectures at Cambridge in 1961 E.H. Carr also denounced 'the parochialism of English history', which lay like 'a dead hand on our curriculum', and he rejected the austere academic ideals which he saw as typical of Namier and the conservative or empiricist school of historians. It was the dual function of history 'to enable man to understand the society of the past, and to increase his mastery over the society of the present'.[14]

Such ideas were rejected *in toto* by Geoffrey Elton, who at times in the late 1960s seemed to be fighting the battle for conventional history alone, and to be in danger of losing it; not by straight defeat, but by sheer weight of numbers. *The Practice of History* (1967) was not strictly speaking defensive – none of Elton's work, in fact, can be so described – nor was it entirely an attack on the 'new history'. It was a firm reassertion of professional as against amateur standards, and its probable starting-point was Trevor-Roper's inaugural lecture ten years before. He also took grave exception to R.W. Southern's inaugural lecture as Chichele professor in 1961, 'The Shape and Substance of Academic History', which seemed to him 'an unacceptable plea for the superiority of the study of mind over the study of matter'. Amongst the amateurs he counted Trevelyan and Acton ('prince of amateurs'), and he contrasted them pointedly with Namier, whose ultimate aims might be wrong-headed, but whose thoroughly professional methods had carried him through to a new plateau of scholarship.[15] The *Annales* school represented 'a valuable, perhaps necessary, stage in the development of historical writing', and in the hands of men of stature, like Braudel or Marc Bloch, it had been remarkably successful. But it had 'lost itself in rhetoric and self-adulation', and in any case he warned: 'In many fields of history it is either clearly insufficient or has already done its work … It can no more answer all the important questions of history than any other method.' But he himself had a longstanding prejudice against historical biography and against narrative for narrative's sake – 'narrative that depends on art superficially imposed on simplicity and ignorance' – and what he called the 'serious popular historians' remained his principal target, though apart from Trevelyan he did not name any. His view was that:

'It is perfectly possible to feel respect and liking for the writings of the serious popular historians without believing that theirs is the highest form of history or the model to follow. Among them are notable practitioners of a far from easy skill; it would not be difficult to bias the argument by looking at the lesser lights; but even the best lack the searching depth of investigation, the establishment of solid truths, and the accumulation of fruitfully illuminating explanations which professional history must and can provide'.[16]

As for teaching, he rejected the current fad, as he saw it, for recent or contemporary history, for the abandonment of defined 'periods' in favour of a vague, conceptual approach, and for the imposition of modern sociological techniques on ages for which the evidence was insufficient to support them. He firmly denied the 'relevance' of historical study: 'It should be said, with regret, that there is no proof that a knowledge of history, recent or distant, at B.A. level succeeds in giving a man much understanding of his own time.' On the contrary, the study of history was an abstract intellectual training, directed towards 'a sharpening of the critical analytical faculty, and a deepening of the imaginative and constructive faculty'. For this almost any period of history would do, provided there was sufficient evidence to sustain the investigation, and provided it was taught according to a rigorous professional method. His standards were indeed rigorous; he reproved his own profession for slackness and for taking easy short cuts. 'We must never cease to work towards a situation', he said, 'in which the active labours of teaching and study fill the year and every day of it.'[17]

He reinforced his views on university teaching two years later, in a pithy retort to Brian Harrison's rather sunny view of the 'new history'. It was wrong, said Elton, to study history, be it ancient, medieval or modern, with the preoccupations of the present day in the forefront of one's mind: there was enough unconscious distortion as it was, without adding conscious distortion. He was deeply sceptical of foundation or freshman courses in 'world history', which could never amount to more than 'wide waffle or a galloping scamper';* but he was even more sceptical of new courses in out-of-the-way parts of Asia or Africa which had no academic back-up:

> 'Subjects taught by single teachers often with the sole help of books and articles written by themselves and a small group of their contemporaries, to students so ignorant of the first thing about these matters that they are bound to accept whatever is told them'.

He summed up these new trends in university education as:

> 'The abandonment of historical studies as an intellectual enterprise capable of training the critical faculty, in favour of such studies as an education in self-adjustment and a training ground for good and aware citizens'.[18]

Finally, in 1970 he issued a further defence of political history as the basis of any curriculum:

> 'All the forms of history that have existed, exist now, or may yet come to exist belong to the world which the political historian inhabits. If at times he may feel, perhaps too arrogantly, that they exist only in order to amplify, explain and put right his political story, he needs to be humbler and recall that politics are not for most people the content of daily life; yet all things are relevant to politics'.

Even narrative was better than a static analysis which was no better than a post-mortem:

> 'The whole difficulty of historical reconstruction and writing lies in this fundamental truth about history: it contains a multiple situation forever on the move. Narrative tends to fall victim to the need to simplify the multiplicity and to disregard too many facets of the moving situation. But analysis, especially the more it succeeds in accommodating the multiple, has to help itself by ignoring the fact of motion. It may be only a matter of personal opinion which of these deficiencies one fears the more, but I should like to suggest that something a little more essential is involved. Without a very present sense of time and change, of life and death, history ceases altogether to be history, whereas a narrative devoid of the full range of past experience is still history, only not altogether adequate or satisfactory history. That is to say, the dangers inherent in analysis are fatal, those inherent in narrative only damaging'.[19]

But in the early 1970s the 'new history' of the 1960s peaked and began to decline. This decline was charted in a classic résumé by one of its most able

---

* According to one apocryphal story, Namier also dismissed global history as 'All balls'.

exponents, Lawrence Stone, in two forthright articles published in 1976 and 1979, the second bearing the significant title, 'The Revival of Narrative'.[20] The adoption of mixed economies in the West, he said, had accelerated the intellectual decline of Marxism, and removed the pressure of inquiry from such key questions as the viability of American slavery, the origins of the English Civil War or the causes of the French Revolution. But in any case the new and vaunted methods of quantification and computerization had failed to resolve such problems, and had resulted in a great deal of trivial and meretricious work. The attempts of the *annalistes* to erect a macroeconomic and social model of European history had similarly failed. Sociology had already been found wanting, and it had proved too susceptible to the kind of contemporary pressure which had produced the inanities of 'women's history' and 'black history'. True, social history had been enormously strengthened by the new techniques, as a comparison of Trevelyan's *English Social History* with almost any similar survey published in the 1970s would show, and the reconstitution of the life of the working classes before 1800, once regretfully dismissed as impossible, was well under way; but that was almost the sole permanent gain. Stone still reacted strongly against what he called the 'antiquarian empiricists', led by Elton, who according to him regarded history as mindless and soulless, but he now accepted that narrative, long treated with disdain by social historians, had recaptured much of the ground it had lost.

The decline of sociology was not so observable in Britain, where it had never established a firm foothold. The inferior scholars who had to be drafted in to meet student demand in the 1960s were no credit to the discipline in the cold light of the 1970s, and student reaction, as we have seen, was crucial, here and elsewhere. As for the history departments, hastily cobbled-up courses on Indonesia or West Africa faded away as soon as these areas ceased to be of immediate current concern;* students also found that such arcane courses, for which external examiners at degree level could rarely be provided, left them at the mercy of their tutor's whims and prejudices. New difficulties in finding postgraduate employment no doubt weaned other students away from 'fancy' degree combinations. Young lecturers, growing older, tended to revise their courses in the direction of greater conventionality or even change them entirely, and the 'freeze' on academic appointments since about 1972 has hindered the recruitment of the next generation of radicals. In Britain the academic profession is now predominantly middle-aged, and radicalism often finds its last refuge amongst the professoriate – men who entered the profession in the 1960s full of new ideas, and rose to the top quickly enough to evade the reaction.

---

*It is strange that despite the continuing strength of the anti-apartheid movement amongst students, South African history was never in vogue.

Toynbee, too, has peaked and faded. The great Toynbee Cult, which some had seen as an indirect threat to Western civilization, proved less enduring and no more significant in the long run than the similar Tolkien Cult. Toynbee's heavy, latinate prose had never been easy reading, and his ideas had permeated the reading public mainly through abridgements; he was pre-eminently the kind of authority more discussed than read, like Marx. Moreover, the extraordinary religious mysticism evident in his later volumes, his claim to supernatural historical visions, could only undermine his intellectual stature, especially (one feels) when they occurred in prosaic venues like Buckingham Palace Road:

> 'In London in the southern section of Buckingham Palace Road, walking southward along the pavement skirting the west wall of Victoria Station, the writer, once, one afternoon not long after the end of the First World War, had found himself in communion, not just with this or that episode in History, but with all that had been, and was, and was to come. In that instant he was directly aware of the passage of History gently flowing through him like a mighty current, and of his own life welling like a wave in the flow of this vast tide. The experience lasted long enough for him to take visual note of the Edwardian red brick surface and white stone facings of the station wall gliding past him on his left, and to wonder – half amazed and half amused – why this incongruously prosaic scene should have been the physical setting of a mental illumination'.[21]

His reputation has comfortably subsided to a more natural level, especially after his death in 1975, and a new abridgement of *A Study of History*, lavishly illustrated, is now it seems marketed rather as an idiosyncratic history of the world than as a blueprint for the future.[22]

Where does this leave the profession of history in the closing decades of the twentieth century? The 'New Wave' has certainly receded, but it has not receded completely; nor is it desirable that it should. As I have said, the advances made in economic and social history – stripped of their hampering Marxist bias – represent a wonderful advance, which could not have been foreseen twenty or thirty years ago. Even Elton concedes that: 'The political historian must certainly know the duty of understanding what his colleagues are doing and saying, he must absorb their answers to their problems if his answers to his are to have virtue and validity.'[23]

As Elton and Trevor-Roper appreciated, the real divide is still between the popular and the academic historian, between the artist and the scientist. Professor Thomas Heyck has traced the process by which the professional scholar abdicated from the literary profession at the turn of the century, often by a conscious act of will. The literary reviews collapsed one by one, and the once honourable term 'man of letters' acquired a faintly patronizing aura. Heyck says that:

'To be a professional required acceptance of certain standards and procedures in intellectual work: concentration on original research; care in the use of evidence; non-partisanship with regard to current politics and theology; valuation of work according to the idea of a 'contribution' seen as relevant to the field itself; and acceptance of the circle of fellow researchers in a field as the significant audience. The new academic professionals looked upon acceptance of these principles as morally elevating; indeed, they felt that their respective disciplines, and professional academic work in general, were a calling. Even though they had sought remunerative careers in science and scholarship, they pictured these careers to themselves as selfless devotion to a high ideal rather than as labour for personal gain. The much used term "disinterested" meant to them "not-for-self-interest" as well as non-partisan. In this way the professional academics imitated the old professions – the clergy, the bar and medicine – in adopting an ideology as close as possible to the landed orders'.[24]

It is perhaps significant that it was a member of the true landed gentry, G.M. Trevelyan, who led the attack on scientific history, divorced himself from the profession for the middle decades of his career, and was regarded, even after his return to Cambridge, as the champion of history-as-literature.[25] It is an issue which can still divide the profession, whose polarities are marked by Elton and J.H. Plumb. And the touchstone is Namier, still a controversial figure twenty years after his death. Though Elton was not so far behind Butterfield in his condemnation of the excesses of the Namier School he endorsed his general interpretation – 'Namier introduced the disorder of reality into what had been a well-fixed and ordered arrangement based on fundamental misunderstandings' – and pointed out that even his most violent critics wrote in terms entirely established by him, and this was because of 'his firm foundation of scholarship': 'He was studying history – trying to find out – not promoting a personal point of view, or merely (as some do) wishing to create a stir by being different.'[26] Plumb was always much more reserved,* and with the passing of the years, when approached about Namier, he has increasingly fallen back on one of Trevelyan's gnomic utterances, 'Namier – great research worker, no historian' – a remark he also made to A.L. Rowse at one time. He has compared him with that destructive miniaturist J.H. Round: 'He quoted too much, and flogged his concepts nearly to death.'[27]

---

* See p. 267 above.

But as the concept of history as science has declined, so has the concept of history as literature, and with it 'popular history' in general. For one thing, the idea that popular historians had a monopoly of literary excellence or sheer readability has now been abandoned; it is doubtful if it ever had any truth, but it was sedulously encouraged by Trevelyan and his disciples, who all conspired to inflate the master's modest literary gifts. As early as 1945, in his inaugural lecture at Edinburgh, Richard Pares forthrightly said: 'The general reader believes that he cannot endure the works of professional historians because they are badly written. I may be biased, but I think the style of professional historians is generally good.'[28] Even C.V. Wedgwood later acknowledged that bad writing was far from being the prerogative of professional historians:

'It often happens that the outstanding scholar has gifts of exposition that put him higher among masters of English prose than some altogether lesser man who puts forth all his conscious artistry to write history as literature'.

In fact, she admitted that an academic training was the foundation of good prose:

'The capacity to weight and to use words correctly, the shaping of sentences, and the structure and presentation of a scene, a fact or an exposition are the natural concomitants of the clear, inquiring and imaginative mind which is needed for historical research'.[29]

The imputation of unreadability has passed elsewhere, and when a reviewer writes: 'Skill in the deployment of words has come to be distrusted, and a sense of moral rectitude now hangs about sentences that have nothing in the world to recommend them beyond their claim to be true', it is of linguistics that he speaks.[30]

Moreover, the sheer feebleness of so much popular history and historical biography since the death of Trevelyan has weakened its grip on the public mind, and its cause has been ill-served by such jejune and over-inflated compilations as Churchill's *History of the English-Speaking Peoples*. The number of worthwhile popular historians was never in fact very large, as is suggested by attempts to claim membership for Neale on the one hand and Hilaire Belloc on the other. (Any cause which has to recruit Belloc is doomed indeed.)[31] Now that Wedgwood has apparently laid down her pen – her last book was *The Trial of Charles I*, in 1964 – and so has Sir Arthur Bryant, popular history is represented in England by the remarkable Pakenham family, Elizabeth Longford and her children Antonia Fraser and Thomas Pakenham, and by the American Barbara Tuchman, author notably of *The Proud Tower* and *The Guns of August*.

These historians are skilful biographers and descriptive artists, but little more. Even when Wedgwood essayed a history of the Thirty Years War or Tuchman traced the convulsions of the fifteenth century in *A Distant Mirror* they had little concern with causation beyond the political. It is this strange gap in their armour which earned Wedgwood's *The King's Peace* and *The King's War* a distinctly cool academic reception in 1955 and 1958, apparently bringing her projected history of the Great Rebellion to a halt. Conversely, the increased cost of printing has combed out of most publishers' lists the frankly bad professional historians, thus refining the breed. It can only be a subjective impression, but with men like Plumb, Elton, Trevor-Roper and Owen Chadwick still writing, with a younger generation coming up behind which includes – taking names at random – Keith Thomas, Blair Worden and John Burrow, professional history in the 1980s is in a strong literary position.

At undergraduate level, too, with the decline in the social sciences and even modern languages, history has continued to hold its own as one of the two most popular arts-based subjects of study (the other being English), and the natural successor to classics as a general intellectual training for those entering business or the professions, even the Church. Nor, despite shrinking opportunities of employment in higher education, does the number of research students in history seem to have diminished; in 1980 177 were registered for the Ph.D. or the M.Litt. at Cambridge alone.* Even so, in his address to the Royal Historical Society in 1976, his last as President, Geoffrey Elton still sounded a note of warning. The enemies of history were no longer so formidable, but they still existed, 'some lurking in thickets, some boldly skirmishing across the plain'; they were ensconced in colleges of education, schools, and even in the Department of Education and Science.[32]

He was still conscious of the weakness of history, its lack of a defined purpose, and feared that it might be reduced to the status of intellectual gymnastics. It was not and is not the function of this book to examine the purpose of history, or the nature of historical explanation, on which the bibliography is already enormous. Enough to say that Elton argues that history is the only truly empirical discipline, the only discipline in which the writer does not, or should not, begin with a predetermined thesis or paradigm which it is his intention to test; the natural procedure in the social sciences as well as the physical sciences. The function of the historian, then, is to monitor the methods of other disciplines:

'Our peculiar method of working, which renders us incapable of seeking "maturity" in the production of a universal law or system, enables us, and our social duty obliges us, to subject the paradigmatic structures of others

* I have omitted sixty-nine foreign students, who will presumably return home eventually.

to criticism and if necessary to demolition by applying our own unhindered, unauthoritative, pragmatic and sometimes simplistic doubts to their claims to authority – especially when that authority moves from intellectual concerns (where after all it only constrains other practitioners of the same discipline) to political, where it constrains us all'.[33]

This is an allowable claim, and a justified one. Historical method has been the main bulwark against Marxism, as it has been one of the main solvents of Christianity. But is Elton wise to dismiss as categorically as he does the commonly received idea that the study of history enhances our understanding of the present, and perhaps even enables us to some extent to predict, if not the whole future, then what might happen next?[34] It is the general, or popular, expectation that history should teach lessons, and it is unwise for historians publicly to disown a role to which they have, as it were, been elected. As Elton himself says, 'Historians cannot exist in a vacuum; they live in the society of men, influence it whether they like it or not, and should therefore be conscious of what they are about.'[35] Gardiner was a Whig historian, and at the same time a disciple of Ranke. He disowned any attempt to project the present back into the past: 'He who studies the history of the past', he said, 'will be of greater service to the society of the present in proportion as he leaves it out of account.' Yet he still thought that history had an informative role:

'The statesman uses his imagination to predict the result of changes to be produced in the actually existing state of society, either by the natural forces which govern it, or by his own action. The historian uses his imagination in tracing the causes which produced the existing state of society ... Where they meet is in the effort to reach a full comprehension of the existing facts'.[36]

Elton cannot be persuaded 'that a minister of foreign affairs is better able to discharge his office because he once investigated the career of Metternich'.[37] Other things being equal, I would rather he had.

Of course, the imposition of a rigid, determinist structure on history, whether Marxist or Toynbeean, making the general course of future history entirely predictable, is to be deplored, and combated. But that does not rule out tentative predictions in short-term situations; after all, economists have no hesitation in foretelling the future, though few would be so bold as to describe economics as a science. The enormous popularity of Arnold Toynbee in his lifetime bespoke a public longing for *order* in history, for *system*, and above all, I think, for prophecy. The system he evolved was, of course, predeterminate; he laid the whole of human history on the procrustean bed of theory, and much of it had to be stretched too far to fit, and some of it cut off. But his work did suggest that history is not entirely random; it never exactly repeats itself, but there are significant echoes which we can sometimes pick up. Situations dissolve, and a generation later, or a century, they re-form, though in a slightly different pattern. We know this, and the public knows it – witness the spate of books in the early 1940s on Napoleon and William Pitt.

In fact, it is arguable that men mould the past to fit their expectations of the future. As Namier once said:

'One would expect people to remember the past and imagine the future. But in fact, when discoursing or writing about history, they imagine it in terms of their own experience, and when trying to gauge the future they cite supposed analogies from the past; till, by a double process of repetition, they imagine the past and remember the future'.[38]

Namier viewed this process with austere dismay; so did Plumb, when he put into the mouths of his critics the statement that 'History is a present world, it can never be the past; it is a dream world made up of actual events.'[39]

Yet if this book has shown anything, it is that the past *is* a dream world, and we *do* have to imagine it. We try to reconstruct men's motives from their statements and actions, and the remarks of other people about them, but this is really only conjecture. The popular historian is always trying to recreate the past *in toto*; so we hear a great deal of loose talk about getting under people's skin, looking at things through their eyes. The professional historian can do no more than create a skeleton of the past. Of course, the past must be largely imaginary; even I, who was growing up in the 1930s, cannot accurately assess what it was like to be an adult in that decade. How much less can I assess this for the 1630s, or the 1830s? All historians, consciously or uncon-sciously, and however scrupulous they may be, fill out their skeleton of the past with conjectured flesh which accords with their conception of the present and confirms their hopes or fears for the future. Or, to switch metaphors, the historical past is a grid, or a board for the great game which embraces also the present and the future. We must imagine the past, so that we can remember the future.

Notes

Abbreviations

BIHR *Bulletin of the Institute of Historical Research*
CHJ   *Cambridge Historical Journal*
DNB   *Dictionary of National Biography*
EHR   *English Historical Review*
HJ   *Historical Journal*
PBA   *Proceedings of the British Academy*
TLS   *Times Literary Supplement*
TRHS *Transactions of the Royal Historical Society*

Note. The place of publication of books is London unless otherwise stated.

One **Introduction**

1 Herschel Baker, *The Race of Time* (Toronto 1967), pp. 16, 45, 86.
2 qu. C.H. Firth, *Essays Historical and Literary* (Oxford 1938), p. 43.
3 Graham Greene, *Lord Rochester's Monkey* (1974), p. 198; Kevin Sharpe, *Sir Robert Cotton* (Oxford 1979), p. 27.
4 There is a good edition of the *Historia* by Lewis Thorne in the Penguin Classics series (1966).
5 Denys Hay, *Polydore Vergil* (Oxford 1952), p. 151.
6 ibid., pp. 157–8.
7 ibid., pp. 136–45.
8 For a more detailed examination of these points see William J. Brandt, *The Shape of Medieval History* (Yale 1966).
9 S.R. Gardiner, *History of England 1603–1642* (1884), II, 77.
10 Preface to his translation of Thucydides, *English Works*, ed. Sir William Molesworth (1843), VIII, p. ix.
11 Herbert Butterfield, *Magna Carta in the Historiography of the Sixteenth and Seventeenth Centuries* (Reading 1969), p. 5.
12 *Leviathan*, pt. II, ch. 29.
13 Joan Simon, *Education and Society in Tudor England* (Cambridge 1966), p. 324.

14 'Ancient History and the Antiquarian', *Jnl Warburg & Courtauld Institute*, xiii (1950), 286.
15 George Huppert, *The Idea of Perfect History* (Urbana, Illinois, 1970), chs 2–4; Donald R. Kelley, *Foundations of Modern Historical Scholarship* (New York 1970), passim.
16 F.J. Levy, *Tudor Historical Thought* (San Marino, California, 1967), pp. 184–6.
17 *History of the Reformation*, vol. I (1679), preface.
18 Levy, op. cit., p. 193.
19 *DNB*, sub 'Holinshed'.
20 *DNB*, sub 'Hayward'.
21 Joan Evans, *History of the Society of Antiquaries* (Oxford 1956), p. 14.
22 Sharpe, op. cit., pp. 142, 238–40.
23 H.R. Trevor-Roper, *Queen Elizabeth's First Historian* (1971). There is a modern abridgement of Camden's *Elizabeth*, edited by W.T. MacCaffrey (Chicago 1971).
24 Trevor-Roper, op. cit., p. 11. See also Levy, op. cit., pp. 279–85, and F. Smith Fussner, *The Historical Revolution 1580–1640* (1962), pp. 230–32.
25 Stuart Piggott, *Ruins in a Landscape* (Edinburgh 1976), p. 41.
26 Levy, op. cit., pp. 196–9.
27 Arthur B. Ferguson, 'Samuel Daniel', *Jnl Hist. Ideas*, xxxii (1971), 185–202.
28 Levy, op. cit., p. 279.
29 Folio Society edition, ed. Roger Lockyer (1971), p. 146.
30 ibid., pp. 230–1, 233–4.
31 The whole subject is thoroughly discussed by Joseph H. Preston, in 'Was there an Historical Revolution?' *Jnl Hist. Ideas*, xxxviii (1977), 353–64.
32 T.D. Kendrick, *British Antiquity* (1950), p. 117.
33 David Douglas, *English Scholars 1660–1730* (2nd ed. 1951), p. 53.
34 G.V. Bennett, *White Kennett bishop of Peterborough 1660–1728* (1957), p. 164.
35 J.G.A. Pocock, *The Ancient Constitution & the Feudal Law* (Cambridge 1957), pp. 66–7.
36 ibid., p. 111.
37 Though John Morris's *The Age of Arthur* (1973) now gives a more coherent account of the Dark Ages.
38 Kendrick, op. cit., p. 58.
39 J.E. Sandys, *A History of Classical Scholarship*, vol. II (Cambridge 1908), pp. 333–4.
40 Piggott, *Ruins*, pp. 8–9; idem, *The Druids* (1968), p. 137; Kendrick, op. cit., pp. 121–3.
41 Piggott, *William Stukeley* (1950), pp. 54–6; T.D. Kendrick, *The Druids* (1927), pp. 4–5, 7–11.

Two The Seventeenth Century

1 First edition (1614), preface.
2 qu. J.P. Kenyon, *Stuart England* (1978), p. 52.

3 J.P. Kenyon, *The Stuart Constitution* (Cambridge 1966), p. 40.

4 ibid., p. 101.

5 J.W. Allen, *English Political Thought 1603–60* (1938), I, 442.

6 Herbert Butterfield, *The Englishman and his History* (2nd ed. New York 1970), pp. 54–62; Butterfield, *Magna Carta*, passim; Levi Fox (ed.), *English Historical Scholarship in the Sixteenth and Seventeenth Centuries* (Oxford 1956), pp. 59–60.

7 Butterfield, *Magna Carta*, p. 5; Faith Thompson, *Magna Carta 1300–1629* (Minneapolis 1948), pp. 335ff.; Stephen D. White, *Sir Edward Coke and the Grievances of the Commonwealth* (Chapel Hill 1979), pp. 121–2, 245ff.

8 In fact, Cotton roused suspicion by reprinting a pamphlet with the title, 'A Proposition for his Majesty's Service to bridle the Impertinency of Parliaments'. (Sharpe, *Cotton*, pp. 80–82.)

9 J.W. Allen, op. cit., I, 439–40.

10 Kenyon, *Stuart Constitution*, pp. 13–14.

11 ibid., pp. 21–3.

12 Pocock, *Ancient Constitution*, ch. 8.

13 Quentin Skinner, 'History and Ideology in the English Revolution', *HJ*, viii (1965), 159–60.

14 *Locke's Two Treatises*, ed. Peter Laslett (Cambridge 1960), ch. 16, also p. 403n.

15 J.P. Kenyon, *Revolution Principles* (Cambridge 1977), pp. 37, 108.

16 Royce MacGillivray, *Restoration Historians and the English Civil War* (The Hague 1974), p. 37.

17 ibid., pp. 55–7.

18 ibid., pp. 40, 74.

19 ibid., pp. 112, 114.

20 ibid., p. 27.

21 M.P. Hartman, 'Contemporary Explanations of the English Revolution', Cambridge Ph.D. dissertation (1977), ch. 4.

22 ibid., ch. 5.

23 *Diary*, ed. Robert Latham (1970–1), iv, 395, 435.

24 R.C. Richardson, *The Debate on the English Revolution* (1977), pp. 15ff.; MacGillivray, op. cit., ch. 4.

25 Ruth Spalding, *The Improbable Puritan* (1975) supersedes all previous accounts of Whitelocke.

26 Kenyon, *Revolution Principles*, pp. 50–51 and ch. 5 passim; A.B. Worden (ed.), *Edmund Ludlow: A Voice from the Watchtower*, Camden Society, 4th ser., xxi (1978), introduction.

27 Richardson, op. cit., p. 25; H.R. Trevor-Roper, *Clarendon* (Oxford 1975), p. 8. The best account is still that of B.H.G. Wormald, *Clarendon: Politics, History & Religion* (Cambridge 1951), pp. 230–9, but see also MacGillivray, op. cit., ch. 8.

28 See the three articles by C.H. Firth in *EHR*, xix (1904), 26, 246, 464.

29 *History*, IX: 241 (iv, 490 in the standard edition by W.D. MacCray, Oxford 1888).

30 ibid., IX: 240, 243 (iv, 490, 492).

31 ibid., XV, 147, 152, 156 (vi, 91, 94, 97).

32 *History of My Own Time* (6 vols, Oxford 1833), VI, 180, 207–8, 210.

33 H. Trevor Colbourn, *The Lamp of Experience: Whig History and the Intellectual Origins of the American Revolution* (Chapel Hill 1965), pp. 48, 66 and passim.

34 T.E.S. Clarke and H.C. Foxcroft, *A Life of Gilbert Burnet* (Cambridge 1907), pp. 157, 166, 169.

35 ibid., p. 199.

36 qu. Kenyon, *Revolution Principles*, p. 163.

37 Clarke & Foxcroft, op. cit., pp. 152, 493.

38 *History of the Reformation*, ed. N. Pocock (Oxford 1865), II, 2–3.

39 Ranke, *History of England* (6 vols, Oxford 1875), VI, 48.

40 *Reformation*, I, 2.

41 ibid., I, 11–17.

42 ibid., I, 3.

43 *Typical English Churchmen*, ed. W.E. Collins (1902), I, 174.

44 qu. James Sutherland, *English Literature of the Later Seventeenth Century* (Oxford 1969), p. 282. I have been unable to trace this quotation to its original source.

45 Firth, in his introduction to Clarke & Foxcroft, op. cit., p. xxxix. Cf A.W. Ward, in *The Cambridge History of English Literature*, vol. IX (1912), p. 208.

46 Sutherland, op. cit., pp. 283–4. For another favourable modern opinion, see K.G. Hamilton, in Harold Love (ed.), *Restoration Literature: Critical Approaches* (1972), pp. 205–23. The Victorian view of the matter is put by Osmund Airy in *DNB*, III, 404.

Three   **The Enlightenment and Neo-Whiggism**

1 M.A. Goldie, 'Tory Political Thought 1689–1714', Cambridge Ph.D. dissertation (1978), p. 205.

2 See Quentin Skinner, 'The principles and practice of opposition', in *Historical Perspectives*, ed. Neil McKendrick (1974), pp. 93–128.

3 Isaac Kramnick, 'Augustan Politics and English Historiography', *History & Theory*, vi (1967), 33–56, and *Bolingbroke and his Circle* (Harvard 1968), passim; also Gerald Straka, '1688 as the Year One of English Liberty', in *Studies in Eighteenth-Century Culture*, ed. Louis T. Milic (Cleveland 1971).

4 Kramnick, 'Augustan Politics', p. 54.

5 ibid., p. 54.

6 'The Idea of the Decline and Fall of the Roman Empire', in *The Age of the Enlightenment: Studies presented to Theodore Bestermann* (Edinburgh 1967), pp. 413–30. See also, by the same author, 'The Historical Philosophy of the Enlightenment' and 'The Scottish Enlightenment', in *Studies in Voltaire and the Eighteenth Century*, xxvii (1963), 1667–87, lviii (1967), 1635–58; and Robert Ginsberg, 'David Hume *versus* the Enlightenment', ibid., lxxxviii (1972), 598–650. For the quotation from Hume see Ernest Campbell Mossner, *The Life of David Hume* (1954), p. 301.

7 Ginsberg, art. cit., pp. 604–7. Cf. Duncan Forbes, *Hume's Philosophical Politics* (Cambridge 1975), pp. 92–3, 141.

8 *History of England* (5 vols 1864), V, 470. See Forbes, op. cit., pp. 152, 168, and his introduction to *Hume's History of Great Britain* (Pelican ed. 1970), p. 20.

9 *History*, iv, 127; *The Letters of David Hume*, ed. J.Y.T. Greig (Oxford 1932), I, 170, 179.

10 The phrase is Trevor-Roper's, in *David Hume: a Symposium*, ed. D.F. Pears (1963), p. 93.

11 *History*, i, p. vii; *Letters*, I, 214; Mossner, *Hume*, ch. 23.

12 Mossner, pp. 305-11; Victor G. Wexler, *David Hume and the History of England* (Philadelphia 1979), pp. 26-7.

13 *History*, iv, 165.

14 *Essays* (Everyman ed.), I, 331, 333, 405.

15 *History*, iv, 219.

16 ibid., 273.

17 ibid., 132, 137, 273.

18 ibid., 506-7.

19 *History*, v, 470.

20 ibid., 471.

21 ibid., 472.

22 ibid., 472-3.

23 Wexler, op. cit., p. 66.

24 *History*, iii, 62.

25 Forbes, *Hume's Politics*, pp. 245-8.

26 *History*, iii, 545, 546.

27 ibid., 546-7, 550, 552.

28 *History*, i, 428, 449-50, 469; ii, 372. Cf. Wexler, ch. 4.

29 *History*, ii, 365.

30 Edward Gibbon, *Memoirs of My Life*, ed. Georges A. Bonnard (1966), p. 99; Wexler, p. 90.

31 Mossner, *Hume*, pp. 318, 402-3.

32 ibid., pp. 370, 405, 445.

33 ibid., p. 318.

34 Lawrence L. Bongie, *David Hume: Prophet of the Counter Revolution* (Oxford 1965), ch. 4; Mossner, chs. 31-2.

35 Mossner, p. 445.

36 ibid., p. 474.

37 Trevor-Roper, 'The Idea of the Decline and Fall', pp. 426-7 (cited n. 6 above).

38 Mossner, p. 535; *Letters*, II, 242n.

39 Gibbon, *Memoirs*, pp. 167-8; *Letters*, II, 269.

40 Mossner, p. 591.

41 Wexler, pp. 69-70.

42 *History*, iv, 578n.; Wexler, p. 23.

43 *Letters*, II, 238, 278. Cf. *History*, v, 140n., 228n., 249, 252, 256, 258n., 292.

44 qu. Wexler, p. 100.

45 *Quarterly Review*, lxxiii (1844), 554.

46 *Letters*, I, 167.

47 Forbes, in *Hume's History* (Pelican), p. 10.
48 Lynne E. Withey, 'Catherine Macaulay and the Uses of History', *Jnl British Studies*, xvi (1976), 59–83. See also Caroline Robbins, *The Eighteenth-Century Commonwealthsman* (Harvard 1959), pp. 265–7, 358–61; Thomas Preston Peardon, *The Transition in English Historical Writing 1760–1830* (New York 1933), pp. 80–82.
49 See the introduction to her *History*, I, pp. vii–xvii.
50 *New Letters of David Hume*, ed. R. Klibansky & E.C. Mossner (Oxford 1954), pp. 81–2 (Paris, 29 Mar. 1764).
51 Notably John Hampden; see vol. III (1767), p. 445.
52 *Letters*, II, 199, 242, 321.
53 *Edinburgh Review*, xii (1808), 276n.
54 *Miscellaneous Essays* (Everyman ed.), p. 31.
55 Roy Strong, *And When Did You Last see Your Father?* (1978), p. 21.
56 *Lectures on Modern History* (2 vols 1848), I, 126.
57 See Robert Birley, *Sunk Without Trace* (1962), ch. 4.
58 Trevor-Roper, 'Historical Philosophy of the Enlightenment', pp. 1673–4 (cited n. 6 above).
59 qu. Peardon, op. cit., p. 53.
60 qu. ibid., p. 27.
61 *Cambridge History of English Literature*, X, 290.
62 Peardon, op. cit., pp. 64–5.
63 I am indebted to Dr R.G. Cant for this information, and much else dealing with university education in Scotland.
64 C.H. Firth, 'Modern History in Oxford 1724–1841', *EHR*, xxxii (1917), 1–16. Also Firth, *Modern Languages at Oxford 1724–1929* (Oxford 1929), ch. 1; V.H.H. Green, *A History of the University of Oxford* (1974), pp. 97–8; and W.R. Ward, *Georgian Oxford* (Oxford 1958), pp. 132–3.
65 D.A. Winstanley, *Unreformed Cambridge* (Cambridge 1935), pp. 155–7; *Jenkinson Papers 1760–66*, ed. N. Jucker (1949), p. 68.
66 See the specimen syllabus, for an academy at Knibworth, printed by Irene Parker, *Dissenting Academies in England* (Cambridge 1914), pp. 143–6; also H. McLachlan, *English Education under the Test Acts* (Manchester 1931), passim.
67 Peardon, op. cit., pp. 59–60.
68 H.R. Trevor-Roper, 'The Idea of the Decline and Fall', pp. 413–30 (cited in n. 6 above).
69 H.T. Dickinson, 'The Politics of Edward Gibbon', *Literature & History*, viii (1978), 175–96.
70 G.M. Young, *Gibbon* (2nd ed. 1943), p. 116. See also H.R. Trevor-Roper's introduction to the volume on Gibbon in the 'Great Histories' series (New York 1963, London 1966).
71 Trevor-Roper, op. cit., pp. 34–5.
72 ibid., pp. xxii–xxv.
73 *The Works of William Robertson* (8 vols 1840), VI, pp. iv–ix.
74 *Cambridge History of English Literature*, X, 298.

75 Peter Gay, *Style in History* (1975), ch. 1.

76 qu. Duncan Forbes, *The Liberal Anglican Idea of History* (Cambridge 1952), p. 14.

77 Forbes, pp. 20–21, 38, 63, 65; Herbert Butterfield, *Man on his Past* (Cambridge 1955), p. 47.

78 qu. V.H. Galbraith, *An Introduction to the Study of History* (1964), p. 77.

79 *A Bibliography of Parliamentary Debates*, House of Commons Library Document No. 2 (1956).

80 vol. II, app. I, p. 228.

81 vol. II, preface, p. vii.

82 ibid., pp. v, vii.

83 qu. Peardon, op. cit., p. 77.

84 Macpherson's extracts appear to be from James's own notes, not the fake autobiography concocted from them by Thomas Dicconson and eventually printed in 1816. See Godfrey Davies, 'James Macpherson and the Nairne Papers', *EHR*, xxxv (1920), 367–76; also Winston Churchill, *Marlborough*, vol. I (1933), ch. 21, and John Miller, *James II* (1978), pp. 243–5.

85 Peardon, op. cit., p. 194; M.A. Thomson, *Some Developments in English Historiography during the Eighteenth Century* (1957), pp. 15–16.

86 *Essays* (Everyman ed.), I, 3–5.

87 *Constitutional History* (Everyman ed.), III, 177–8.

88 John Clive, *Thomas Babington Macaulay: the Shaping of the Historian* (1976). The letters, edited by Thomas Pinney, are now complete in five volumes (Cambridge 1974–80), and are cited hereafter as '*Letters*'. The journal is being edited by W.R. Robson. Apart from Clive, one of the most useful studies of Macaulay is by Jane Millgate (1973). The most recent discussion is by John Burrow, in *A Liberal Descent* (Cambridge 1981).

89 *Macaulay's Napoleon and the Restoration of the Bourbons*, ed. Joseph Hamburger (1976), p. 49.

90 *Quarterly Review*, cxlii (1876), 2.

91 qu. Clive, *Macaulay*, p. 164.

92 30 Mar. 1831, *Letters*, II, 9–11.

93 See Sir George Trevelyan's remarks in *The Life and Letters of Lord Macaulay* (1893), p. 207.

94 20 July 1838, *Letters*, III, 252.

95 *Letters*, IV, 365n., 382.

96 Trevelyan, *Life*, pp. 517, 518, 522.

97 ibid., pp. 527–8.

98 ibid., pp. 617–18.

99 qu. in H.R. Trevor-Roper's introduction to *Lord Macaulay's History of England* (Penguin 1979), p. 24.

100 *Letters*, III, 206–8 (31 Dec. 1836); *Essays*, II, 73ff.

101 See, for instance, *Letters*, IV, 255–8; Trevelyan, *Life*, pp. 408n., 633; Aubrey Newman, *The Stanhopes of Chevening* (1969), pp. 293–4.

102 Apart from the abridgement cited above (n. 99), it is still in print in the Everyman series.

103 H.R. Trevor-Roper, *The Romantic Movement and the Study of History* (1969). See also Macaulay's own remarks, *Essays*, I, 1-2.

104 Trevelyan, *Life*, p. 497.

105 *Quarterly Review*, cxliii (1976), 20; *Edinburgh Review*, xc (1849), 250.

106 qu. Butterfield, *Man on his Past*, p. 228; *Edinburgh Review*, xc, 259.

107 *Macmillans Magazine*, xl (1879), 291.

108 Trevelyan, *Life*, pp. 503-4.

109 ibid., pp. 502, 505.

110 ibid., pp. 539, 540.

111 *Essays*, II, 541.

112 *History of England* (Everyman ed. 1906), III, 269-70.

113 *Letters*, III, 286 (3 May 1839).

114 Alan Macfarlane, *The Origins of English Individualism* (1979), pp. 35-7, 52, 54.

115 *Edinburgh Review*, cv (1857), 154-5.

116 *Essays*, I, 5, 10, 17, 19, 25-6, 28, 97-8, 109, 120.

117 ibid., 18, 103, 149.

118 ibid., 48-53. Cf. Hallam, II, 242-3.

119 *Essays*, I, 55-60. He returned to the same theme later in his essay on William Temple, pp. 200-2.

120 ibid. 64-5.

121 Joseph Hamburger, *Macaulay and the Whig Tradition* (Chicago 1976), passim. For the more conventional view of Macaulay, see H.A.L. Fisher, 'The Whig Historians', *PBA*, xiv (1928), 297-339.

122 H.R. Trevor-Roper, introduction to *Macaulay's History*, pp. 11-13 (cited n. 99 above).

123 *History*, i, 9, 10.

124 ibid., ii, 214-15.

125 Trevelyan, *Life*, p. 507.

126 T.E. Jessop, *A Bibliography of David Hume* (1938), p. 31.

127 Sir Charles Firth, *A Commentary on Macaulay's History of England* (1938), pp. 254-5; *Letters*, III, 268, 325-6.

128 Ranke, *History of England* (Oxford 1875), IV, 364; also VI, 144, and Trevelyan, *Life*, p. 622.

129 Ranke, *History*, I, p. xvi.

130 *Letters of Lord Acton to Mary Gladstone*, ed. Herbert Paul (1913), pp. 139, 168; David Mathew, *Lord Acton and his Times* (1968), pp. 93-4; Butterfield, *Man on his Past*, pp. 92, 138n.; *Home & Foreign Review*, ii (1863), 257-60.

Four The High Victorians

1 J.W. Burrow, *A Liberal Descent: Victorian Historians and the English Past* (Cambridge 1981), pp. 59-60.

2 MS Journal, Trinity College, Cambridge, 23 June 1849.

3 Martin Haile & Edwin Bonney, *Life and Letters of John Lingard* (1912), pp. 182, 195, 347; Sheridan Gilley, 'John Lingard and the Catholic Revival', *Jnl Eccl.*

Hist., xxix (1978), 325; Edwin Jones, 'John Lingard and the Simancas Archives', *HJ*, x (1967), 73–4.

4 *History of England*, 6th ed. (10 vols 1852), VI, 322.

5 Haile & Bonney, pp. 167–8.

6 Gilley, art. cit., pp. 317–18; Donald F. O'Shea, *The English Ranke: John Lingard* (New York 1969), p. 77.

7 *History*, i, 8. Cf. O'Shea, pp. 34, 65; Haile & Bonney, pp. 334, 342.

8 Philip Hughes, 'Lingard and St Bartholomew', in *From the Renaissance to the Counter-Reformation*, ed. Charles H. Carter (1966), pp. 179–204.

9 Haile & Bonney, p. 194.

10 *History*, i, 5. Cf. Haile & Bonney, p. 343.

11 Haile & Bonney's only reference to the State Paper Office and the British Museum (p. 137) is extremely vague.

12 ibid., p. 181.

13 ibid., pp. 152, 157.

14 For a short history of the SPO, and a calendar of relevant documents, see *Thirtieth Report Deputy Keeper Public Records* (1869), App., pp. 212–93.

15 Burnet, *History of the Reformation* (6 vols, Oxford 1865), I, 8.

16 J.G.A. Pocock, 'Robert Brady', *CHJ*, x (1951), 196–8.

17 *Twenty-Third Report Deputy Keeper Public Records* (1862), pp. 57–60; F.S. Thomas, *A History of the State Paper Office* (1849), pp. 8–9.

18 *Guide to the Public Records*, Part I (1949), pp. 9–10.

19 *1st Report* (1874), pp. 1–10; M.F. Bond, *Guide to the Records of Parliament* (1971), p. 4.

20 *1st Report*, pp. 14, 117.

21 *3rd Report* (1872), p. 147.

22 See, for instance, the report on the papers of William King, *2nd Report*, pp. 231–57.

23 *The Collected Letters of the Carlyles* (Durham, NC, 1970), V, 416 (11 Sept. 1831).

24 The best short account is by P.R. Harris, *The Reading Room* (BL Pubs 1979).

25 Sir George Trevelyan, *Life & Letters of Lord Macaulay* (1907), pp. 623–4.

26 H.R. Trevor-Roper, 'Thomas Carlyle's Historical Philosophy', *TLS*, 26 June 1981, pp. 731–4, an essay to which I am greatly indebted.

27 *Letters*, I, 252.

28 K.J. Fielding & R.L. Tarr (eds), *Carlyle Past and Present* (1976), p. 14; James Pope-Hennessey, *Monckton Milnes: the Years of Promise* (1949), p. 184. (I owe this reference to Professor J.V. Chapple.)

29 Mary Moorman, *George Macaulay Trevelyan: a Memoir* (1980), p. 89.

30 Trevor-Roper, loc. cit.

31 J.A. Froude, *Thomas Carlyle ... Life in London* (1885), I, 85; *Letters*, VII, 306 (21 Sept. 1834). See also Hevda Ben-Israel's valuable study, *English Historians on the French Revolution* (Cambridge 1968), ch. 8.

32 Pt. III, bk. I, ch. 1.

33 Pt. III, bk. I, ch. 4.

34 Pt. III, bk. VII, ch. 8.

35 Pt. III, bk. III, ch. 1. Cf. G.M. Trevelyan, *Clio a Muse* (1913), p. 9.

36 vol. I, p. xiv (1853 ed.). Cf. Disraeli, *Coningsby*, bk. III, ch. 2.

37 MS. Journal, 4 Apr. 1850.

38 Even Buckle thought this 'the most eccentric eulogy ever passed on William III', *History of Civilisation* (Worlds Classics), I, 252n. Cf. Ben-Israel, op. cit., pp. 152–3.

39 Acton, *Lectures on the French Revolution* (1910), p. 358.

40 Pt. III, bk. V, ch. 1. Cf. Hannah Arendt, *On Revolution* (Pelican ed. 1973), pp. 48–9.

41 *Barclay Fox's Journal*, ed. R.L. Brett (1979), p. 192.

42 Acton, loc. cit.

43 *Letters*, II, 294.

44 His labours on this biography are discussed in Fielding & Tarr, op. cit., pp. 14–18.

45 Peter Karsten, *Patriot Heroes in England and America* (Wisconsin 1980), pp. 142–4.

46 P.B.M. Blaas, *Continuity and Anachronism 1890-1930* (The Hague 1978), pp. 105–7, 143–5; Christopher Hill, *God's Englishman* (1970), pp. 265ff.; W.C. Abbott, 'The Fame of Cromwell', in *Writings and Speeches of Oliver Cromwell*, vol. IV (Harvard 1947), pp. 882–99; and C.H. Firth's introduction to the S.C. Lomas edition of Carlyle's *Cromwell* (3 vols 1904), I, pp. xxi-lii.

47 *Heroes and Hero-Worship* (Everyman 1954), p. 434.

48 *Past and Present* (Everyman 1938), p. 19.

49 *Heroes*, pp. 441–2.

50 Acton, loc. cit.; Froude, *Carlyle in London*, II, 137, also I, 151–2, 188–9; *Letters*, V, 416, 426, VII, 259; Ben-Israel, op. cit., pp. 138–9; Alan Bell, 'Thomas Carlyle and the London Library', *TLS*, 29 May 1981, pp. 611–12.

51 Everyman ed. (1907), I, 12–13.

52 ibid., I, 8.

53 ibid., I, 64; II, 291.

54 ibid., II, 24–7.

55 Abbott, op, cit., IV, 892.

56 Firth, op. cit., p. xxxv; Karsten, op. cit., illustrations 28–33; Roy Strong, *And When Did You Last See Your Father?* (1978), pp. 146–51.

57 Waldo H. Dunn, *Froude* (Oxford 1961–3), II, 264; Trevor-Roper, loc. cit.

58 *DNB*, III, 211.

59 For this and for much of what follows I have relied on *A Victorian Eminence* by Giles St Aubyn (1958), and the *DNB* entry by Leslie Stephen. See also H.J. Hanham's introduction to *Buckle on Scotland and the Scotch Intellect* (Chicago 1970).

60 *Miscellaneous and Posthumous Works of H.T. Buckle*, ed. Helen Taylor (3 vols 1872), I, 84–135; III, 601–47.

61 ibid., I, p. xxiii.

62 ibid., I, 139.

63 ibid., I, 495–501.

64 ibid., II, 394–7.

65   Cambridge University Library, Acton c. 51, 79–81.
66   St Aubyn, op. cit., p. 12.
67   *Buckle and his Critics* (1895), p. 47.
68   *History of Civilisation* (1878 ed.), I, 373, 387.
69   *Fortnightly Review*, xxxvii (1880), 673.
70   *History*, i, 65–6, 101–7.
71   ed. H. J. Hanham (Chicago University Press).
72   Trevelyan, *Macaulay*, p. 673n.
73   J.M. Robertson, *Buckle and his Critics*, p. 25.
74   Charles Gavan Duffy, *Conversations with Carlyle* (1892), p. 108.
75   Acton, *Historical Essays* (1907), pp. 305–43.
76   St Aubyn, op. cit., pp. 30–33; Robertson, passim; B. & H. Wedgwood, *The Wedgwood Circle 1738–1897* (1980), p. 262. His financial rewards, initially at least, were not great. He published the first volume at his own expense, and cleared £506 on an edition of 1500. He sold the second volume, in an edition of 3000, for £600. However, the first volume was reprinted twice in his lifetime.
77   St Aubyn, p. 69n.
78   ibid., pp. 99–100.
79   *Fortnightly Review*, art. cit., 672, 673, 695.
80   Waldo Hilary Dunn, *James Anthony Froude* (2 vols, Oxford 1961–3), II, 511. Dunn is comprehensive but pedestrian; Herbert Paul's biography of 1905 is livelier and more perceptive. See also Basil Willey, *More Nineteenth-Century Studies* (1956), ch. 3.
81   Dunn, I, 94.
82   Dunn, I, 72; *Short Studies in Great Subjects* (1891), I, 37.
83   *Short Studies*, I, 25, 37; Dunn, I, 94.
84   Dunn, I, 173, 178–9.
85   Dunn, II, 267.
86   Dunn, II, 292.
87   *The Writing of History* (1926), p. 19.
88   Dunn, II, 310.
89   Herbert Paul, *Froude*, pp. 152–3.
90   W.R. Ward, *Victorian Oxford* (1965), p. 236; *Life & Letters of E.A. Freeman*, ed. W.R.W. Stephens (2 vols 1895), II, 302; Creighton, *Life and Letters* (2 vols 1913), I, 337; *The Letters of J.R. Green*, ed. Leslie Stephen (1901), p. 315; Oliver Elton, *Frederick York Powell* (Oxford 1906), I, 169–71.
91   Dunn, I, 8; Fortescue, loc. cit.
92   Dunn, II, 281.
93   *Short Studies*, I, 1.
94   1870 ed., VI, 101–2.
95   Dunn, II, 310.
96   Dunn, II, 313.
97   X, 317, 318–19 and note.
98   XII, 491, 501, 506.
99   XII, 510.
100 XII, 475.

101   *A History of England from the Defeat of the Armada to the Death of Elizabeth* (2 vols, New York 1914, 1926).

102   *Biographical Essays* (1948), pp. 262-3; Dunn, II, 543.

103   *Bibliography of British History: Tudor Period*, ed. Conyers Read, 2nd ed. (Oxford 1959), p. 30.

104   Dunn, II, 371ff. Pollard passes this over in the *DNB*.

105   Strachey, op. cit., p. 257.

106   *DNB Supp.*, sub 'Allen'.

107   Lord Edmund Fitzmaurice, *Life of ... the 2nd Earl Granville* (2 vols 1905), I, 258, 262, 305.

108   Owen Chadwick, *Acton and Gladstone* (1976), p. 6.

109   Lytton Strachey, *Eminent Victorians* (1948 ed.), p. 102.

110   6 Oct. 1862, *Correspondence of Lord Acton and Richard Simpson*, ed. Joseph L. Altholz et al., vol. III (Cambridge 1975), 25.

111   Robert Schuettinger, *Lord Acton: Historian of Liberty* (La Salle, Illinois, 1976), p. 108.

112   F. Engel de Janösi, 'Correspondence between Lord Acton and Bishop Creighton', *CHJ*, vi (1940), 316-17.

113   Chadwick, op. cit., pp. 7-8, 48-9.

114   Fitzmaurice, *Granville*, I, 358. For Fisher, see Schuettinger, op. cit., p. 155.

115   The best general account of the library is in David Mathew, *Lord Acton and his Times* (1968), ch. 9.

116   Herbert Butterfield, *Man on his Past* (Cambridge 1955), ch. 3; 'Acton: his training, methods and intellectual system', *Studies in Diplomatic History and Historiography in honour of G.P. Gooch*, ed. A.O. Sarkissian (1961), pp. 169-98.

117   Mathew, op. cit., p. 330.

118   *The Tales of Henry James* (Oxford 1978), II, 221.

119   Chadwick, op. cit., p. 22; *Letters of Lord Acton to Mary Gladstone*, ed. Herbert Paul (1906), pp. 126, 150.

120   Chadwick, op. cit., p. 19.

121   ibid., pp. 25-7.

122   ibid., p. 21; *Diaries and Letters of Mary Gladstone*, ed. Lucy Masterman (1928), p. 17.

123   James Bryce, *Studies in Contemporary Biography* (1903), pp. 396-7.

124   Butterfield, loc. cit. Compare Acton on Ranke in 1886 and 1895: *Historical Essays*, pp. 352-3, and *Lectures on Modern History* (Fontana 1960), pp. 32-3.

125   A. Watkin, 'Gasquet and the Acton-Simpson Correspondence', *CHJ*, x (1950), 101; Acton, *Modern History*, p. 29; Butterfield, in *TRHS*, 5th ser., xix (1969), 167-8; Ben-Israel, op. cit., pp. 254-5, 268-9.

126   Butterfield, loc. cit., and in *Man on his Past*, ch. 6; Ben-Israel, pp. 250-4, 305-6.

127   Gertrude Himmelfarb, *Lord Acton: a Study in Conscience and Politics* (1952), p. 204.

128   *EHR*, ii (1887), 571-2, 573, 577-8.

129   Janösi, art. cit., p. 316; Creighton, *Life and Letters* (2 vols 1913), I, 227-9, 368-76.

130   Janösi, p. 313n.

131 Himmelfarb, op. cit., p. 207; *Historical Essays*, p. 353.
132 Ben-Israel, op. cit., pp. 272-3; *Lectures on Modern History*, pp. 33, 38.
133 H.A.L. Fisher, Studies in *History and Politics* (Oxford 1920), p. 90.
134 *Lectures on Modern History*, p. 221.
135 *Lectures on the French Revolution*, p. 373.
136 Letter to contributors to the Cambridge Modern History, *Lectures in Modern History*, pp. 315-18.
137 Chadwick, op. cit., pp. 34-48.
138 Fisher, op. cit., p. 97; 'Lord Acton's Lectures', *Independent Review*, xi (1906), 225; Trevelyan, *Clio a Muse* (1930 ed.), p. 183.
139 Chadwick, op. cit., p. 50; Mathew, op. cit., pp. 356-7.
140 *The Athenaeum*, 28 June 1902; *The Letters of F.W. Maitland*, ed. C.H.S. Fifoot (Cambridge 1965), nos 317-19, 332.
141 G.N. Clark, 'The Origin of the Cambridge Modern History', *CHJ*, viii (1945), 57-64; Mathew, op. cit., p. 361.
142 Cambridge University Library, Add. MS. 6643. Other material on the Cambridge Modern History is in Add. 5524, 7729.
143 Creighton, *Life & Letters*, II, 203-5; Jänösi, art. cit., pp. 320-1.
144 *Cambridge Modern History*, vol. I (1902), 1-6.
145 *The Times*, 20 June 1902.
146 *On the Writing of History* (1939), pp. 209-10.
147 Maitland, *Letters*, no. 261.
148 Clark, art. cit.; Stanley Leathes, 'The Editorial Methods of Sir Adolphus William Ward', *CHJ*, i (1924), 219-20. Volume I appeared in November 1902, volume XII, 'The Latest Age', in 1910. The Index (vol. XIII) and the Atlas were published in 1911 and 1912 respectively.

Five **The Professionalization of History**

1 *A Historical Register of the University of Oxford* (Oxford 1900), pp. 191-3; *A Historical Register of the University of Cambridge*, ed. J.R. Tanner (Cambridge 1917), pp. 348-54; Jean O. McLachlan, 'The origin and early development of the Cambridge Historical Tripos', *CHJ*, ix (1946), 78-104.
2 K.T.B. Butler, 'A Petty Professor', *CHJ*, ix (1948), 217-38. For the chair in general, see G.P. Gooch, 'The Cambridge Chair of Modern History', in *Maria Theresa and other studies* (1951), pp. 297-331.
3 *Report of the Royal Commission* (1852), Pt II (Evidence), pp. 111-12.
4 Owen Chadwick, 'Charles Kingsley at Cambridge', *HJ*, xviii (1975), 303-25, takes a more favourable view of his professorship than is usual.
5 C.H. Firth, 'Modern History in Oxford 1724-1841', *EHR*, xxxii (1917), 19.
6 Firth, *Modern History in Oxford 1841-1918* (Oxford 1920), p. 4.
7 E.G.W. Bill, *University Reform in Nineteenth-century Oxford: a study of Henry Halford Vaughan* (Oxford 1973), passim; esp. ch. 9 and App. B.
8 Ward, op. cit., p. 212.
9 See T.F. Tout's important memoir in *DNB Supp. I*, pp. 444-51; also Helen Cam, 'Stubbs Seventy Years After', *CHJ*, ix (1948), 129-47; and J.G. Edwards,

William Stubbs (Hist. Assoc. 1952). The opposing view is put with great vigour in *The Governance of Medieval England*, by H.G. Richardson and G.O. Sayles (Edinburgh 1963), pp. 1-21.

10   Firth, loc. cit.

11   Maitland, *Collected Papers* (Cambridge 1911), III, 455; and in general, G.P. Gooch, *History and Historians in the Nineteenth Century* (1920), pp. 286-90, and P.B.M. Blaas, *Continuity and Anachronism 1890-1930* (The Hague 1978), pp. 76-83.

12   David Knowles, *Great Historical Enterprises* (1963), ch. 4; *Texts and Calendars*, ed. E.L.C. Mullins (RHS 1958), pp. 42-60.

13   Maitland, *Collected Papers*, III, 456.

14   Knowles, op. cit., pp. 105-6, 131.

15   N.J. Williams, 'Stubbs's appointment as regius professor', *BIHR*, xxxiii (1960), 121-5.

16   James Bryce, *Studies in Contemporary Biography* (1903), pp. 289-90.

17   *Collected Papers*, *III*, 498; Robert Brentano, 'The Sound of Stubbs', *Jnl British Studies*, vi (1967), 1; Helen Cam, art. cit.

18   Norman Cantor, *William Stubbs on the English Constitution* (New York 1966), p. 7; Knowles in 5 *TRHS*, xix (1969), 144; Maitland, *Collected Papers*, III, 458.

19   Blaas, op. cit., pp. 174-83.

20   Cantor, op. cit., p. 12.

21   W.R.W. Stephens, *The Life and Letters of E.A. Freeman* (2 vols 1895), II, 67-8.

22   Bryce, op. cit., pp. 263-4.

23   Stephens, *Freeman*, I, 256-8.

24   Ibid., II, 379.

25   H.A. Cronne, 'Edward Augustus Freeman', *History*, xxviii (1943), 81.

26   Stephens, *Freeman*, II, 471-2.

27   *The Life and Letters of Mandell Creighton* (2 vols 1913), I, 264; F.W. Maitland, *Life and Letters of Leslie Stephen* (1906), pp. 367-8; C.H.S. Fifoot (ed.), *The Letters of F.W. Maitland* (Cambridge 1965), no. 175.

28   J.W. Burrow, introduction to the abridged edition of Freeman's *Norman Conquest* (Chicago 1974), p. xxiii. See also Burrow's *A Liberal Descent* (Cambridge 1981), chs 7, 8.

29   Stephens, *Freeman*, I, 125; Blaas, op. cit., p. 190.

30   Stephens, *Freeman*, II, 266, 400-1, 450.

31   ibid., I, 118-23; *Report of the Royal Commission* (1852), Part II (Evidence), pp. 138-9.

32   Stephens, *Freeman*, II, 279; Creighton, *Life & Letters*, I, 244.

33   Stephens, *Freeman*, II, 366; Charles Oman, *Memories of Victorian Oxford* (1941), p. 238; D.J. Palmer, *The Rise of English Studies* (Oxford 1965), pp. 96-100.

34   Stephens, *Freeman*, II, 334.

35   Oman, *Memories*, p. 236.

36   Stephens, *Freeman*, II, 289.

37 E.L. Woodward, 'The Rise of the Professional Historian in England', in *Studies in International History*, ed. K. Bourne and D.C. Watt (1967), p. 32n.; Firth, *Modern History 1841-1918*, pp. 32-3; J.A.R. Marriott, *Memories of Four-Score Years* (1946), p. 60.

38 Deborah Wormell, *Sir John Seeley and the Uses of History* (Cambridge 1980), p. 113.

39 Charles Oman, *On the Writing of History* (1939), p. 237.

40 Stephens, *Freeman*, II, 459-62; Strachey, *Biographical Essays* (1948), pp. 260-1.

41 *DNB Supp. I*, p. 685.

42 See Creighton's memoir in *DNB*, and Bryce's in *Studies in Contemporary Biography*.

43 *The Letters of J.R. Green*, ed. Leslie Stephen (1901), pp. 246, 317-18.

44 ibid., p. 254.

45 Bryce, op. cit., p. 265.

46 *Letters*, pp. 364-5.

47 ibid., p. 240; Simon Nowell Smith (ed.), *Letters to Macmillan* (1967), pp. 117-19.

48 *Letters*, p. 245.

49 *Short History* (Everyman 1915), I, p. xi.

50 ibid., I, 314.

51 ibid., I, 352.

52 ibid., II, 485.

53 Bryce, op. cit., p. 165.

54 *Letters*, p. 302; Bryce, p. 143.

55 R.B. McDowell, *Alice Stopford Green: a passionate historian* (Dublin 1967).

56 'Du progrès des études historiques', *Revue Historique*, i, 29.

57 R.W. Southern, *The Shape and Substance of Academic History* (Oxford 1961), p. 11.

58 Sheldon Rothblatt, *The Revolution of the Dons* (1968), p. 185.

59 Oliver Elton, *Frederick York Powell* (Oxford 1906), I, 174. See J.P.D. Dunbabin, 'Oxford and Cambridge Finances 1871-1913', *Econ. Hist. Review*, xxviii (1975), and the comment by Arthur Engel, ibid., xxxi (1978).

60 Arthur Engel, 'From Clergyman to Don: the Rise of the Academic Profession in Nineteenth-century Oxford', Princeton Ph.D. dissertation (1975), pp. 180-2, 204-11; Creighton, *Life & Letters*, I, 134-5, 141-3. Cf. John Sparrow, *Mark Pattison and the Idea of a University* (Cambridge 1967).

61 Creighton, *Life and Letters*, I, 62, 276-7, 281-2; *Lectures and Addresses* (1904), p. 27.

62 Engel, op. cit., p. 221.

63 E.G.W. Bill, op. cit., pp. 186-8; Oman, *Writing of History*, p. 234.

64 C.H. Mallett, *History of the University of Oxford*, vol. III (1927), p. 455; Oman, *Memories*, pp. 104-5; Stubbs, *Two Lectures on the Present State and Prospects of Historical Study* (Oxford 1876), p. 7.

65 Oman, *Memories*, pp. 258-9, 264; Marriott, *Four-Score Years*, p. 61.

66 J.R. Tanner, in *Essays on the Teaching of History*, ed. W.A.J. Archbold (Cambridge 1901), p. 54. For Knowles see 5 *TRHS*, xix (1969), 143.

67 *Seventeen Lectures* (1886), pp. 40, 57, 381–3.
68 Engel, op. cit., pp. 139, 146, and 'The emerging concept of the academic profession at Oxford 1800-54', in Lawrence Stone (ed.), *The University and Society* (Princeton 1973), I, 347-50; C.H. Firth, *The Faculties and their Powers* (Oxford 1909), pp. 5-6, 12.
69 The main authority for Seeley's career is now Deborah Wormell, cited n. 38 above. See also Rothblatt, op. cit., ch. 5.
70 Wormell, p. 41.
71 Paul Frédéricq, 'The Study of History in England and Scotland', *Johns Hopkins University Studies in History*, no. 10 (1887), pp. 28-31; Rothblatt, op. cit., p. 180; Memoir by G.W. Prothero in *DNB* sub 'Seeley'.
72 *The Expansion of Europe*, ed. John Gross (Chicago 1971), p. xii.
73 Wormell, *Seeley*, p. 93.
74 ibid., p. 126; Trevelyan, *An Autobiography* (1949), p. 17.
75 *Expansion*, ed. cit., pp. 114-15.
76 Wormell, *Seeley*, p. 130.
77 *Expansion*, p. 11.
78 For a specimen Tripos paper, see McLachlan, art. cit., p. 100.
79 Wormell, p. 113; Frédéricq, op. cit., pp. 34-5; McLachlan, art. cit., pp. 84-5.
80 *Cambridge Review*, vi (1885) 194. Cf. McLachlan, p. 89. There is considerable divergence between McLachlan and Rothblatt and Wormell on the degree to which Seeley opposed Tripos reform. See also G.S.R. Kitson Clark, 'History at Cambridge 1873-1973', *HJ*, xvi (1975), 541-2.
81 Wormell, p. 120; J.R. Tanner, in *Essays* (cit. n. 66 above), p. 58.
82 McLachlan, art. cit., p. 91.
83 ibid., pp. 92-5.
84 Maitland, *Letters*, nos 343, 348, 350.
85 Creighton, *Life*, I, 281, 283, and *Lectures and Addresses*, p. 27; Seeley, 'History and Politics', *Macmillans Magazine*, xl (1879), 295.
86 *TRHS*, NS, xvi (1902), pp. xviii-xix; R.H. Humphrey, *The Royal Historical Society 1868-1968* (RHS 1969), pp. 28-9.
87 *Selected Essays*, ed. Harold Temperley (Cambridge 1930), p. 13.
88 Doris S. Goldstein, 'J.B. Bury's Philosophy of History', *Amer. Hist. Review*, lxxxii (1977), 896-919.
89 *Selected Essays*, p. 18.
90 ibid., p. 52.
91 qu. William R. Keylor, *Academy and Community; the Foundation of the French Historical Profession* (Harvard 1975), p. 59.
92 *TRHS*, NS, xix (1905), 17-25; Trevelyan, *Clio a Muse* (1913), pp. 1-55. Trevelyan may have borrowed his title from Prothero, who said on this occasion: 'Clio, let us not forget, was a Muse.'
93 *DNB Supp. I*, sub 'Burrows'; Oman, *Writing of History*, p. 234; D.M. Owen, 'The Chichele Professorship of Modern History, 1862', *BIHR*, xxxiv (1961), 217-20. Burrows was well aware of his own limitations, but braved the matter out; see his *Autobiography*, ed. S.M. Burrows (1908), esp. pp. 215-17.
94 Elton, *Frederick York Powell*, I, passim; esp. pp. 27, 174.

95 Oman, *Memories*, pp. 204–6, 259.

96 Charles V. Langlois and Charles Seignobos, *Introduction to the Study of History* (1898), p. vii.

97 Elton, *York Powell*, I, 190, 344–6, II, 1–3 passim, 39, 85; Firth, *Modern History 1841–1918*, p. 36.

98 *A Plea for the Historical Teaching of History* (Oxford 1905), pp. 14–29 passim. Cf. obituaries by Sir George Clark, *DNB Supp. 1931–50*, and Godfrey Davies in *PBA*, xxii (1936); J.C. Masterman, *On the Chariot Wheel* (Oxford 1975), pp. 148–9; and Marriott, *Four-Score Years*, pp. 61–2. There are also two relevant articles by R.I. Moore, 'Stubbs, Tout and undergraduate history', *Durham University Jnl*, NS, xl (1978), 9–16, and 'History Teaching: Prisoner of its own Past', *Times Higher Educational Supplement*, 28 Jan. 1977.

99 *The Study of History* (Oxford 1906), pp. 14–21.

100 Firth, *Modern History 1841–1918*, pp. 46–7; *PBA 1912–13*, pp. 142–3.

101 Masterman, op. cit., pp. 149–50; private information from Lord Dacre of Glanton.

102 C.J.W. Parker, 'The Development of History Courses in British Universities 1850–1975', Exeter M.A. Dissertation (1976), pp. 94–6.

103 *DNB Supp. 1931–50*, pp. 642–4 (quite the most unkind entry I have noticed in the modern *DNB*).

104 Parker, op. cit., pp. 125–6, 129–34; *Collected Papers of T.F. Tout*, vol. I (Manchester 1932), particularly the memoir of Tout (pp. 1–24), and Tout's own account of his stewardship (pp. 60–109). See also F.M. Powicke, 'The Manchester History School', in *Modern Historians and the Study of History* (1955), pp. 19–95.

105 *Collected Papers*, I, 76–9, 93–109 (esp. pp. 99, 107–8).

106 Parker, op. cit., pp. 114–15, and 'Academic History: Paradigms and Dialectic', *Literature & History*, v (1979), 176.

107 The following is based mainly on W.H.G. Armytage, *Civic Universities: Aspects of a British Tradition* (1955).

108 *Collected Papers*, I, 95.

109 'History at Leeds 1877–1974: the evolution of a discipline', *Northern History*, x (1975), 141–64.

110 Frédéricq, op. cit., pp. 20, 35–7.

111 Taylor, art. cit., p. 152.

112 Armytage, op. cit., p. 250; *Victoria County History: Cambridge*, vol. III (1959), p. 289. I am also grateful to the Secretary of the Board of Graduate Studies at Cambridge for lending me a paper on the evolution of research status by the late W.J. Sartain.

113 Professor G.R. Elton, in private correspondence.

114 *Modern Historians*, p. 202.

115 Elton, *York Powell*, I, 84–5.

116 *Letters of J.R. Green*, p. 173.

117 ibid., pp. 433–7.

118 Creighton, *Life & Letters*, I, 334–5.

119 F.E. de Janösi, 'The Acton-Creighton Correspondence', *CHJ*, vi (1940), 313.

120   *EHR*, ii (1887), 281–302.
121   Janösi, art. cit., p. 314.
122   Humphrey, *Royal Historical Society*, pp. 1–26.
123   Maitland, *Leslie Stephen*, pp. 353–6, 365–404; Statistical Account, *DNB*, vol. LXIII (1901), pp. lxi–lxxvi; Memoir of George Smith, *DNB* (1909 ed.), I, pp. xxiff., esp. pp. lv–lix; Memoir of Sir Sidney Lee, *DNB Supp. 1912–21*, pp. xiii–xxvi; A.F. Pollard, 'Sir Sidney Lee', *BIHR*, iv (1926), 1–13.
124   *DNB Supp. 1941–50*, pp. 679–81; *PBA*, xxxv (1949), 257–74; *EHR*, lxiv (1949), 198–205; *BIHR*, xxii (1949), 1–10; Pollard, *Factors in Modern History* (3rd ed. 1932), pp. 234–97.
125   *Historical Register: Supplement 1921–30* (Cambridge 1932), p. 21.
126   Parker, 'History Courses', pp. 139–41, 159–80; B.P. Lenman, 'The Teaching of Scottish History in the Scottish Universities', *Scottish Historical Review*, lii (1973), 174.

Six   The Fruits of Research

1   Roy Stone de Montpensier, 'Maitland and the Interpretation of History', *Amer. Jnl Legal History*, x (1966), 260.
2   *Life and Letters* (1913), I, 288.
3   *Studies in Tudor and Stuart Politics and Government* (Cambridge 1974), I, 240–2.
4   1900 ed., pp. 306–7.
5   *Reappraisals in History* (1961), ch. 3.
6   ibid., pp. 26–7, 40.
7   For Pollard's methods, see P.B.M. Blaas, *Continuity and Anachronism* (Hague 1978), pp. 277–8, and Elton, *Studies*, I, 110–15.
8   *Henry VIII: an Essay in Revision* (Hist. Assoc. 1962), p. 5.
9   Blaas, op. cit., p. 302; Elton, loc. cit.
10   *Political History of England 1547–1603* (1910), p. 475.
11   1947 ed., pp. 163–4.
12   G.R. Elton, 'Fifty Years of Tudor Studies at London University', *TLS*, 6 Jan. 1956.
13   Nora M. Fuidge, 'Joel Hurstfield and the Tudor Seminar', in *The English Commonwealth 1547–1640*, ed. Peter Clark et al. (1979), pp. 17–22.
14   *PBA*, lxiii (1977), 403–21; *The Times*, 4 Sept. 1975.
15   *PBA*, pp. 408–9; Elton, *Studies*, I, 241.
16   *Mr Secretary Cecil and Queen Elizabeth* (1955), and *Lord Burleigh and Queen Elizabeth* (1960).
17   *Essays in Elizabethan History* (1958), pp. 59–84. For Elton's view, see *Studies*, I, 241, and *England under the Tudors* (1955), pp. 262, 398.
18   *Elizabethan House of Commons*, p. 15; *Elizabeth I and her Parliaments*, I, 370, 417–18, II, 13, 436.
19   *PBA*, p. 418. Cf. *Elizabeth I and her Parliaments*, II, 436.
20   See Elton's Neale Memorial Lecture for 1978, 'Parliament in the Sixteenth Century: Functions and Fortunes', *HJ*, xxii (1979), 255–78; Conrad Russell, 'Parliamentary History in Perspective 1602–29', *History*, lxi (1976), 1–27.

21 Elton, *Studies*, I, 39.

22 See his revisionist essay in *History* in 1954, repr. *Studies*, I, 173–88; his Hist. Assoc. pamphlet cited in n. 8 above, and his review of Scarisbrick's book, repr. *Studies*, I, 100–8.

23 *The Past & the Present* (1981), p. 107.

24 J.A. Guy, 'The Tudor Commonwealth: revising Thomas Cromwell', *HJ*, xxiii (1980), 681–8.

25 The future workings of his mind are also foreshadowed in his presidential addresses to the Royal Historical Society 1974–6, printed in 5 *TRHS*, vols xxiv– vi.

26 C.H. Firth, in *DNB Supp. 1901–11*, pp. 75–8; York Powell, in *EHR*, xvii (1902), 276–9; *The Athenaeum*, 1 & 8 March 1902, pp. 272–3, 307–8.

27 *Quarterly Review*, cxcv (1902), 535.

28 *Factors in Modern History* (3rd ed. 1932), pp. 238, 309.

29 *History of England 1603–1642* (1884), X, pp. vii–ix.

30 *England under the Duke of Buckingham and Charles I* (1875), I, p. vi; *The Personal Government of Charles I* (1877), I, pp. vii–viii. [These prefaces were not reprinted in the octavo edition.]

31 Blaas, op. cit., pp. 149–50.

32 *TLS*, 9 Oct. 1919.

33 *TLS*, 6 & 13 Nov. 1919.

34 Usher, pp. 129–30. Even today Usher's book is not widely known, and remarkably little attention has been paid to this controversy, except by David A. Fahey, in a very slight article, 'Gardiner and Usher in perspective', *Jnl Hist. Studies*, i (1968), 137–50.

35 Usher, p. 74.

36 ibid., p. 72.

37 ibid., p. 125.

38 ibid., p. 88n.

39 ibid., pp. 77–8.

40 ibid., pp. 84, 90.

41 ibid., pp. 61–2, 63, 78.

42 ibid., p. 69.

43 Conrad Russell (ed.), *The Origins of the English Civil War* (1973), and *Parliaments and English Politics 1621–29* (Oxford 1979). See also Kevin Sharpe (ed.), *Faction and Parliament* (Oxford 1978), Robert Zaller, *The Parliament of 1621* (Berkeley 1971), and Robert E. Ruigh, *The Parliament of 1624* (Harvard 1971).

44 *The Fall of the Monarchy of Charles I*, I, p. vii.

45 ibid., p. vi.

46 *Prince Charles and the Spanish Marriage* (1869), I, p. v.

47 G.N. Clark, in *DNB Supp. 1931–40*, pp. 272–5; also obituaries by Clark again, in *EHR*, li (1936), 257–63; by Godfrey Davies, in *PBA*, xxii (1936), 380–400; and by E.S. de Beer, in *History*, xxi (1936), 1–13.

48 See his review of Gardiner's achievement in *Quarterly Review*, cxcv (1902), 547–66.

49 ibid., p. 559.

50 G.M. Young, introduction to Firth's *Oliver Cromwell* (Worlds Classics 1953), p. v; *DNB Supp.*, pp. 274-5.

51 *Essays Historical and Literary*, ed. Godfrey Davies (Oxford 1939), p. 119.

52 *EHR*, xv (1900), 171-5, 803-7.

53 ed. cit., pp. 478-9.

54 Peter Karsten, *Patriot Heroes in England and America* (Wisconsin 1980), pp. 157-8.

55 An updated edition of Davies's volume, by Mary Frear Keeler, was published in 1970.

56 *The Early Stuarts* (2nd ed. Oxford 1959), p. xvii.

57 To R.C. Trevelyan, 9 July 1900, Trinity College, Cambridge, RCT 14(43); *Autobiography and other essays* (1949), p. 46.

58 *Autobiography*, pp. 17, 18. See also G.S.R. Kitson Clark's sensitive memoir in *Durham University Journal*, lv (1962), 1-4, which I have used extensively, together with G.N. Clark's obituary in *PBA*, xlix (1963), 375-86. See also Joseph M. Hernan, 'The last Whig historian and consensus history', *Amer. Hist. Review*, lxxxi (1976), 66-97.

59 The incident is discussed by Owen Chadwick, *Freedom and the Historian* (Cambridge 1969), pp. 20-1, and J.H. Plumb, *Trevelyan* (1951), p. 14.

60 To R.C. Trevelyan, 24 May 1910, Trinity College RCT 14(79); A.L. Rowse, *Memories of Men and Women* (1980), pp. 96, 119.

61 1925 ed., pp. 238, 258.

62 ibid., pp. 35-6.

63 Rowse, *Memories*, p. 101.

64 *England under the Stuarts* (1925 ed.), p. 516.

65 ibid., pp. 71, 130.

66 ibid., p. 291.

67 ibid., p. 232.

68 ibid., pp. 229-30.

69 ibid., p. 195. It is significant that this is one of the few passages which Trevelyan altered for the 1925 edition in search of stylistic improvement, without changing the sense.

70 Chadwick, op. cit., pp. 37-8; Ved Mehta, *Fly and Fly Bottle* (1963), pp. 205-6. Clark (*PBA*, ut supra, p. 385) thought it was at least partly directed at Trevelyan.

71 pp. v, 3, 41, 105.

72 It is sometimes said that he undertook this after he arrived in Cambridge, but in a letter to his brother announcing his appointment he says: 'Queen Anne will move more slowly, but she will move'; Trinity College RCT 14(116), 16 June 1927.

73 J.H. Plumb, *TLS*, 2 May 1980.

74 Rowse, *Memories*, p. 131.

75 *Death of the Past*, p. 144.

76 Kitson Clark, op. cit., p. 2.

77 Plumb, *Trevelyan*, p. 29.

78 C.W. Crawley, 'Sir George Prothero and his Circle', 5 *TRHS*, xx (1970), 115.

79 4 Oct. 1939, Trinity College, RCT 14(149).

80 Plumb, op. cit., pp. 32-3.
81 Ross Terrill, *R.H. Tawney and his Times* (1973), p. 58. I have also drawn on other studies of Tawney, by T.S. Ashton in *PBA*, xlviii (1962), 461-81, and W.H.B. Court, in *Scarcity and Choice in History* (1970), pp. 127-40.
82 See the account by N.S.B. Gras, in *Econ. Hist. Review*, i (1927), 12-34; also N.B. Harte's introduction to *The Study of Economic History* (1971).
83 C.J.W. Parker, 'The Development of History Courses in British Universities 1850-1975', Exeter M.A. dissertation (1976), pp. 91-3, 96.
84 *PBA*, ix (1920), 465-74.
85 ibid., xxxii (1946), 342.
86 Parker, op. cit., pp. 114, 116.
87 Harte, op. cit., p. xxiv. For Cunningham see also C.J.W. Parker, *History as Present Politics* (Winchester 1980), p. 18.
88 F.A. Hayek, 'The London School of Economics 1895-1945', *Economica*, xiii (1946), 1-31.
89 Peter Clarke, *Liberals and Social Democrats* (Cambridge 1978), pp. 74-82, 154-60, 187-90, 243, 247-51.
90 ibid., pp. 155, 162.
91 Arthur J. Taylor (ed.), *The Standard of Living in Britain in the Industrial Revolution* (1975). For the earlier stages of the debate, see Clarke, op. cit., pp. 244-7, 325-8.
92 Clarke, op. cit., p. 189; *The Agricultural Problem of the Sixteenth Century* (1912), p. vii.
93 Terrill, op. cit., p. 189; *R.H. Tawney's Commonplace Book*, ed. J.M. Winter & D.M. Joslin (Cambridge 1972), pp. 10-11, 72.
94 *Agricultural Problem*, p. 402.
95 *Commonplace Book*, pp. 9, 22.
96 *Agricultural Problem*, p. 316.
97 Terrill, op. cit., p. 44.
98 *Religion and the Rise of Capitalism* (1960 ed.), p. 138.
99 ibid., p. 286.
100 *Reformation Europe* (Fontana 1963), p. 315.
101 *Religion and the Rise of Capitalism*, p. 197.
102 The bibliography on the Levellers is now extensive. See that printed in Gerald Aylmer, *The Levellers and the English Revolution* (1975), pp. 172-4, and add to it two typical modern socialist studies: A.L. Morton (ed.), *Freedom in Arms* (1975), and Fenner Brockway, *Britain's First Socialists* (1980).
103 *The Causes of the English Revolution 1529-1642* (1972), p. 99. See Charles H. & Katherine George, *The Protestant Mind of the English Reformation 1570-1640* (Princeton 1961); John F. New, *Anglican and Puritan 1558-1640* (1964); Basil Hall, 'Puritanism: the problem of definition', *Studies in Church History*, ed. G.J. Cuming, vol. II (1965), pp. 283-96; C.H. George, 'Puritanism as History and Historiography', *Past & Present*, no. 41 (1968), 77-104; Patrick Collinson, 'A Comment: concerning the name Puritan', *Jnl Eccl. History*, xxxi (1980), 483-8.
104 *Econ. Hist. Review*, xi (1941), 1-38, reprinted *History and Society: Essays by*

R.H. Tawney, ed. J.M. Winter (1978), pp. 85-119. It was preceded in 1940 by a British Academy lecture on the same theme, 'Harrington's Interpretation of his Age', reprinted Winter, pp. 66-84.

105 *Econ. Hist. Review*, xviii (1948).
106 ibid., 2nd ser., iii (1951).
107 *Social Change and Revolution in England 1540-1640* (1965), p. xi; Hexter, *Reappraisals*, p. 138.
108 'The Rise of the Gentry: a postscript', *Econ. Hist. Review*, 2nd ser., vii (1954), repr. Winter, op. cit., pp. 119-28.
109 *Agrarian Problems in the Sixteenth Century and After* (1969), Introduction.
110 *TLS*, 11 Feb. 1977.
111 *The Times*, 2 Dec. 1980.
112 Stone, *Social Change*, p. xvi.
113 The literature is extensive. See, in particular, Alan Everitt, *Change in the Provinces: the Seventeenth Century* (Leicester 1969), and John Morrill, *The Revolt of the Provinces* (1976). The whole question is reviewed by Christopher Hill, 'Parliament and People in Seventeenth-Century England'. *Past & Present*, no. 92 (1981), 100-124, and by David Underdown, 'Community and Class: theories of local politics in the English Revolution', in *After the Reformation*, ed. Barbara C. Malament (Manchester 1980), pp. 147-65.
114 The most important contributions to this debate were reprinted in *Crisis in Europe 1560-1660*, ed. Trevor Aston (1965).
115 *HJ*, xvi (1973), 205-8.
116 *Three British Revolutions*, ed. J.G.A. Pocock (Princeton 1980), pp. 23-108.
117 *Prince Charles and the Spanish Marriage* (1869), I, p. v.
118 *Macmillans Magazine*, xlv (1881), 46.
119 *Essays* (Everyman ed.), I, 348, 350, 359.
120 ibid., I, 363-4, 368, 386, 409.
121 ibid., I, 460; Hallam, *Constitutional History* (Everyman ed.), III, 232.
122 Lecky, *History of England in the Eighteenth Century* (1879), I, 366-9; Stanhope, *History of England from the Peace of Utrecht to the Peace of Versailles* (4th ed. 1853), III, 158.
123 pp. 120-22.
124 See Herbert Butterfield, *George III and the Historians* (1957), bk. II.
125 Julia Namier, *Lewis Namier* (1971). I have also drawn on the obituary by Lucy Sutherland in *PBA*, xlviii (1962), 371-85; J.L. Talmon, 'The Ordeal of Sir Lewis Namier', *Commentary*, 33 (1962), 237-45; and John C. Cairns, 'Sir Lewis Namier and the History of Europe', *Historical Reflections*, i, (1974), 3-35. The latest book on Namier, *Lewis Namier and Zionism*, by Norman Rose (Oxford 1980), also contains more evidence of a general nature than its title would suggest. I am grateful to former friends and colleagues of Namier's who corresponded with me about him, particularly John Brooke.
126 Lord Boothby, in *My Oxford*, ed. Ann Thwaite (1977), pp. 32-3.
127 Arnold Toynbee, *Acquaintances* (Oxford 1967), p. 63. See also Isaiah Berlin, in *Encounter*, Nov. 1966, pp. 32-42.
128 J.H. Plumb in *New Statesman*, 1 Aug. 1969, 'The Atomic Historian'.

129 *England in the Age of the American Revolution* (1930), p. 18.

130 *Structure of Politics* (2nd ed. 1957), p. 104.

131 There have been many expositions of Namier's methods and achievements. The best are 'The Namier View of History', *TLS*, 28 Aug. 1953; E.A. Smith, 'Sir Lewis Namier and British Eighteenth-Century History', *Parliamentary Affairs*, 17 (1963-4), 465-9; and Romney Sedgwick, 'The Namier Revolution', *History Today*, 10 (1960), 723-4.

132 Norman Rose, op. cit., p. 50n.

133 *Additions and Corrections to Sir John Fortescue's Edition of the Correspondence of George III Volume I* (Manchester 1937). For Churchill, see Julia Namier, pp. 228-30.

134 Rowse, *Memories*, p. 131.

135 See Stone's essay on 'Prosopography' in *The Past & the Present* (1981), pp. 45-73.

136 Rose, op. cit., p. 37.

137 These fragments, edited by Lucy Sutherland and John Brooke, were published in *Crossroads of Power* (1962), pp. 73-117.

138 See Maurice Cowling, *Religion and Public Order in England* (1980), pp. 237-59 passim.

139 *Christianity and History*, pp. 52, 54, 64.

140 'The Originality of the Namier School', *Cambridge Review*, 25 May 1957.

141 'Namier and his Critics', *Encounter*, Feb. 1965, p. 48.

142 Ved Mehta, *Fly and Flybottle* (1963), p. 196.

143 'Professor Butterfield and the Namier School', *Cambridge Review*, 10 May 1958.

144 ibid., 25 May 1957.

145 *George III and the Historians*, pp. 207, 208, 211, 212, 298.

146 *TLS*, 22 Nov. 1957.

147 *George III and the Historians*, pp. 200, 202.

148 ibid., pp. 10, 206, 207, 235; *Cambridge Review*, vol. 78, p. 616.

149 vol. 79, pp. 528-31 (10 May 1958).

150 'Sir Lewis Namier as Historian', *The Listener*, 18 May 1961 (pp. 873-6). See also his review of Lady Namier's biography, in *History*, lviii (1973), 410-11, and his interview with Ved Mehta, *Fly and Flybottle*, pp. 195-7.

151 'Party and Progress in Eighteenth-Century Britain', *The Listener*, 8 June 1961, pp. 1008-10. See also the letters of 22 June, pp. 1096-7.

152 Jacob M. Price, 'Party, Purpose and Pattern: Sir Lewis Namier and his Critics', i (1961), 71; Harvey C. Mansfield, 'Sir Lewis Namier Considered', ii (1962), 28; Robert Walcott, ' "Sir Lewis Namier Considered" considered', iii (1964), 85; Harvey C. Mansfield, 'Sir Lewis Namier again considered', iii (1964), 109. (All *Journal of British Studies*.)

153 Brooke, 'Namier and Namierism', *History & Theory*, 3 (1963-4), 331-47, and 'Namier and his Critics', *Encounter*, Feb. 1965, pp. 47-9; John Owen, 'The Namier Way', *New Statesman*, 26 Jan. 1962. See also Ved Mehta's interviews with Brooke and Lady Namier, *Fly and Flybottle*, pp. 175-90, 206-13, and an important review of Lady Namier's biography in *TLS*, 21 May 1971.

154 'The Atomic Historian', *New Statesman*, 1 Aug. 1969.

155   *The Future of the Past* (Cambridge 1968), p. 8n.
156   *History & Theory*, 3 (1963–4), 332–3.
157   *Conflicts: Studies in Contemporary History* (1942), pp. 69–70.
158   Mehta, op. cit., p. 211.
159   *King George III and the Politicians* (Oxford 1953), p. 176.

Seven   **Conclusion: History in the Twentieth Century**

1   *History Professional and Lay* (Oxford 1957), p. 1.
2   See, for instance, Barbara Tuchman, *Practicing History* (1982), p. 15.
3   *Macmillans Magazine*, xl (1879), 293.
4   *Velvet Studies* (1946), pp. 155, 157.
5   *Truth and Opinion* (1960), p. 53.
6   Trevor-Roper, op. cit., pp. 5, 12; Elton, *The Practice of History* (Sydney 1967), p. 72.
7   *New Republic*, 8 Nov. 1954.
8   'Arnold Toynbee's Millennium', *Encounter*, June 1957.
9   See the very frank survey by Lawrence Stone, in *The Past and the Present* (1981), ch. 1, reviewed by Keith Thomas, *TLS*, 30 Apr. 1982.
10   See R.H.C. Davies, 'The Content of History', *History*, lxvi (1981), 367.
11   Brian Harrison, 'History at the Universities: a Commentary', ibid., liii (1968), 357–80, paints a gloomier (or happier) picture than emerges from R.P. Blows, *History at the Universities* (1971).
12   Harrison, art. cit., p. 363.
13   *Crisis in the Humanities* (1964), pp. 28, 34.
14   *What is History?* (1961), pp. 55, 150, 155.
15   *The Practice of History*, pp. 103–4. Cf. pp. 72, 148.
16   ibid., pp. 133–4.
17   ibid., pp. 148–9, 163.
18   'Second Thoughts on History at the Universities', *History*, liv (1969), 60, 61, 63.
19   *Political History: Principles and Practice* (1970), pp. 160–1, 177.
20   *The Past and the Present*, chs 1, 3.
21   *A Study of History*, x (1954), 139.
22   Edited by Toynbee and Joan Caplan (Thames & Hudson 1972).
23   *Political History*, p. 177.
24   T.W. Heyck, *The Transformation of Intellectual Life in Victorian England* (1982), p. 226.
25   C.V. Wedgwood, 'History as Literature', *TLS*, 6 Jan. 1956, is a panegyric on Trevelyan.
26   *Practice of History*, pp. 103–4; *Political History*, pp. 35, 109.
27   *TLS*, 2 May 1980. Cf. Rowse, *Memories of Men and Women* (1980), p. 131. (The *TLS* review, of a biography of Trevelyan, is largely devoted to criticism of Namier.) See also Plumb's remarks in a BBC radio programme on Namier, 'Not a Place for Happiness at All', broadcast 11 May 1982.
28   *The Historian's Business* (Oxford 1961), p. 2.
29   *TLS*, 6 Jan. 1956; *Truth and Opinion*, p. 74.

30 *TLS*, 13 Mar. 1981 (Liam Hudson).
31 Wedgwood, *TLS*, 6 Jan. 1956.
32 5 *TRHS*, xxvii (1977), 197.
33 ibid., p. 210.
34 ibid., p. 198.
35 *Practice of History*, pp. 41–2.
36 *History of England* (1883–4), X, pp. vii–ix.
37 art. cit., p. 199.
38 *Conflicts* (1942), pp. 69–70.
39 *Crisis in the Humanities*, p. 30.

Index